P9-DVZ-605

"Nolo's home pa~ ~~~~~ ~~~~marking.
—WALL STREET JOURNAL

LEGAL INFORMATION ONLINE

www.nolo.com

2 4 h⊙urs a day
find:

- Nolo's comprehensive Legal Encyclopedia

- SharkTalk: Everybody's Legal Dictionary

- Auntie Nolo—if you've got questions, Auntie's got answers

- Update information on Nolo books and software

- The Law Store—over 250 self-help legal products

- Discounts, good deals, and our hilarious Shark Talk game

- Our ever-popular lawyer jokes

- NoloBrief, our monthly email newsletter

Quality LAW BOOKS & SOFTWARE FOR NON-LAWYERS

Nolo legal books and software are consistently rated Number 1 because:

- A dozen in-house Nolo legal editors, working with highly skilled authors, ensure that our products are accurate, up-to-date and easy to use.

- We know our books get better when we listen to what our customers tell us. Please fill out and return the card at the back of this book.)

- We are maniacal about updating every book and software program to keep up with changes in the law.

2nd Edition

Trouble-Free

Travel

... And What to Do
When Things Go Wrong

By Attorneys Stephen D. Colwell & Ann R. Shulman

Riverside Community College
OCT '01   Library
4800 Magnolia Avenue
Riverside, CA 92506

G151 .C65 1998
Colwell, Stephen D.
Trouble-free travel...and
what to do when things go
wrong

Self-Help Law Book

ate information in this book. But
bject to differing interpretations.
ee a lawyer. If you use this book,
and general advice contained in it
are applicable to your situation.

Keeping Up to Date

To keep its books up to date, Nolo issues new printings and new editions
periodically. New printings reflect minor legal changes and technical corrections.
New editions contain major legal changes, major text additions or major reorganiza-
tions. To find out if a later printing or edition of any Nolo book is available, call
Nolo at 510-549-1976 or check our website at www.nolo.com.

To stay current, follow the "Update" service at our website:www.nolo.com. In
another effort to help you use Nolo's latest materials, we offer a 35% discount off
the purchase of the new edition of your Nolo book if you turn in the cover of an
earlier edition. (See the "Recycle Offer" in the back of this book.) This book was
last revised in **September 1998**.

Second Edition	SEPTEMBER 1998
Editors	ROBIN LEONARD
Cover & Book Design	TERRI HEARSH
Index	SAYRE VAN YOUNG
Proofreading	JOE SADUSKY
Printing	BERTELSMANN INDUSTRY SERVICES, INC.

Colwell, Stephen D.
   Trouble-free travel...and what to do when things go wrong / by
Attorneys Stephen D. Colwell & Ann R. Shulman. -- 2nd ed.
     p. cm.
   Includes bibliographical references and index.
   ISBN 0-87337-478-9
   1. Travel.   I. Shulman, Ann R.   II. Title.
G151.C65 1998
910' .2'02--dc21   98-13690
                                             CIP

Copyright © 1996 and 1998 Stephen D. Colwell and Ann R. Shulman.
ALL RIGHTS RESERVED. Printed in the U.S.A.

No part of this publication may be reproduced, stored in a retrieval system or transmitted in
any form or by any means, electronic, mechanical, photocopying, recording or otherwise
without the prior written permission of the publisher and the author. Reproduction prohibitions
do not apply to the forms contained in this product when reproduced for personal use.

For information on bulk purchases or corporate premium sales, please contact the Special
Sales Department. For academic sales or textbook adoptions, ask for Academic Sales. Call
800-955-4775 or write to Nolo.com, Inc., 950 Parker Street, Berkeley, CA 94710.

Dedication

In loving memory of

Dr. Nahum Raphael Shulman

who knew that the best part of traveling was coming home.

The second edition is also dedicated to our newest addition, sweet baby James.

Acknowledgments

Writing this book was a lot like driving down a long and winding road at night wearing sunglasses. We got stuck a number of times and often wondered if we were headed in the right direction. We send our sincere thanks to many fellow travelers for their guidance and encouragement along the way, especially to:

Robin Leonard for her patience, reassurance and kindness as we muddled through.

Marcia Stewart, Terri Hearsh, Stan Jacobsen and the rest of the delightful gang at Nolo Press for all that they did to bring the book to life.

Laurel Pallock, of the San Francisco District Attorney's Consumer Fraud office, for reviewing the material on travel scams.

James and Mary Anna Colwell, whose zest for travel is contagious and inspiring.

Ilene Shulman, a terrific travel companion and steadfast fan.

Friends and family who haven't seen much of us for a while and who are bound to see us in a better mood now.

Each other—because two minds (and hearts) are better than one on the voyage of life.

Table of Contents

Introduction

1 Traveling by Plane

2 Renting a Car

7 Travel Scams and Questionable Travel Providers

8 Travel Insurance and Travel Assistance

9 Foreign Travel

10 Returning to the United States From Abroad

11 Discrimination and Travel Restrictions

12 Is It Tax Deductible? Traveling for Business or Charity

13 Resolving Your Travel Dispute: Let's Make a Deal

Appendix

Contacting a Travel Supplier

Introduction

Have you ever wondered …

- whether you really need extra insurance for a rental car?
- what an airline must pay you if it loses your bags or if your flight is delayed or overbooked?
- how to make your travel tax deductible?
- who to talk to if a hotel "can't find" your reservation?
- how to get a refund if you have to cancel a pre-paid trip?
- why some discount travel offers sound "too good to be true"?

If so, then you need to read this book! Whether you travel for business or pleasure, this book will answer vital questions about your rights as a traveler.

Travel and tourism is the largest industry in the world, with an army of lawyers behind it. If you want to travel smart, you need to be informed. You need inside information to defend your rights when you travel. By reading this book, you will be able to stand up for your rights without paying for a lawyer. This book shows you how to negotiate with travel suppliers when trouble arises and how to write effective letters after the fact that get you the compensation you deserve.

Each chapter covers a different aspect of traveling—from traveling on an airplane (Chapter 1), to using a travel agent (Chapter 5), to deducting travel expenses (Chapter 12). You learn practical tips for avoiding trouble while traveling, as well as information to help work things out when they go wrong.

How to Use This Book

Each chapter explains how to avoid common problems with travel suppliers, describes your rights and gives examples of what to do if you have a problem. If you are about to take a trip, read the chapters that cover the kind of travel suppliers you will be using to protect yourself from trouble—before it happens. If you've had a problem with a particular travel supplier, turn first to the chapter that talks about that kind of supplier to learn more about your specific rights. Then read Chapter 13 to find out what you can do to resolve the problem quickly and effectively.

Most people find out about the traps for unwary travelers when it is too late. Consider the following:

- An airline lost a professional courier's checked piece of luggage containing $2 million in cash, and the airline was only required to pay him $1,250 in compensation. Chapter 1 helps you handle problems with airlines including baggage, overbooking and delays.
- Because a traveler had to return her rental car one day early, her special weekly rate was invalidated and she was charged 35% more for using the car one day *less*. Chapter 2 explains how to avoid this and other surprise charges when renting a car.
- An unsuspecting cruise passenger was shocked to learn that she would get no compensation for $65,000 worth of personal property destroyed during a ship fire—because she didn't file a claim with the cruise line within ten

days. Chapter 3 demystifies your rights as a cruise passenger.

- Over $10 billion a year is lost to phony contests and other travel scams in the U.S. Read Chapter 7 to learn how to recognize travel scams and avoid being defrauded by scam artists.

- A couple arrived in Asia and got sick two days before their tour began. They were surprised to learn that although they had purchased trip cancellation insurance, they could get no refund because their coverage ended as soon as they left home. Chapter 8 will help you to determine the type of travel insurance you need.

You don't have to learn these lessons the hard way. By using this book, you can become a smarter traveler.

Travel "Law"

To assert your rights in these and the other situations covered by this book, you may have to learn a little bit of law in one or more of the following areas:

- contract law—which governs your tickets, insurance policies and reservations

- tort law—for example, if you are injured while traveling

- maritime law—which governs virtually everything that happens on a cruise

- consumer fraud—especially if you're the victim of a travel scam, questionable tour operator or misleading advertisement, or

- discrimination law—if you feel you were mistreated because of your race, sex, age, disability or other characteristic.

Don't worry—in most cases, everything you need to know is discussed in this book. Pay attention to the rules as we explain them, and if your situation is complex, you may need to do some extra research. Knowledge is power—knowing and asserting your rights will make your demands for compensation more forceful than simply accusing the travel supplier of incompetence and stupidity.

General Travel Tips

As you read about your travel rights in specific circumstances, keep in mind the following general travel tips:

Do your homework. When planning your trip, compare more than price. While the deals offered by different airlines, hotels, rental car agencies, tour operators and other travel suppliers may look the same, the terms of the deals often contain differences that can significantly affect the quality of your trip. You should also research health risks, weather, crime, political situations and other conditions that could cause problems. Many travel problems can be avoided by doing some background research before your trip.

Throughout this book, you'll find references to some of the most important sources of information. You can get additional information from travel agents and travel associations; visitor centers, travel and information offices and tourist bureaus;

government agencies, including the U.S. State Department; travel guides, magazines and newspaper sections; and online services.

Choose your travel agent carefully. A good travel agent can be the difference between a good trip and a bad one. If things do go wrong, your best ally may be your travel agent. (See Chapter 5.)

Know what you are buying. Read the ticket—airline or cruise—carefully, including all the fine print. Also read your rental car contract, travel insurance policy and all other papers you get. These are your contracts, and they determine your legal rights. Many key provisions—particularly about refunds or exclusions—are hidden. This book will help you uncover many of these important hidden terms.

Keep a paper trail. Keep tickets, contracts, policies, ads that lured you into buying a product, confirmation letters, receipts, bills and all other documents. You will need these later if a dispute arises.

Use your clout. If you use the same travel agent, airline, car rental company or hotel frequently, use your pull as a long-time customer (perhaps as a member of a frequent flyer, renter or guest program) to work out a settlement or resolve your dispute. (See Chapter 13.)

Icons to Help You Along

Throughout this book, you will encounter the following icons:

 When you see the "fast track" icon, you'll be alerted to a chance to skip some material you may not need to read.

 This icon cautions you about potential problems.

 Suggested references for additional information follow this icon.

 This icon cross-references another chapter of book.

 This icon lets you know that we are introducing a legal concept.

 This icon provides the name and address or phone number of a person, organization or agency that can provide you with more information.

While we can't guarantee that the food on your next flight will be delicious or that customs officials will become friendly overnight, this book will help make your next trip as "trouble-free" as possible.

May the wind be at your back and the road rise up to greet you!
Bon voyage! Buon viaggio!
Gute reise! Buon viaje!

Chapter 1

Traveling by Plane

An Introduction to Airlines

Every day, over a million Americans take a trip by airplane. During the past few decades, airlines have become some of the largest and most powerful businesses in the travel industry. Airline travel is subject to federal laws and regulations, although to a much lesser degree than 25 years ago. This deregulation has led to competition among airlines and a variety of benefits for passengers, including fare wars and frequent flyer programs. Because your airline ticket is a contract between you and the airline, many of your rights are governed by the terms of this contract. This chapter summarizes your most important rights as an airline passenger and describes some ways to make sure that the airlines do not take advantage of you.

Before You Fly

Make your flying as trouble-free as possible by following these suggestions before you fly:

- Your relationship with the airline is governed not only by the visible terms of your ticket, but also by hidden terms known as the "Conditions of Carriage," such as boarding priorities and compensation for injuries. These conditions are not given to you—you must ask for them, and you should do so if you believe your rights are being violated. Don't be put off if an airline representative is reluctant to provide them; be persistent. You may need to speak to a supervisor.

- Be sure you ask about all restrictions on a ticket before you buy—such as penalties for cancellation or changes in your itinerary, blackout periods and whether frequent flyer points are awarded.

- Be aware that airline fares change rapidly and that you can often save 20% to 30% by comparison shopping and/or adjusting your schedule by one or two days. Ticket sellers are not obliged to tell you that small changes could save you big money, so ask a lot of questions.

- When you receive your airline ticket from a travel agent or other ticket seller, check the name of the airline, date, time and fare on the ticket for accuracy.

Airline Switcheroo

Your next flight may be on an airline you have never heard of, even if your reservation is with your favorite U.S. airline. With the approval of the Department of Transportation, U.S. airlines are allowed to enter into agreements (called code-sharing) with other carriers, which means that the airlines team up, particularly on international flights. For example: You buy a ticket for an American Airlines flight to Brazil, which requires you to change planes in New York. In New York, you are switched to a plane operated by China Air Lines for the rest of your flight. Sometimes, the international airline may be better than the domestic one, but if you want to avoid a surprise, ask your ticketing agent whether there is code-sharing on the flight, and if so, which airline will be responsible for each leg of the flight.

- Make sure you have proper identification with you. Airlines require that all passengers show a photo ID to travel. The ID must be one issued by a government agency, such as a driver's license or passport. Sometimes, airlines can be quite sticky about the rules. In one case, a college-age daughter traveling with her parents was denied boarding even though she had a university ID. Travelers using e-tickets will also need to produce the credit card used to pay for the ticket. If you live in a state that does not put photos on drivers' licenses (such as New Jersey) and you don't have a current passport, be sure to find out from the airline other forms of acceptable ID.

- As you are boarding an airplane, double-check your ticket: Make sure the ticket agent has taken the correct ticket coupon so you still have the coupon needed for your return flight.

- If your flight is overbooked, you are entitled to compensation if you are involuntarily "bumped" (denied boarding). You can receive from $200 to $400 from the airline, depending on how long you are delayed in reaching your destination. The airline may offer free or discounted travel in the future, but you are entitled to cash if you want it.

- If your flight is overbooked and you are not in a hurry, you can volunteer to be bumped and receive a free ticket or travel discount from the airline. If you need to be on the flight, insist on seeing the airline's boarding procedures in order to ensure that no one lower in the boarding priority list gets your seat.

- Don't put medicines, watches, jewelry or other valuable or necessary items in your checked baggage. If you transport valuable items in your luggage, the compensation you receive is unlikely to be complete if your luggage is damaged or lost.

- Join more than one frequent flyer program. Although you can get travel awards faster by concentrating your travel on one airline, you may miss some low-fare deals or better connections on other airlines. Frequent flyer miles are worth only about 2¢ per mile; use that figure to help calculate your best option.

Second-Class Treatment

It seems a lawyer seated in the coach section of the airplane needed to use the lavatory. All the lavatories in coach were occupied, so she walked forward to use the lavatory in the first-class section. A first-class passenger, also a lawyer, barred her way and told her that the first-class lavatories were for first-class passengers only. This led to a heated argument, a fistfight and eventually a lawsuit. The court ruled that the coach passenger was in the wrong and that, in fact, under the terms of the airline's policies, she could only use the coach lavatories. The moral of the story? Beware of "first-class" lawyers (and hidden airline policies), especially if you are in desperate need of relief.

Laws Covering Air Travel

Your Airline Ticket Is a Contract With the Airline

Your airline ticket is a contract between you and the airline, but it is heavily one-sided. You can't negotiate the terms, and most of the conditions are placed there for the benefit of the airline and restrict your rights. If that isn't bad enough, the majority of the important terms of the contract are hidden.

The back of all standard airline tickets has at least 11 paragraphs of fine print under the heading "Conditions of Contract." In Paragraph 3 is a statement that various "applicable tariffs" and the "Carrier's Conditions of Carriage and Related Regulations" are incorporated into the contract. This means that the airline has filed with the U.S. Department of Transportation a series of statements about its obligations to its passengers and its limitations of liability. These tariffs and conditions are the hidden terms of your contract with the airline. As mentioned earlier, you can see them by asking the airline for a copy of its Conditions of Carriage. Anyone who sells tickets for an airline is legally required to let you see a copy upon request.[1]

The Conditions of Carriage cover everything from the number of bags you can check to the type of compensation you receive if your flight is delayed or canceled. Boarding priority, check-in requirements and most of the other fine-print terms that describe an airline's rights and responsibilities to its passengers are set forth in the Conditions of Carriage.

Conditions of Carriage vary from airline to airline. Although most airline tickets look identical, the subtle differences in the hidden terms can make a substantial difference in your rights as a passenger.

> **Example:** Raphael takes a flight from New York to Atlanta on Standard Air Lines. Unfortunately, when he arrives, his checked bag containing camera equipment (worth $1,000) and clothes (worth $500) is missing. Under Standard Air's Conditions of Carriage, the airline has no liability for lost camera equipment unless the passenger purchases specific baggage valuation (which Raphael did not), so the most he can recover is $500—the value of his clothes. If he had flown Ether Air Line, which has no restriction on camera

equipment in its Conditions of Carriage, he would have been able to recover $1,250—the maximum allowed by Ether Air under its Conditions of Carriage (still less than the full $1,500 he lost).

 You can obtain a summary of the hidden terms and conditions of most major airlines' contracts by requesting a copy of United States Air Carriers, Conditions of Carriage, Summary of Incorporated Terms (Domestic Air Transportation) from the Air Transport Association, 1301 Pennsylvania Avenue, NW, Suite 1100, Washington, DC 20004; 800-497-3326 (phone); 202-626-4166 (fax); http://www.air-transport.org (Web). You can send a check for $55, or you can call or visit the Web page and provide your credit card number and expiration date. Also, your travel agent might have a copy of the Conditions of Contract.

If an airline violates your contract (the ticket) or the Conditions of Carriage, you may be able to recover compensation from the airline for its breach of contract. Your rights to recover compensation are restricted by certain national and international laws, discussed throughout this chapter.

Your Rights Under U.S. Law

Your rights on domestic flights in the U.S. are governed by the Federal Aviation Act.[2] The Department of Transportation has the power to create regulations based on the Act which affect an airline passenger's rights. Generally, any state laws which attempt to regulate the airline industry are preempted by the Act and will be ignored by a court.

Certain rights, however, are so important that they are not preempted by the Act. These include civil rights protection against racial or religious discrimination, access for the disabled and some common-law contract rights, such as a prohibition against an airline retroactively raising the price of a ticket after it's purchased. For a long time, courts disagreed as to whether certain state laws, such as consumer protection laws, applied to airlines. In 1995, the U.S. Supreme Court ruled that most state regulations are preempted by federal regulations—that is, they do not apply to airlines.[3]

Your Rights Under International Law

Your rights on international flights are governed by an international agreement known as the Warsaw Convention.[4] This agreement defines an airline's liability for damages you incur due to lost, delayed or damaged baggage or a flight delay, when you are "engaged in international travel." You are considered to be engaged in international travel if your ticket specifies on its face that:

- you will fly from one country that has signed the Warsaw Convention to another country that has signed the Convention (virtually all countries have signed the Warsaw Convention), or
- en route to your final destination, you will stop over in a foreign country.

The law focuses on what was *intended* and listed on your ticket, not what actually happened.

Example: On your flight from Texas to California, the plane crashed in Mexico and you were hurt. This would not be considered an international flight, and thus would not be covered by the Warsaw Convention. If, however, your flight from New York to Montreal crashes in Massachusetts, it would be covered by the Warsaw Convention because international transit was originally intended.

The Warsaw Convention is written in very technical legal language. Most of the important provisions are covered in this chapter. The Convention applies in nearly all countries, with some minor variations.

New Ways to Book Flights: Electronic Tickets and Web Tickets

Many airlines now offer electronic tickets as an alternative to standard paper tickets. You are given a record locator number, sent a written receipt and must show an appropriate photo ID at the airport. Your rights and responsibilities are supposed to be the same whether the ticket is electronic or paper. However, new legal issues are sure to develop with electronic tickets. For example, if you don't receive a written ticket before you fly and have no opportunity to read the terms of your ticket, how can you be deemed to have agreed to these terms? Or, if you purchase the ticket shortly before you travel and don't receive the receipt before you depart, and the airline loses your electronic ticket in its computer, how can you prove you bought the ticket and avoid having to pay much more at the airport on the day of your flight? To protect yourself in this situation, when you make your reservation, note the name of the ticketing agent and the date and time you purchased the electronic ticket, and ask the agent to fax, mail or e-mail you an itinerary indicating that you have purchased an electronic ticket.

In one recent case, a passenger who did not have a paper confirmation of his electronic ticket was pulled off a plane because the computer did not show any credit card information in the record. The traveler had purchased the e-ticket with a check.

E-tickets aren't the only innovation brought on by the computer age. Many World Wide Web sites have sprung up to service travelers. Occasionally, they offer deals, particularly for departures with little or no advance notice that help airlines fill empty seats. Booking online, however, is not always the best deal. Consumer advocates have found substantial variations in price, and travel agents may be able to do better than you using their computerized reservation service. Some sites offer online auctions where you bid online for a particular destination. For others, you state where you want to go and how much you are willing to pay, and the service finds the best deal within that price range. Beware of the restrictions on such tickets. Often they are nonrefundable, nonchangeable and nonendorseable, which means that if you must make a change, the ticket could be worth nothing.

Ticket Consolidators

Have you ever been tempted by the really cheap international flights advertised in the travel section of your local newspaper? Some of these ads are placed by people operating travel scams (see Chapter 7), but others are legitimate discount tickets offered by companies known as ticket brokers or consolidators. Ticket consolidators buy tickets in bulk from airlines, often at a substantial discount, and then resell them either to the public or through travel agents.

Although purchasing tickets from a consolidators may save you money, there are a few traps to be wary of:

- Consolidator tickets are often non-refundable and nonexchangeable, so if you need to change your travel plans, you may be stuck.
- Consolidator tickets are not always the cheapest available—especially during fare wars—and there are often hidden charges such as a fee for using a credit card.
- You may not get frequent flyer miles on a consolidator ticket. Ask before you buy.
- There may be a delay in getting the tickets to you—sometimes you will get your tickets only days before the flight, even if you have made your purchase weeks before.

There are a few ways to protect yourself: go through a travel agent to purchase a consolidator ticket, pay with a credit card and think about travel cancellation insurance if your ticket isn't refundable. For more information on consolidators, see Chapter 5.

Ticket Fares and Restrictions

How Airlines Calculate Fares

The price of most air fares is determined by complicated computer programs which calculate how many passengers are likely to book seats on any given flight. Airlines hate to fly with empty seats, so often they are willing to lower prices to get at least some money for seats that would otherwise be empty. An airline's desire to build up a certain route, or to meet discounted prices offered by competitors, also affects the final price of a ticket. The result is that passengers on the same flight could be paying as many as a dozen different fares. While this is perfectly legal, it often leads to resentment on the part of the passengers who paid substantially more for exactly the same service. In some instances, an airline may be willing to reticket passengers (before the flight) who purchased tickets before a special promotion or discount fare was announced, but an airline is not obliged to do so. If you are allowed to reticket, you are likely to be charged a fee of $25 to $100.

Restricted Tickets

Before the substantial deregulation of the airline industry in the 1980s, fares were determined by agreements (called "tariffs") filed by the airlines with the Civil Aeronautics Board (CAB), the federal agency that formerly regulated airlines. Unused tickets were almost as good as cash—tickets could be cashed in, traded and even used on other airlines. This is still true for many full-fare, unrestricted tickets.

Most tickets, however, carry some sort of restrictions. Today, tickets usually:

- are nontransferable (you can't give your ticket to another person)
- are nonrefundable (you can't get your money back), and/or
- have penalties if you cancel or make changes.

These restrictions should be stated explicitly on the face of the ticket itself, and the travel agent or airline employee selling the ticket is required to inform you of the restrictions before you purchase the ticket. If you are not warned of the restrictions, they cannot be enforced against you, but otherwise they are strictly enforced. One passenger who recently purchased two nonrefundable tickets found this out the hard way. An hour after purchasing the tickets by phone (with his credit card), he canceled them. The airline still charged him for the entire price of the tickets because he was warned that they were nonrefundable, even though he never even received his tickets.

Nontransferable, Nonrefundable Tickets

Most economy seats are sold as "nontransferable, nonrefundable." What do these terms really mean?

Nontransferable:

A nontransferable ticket can be used only by the passenger whose name appears on the face of the ticket. In the past, domestic tickets were fairly easy to transfer, but increasingly, airlines ask passengers to show ID when they check in. If the names on the ID and the ticket do not match, the airline can confiscate the ticket. If a ticket is nontransferable but refundable, try cashing in the old ticket and buying a new one with the new passenger's name.

Nonrefundable:

A nonrefundable ticket generally means that you cannot get your money back if you decide not to travel; however, each airline sets its own policies and exceptions. If you cannot make a flight for which you have a nonrefundable ticket, you may be able to apply the ticket toward a future flight or exchange it for credit toward future travel. If the fare has dropped on a flight for which you have a nonrefundable ticket, you may be able to get "reticketed." In either situation, you will probably have to pay a fee to make the change.

Trying to Get Around Airline Restrictions

Every time an airline creates a ticket with an unusual (high) fare or restriction, some wily travel agent or passenger figures out a way to get around it. For instance, when airlines set fares making travel to or from a particular airport more expensive than simply passing through that airport, travel agents and passengers developed the "hidden-city" technique.

Here is how the hidden-city technique works. A round-trip ticket on a flight between Los Angeles and New York, a very competitive route, might be less expensive than a round trip between Los Angeles and St. Louis. To take advantage of the lower price, a passenger wanting to visit St. Louis could purchase a flight between Los Angeles and New York with a change of planes in St. Louis. When the passenger arrived in St. Louis, she could simply throw away the portions of the ticket between St. Louis and New York, and use the last coupon to return to Los Angeles from St. Louis.

Airlines combat this technique by keeping track of "no-shows" on flights (such as the St. Louis to New York and New York to St. Louis flights) to determine who is using the hidden-city technique. If you are caught, the airline can cancel your reservation on the return flight, may attempt to charge you or your travel agent for the regular full-fare ticket between Los Angeles and St. Louis and might even confiscate your return ticket.

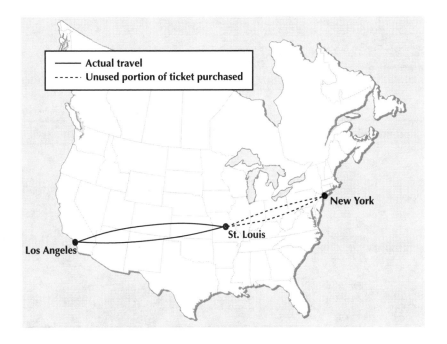

Actual travel
Unused portion of ticket purchased

New York
St. Louis
Los Angeles

A second technique, known as "back-to-back" or "nested" ticketing, allows business travelers to take advantage of cheaper fares available only with a Saturday night stay-over by buying two sets of round-trip tickets that overlap.

Example: Tony knows that he needs to make two business trips between Dallas and Chicago. On the first trip, he plans to be in Chicago from Monday, the 1st, until Friday, the 5th. On the next trip, he plans to be in Chicago from Monday, the 15th, until Friday, the 20th. Under most airlines' fare schedules, Tony would be required to pay full fare for both of those trips because he does not have a Saturday night stay-over. If, however, Tony purchases one round trip from Dallas to Chicago on the 1st, returning on the 20th, and a second ticket from Chicago to Dallas on the 5th, returning on the 15th, both of his tickets qualify as excursion fares because of the Saturday night stay-overs.

Airlines consider this an abuse of the excursion fare and have tried charging travel agents and sometimes passengers when the airlines determine, by using computerized reservations and frequent flyer records, that passengers are essentially on two trips at once. In the past, the airlines' attempts to enforce their policy against back-to-back travel have been frustrated, however, because passengers and travel agents figured out that by booking one of the tickets on one airline and the second on a different airline, the back-to-back bookings could not be discovered.

Airlines now use more sophisticated computer techniques to try to trace back-to-back bookings. The airlines attempt different means of enforcement by threatening cancellation of frequent flyer privileges and/or limiting excursion rates to 30 days (thereby eliminating long-term back-to-backs). Most aviation attorneys who represent passengers claim that unless the restriction on multiple trips is explicitly included in the passenger's ticket, the

Sun	Mon.	Tues.	Wed.	Thurs.	Fri.	Sat.
	1 Dallas to Chicago Ticket 1	2 Chicago	3 Chicago	4 Chicago	5 Chicago to Dallas Ticket 2	6
7	8	9	10	11	12	13
14	15 Dallas to Chicago Ticket 2	16 Chicago	17 Chicago	18 Chicago	19 Chicago to Dallas Ticket 1	20

passenger is not doing anything wrong by using the back-to-back technique. Some airlines have given up trying to enforce the ban on back-to-back ticketing.

Tickets for Infants

Many U.S. airlines sell half-fare tickets for infants under two. The infant is given a reserved seat where a child safety seat can be used. In the past, the only options available for people traveling with infants were having the child sit on a parent's lap or buying a full-fare ticket. Each airline has its own restrictions, so check for details in advance.

Ticket Changes Because of Death or Serious Illness

In certain exceptional cases, the airlines will allow nonrefundable tickets to be refunded if you cancel because of illness or the death of a friend or relative. Sometimes, an airline needs to be persuaded to be generous. One frequent flyer was told that her ticket was nonrefundable despite the death of a relative which caused cancellation of a trip. The airline acquiesced quickly when the passenger explained to the ticket seller's supervisor that she was a frequent customer who was willing to take her business elsewhere if the airline could not see its way to allowing a refund.

Ticket Purchases Because of Death or Serious Illness

In certain exceptional cases, an airline will offer a discounted fare (sometimes minor, sometimes generous) even if you do not meet the advance-purchase or stay-over requirements for that fare. Generally, this occurs when a member of your immediate family becomes seriously ill or dies, and you need to travel without any advanced planning. Precisely who must be ill or have died in order for you to obtain a "bereavement fare" is an aspect that varies among airlines—for example, some airlines will give a discounted fare to attend the funeral of a parent, child, sibling, spouse or in-law only, while other airlines include the immediate relatives of your nonmarital partner. It is worth doing some comparison shopping if you must suddenly travel due to a relative's illness or death.

Also, you will probably have to provide the airline with information it can use to verify the illness or death before giving you the discounted fare. In the case of illness, be ready to provide the name of a hospital and the name and phone number of the treating physician. In the case of death, you'll probably need to provide the name and phone number of the funeral home.

Lost Tickets

If you lose your airline ticket, you must fill out a lost-ticket application. The airline will either issue a replacement ticket (after you sign an agreement to reimburse the airline for the cost of the replacement ticket if someone uses your lost ticket) or force you to purchase a replacement ticket at the currently available fare (often outrageously expensive because you don't get any advance-purchase discounts). In addition, you usually have to pay some sort of service charge or penalty for a replacement ticket.

After a waiting period of three months to a year, the airline will issue you a refund for the price of your replacement ticket if your lost ticket was not used during that time.

The policies on lost tickets vary among airlines. Policies are generally looser on international flights.

Unfortunately, sometimes a part of your ticket may be "lost" because the ticket agent at the gate takes the wrong coupon from your ticket. For example, if on the first leg of a round trip between Boston and New York, the agent takes your New York to Boston coupon by mistake, you will be left in New York with a seemingly worthless Boston to New York ticket. In such cases, the airline may honor that coupon for the return trip; but if it is particularly strict, it may force you to purchase a separate one-way New York to Boston ticket. You can avoid this predicament by double-checking your remaining ticket coupon as soon as you enter the aircraft.

Lost Ticket, Happy Ending

I recently sat in a small claims court and witnessed the following case: A student from San Francisco traveled to London for the summer. The return trip was booked London to New York and New York to San Francisco. The student stated that when she arrived in New York, she discovered both the London to New York coupon and the New York to San Francisco coupon had been removed from her ticket so that she had no way to return to San Francisco. Her conclusion was that the gate agent had mistakenly taken both coupons from her ticket when she left London. The airline was unsympathetic and required her to purchase a full-fare, one-way ticket between New York and San Francisco. The student felt that she should not have had to pay for a second ticket because the airline employee was at fault.

After she presented her side of the story to the judge, the airline's represen-tative argued first, that the gate agent could not have taken both coupons and second, that the student's claim for a refund, if any, should be against her original travel agent rather than the airline because the terms of her ticket contained a standard provision requiring any claim for "lost" tickets to be pro-cessed through the ticketing travel agent. The judge's response brought laughter to the entire court. He told the airline's representative: "Unfortunately for you, this has happened to me." He stated that it was very probable that the gate agent had taken both coupons and so the student was entitled to a refund on the second ticket. He also noted that the airline, and not the student's travel agent, was responsible for the refund because the coupon had not been "lost," it had been taken by the airline. In this case, the ticket agent may have been blind, but justice wasn't.

Overbooking and Bumping

In most industries, accepting more reservations than there are seats would be considered illegal. Overbooking in the airline industry, however, is completely legal and permitted by federal law. Airlines count on the fact that a certain percentage of passengers will not show up for a given flight.

Of course, when all passengers do show up, conflicts often arise. Over half a million passengers are denied boarding—or bumped—each year. Although your chances of being bumped involuntarily are only about 1 in 10,000, those odds increase considerably during peak flying times, particularly around Thanksgiving and during the December holiday season.

If a flight is overbooked, the airline is required to ask passengers if anyone is willing to volunteer to take a later flight.[5] Normally, the airline will offer some kind of incentive such as a free or discounted round-trip ticket (some restrictions, such as blackout dates or use within one year, may apply). Over 90% of U.S. passengers who are bumped are volunteers. If an insufficient number of passengers volunteer to be bumped from the flight, the airline must begin involuntary bumping. Each airline has

its own set of policies and procedures to determine who will be bumped. Generally, passengers with the most recent reservations or those who checked in the latest are the first to be bumped.

When to Bargain

If you discover, at the airport, that your flight is very full and some passengers are likely to be bumped, you can volunteer to be bumped even before the airline makes any requests. Simply go to the ticket counter at the desk and inform the ticket agent that you are willing to be bumped. If you are offered compensation which does not seem high enough, you can bargain with the airline, keeping in mind the maximum amounts the airline would have to pay (these are discussed below) if it involuntarily bumped a passenger.

When You Are Bumped Involuntarily: Denied Boarding Compensation

If you are denied boarding, you must have a confirmed reservation (your tickets should have an "ok" or "hk" in the "Status" column), and the scheduled plane must have a seating capacity of more than 60 passengers (this eliminates many commuter flights) to be eligible for compensation.

Even if you meet both of those requirements, the airline might refuse to compensate you if any of the following is true:[6]

- You have not fully complied with the airline's ticketing, check-in and reconfirmation requirements—such as arriving at an airport one hour before a flight or reconfirming an international flight as required.

- You are not acceptable for transportation under the airline's usual rules and practices—for example, you are drunk.
- The entire flight was canceled.
- A smaller aircraft was substituted for safety or operational reasons—for example, the airplane that was scheduled to make the flight broke down, and the only available replacement was smaller than the original plane.
- You refuse an offer to take a seat in a different section (class) of the aircraft at no extra charge. Normally, this is not a problem for economy passengers; very few people refuse to be upgraded to business or first class. Business or first-class passengers, however, may resist being placed in economy class even though they are entitled to a refund of the difference in the ticket price.
- The airline offers to place you on another flight or flights scheduled to reach your final destination within one hour of the scheduled arrival of the original flight.

Sometimes, it is worth putting up a fight if you are bumped involuntarily and won't be compensated (for example, if you arrive late at the airport) or if you absolutely must be on a flight. Here are some suggestions:

- Emphasize why you must reach your destination on time by explaining the specific harm or loss you would suffer if you are not on the flight.
- Ask to see the airline's rules for boarding priority. The airline is required to make this list available to you at all of

its ticket selling and boarding locations.[7] Insist that the airline enforce its own boarding priority policies. For example, the policy may be that passengers with the most recent reservations are bumped first.

- Demand that the airline make a greater effort to get volunteers.

Domestic Flights

The amount of denied boarding compensation generally depends on how long the airline makes you wait. If the airline places you on a flight scheduled to arrive within an hour of your original arrival time, the airline is not required to pay you anything. If the airline can place you on a flight that is scheduled to arrive at your destination more than one hour but less than two hours after your original arrival time, the airline must pay you an amount equal to the value of that segment of your ticket, with a maximum of $200.

If the next flight the airline can arrange for you is scheduled to arrive more than two hours after your original flight, you are entitled to compensation of two times the value of that segment of your ticket, with a maximum of $400. In practice, airlines will typically offer vouchers for future flights instead of cash, but, by law, you are entitled to cash or a check from the airline.[8] Note that the rules focus on when the replacement flight is scheduled to arrive, not when it actually arrives.

Example 1: Fernando is bumped involuntarily from his 2:00 p.m. flight from Chicago to New York, which was scheduled to arrive at 4:00 p.m. The next available flight that the airline can put him on is not scheduled to arrive until 7:00 p.m. His one-way ticket from Chicago to New York cost $350. Because the next available flight is scheduled to arrive more than two hours after his originally scheduled arrival time, Fernando is entitled to two times the value of that segment of his ticket, up to $400. Because two times the value of his ticket is $700, he gets only $400.

Example 2: Teresa is bumped involuntarily from her 1:00 p.m. flight from San Francisco to San Diego, which is scheduled to arrive at 2:30 p.m. Her round-trip ticket cost $300. The airline arranges a flight for her that is scheduled to arrive at 4:00 p.m. Because this is more than one but less than two hours after her originally scheduled arrival time, she is entitled to $150 compensation, which equals the value of that segment of her ticket.

Example 3: Larry is also bumped involuntarily from the San Francisco to San Diego flight, but the airline is able to place him on a flight that is scheduled to arrive at 3:25. Because this flight is scheduled to arrive only 55 minutes after the original flight, he receives no compensation because the airlines do not have to pay for delays of less than one hour. Even if Larry's substitute flight develops mechanical problems and he is actually several hours late, he will not be eligible for denied boarding compensation.

Compensation for Involuntary Bumping (Flights Within or Leaving U.S.)

Scheduled Arrival of New Flight	Domestic Flights	International Flights (Departing From the U.S.)
New flight scheduled to arrive less than one hour after original flight	No compensation	No compensation
New flight scheduled to arrive between one and two hours after original flight (one to four hours for international flights)	Value of ticket segment, $200 maximum	Value of ticket segment, $200 maximum
New flight scheduled to arrive more than two hours after original flight (domestic only)	Twice the value of ticket segment, $400 maximum	N/A
New flight scheduled to arrive more than four hours after original flight (international only)	N/A	Twice the value of ticket segment, $400 maximum

International Flights

On international flights departing from the U.S., the compensation is the same as on domestic flights, but the time requirements are different. If the airline can get you on a flight that is scheduled to arrive within an hour of your original flight, you won't receive any compensation. If the flight is scheduled to arrive between one and four hours of your originally scheduled flight, the required compensation is the value of that segment of your ticket, up to a maximum of $200. If the next available flight is scheduled to arrive more than four hours after your originally scheduled flight, you are entitled to compensation of two times the value of that segment of your ticket, up to $400 maximum.

These compensation amounts do not apply to flights departing from other countries and arriving in the U.S. Some other countries provide compensation, but generally for lower amounts. For instance, if you are bumped involuntarily from an international flight departing from one of the 15 European Union (EU) countries, you are entitled to the compensation indicated below, paid in European Community Units (ECUs):[9]

Stopover Cities—Domestic or International Flights

If your original flight has a scheduled stop-over of four or more hours and you are bumped involuntarily, the airline must compensate you if it cannot get you to either your stopover city or your final destination within the time limits described for flights within or leaving the U.S.[10]

Example: You are flying from Los Angeles to Boston with a five-hour stopover in St. Louis and are involuntarily denied boarding on the Los Angeles to St. Louis flight. The airline is only liable to pay you compensation for the Los Angeles to St. Louis segment of your trip. You are not entitled to compensation for the St. Louis to Boston trip even if you arrive in

Compensation for Involuntary Bumping (Flights Leaving European Union Country)

Scheduled Duration or Distance of Original Flight	Arrival at ...ÚÚDestination	Compensation
Less than two hours or 3,500 kilometers	Within two hours of originally scheduled arrival	75 ECUs (approximately $50)
Less than two hours or 3,500 kilometers	More than two hours late	150 ECUs (approximately $100)
Over two hours or over 3,500 kilometers	Within two hours of originally scheduled arrival	150 ECUs (approximately $100)
Over two hours or over 3,500 kilometers	More than two hours late	300 ECUs (approximately $200)

St. Louis so late that you miss your St. Louis to Boston flight. (In practice, the airline would probably try to find an alternate route for you if your true destination is Boston).

If your connection time between flights is less than four hours, legally your flight does not qualify as a stop-over. This means that if you are bumped involuntarily, the airline must get you to your final destination within the time limits described earlier or pay you the required compensation.

Refusing the Offered Compensation

The overbooking law contains a provision stating that you may reject the compensation offered by the airline and "seek to recover damages in a court of law or in some other manner."[11] Generally speaking, you should accept the offer of compensation unless all of the following are true:

- you will suffer some special damage or loss if you are involuntarily bumped
- you have informed the airline of the potential damage or loss, and
- the airline still refuses to board you or give you additional compensation.

Example: You are a singer on the way to perform in a show in another city, are involuntarily refused boarding, explain your potential financial loss to the airline, are still denied boarding and do not arrive in time to perform. The income you lost by not performing is a type of consequential damage that may greatly exceed the value of any compensation offered by the airline.

Suing to recover your losses is particularly likely to succeed if the airline does not follow its own rules and policies. In one case, an economy-class passenger recovered $5,000 in a case against an airline when his coach seat was given to a first-class passenger when the first-class section was overbooked. The court ruled that the airline should have followed its own procedure, which was to board passengers with the earliest reservations first, even if it meant denying boarding to a first-class passenger.[12]

Before rejecting the compensation offered by the airline, weigh carefully what you are likely to recover even if you succeed in a lawsuit against the airline. For instance, in one case, a passenger who was flying to attend a wedding the next day was involuntarily bumped, and instead of arriving at his destination at night he arrived early in the morning, missing the rehearsal dinner. He claimed that he suffered "humiliation, annoyance and distress." After a long and expensive legal struggle he finally won—$450—less than the original compensation offered by the airline.[13] Of course, the court probably would have been more sympathetic if he was actually getting married, rather than just attending the wedding as a guest.[14]

If you do reject the airline's compensation and plan to fight for more, consider writing a Solution Letter™ or using mediation or arbitration to resolve your dispute (see discussion in Chapter 13). Because of the small amounts of money normally involved in overbooking cases, legal fees are likely to eat up any potential recovery. Sometimes, of course, passengers sue just to prove a point. For instance, when consumer activist Ralph Nader was denied boarding on a flight in

1972, he and the public interest group before which he was scheduled to speak sued the airline. Although the ultimate recovery was very small, the publicity generated by the case served to heighten passengers' awareness of their rights as travelers.[15]

Delayed, Diverted and Canceled Flights

A flight is considered on time by the Department of Transportation if it arrives at its destination within 15 minutes of the scheduled arrival time. Generally, a 15-minute delay will not affect your schedule very much. Longer delays can have serious consequences, particularly if you cannot make a connecting flight because of the delay. In such cases, you may be forced to waste hours in an airport waiting for the next available flight and may even have to stay overnight if the next flight does not leave until the following day.

If your trip is delayed because of overbooking, the rules discussed in the previous section apply. If the delay is caused by any other reason, your rights on a domestic flight are largely determined by the hidden terms of your ticket. On international flights, your rights are largely determined by the Warsaw Convention.

Domestic Flights

In their Conditions of Carriage, most airlines include terms which set forth the airline's obligations if a flight is delayed, diverted or canceled. In some cases, the terms are quite specific and promise compensation, such as meals while you wait and a hotel room if the delay is overnight.

Generally, airlines are not obliged to provide any compensation if the delay, diversion or cancellation was caused by factors outside of the airline's control, such as bad weather or air traffic congestion at a particular airport. On the other hand, airlines may be required to compensate you for problems deemed in their control, such as scheduling problems or late-arriving crew members, if it says so in the Conditions of Carriage.

The offered compensation can vary substantially among airlines—full-service airlines are likely to offer more generous terms, such as hotel and meal vouchers, while budget or no-frills airlines may not offer any compensation.

If your flight is substantially delayed and the airline offers no compensation or much less than you believe is fair, you can challenge the airline. If you take your challenge to court, your chance of success depends on the relevant terms in your ticket and the particular facts in your case. A court will generally award compensation only if it finds that the airline has broken its contract with you, or if the terms of the contract are so unreasonable, such as denying all responsibility for any delays, that the court will not enforce them.

The airlines' limitations of liability are usually upheld by the courts.[16] If, however, an airline misleads you about alternative flights or the expected duration of the delay, a court may conclude that the airline did not live up to its contractual promises. In such a situation, a court may rule that an airline cannot use the limitations it placed in the contract to avoid paying you damages. In a successful lawsuit, the court may award you direct or consequential damages—punitive damages might be obtained in only the most extreme cases. (See below.)

Any damages a court might award will vary substantially depending on your situation, and often the expense of pursuing a case against an airline will be greater than your damages. In a situation where you have real, provable damages, but they are not large enough to justify suing, consider an alternative dispute resolution procedure such as mediation or arbitration (discussed in Chapter 13).

Direct Damages

The most immediate loss or expense incurred on a delayed or canceled flight is money spent for meals, phone calls, hotel rooms or alternative transportation. These are direct damages and are usually fairly easy to calculate.

Consequential Damages

Consequential damages cover losses that naturally occurred because of the delay. For instance, if you are on a delayed or canceled flight and miss an important meeting or event, you can claim you suffered consequential damages. A court will generally force an airline to pay consequential damages only if the following are true:

- the damages are of a type that the airline knew would result or should have foreseen would result because of the delay—such as if you cannot get back to work and are docked a day's wages

- the amount of loss can be calculated in dollar terms—in the above example, you could make a claim for the lost wages, but not for the hypothetical goodwill that you would have earned in the eyes of your employer if you had made it back, and

- the loss was caused by some act of the airline or its employees, rather than an event outside of the control of the airline, such as weather, a war or a natural disaster.

The idea is that you should be placed in as good a position as if the airline had fulfilled its obligations under the contract. You are most likely to recover consequential damages if you can prove that the flight delay or cancellation was solely for the convenience of the airline or to save the airline money.

Example: An airline operates several flights a day from New York to Los Angeles using jumbo jets. Just before a flight is scheduled to depart, a large number of passengers cancel. The airline, knowing it will lose a great deal of money flying a practically empty airplane across the country, cancels the flight and puts the passengers on a later flight in the afternoon. In this circumstance, the airline is placing its commercial interests ahead of the interests of the passengers and could be responsible for paying the passengers' consequential damages.

International Flights

Recovering damages for an international flight delay is very difficult if the delay was caused by anything other than the airline's overbooking. Airlines have a number of ways to avoid paying damages for any flight delay. To begin with, under the Warsaw Convention, an airline can escape liability for damages caused by a flight delay if it can show that it took "all necessary measures to avoid the damage or [it was impossible] to take such measures."[17]

> **Example:** A passenger who had just returned from Europe was delayed over four hours on his flight from New York to Chicago. Although the passenger claimed that the New York to Chicago leg was exclusively domestic, the court ruled that because that flight was part of a larger series of flights including international transit, his flight between New York and Chicago was international travel and was therefore covered by the Warsaw Convention. Since the delay was caused by mechanical difficulties, the airline was not liable for damages caused by the delay because the repairs were necessary to ensure the safety of the passengers.[18]

In similar cases, courts have ruled that if an airline provides passengers with an alternate means of reaching their destination, such as tickets on another airline, the requirement of taking all necessary measures to avoid the damage is satisfied—even if the replacement airline also suffers delays.[19] Courts have also ruled that an airline can limit its liability if it can show that the damage suffered was contributed to or caused by the passenger's negligence.[20]

If your international flight is delayed, you may be able to persuade the airline that it should cover direct costs caused by the delay such as meal, hotel or telephone expenses. To back up your argument, you can quote Article 19 of the Warsaw Convention, which states: "The Carrier shall be liable for damages occasioned by delay in the transportation by air of passengers, baggage or goods."

Remember that, in addition to the protection offered by the Warsaw Convention, an airline may try to protect itself further by asserting the hidden terms of its Conditions of Carriage. These terms are generally upheld by the courts, but not always.

> **Example:** In one case, a flight from Alabama to Italy was delayed for 32 hours. The airline claimed that it was protected by its Conditions of Carriage, which stated that the airline would provide alternate transportation if a delay lasted more than 48 hours. The court determined that even though the delay was less than 48 hours, the passengers might have a right to recover damages against the airline for the 32-hour delay.[21]

Lost or Damaged Baggage

The airlines' treatment of baggage is a constant source of passenger complaints. Nearly every airline passenger, at some point, has waited for what seemed like an eternity for his or her baggage to show up on the baggage carousel. Many passengers can identify with the old suitcase commercial which showed a gorilla jumping up and down on a passenger's bags and throwing the passenger's suitcase around a room.

To be fair, most of the time baggage does arrive, in good shape, on the same flight you were on. When your luggage is damaged, delayed, stolen or lost, however, the results can be disastrous. The best way to protect yourself from the most serious losses is to follow one simple rule: Never put anything valuable or irreplaceable (such as jewelry), or that you might urgently need (such as medications), in checked baggage. You will be compensated by the airline for lost or damaged baggage or items taken from your baggage, but this compensation rarely covers your actual loss.

What Not to Pack in Your Checked Luggage

What some people pack in their checked luggage is astounding. In one case, a salesman made a claim for $175,000 in jewelry which disappeared; in another case, a professional courier lost a checked piece of luggage containing $2 million in cash; and in several cases, passengers packed urgently needed medicine in checked baggage that was lost or delayed by the airlines. Although airline baggage services are normally reliable, do not let this lull you into a false sense of security. Do not pack extremely valuable or urgently needed items in your checked baggage—ever.

In addition, airlines prohibit passengers from packing several items in checked baggage. You might guess that explosives, fireworks and loaded guns are not allowed. It might surprise you to know, however, that matches and lighters (which might ignite by friction), flammable liquids such as camping gas or other fuels, paints, solvents and adhesives are also prohibited, as well as many household items such as bleaches, drain cleaners, many aerosols, mercury and other dangerous chemicals which could cause toxic fumes or corrosion. Information on other forbidden items can be obtained from the airline or your travel agent.

In addition, a pamphlet entitled *These Fly, These May Not* outlining the hazardous materials restrictions is available from the Federal Aviation Administration at FAA, AS4-20, 400 7th Street, SW, Washington, DC 20590, 202-267-7770 (phone); or visit http://www.faa.gov (World Wide Web).

Domestic Flights

Under federal regulations, an airline can limit the amount it must pay if baggage is lost, stolen, damaged or delayed, but the airline cannot limit its liability to less than $1,250 per passenger.[22] Most airlines, therefore, limit their maximum liability to $1,250. You can get around this by declaring at check-in a higher value for the baggage up to the airline's maximum, which is likely to be between $2,500 and $5,000. If you declare a higher value, the airline will charge you a fee, generally based on a percentage of the declared value. The airline then becomes liable up to the declared value if it loses, damages or delays delivery of the baggage, unless the airline can prove that the actual loss was lower than the declared value.

Another source of protection is baggage insurance. Many travel insurance policies, some homeowners' policies and even some credit cards offer reimbursement for lost or damaged baggage. Check your policies before traveling so that you can calculate whether it is worth declaring (and paying for) the excess value.

Limitations on Luggage

Airlines can set reasonable limitations on the size, weight and number of bags you can check. These limitations are set forth in the Conditions of Carriage. You may be able to transport oversized, overweight or extra bags by paying a fee.

 Chapter 8 contains information on baggage insurance.

If your baggage appears to be lost or delayed, your first step is to check with the airline's baggage agent. Because most airline baggage services are computerized, the agent can often determine where the baggage is and how long it will take to arrive. If your baggage will be delayed, most airlines are obligated by the terms of their Conditions of Carriage to deliver the bags to you free of charge wherever you are. If your baggage arrives before you do, the airline has the responsibility to safeguard it for you.

To protect your rights, you must fill out a written claim for lost or delayed baggage. Most airlines have their own forms; when filling any of them out, describe your baggage and its contents as completely and accurately as possible. (When you pack, make a list of what you are putting into your baggage and put the list in a bag you carry onto the plane.) If your baggage is never found, the claim will probably be the basis upon which the airline determines how much your bags and their contents were worth—meaning that you are not automatically entitled to $1,250. The terms of most tickets will prevent you from recovering anything if you do not make a written claim.

Recovering More Than $1,250

Your right to recover more than the normal $1,250 limitation amount often depends more on the airline's behavior than on the value of the baggage. Courts will sometimes ignore the $1,250 limit if you can show that the airline engaged in willful misconduct. The term "willful" is somewhat deceiving. It is not necessary to prove that the airline intended to lose or damage the baggage, but only that it intentionally took some action that it should not have taken that led to the damage.

In one case, a passenger who changed his travel plans requested that the airline remove his baggage from the plane. The airline refused, the plane departed and the plaintiff's baggage was never recovered.[23] In another case, the court stated that a series of actions by the airline constituted willful misconduct: the airline incorrectly ticketed the baggage, refused to correctly ticket the baggage when it was requested to do so by the passenger, refused to verify the whereabouts of the baggage, did not retrieve the lost baggage for 15 days and misled the passenger by telling him that the baggage would be returned the next day.[24] In such cases, courts generally allow a passenger to recover more than the $1,250 limit.

The airline's limitation of liability provision is most likely to be rejected if the airline does not follow its own policies and rules regarding baggage, or when it puts its own economic interests ahead of the passenger's rights. For example, in one case, an airline that uses small airplanes unloaded one passenger's baggage in order to stay below its weight limitations and accommodate several additional passengers. The airline did not inform the passenger ahead of time in order to give him an option to choose a different airline, and the passenger arrived at his destination without any of his luggage. The passenger was traveling to a convention and was greatly inconvenienced by not having a change of clothing. The court ruled that the airline's failure to notify the passenger that his luggage would not be traveling with him constituted misrepresentation and concealment, which are types of fraud, and therefore the airline could not limit its damage to $1,250.[25]

Passengers have attempted to claim damages for emotional distress, discomfort, humiliation or annoyance because of loss, damage or delay of baggage, but courts generally do not allow such damages.

Damages for Delayed Baggage

Most of the time when your baggage is delayed, the airline puts the baggage on the next flight heading to where you are and delivers the bag to you the same day. Nonetheless, a delay of even several hours can be very significant if, for instance, you packed medicine that you need to take in your checked bags. However long the delay, the airline is generally responsible for paying any reasonable expenses that you incur because of the delay. To reduce their costs, many airlines have put together their own overnight kits, which include most basic toiletries, to give to passengers whose bags are lost or delayed and cannot be delivered until the next day.

Often, however, you will need more than toiletries. If you anticipate additional expenses, such as underwear and a shirt for the next day or necessary medications, request a check from the airline to cover the expenses. The airline agent may resist making up-front payments, in which case you should purchase what you need and bill the airline for the expenses. This is not a license to go on a spending spree. The airline will compensate you for reasonable and documented expenses only. Of course, if you arrive in town for a business meeting wearing casual clothes, and your bag contained your business clothes, you have a good argument that you are entitled to purchase whatever business apparel you need if you need it right away. Be prepared to prove how much you spent (keep your receipts) and why you needed the items you bought.

If you can prove that the airline's acts caused a significant delay or the loss of your luggage, you may be able to obtain more than the value of your baggage. In one case, a golfer purchased a package tour which included air travel, hotel and golfing privileges. The passenger's baggage, including his golf clubs, was not delivered to him until after his vacation was over. The court allowed him to recover not only his expenses for the golfing equipment and other items he had to purchase, but also for the reduced value of his vacation.[26]

International Flights

The Warsaw Convention provides the rules under which liability for lost, delayed or damaged baggage is determined on international flights. Everyone (except the airlines) agrees that the limits under the Warsaw Convention are ridiculous. To begin with, damages are calculated based on the weight of the baggage. Regardless of the real value of the baggage or its contents, the Warsaw Convention states that the value for lost or damaged baggage is $9.07 per pound (or $20 per kilogram).

If your bag was weighed before the flight, then the value is determined by multiplying the weight of the bag times $9.07. For example, a 20-pound bag would be valued at $181.40. If your bags were not weighed,

the airline will generally assume that all of your bags weighed a total of 70 pounds, and will reimburse you $634.90. The $9.07 per pound limitation has been upheld by the Supreme Court.[27] It has been applied even when the bags lost contained $2 million in cash.[28]

To add insult to injury, an airline can completely avoid responsibility for lost or damaged baggage if it can prove "that the damage was occasioned by error in piloting, in the handling of the aircraft or in navigation" and that, in all other respects, "the airline and its agents have taken all necessary measures to avoid the damage."[29] It is difficult to understand why an airline should not be liable for your lost or damaged baggage if one of its pilots mishandles the airplane. On the other hand, if the pilot seriously mishandles the plane, your baggage may be the least of your concerns.

Time Limits to File Your Written Complaint

To make the limitation of damages for baggage even more one-sided, the Warsaw Convention sets forth very strict time limits for filing complaints about baggage:[30]

- If your baggage is damaged (if something is missing from your bag, it qualifies as damaged), you must notify the airline in writing within a maximum of three days of receiving the bag. A shipper sending commercial goods rather than personal baggage has seven days to file a complaint.

- If your baggage is delayed or lost, you must make a written complaint to the airline within 14 days of the date you checked your baggage in with the airline.

These restrictions are particularly difficult for passengers who arrive in a foreign country, may not speak the language and cannot wait at the airport for their baggage to arrive. To be safe, any time your baggage is delayed, immediately fill out a written claim, even if an airline employee assures you that your baggage will arrive on the next flight. State that you believe that your baggage has been delayed, lost or stolen, given that you don't actually know what happened to your baggage until it arrives. Keep a copy of your written claim as proof that you filed it. Also, take an extra blank copy of the claim with you in case your baggage is damaged when it arrives. The odds that something may have been taken from your baggage increase dramatically the longer your baggage is delayed or lost.

Recovering More Than the Warsaw Convention Provides

Under the Warsaw Convention, an airline must do the following:

- provide notice that the Warsaw Convention applies
- provide a baggage check (a notice that your bags were taken, normally part of your ticket; it is not the baggage ticket stub, normally stapled to your ticket envelope), and
- weigh the baggage.

If you can show that the airline did not do one or more of the above, a court may permit you to recover more than the limit.[31] On the other hand, a court might decide that the airline's failure to follow the Warsaw Convention procedures is merely technical and doesn't permit you to recover more than the limit. For example, if an airline fails to weigh your bags, the court may rule that the airline is required merely to pay you as though the bags weighed 70 pounds, the maximum allowable baggage per customer.[32]

One way to protect yourself, if you are concerned about lost, delayed or damaged baggage on an international flight, is to make a declaration of "excess value." That is, when you check your baggage in, declare the estimated value of the baggage and its contents. The airline will then be liable for the entire declared amount if the baggage is lost or damaged, unless the airline can prove that the value was actually less than what you declared. The only hitch, of course, is that the airline will charge you a surcharge for any declared value in excess of $9.07 per pound.

Carry-On Bags

More and more passengers bring most, if not all, of their baggage with them on board the plane as carry-on bags. Airlines can and do place limitations on the number and size of carry-on bags. Most airlines permit two carry-on bags per passenger, and at least one of the bags must be small enough to fit under the seat in front of you. Airlines are tightening restrictions on carry-on baggage. Many now limit economy class passengers to one carry-on bag in addition to a briefcase or purse. Computer bags and hanging garment bags—which used to be considered allowable "extra" bags—are now counted in the one carry-on bag limit. These restrictions make it even more important to plan ahead, and make sure you can keep medicines, jewelry and other items of value with you, and not in a bag that might have to be checked. If the flight is not full, the airline may be more lenient, but don't count on it. First-class and business class travelers are often exempted from the more stringent restrictions. Some airlines also make provisions for passengers belonging to their very frequent flyer programs.

These limits are set forth in each airline's Conditions of Carriage. (Certain other restrictions, such as prohibitions on carrying on weapons or explosives, are imposed by federal law.)

On domestic flights, the limitations of liability that apply to checked-in baggage also apply to carry-on baggage. Thus, if a carry-on bag is damaged or stolen on a domestic flight, the airline's liability is limited to $1,250. On an international flight, the airline's liability is $181.40 per passenger (20 pounds at $9.07 per pound).[33]

Watch Your Bags!

Theft of portable computers, cameras and other small, valuable carry-on items from travelers is now common, particularly in busy airports. Do not leave them unwatched even for a short while. The security checkpoints where your bags are x-rayed is a high-risk area for theft. A common ploy involves several people working together: When you put your portable valuable carry-on items, particularly a personal computer, through the x-ray machine, one person will hold up the line in front of you at the metal detector while his accomplice walks away with your bag. To avoid this scam, wait until you are next in line for the detector before putting your bag through the x-ray machine, and keep an eye on your bag as it comes out the other side. If you are traveling with someone, one of you can stay back with all the valuables to place on the x-ray reader, while the other can go through ahead and retrieve the items on the other side.

 For restrictions on transporting animals, see Chapter 11.

Physical Injuries

While statistics show that you are safer traveling on a commercial airplane than you are in your own car, occasionally, travel by air can cause both physical and emotional injuries. Passengers have been hit on the head by falling luggage, scalded by boiling coffee and run over by food carts, and have slipped and fallen in just about every imaginable part of airplanes and airports.

The most important questions to answer when you are injured are:

- Who is responsible for your injury?
- How much can you recover?

Most air injuries are minor and probably warrant only a Solution Letter™ to the airline (see Chapter 13). When you are not seriously injured, an airline may be willing to pay some small compensation, such as a free or discounted ticket, as a gesture of goodwill.

 For useful information on obtaining compensation if you are injured, see *How to Win Your Personal Injury Claim,* by Joseph L. Matthews (Nolo Press). If, however, your air travel involves serious injuries or even death, you will need to consult a qualified attorney.

Is the Airline Responsible?

To recover against an airline for personal injuries, you must prove that the airline was negligently or intentionally responsible for your injuries. Because intentional injuries are rare, almost all cases are based on the claim of negligence. Airlines are held to a high standard of conduct because they are considered "common carriers" that owe a duty of care to their passengers. If an airline fails to take reasonable care to protect you, you may be entitled to compensation. One way to prove the airline's negligence is to show that it was required to live up to a certain standard of care and failed to do so in your case.

Although some passengers have claimed that an airline breaches its contract when it allows a passenger to be injured, most courts have rejected these claims, stating that airlines are not ensurers of safe travel.

The standards of care an airline must live up to can be found in the following:

- the operational and safety rules and regulations created by the Federal Aviation Administration for airlines
- the airline's own rules as set out in its Conditions of Carriage, or
- the airline's operations and maintenance manual.

If you believe that an airline violated any of these standards, you should mention it in your Solution Letter™ or lawsuit.

Showing that the airline failed to follow its own standard procedures may be enough to prove that the airline failed to take reasonable steps to protect you from injury. In one case, an airline's failure to follow its own procedures for caring for a passenger having a heart attack cost the airline $2.4 million. The airline failed to contact ground personnel for medical assistance, apply proper first aid procedures or land at the first available airport, and the passenger sustained permanent injuries.[34]

Be aware that courts are all over the map in determining an airline's liability. For example, there have been many cases in which a passenger has been hit by falling overhead baggage. In one case, the court determined that the airline was negligent for failing to foresee that the overhead bins would be overfilled and to take reasonable steps to prevent the baggage from falling and injuring passengers. In another case, the court found that the airline was negligent for failing to assist a passenger with carry-on baggage which ultimately fell and injured another passenger.[35]

In several similar cases, however, other courts have found that the airline was not responsible for falling overhead baggage. Also, in one case, an airline was not responsible for an injury to a passenger's neck when the airplane suddenly dropped 500 feet due to clear air turbulence; the court found that this injury was not foreseeable, and, therefore, the airline was not negligent.[36]

In some cases, where both you and the airline were partially responsible for your injury, the amount of damages you can recover may be limited. (See Comparative Negligence, below.)

 Respondeat Superior. Under the legal principle known as "respondeat superior," an employer is responsible for injuries caused by his or her employees in the course and scope of their work. This means that you can recover from an airline if an airline employee causes injury to you while performing a normal part of his work. For instance, an airline would be responsible if a flight attendant dumps an entire tray of airline food onto your lap. On the other hand, if you get into a fistfight with an airline employee over a parking spot in the garage, it is unlikely that the airline would be held responsible unless parking cars was part of the employee's job.

Res ipsa loquitur means that "the thing speaks for itself." It would apply when an airline has complete control over a situation and a passenger is injured—usually in situations in which injuries occur during the navigation or piloting of the airplane. For instance, a court applied the principle of res ipsa loquitur when a passenger was injured when an airplane skidded off the runway during a landing.[37] Even if the passenger could not prove exactly what the airline or captain did wrong, it was clear that the passenger's injury was due to negligence on the part of the airline, not the passenger.

Limitations When Injuries Occur on International Flights

Under the Warsaw Convention, an airline's liability is limited to $75,000 for injuries resulting from an accident on flights with a scheduled departure, arrival or stop in the U.S.[38] Elsewhere the limitation is even lower. Although $75,000 will almost certainly cover minor injuries, it is likely to be insufficient to compensate you in the case of serious injury or the death of a loved one. Several international airlines agree that this limit is too low and that the Warsaw Convention should be changed.

A number of international airlines have realized that this compensation limit is too low and have agreed to waive the Warsaw Convention limits. Under an agreement reached in February 1997 between major international carriers and the Department of Transportation, injured passengers and their families are able to recover up to $139,000 even if the airline can prove that it was not negligent, or the full amount of damages suffered by the passenger or family if the airline was at fault. Prior to this agreement, the only way around the $75,000 limitation was to prove that the airline engaged in willful misconduct or was so neglectful of its responsibilities that its actions equaled willful misconduct, such as allowing a drunk pilot to fly.[39]

Under this new agreement, the law of the passenger's home can now be applied in a lawsuit against an international airline, meaning that a U.S. citizen could ask a court to apply U.S. law, even if she were to sue in a foreign country.

Although most international airlines flying to and from the U.S. are expected to agree to waive the Warsaw convention limitations, not all had done so as of Fall 1998. If you have questions about a particular airline, check with that airline or the Department of Transportation.

Emotional Damages on International Flights

Although old cases allowed passengers to recover for emotional distress even if they did not suffer any actual bodily injury, this is no longer true. In 1991, the U.S. Supreme Court ruled that claims for damages for emotional distress under the Warsaw Convention are not allowed unless you suffer an actual physical injury.[40]

Need for an "Accident"

The Warsaw Convention has historically been interpreted to limit an airline's liability only when a passenger is injured during an "accident." Most courts agree that crash landings, hijackings and problems such as a defective airplane engine, tire or door are accidents.[41] Getting shaken up by turbulence or on a rough landing, however, is usually not considered an accident.[42]

Furthermore, injuries caused by a passenger's own actions do not constitute accidents. So when a passenger got drunk and fell down in the lavatory, there was no accident.[43] By contrast, when a drunk passenger injured another passenger, it was considered an accident.[44]

Finally, injuries caused by a passenger's unusual response to normal airline operations are not considered accidents. The U.S. Supreme Court has observed that "when the injury indisputably results from the passenger's own internal reaction to the usual, normal, and expected operation of the aircraft, it has not been caused by an accident."[45] Applying this principle, courts have held that passengers with heart conditions, hernias, sensitive ears or other medical problems cannot claim that their reaction to air travel was an accident for which the airline is responsible.

One court figured out a way around the Warsaw Convention. In the case, a passenger had a heart attack on board and the airline crew was found to be negligent because it failed to respond properly—ignoring the airline's own procedures for dealing with medical emergencies. The court stated that the Warsaw Convention clearly did not apply because there was no accident. But rather than leave the passenger with no redress, the court allowed the passenger and his wife to recover over $2 million in damages. The case was upheld on appeal and may be a very useful precedent for passengers injured during international flights.[46]

Nonflight Injuries

Airlines may be responsible for injuries that occur before or after a flight, such as an injury to you in the airline terminal.[47] Generally, an airline is liable if the injury is caused by one of the airline's employees in the course of performing his or her work, or if the injury occurs in an area controlled or managed by the airline. For instance, if you slip and fall on the walkway while boarding an airplane, you may have a valid complaint against the airline. If you slip and fall at the curb while waiting for a taxi, however, the airport, not the airline, would be responsible.

Filing a Claim or Lawsuit With an Airline

In most instances, a formal claim should be filed with an airline within a relatively short time after the incident occurs. If you are injured during a flight, make sure a crew member writes an incident report and gives you a copy. You may also want to collect the names of any potential witnesses.

If you eventually sue the airline, you must file your case within your state's time limit for suing in cases of personal injury (called the "statute of limitations"). Statutes of limitations vary from state to state, but are usually between one and three years. For injuries on international flights, many courts have held that a complaint must be filed within two years, or the court will not hear the case.

Where to Sue

Generally, it is easiest to sue in a court close to where you live. If the airline objects, the judge could move the case. Often, in lawsuits for injuries in airline transportation, the laws of several different states may apply. In such a case, you'll want your attorney to investigate the existing laws in all the possible states and file the case in the state where the case law is most heavily in your favor.

 Comparative Negligence. If you are partially responsible for your injury, your compensation for the injury may be limited by a legal doctrine known as "comparative negligence."

In a few states, if the airline can show that you were even slightly negligent, you cannot receive anything for your injury. In most states, however, even if you were partially at fault, you would be entitled to compensation based on the degree of negligence of the airline, as long as you were not more than 50% responsible. If you were more than 50% responsible, you would receive nothing.

Example: You are sitting in your seat when a flight attendant trips and scalds you with a pot of burning coffee. Because you did not cause the injury in any way, you would be entitled to 100% compensation for your injuries.

If, however, you were scalded by hot coffee because you held your coffee cup over your lap and moved it as the flight attendant was pouring, your recovery would depend upon the laws of the state where the accident occurred.

- In a few states, you would receive nothing because you were partially at fault.[48]
- In many states, your compensation would be reduced by the amount of your own negligence; if the

judge or jury decided you were 60% at fault, you would only be entitled to receive 40% of your damages.[49]

- In most states, you would receive partial compensation if you were less than 50% responsible. If you were 50% responsible or more, you would receive nothing.[50]

How Much Can You Receive

The amount of compensation you can receive for an injury on a domestic flight generally depends on the seriousness of the injury, the costs you incur in getting treated and whether you or the airline were primarily responsible.

Generally, you are entitled to receive compensation for direct or consequential damages arising from your injury (see discussion, above). For example, if you broke your leg, you could recover the direct expenses, such as medical bills and the cost of crutches. You might also be able to collect consequential damages, such as the income you lost while you could not work.

In some special cases, you may be able to recover emotional or punitive damages, but these types of damages are hard to prove and often require specific, technical allegations. Before making such claims, talk to an attorney.

On domestic flights, whether or not you can receive compensation for emotional injuries without having been physically injured varies considerably from state to state. One court allowed it when an airplane suddenly dropped 34,000 feet, but many other courts have refused to permit compensation.[51]

Generally, to get punitive damages, you must show that the airline intentionally caused you harm and acted in a "wanton, reckless or malicious manner." This means that you must show that the airline's behavior was so unacceptable that the airline should be penalized as an example and to prevent that airline or other airlines from repeating similar behavior in the future.

Special Air Travel Concerns

Frequent Flyer Programs

Originally designed as a way to encourage brand loyalty for air travelers, frequent flyer programs seem to have become a permanent fixture in the travel industry. Hotels, rental cars, credit cards and even telephone companies now offer frequent flyer points to entice customers with promises of free travel and other gifts. Airlines have been overwhelmed by the numbers of people who signed up—and by the millions of earned but not yet claimed frequent flyer miles. As a result, airlines are looking for ways to minimize the actual number of free trips they must give away (such as by having the miles expire after three years).

While frequent flyer programs can provide you with some travel bargains, understand that there are few legal protections for the credits you earn. Under the rules of almost all frequent flyer programs, the airline can change award levels, have credits expire or even cancel the whole program without warning. And because state laws are preempted by federal laws regarding air travel, state consumer protection laws cannot be used to fight an airline.

The only apparent argument you can make is to sue for breach of contract, asserting that you relied on the frequent flyer program when you made your purchase and so the airline cannot take away or reduce the value of the promised benefits.[52] The question of whether an airline can retroactively reduce the value of miles already earned has not been settled.

Some travelers will pay more for their tickets if they receive frequent flyer credit or will take an indirect or inconvenient flight on an airline in order to get frequent flyer credit. One way to avoid this frequent flyer trap is to join more than one program. Although you can get travel awards faster by concentrating your travel on one airline, you may miss some low-fare deals or better connections if you use only one airline. When you compare tickets, keep in mind that frequent flyer miles are worth approximately 2¢ per mile; use that figure to help calculate which option is best. The 2¢ per mile estimate was calculated by dividing the average cost of a domestic round-trip ticket (approximately $500) by the number of frequent flyer miles needed for such a ticket (25,000 miles).

To make best use of your frequent flyer credit, use miles to pay for expensive trips, such as when you can't meet advance purchase requirements or stay over a Saturday night. Beware that miles do expire and that it may be difficult to use frequent flyer credit during holidays and other peak periods because of the blackout dates created by the airlines.

Contesting Frequent Flyer Mileage Changes

The U.S. Supreme Court recently allowed travelers to sue an airline for breach of contract when the airline increased the number of miles travelers needed to get free airline travel. The travelers claimed that under the original contract, the miles they had already earned had a value that was reduced by the change. For example, if a traveler could earn a domestic ticket with 20,000 miles before the policy change but needed 25,000 miles after the policy change, this effectively reduced the value of the previously earned miles by 25%.

The Supreme Court did not say that reducing the value of frequent flyer miles was a breach of contract. What it did say was that travelers could sue the airline for breach of contract because that kind of lawsuit is different from a lawsuit based on state consumer protection law, which would be barred (preempted) by federal law.

In a not so subtle attempt to reduce the value of frequent flyer miles, most airlines have introduced two classes of frequent flyer awards. What used to be considered standard awards are now called something like "saver" awards, and the airlines have created a new class of standard awards. The advantage of the new "standard" awards is that there are fewer restrictions and blackout dates; the disadvantage is that they cost more frequent flyer miles. For example, a domestic flight using a new standard award is likely to cost 40,000 rather than 25,000 for the saver awards. The airlines also make the saver awards harder to get, essentially forcing more people to use new standard awards. Just a few years ago you could generally fly anywhere domestically for 20,000 miles, meaning that this new program has effec-tively cut the value of your frequent flyer miles in half. When you make a reservation using your frequent flyer miles, make sure that you ask the airline whether there are flights where you can use saver awards.

Trading or Selling Frequent Flyer Awards

You can use your frequent flyer awards or give them to anyone you choose, but you cannot sell or trade them. Despite this clear limitation in all frequent flyer programs, frequent flyer awards are still sold and bartered. Many of the deeply discounted tickets advertised in newspapers are actually tickets obtained by agents using purchased frequent flyer awards. Because airlines require you to present a photo ID when you check in and are traveling on a ticket obtained through a frequent flyer program, it is becoming difficult to use purchased coupons.

If you attempt to use frequent flyer awards that have been purchased, the airline can confiscate your ticket if it believes you violated its rules to obtain the ticket.

Taxing Frequent Flyer Benefits

In the past, the IRS declared that under certain circumstances, frequent flyer credits earned in the course of travel for a business were taxable as personal income to the individual traveler. Because of the enormous public outcry in response to this, the IRS backed off. In fact, legislation has been proposed that specifically excludes frequent flyer points earned during the course of business travel from personal income. As of September 1998, the legislation has not become law, but you do not have to declare frequent flyer miles as personal income.

Inheriting Frequent Flyer Miles

As travelers accumulate hundreds of thou-sands of frequent flyer miles, their frequent flyer accounts have become valuable assets. Many people now include these accounts in their wills. Inheriting the miles is not always simple. Each airline has its own require-ments. All airlines require documentation of proof of death and proof of the heir's right to inherit the miles. In some cases, the miles must specifically be included in a will; in others, a letter of authorization from the executor of the estate may be sufficient. Some airlines charges a transfer fee. For nonairline programs, such as American Express, the miles may be more difficult to inherit. Because charge cards are canceled on notice of death, the accumulated miles may disappear. In this case, the best way to safeguard your miles may be to make sure that the intended heir is listed as a secondary name on the credit card.

When an Airline Files for Bankruptcy

What happens if you hold a ticket on an airline that goes bankrupt? Technically, you become one of the airline's creditors in bankruptcy. If you file a claim in the bankruptcy court, there is a chance you will recover some very small percentage of the value of the ticket, but more likely you will recover nothing at all.

In the past, most airlines would honor a bankrupt airline's ticket and allow you on a substitute flight. Given the competitive nature of the airline industry, however, this is rarely done these days. Sometimes, as a gesture of goodwill (and a way of luring new customers), an airline will offer a special discounted fare for passengers holding tickets on a bankrupt airline. If you have a ticket on a bankrupt airline and are a frequent flyer on another airline, try to negotiate free or discounted travel using the bankrupt airline's ticket. Trip cancellation or trip interruption insurance can sometimes cover the cost of a replacement ticket. (See Chapter 8.)

When Airline Ads Are Deceptive

The U.S. Supreme Court ruled a few years ago that an airline could not be sued for violating a state's "truth in advertising" or other consumer protection law because all state laws related to an airline's rates, routes

or services were preempted (barred) by federal law.[53] Only the U.S. Department of Transportation can sue an airline for disputes involving an airline's rates, routes and services. Given the number of airlines, the competitive nature of the industry and the limited resources of the Department of Transportation, there is a clear opportunity for abuse. (See Chapter 7.)

Airline deceptive practices include:

- failing to inform passengers that only one or two seats per flight are available at low, advertised prices, making them almost impossible to get
- "bait and switch" operations where advertised fares are not available, but the airline suggests that "for just a little more" you can book the same ticket, and
- fine-print restrictions that are not mentioned until the ticket is being sold.

If you believe that an airline has engaged in false or misleading advertising, register a complaint with the U.S. Department of Transportation, C-75, Washington, DC 20590, or call 800-322-7873. Include your name, address, daytime phone number, the name of the airline, the flight number and date, the itinerary and the nature of your complaint. If you think it's crazy that no state can enforce its consumer protection laws against an airline, complain to your Senator and Representative in Congress!

 The Federal Aviation Administration has a series of fact sheets on travel by airplane called *Fly Smart*. To order copies, write to the FAA, AS4-20, 400 7th Street, SW, Washington, DC 20590, call 202-267-7770 or visit their Web page at http://www.

faa.gov. The International Airline Passengers Association (IAPA) provides safety reports and other information on airlines to its members. It sends a copy of a member's complaint (and nonmember complaints, if very serious), as well as its own letter, to the offending airline to try to reach a solution. For more information, contact the IAPA at 4341 Lindburg Dr., Dallas, TX 75244, 972-404-9980.

Long-Distance Travel by Train or Bus

In most parts of the country, air travel has replaced long-distance travel by train and bus. Trains and intercity buses are considered "common carriers" and have a duty to use great care in transporting their passengers and baggage. Train and bus companies can be sued for personal injuries, loss of luggage, breach of contract and other related claims. Be aware also that train and bus companies have "hidden terms" in their ticket contracts. The hidden terms are contained in a set of rules and limitations (called "tariffs") filed with:

- the Surface Transportation Board (formerly the Interstate Commerce Commission), which regulates interstate train and bus travel, and

- various state departments of transportation, which regulate intrastate train and bus travel.

If you have a dispute with a train or bus company, demand a copy of the company's tariffs. They will give you the basic information you need to assess whether the company has fulfilled its obligations to you.

- **Trains.** Copies of the tariffs are supposedly available at all train stations, but rarely are. You can obtain a copy of Amtrak's tariffs from the National Railroad Passenger Corporation, Corporate & Legal Support Services, 60 Massachusetts Ave., NE, Washington, DC 20002, 202-906-2121 (voice), 202-906-2850 (fax), http// www. amtrak.com (Web).

- **Buses.** Contact the individual bus company to receive a copy of its tariffs.

If the company fails to provide the tariffs within a reasonable time, you can file a complaint with the Surface Transportation Board, Office of Compliance and Enforcement, 1925 K St., NW, Washington, DC 20423-0001, 202-565-1500 (voice), 202-565-1905 fax) (for interstate travel) or the state's department of transportation (for intrastate travel).

Endnotes

1 14 C.F.R. § 253.

2 49 U.S.C. § 1381.

3 *American Airlines v. Wolens*, 115 S. Ct. 817 (1995).

4 49 Stat. 3000. The Warsaw Convention, officially named the Convention for Unification of Certain Rules Regarding Transportation by Air, as passed in 1929. Amendments applicable in the U.S. can be found at 31 Fed. Reg. 7302, 14 C.F.R. § 203 and 49 Fed. Reg. 8402.

5 14 C.F.R. § 250.2(b).

6 14 C.F.R. § 250.6.

7 14 C.F.R. § 250.9(a).

8 14 C.F.R. § 250.5(b) and 14 C.F.R. § 250.8.

9 EEC Transportation Regulation no. 2919.

10 14 C.F.R. § 250.5 and 14 C.F.R. § 250.1.

11 14 C.F.R. § 250.5 and 14 C.F.R. § 250.1.

12 *Wills v. Trans World Airways, Inc.*, 200 F. Supp. 360 (S.D. Cal. 1961).

13 *Lopez v. Eastern Airlines*, 677 F. Supp. 183 (S.D.N.Y. 1988).

14 *Smith v. Piedmont Airlines, Inc.*, 728 F. Supp. 914 (S.D.N.Y. 1989).

15 *Nader v. Allegheny Airlines*, 426 U.S. 290 (1976).

16 *Cenci v. Mall Airways, Inc.*, 21 Aviation Cases 17,812 (N.Y. 1988); *Padua v. Eastern Airlines, Inc.*, 21 Aviation Cases 17,716 (P.R. 1988).

17 Warsaw Convention, Article 20(1).

18 *Duff v. TransWorld Airlines, Inc.*, 21 Aviation Cases 17,795 (1988).

19 *Cenci v. Mall Airways, Inc.*, 21 Aviation Cases 17,812 (N.Y. 1988).

20 Warsaw Convention, Article 21.

21 *Newsome v. Trans International Airlines, Inc.*, 492 So. 2nd 592 (Ala. 1986).

22 U.S. Department of Transportation Regulations, Part 254; 14 C.F.R. § 254.

23 *Cohen v. Varig Airlines*, 62 A.D.2d 324, 405 N.Y.S.2d 44 (N.Y. 1978).

24 *Kupferman v. Pakistan International Airlines*, 108 Misc.2d 485, 438 N.Y.S.2d 189 (N.Y. 1981).

25 *Daun v. Sunaire*, 17 Aviation Cases 17,536 (S.L.M.C. 1982).

26 *Seltzer v. American Airlines, Inc.*, New York Law Journal, June 1, 1979, p. 13, col. 6 (N.Y. 1979).

27 *Franklin Mint Corp. v. TransWorld Airways, Inc.*, 46 U.S. 243 (1984).

28 *Republic National Bank of New York v. Eastern Airlines, Inc.*, 815 F.2d 232 (2nd Cir. 1987).

29 Warsaw Convention, Article 20(2).

30 Warsaw Convention, Article 26(2).

31 *Vekris v. People Express Airlines*, 21 Aviation Cases 17,540 (S.D.N.Y 1988), *Maghsoudi v. Trans Mediterranean Airways*, 15 Aviation Cases 17,806 (D. Ha. 1979).

32 *Republic National Bank v. Eastern Airlines, Inc.*, 20 Aviation Cases 17,920 (2d Cir. 1987); *Jalloh v. Trans World Airways, Inc.*, 19 Aviation Cases 17,804 (D.D.C. 1985).

33 Warsaw Convention, Article 22 (3); see *Schedlmayer v. Trans International Airlines, Inc.*, 99 Misc. 2nd 478, 416 N.Y.S. 2d 461 (N.Y. 1979).

34 *Krys v. Luftansa*, Travel Weekly, p.1, March 7, 1996 (Fla. 1996).

35 *Schwamb v. Delta Airlines, Inc.*, 21 Aviation Cases 17,101 (La. 1987); *Brosnhan v. Western Airlines, Inc.*, 22 Aviation Cases 17,710 (8th Cir. 1989); see also *Smith v. Piedmont Airlines, Inc.*, 728 F.

Supp. 914 (S.D.N.Y. 1989) and *Carcone v. Delta Airlines, Inc.*, 21 Aviation Cases 17,668 (S.D.N.Y. 1988).

[36] *Ginter v. Trans World Airways, Inc.*, 21 Aviation Cases 18,205 (N.Y. 1989); *Haley v. United Airlines, Inc.*, 728 F. Supp. 324 (D. Md. 1989); *Kohler v. Aspen Airways, Inc.*, 19 Aviation Cases 18,051 (Cal. 1985).

[37] *Farina v. Pan American World Airways, Inc.*, 19 Aviation Cases 18,199 (N.Y. 1983).

[38] Montreal Agreement § 1(1).

[39] Warsaw Convention, Article 25.

[40] *Eastern Airlines, Inc. v. Floyd*, 499 U.S. 554 (1991).

[41] See *Stanford v. Kuwait Airlines*, 705 F. Supp. 142 (S.D.N.Y. 1986); *Floyd v. Eastern Airlines, Inc.*, 872 F.2d 1462 (11th Cir. 1989); *Arcin v. Trans International Airlines, Inc.*, 19 Aviation Cases 18,311 (E.D.N.Y. 1985); *Striker v. British Airways, Inc.*, 20 Aviation Cases 17,111 (S.D.N.Y. 1986).

[42] *Salce v. Aerlingus Irish Airlines*, 19 Aviation Cases 17,377 (S.D.N.Y. 1985).

[43] *Padilla v. Olympic Airways*, 23 Aviation Cases 17,656 (S.D.N.Y. 1991).

[44] *Oliver v. Scandinavian Airline System*, 17 Aviation Cases 18,283 (D. Md. 1983).

[45] *American Airlines v. Wolens*, 115 S. Ct. 817 (1995).

[46] *Krys v. Luftansa*, No. 96-4430 (11th Cir. 1997).

[47] *Williams v. Aerlingus Irish Airlines*, 20 Aviation Cases 17,900 (S.D.N.Y. 1987).

[48] This is the law in Alabama, the District of Columbia, Maryland, Nebraska, North Carolina, South Carolina, South Dakota, Tennessee and Virginia.

[49] This is the law in Alaska, Arizona, California, Florida, Kentucky, Louisiana, Michigan, Mississippi, Missouri, New Mexico, New York, Rhode Island and Washington.

[50] This is the law in Arkansas, Colorado, Connecticut, Delaware, Georgia, Hawaii, Idaho, Illinois, Indiana, Iowa, Kansas, Maine, Massachusetts, Minnesota, Montana, Nevada, New Hampshire, New Jersey, North Dakota, Ohio, Oklahoma, Oregon, Pennsylvania, Texas, Utah, Vermont, West Virginia, Wisconsin and Wyoming.

[51] *Quill v. Trans World Airways, Inc.*, 19 Aviation Cases 17,330 (Minn. 1985).

[52] *American Airlines v. Wolens*, 115 S. Ct. 817 (1995).

[53] *Morales v. Trans World Airlines, Inc.*, 112 S. Ct. 2031 (1992).

Chapter 2

Renting a Car

An Introduction to Rental Cars

Whether on business or vacation, travelers often use rental cars for at least part of their trip. This chapter outlines some of the basic rights you have as a renter and describes how to handle the most common disputes that arise with rental car companies. Most laws related to rental cars were enacted by state legislatures or derived from cases interpreting those state laws. It is not possible to describe all of the variations in state rules governing car rental, but after reading this chapter, you will understand the most important legal issues involved in renting a car and obtaining compensation if you are entitled to it.

Avoiding Problems When You Rent a Car

You can avoid a lot of frustration and wasted time and money if you follow these suggestions before, during and after you rent a car:

- When making a reservation, ask about extra charges and get the total quoted rental rate, including any extra expenses, in writing by mail or fax.
- Shop around for terms as well as for prices. The lowest rate may not be the best if it does not include unlimited mileage, excludes travel outside the rental state, has cancellation penalties or has other limitations that could inconvenience you or cost you money.
- Examine the coverage offered by your automobile insurance policy and any additional insurance coverage offered through your credit cards before your trip so you can make an intelligent choice to accept or reject coverage—especially the loss damage waiver (LDW)—offered by the rental car company. Don't be bullied or scared by the tactics of sales agents at rental car counters.

- If you are under age 25, have a questionable driving record or have been in any automobile accidents (even as a passenger) in the past few years, ask if the company has any driver restrictions when you make your reservation.
- If you want to pay cash, find out if cash is acceptable and if so, how much of a deposit you will have to put down.
- Before you sign the agreement, read it and clarify any terms and conditions you don't understand.
- Ask when you must return the car in order to avoid late penalties. In some cases, you will be given a 30-60 minute grace period to return the car; but if you return it after the grace period, you may be charged a bundle—up to a full day's rental fee.
- When you return your car to the rental company's parking lot, have the lot attendant inspect the car for damage and "sign off" on the condition of the car before you leave; keep a copy of the sign-off sheet.
- Keep a copy of your completed rental contract and compare it to the final charge that appears on your credit card bill. Rigorously investigate any "mystery charges" that were added after you returned the car.

- If you have an accident or other problem and the charges assessed against you by the rental car company seem unfair, don't be afraid to fight just because the company tells you "it's in the contract." Rental car contracts that give the renter no bargaining power can be contested if they are enforced unfairly. (See Chapter 13.)

Out-of-State Drivers

As a rental car driver, you are subject to the same driving and parking laws and regulations as every other driver in the state where you are driving. Ignorance is no excuse; if the state you are visiting doesn't allow right turns on red or has special speed laws near playgrounds, you are responsible for knowing and abiding by these and all other laws. For an overview of the laws of all 50 states, order a copy of the *Digest of Motor Laws* from your state motor vehicles agency or your local auto club.

Some car renters seem to believe that they are immune from other states' laws, or that the local police won't be able to enforce their tickets. Wrong! When you sign your

rental contract, you agree to pay all moving and parking violations obtained during the rental period. If you do not pay your tickets and they are assessed against the rental company, the company will bill you for the cost of the ticket and often add a service or collection fee for each ticket. If you paid for the rental car with a credit card, the company may have given itself, in your rental agreement, the right to charge your account for unpaid tickets.

Before You Rent: Rental Car Reservations

When you make a reservation to rent a car, you are making a contract with the rental car company. Basically, the company promises to have the type of car you request available for you at the time agreed upon, and you agree to pay for the car rental. In practice, many car renters do not honor their part of the bargain and do not show up. To deal with this "no-show" problem, some rental car companies require deposits or impose no-show penalties. Of course, sometimes the rental car company doesn't live up to its part of the deal.

If a Company Fails to Provide the Type of Car Reserved

A prepaid or guaranteed reservation (where you have given the rental car company your credit card number and are obligated to pay all or part of the rental fee whether or not you show up) is the strongest type of contract you can have with the rental car company. If you have guaranteed payment and the company does not have the car you reserved available for you, the company must do everything it can to find you a different car from its fleet. Theoretically, the company is obligated to help you find a car from another rental car company if it has no suitable substitute, but in practice this rarely happens. If the alternate car found for you is more expensive, the original rental car company should cover the difference because your contract was for a car at a certain price.

If you haven't put down a deposit or guarantee, even though there is no penalty if you do not show up, the company is required to honor its part of the bargain and have the car available. Rental car companies bear the risk that you might not show up, and, as a result, many companies overbook to cover no-shows. This often means that when you do show up, the class of car you reserved is not available. In this situation, the rental car company will usually provide you with a larger, more expensive car (because these tend to be rented less frequently), and may tell you it is giving you a "free upgrade."

If you accept the substitution, you allow the company to change the agreement created by your original reservation. In most cases, renters are happy to accept the upgrade to a larger, more expensive car; in some cases, however, the increased costs for gasoline consumption, insurance or other charges may make this change less of a bargain than it appears. If you accept a smaller, cheaper car than the one you reserved, the rental company is obliged to charge you the lower rate.

If you refuse to accept a substitute car, you may have difficulty obtaining compen-

sation afterwards because a court would likely require you to reduce (mitigate) your damages by accepting a car that was a reasonable substitute for the car you reserved, especially if the substituted car was in a superior class.

If the Company Fails to Provide Any Car

Sometimes, the company's overbooking means that no cars are available when you arrive. In this case, your only alternative may be to find a substitute rental car at a different company, or to take a taxi and seek reimbursement from the original car rental company.

Getting Back What You Lost Directly

Under basic contract law, if you make a reservation and are qualified to rent a car and the company does not produce a car that is reasonably similar to the one you reserved, you are entitled to money that puts you in the same position you would have been in if the company had kept its promise. This type of recovery (called compensatory damages) is the standard form of recovery in breach of contract cases.

> **Example:** Darlene made a reservation to rent a compact car for a week from Acme Rent-a-Car. The reservation was for 9:00 p.m. on Monday at the Houston Airport, at a weekly charge of $250. When Darlene arrives, the Acme agent says, "Sorry, no cars." Darlene finds another company at the airport, Bettah Rent-a-Car, that rents her a similar car for $300. Darlene is entitled to $50, the difference between what she paid for

renting a car from Bettah and what she would have paid if Acme had not broken its promise (breached its contract).

Chapter 13 suggests ways to handle this problem short of suing the company. If you do have to sue, you may have a difficult time finding any published court cases that directly address this point for rental cars. However, the basic contract principle is well established.[1] The lack of published cases may be due to the small amount of money involved. Many renters may not bother to sue for the difference, or they may sue in small claims court. More likely, the rental car company may offer compensation without renters having to sue—probably in the form of future discounts on rentals, rather than cash.

Your case against the rental company will be even stronger if the company's standard rental agreement (that you would have received had you been able to rent a car) includes cancellation charges or no-show fees against you. In general, contracts for use with the general public must be fair—meaning the rights must be reciprocal. If the company includes a provision for it to get paid if you don't show up or cancel in time, then you should be able to collect if the company doesn't hold up its end of the deal.

Getting Back What You Lost Indirectly

Sometimes, your loss may be greater than just the extra money paid to rent another car. For instance, what happens if all of the other car rental companies in the area are sold out—not uncommon if a convention or special event is taking place? In this circumstance, you should demand compensation for the other damages you suffered due to the company's failure to have the car available as agreed.

Example: Darlene made a reservation (leaving her credit card number) for 9:00 p.m. on a Monday at the Houston Airport. When she arrives, the Acme agent says, "Sorry, no cars." Darlene tries unsuccessfully to find another rental car at the airport. In fact, there are no cars available in all of Houston because of a huge convention. Darlene is forced to take cabs everywhere and even has to check out of an inexpensive suburban hotel into a more expensive hotel downtown because she can't get to her business meetings in Houston conveniently without a car. Because Acme breached its contract to provide a car, Darlene is entitled to the cost of the cabs and the difference between what she paid at the downtown hotel and what she would have paid at the cheaper suburban hotel.

There are limits to the recovery of indirect damages. Most important, the damages must be "reasonable" and "foreseeable." In the above example, Darlene could not run up thousands of dollars of additional charges at a deluxe hotel downtown if other downtown hotels of comparable quality to the suburban hotel she had originally booked were available. Similarly, if Darlene claimed that because she had no car, she missed a million dollars worth of additional business contracts, the rental car company would argue that she shouldn't recover because those damages were not foreseeable.

If You Cancel or Are a No-Show

Nearly all rental car companies keep deposits or charge penalties for four-wheel drives, minivans, convertibles and other specialty rentals if you fail to cancel a reservation in advance or are a no-show. Some companies are testing similar policies on their standard rental cars.

For example, at the time of this writing, one company assesses a penalty of one day's rental for no-shows with guaranteed reservations in certain cities. Another company lets you cancel a guaranteed reservation on a regular daily or weekly rental up to two hours prior to the rental with no penalty, but imposes a $50 penalty if you cancel less than two hours ahead. In some cases, you may be charged the full value of the rental if you miss the cancellation deadline. Be aware that other companies may follow suit, and be sure to ask about cancellation rules and no-show penalties when you make a reservation.

These charges are usually legal if you are given reasonable notice when you make the reservation. If a company fails to give reasonable notice when you make your reservation, then you are entitled to challenge the charge. Simply mentioning that "other fees may apply" or putting the charge in fine print in your confirmation without drawing your attention to it may not be reasonable notice—at least while these fees are the exception and not general practice in the rental car industry. Chapter 13 offers suggestions on how to challenge the charges.

Credit Card "No-Show" Penalties

Several major rental car companies have started programs aimed at reducing the number of no-shows during peak seasons by imposing a charge on a credit card if a reservation is not canceled within a specified time before the scheduled pickup. Under contract law, these penalties could be enforced against you if you had sufficient notice, but what constitutes sufficient notice is unclear. If you are charged and did not know about the penalty, you can dispute the charge with the credit card issuer.

Restrictions on Renting a Car

Rental car companies are allowed to place reasonable limitations and conditions on your ability to actually rent a car you have reserved. For example, if you reserve a car for Wednesday and don't show up until Thursday, the rental company is not obliged to hold a car for you, unless you make arrangements ahead of time. In fact, the company may be within its rights to cancel your reservation within minutes of the scheduled pick-up time, if it has warned you that you must pick the car up by a certain time.

Many of the conditions of rental, such as requiring that you have a valid driver's license and are not drunk when you pick up the car, seem reasonable. Other restrictions, such as having a credit card or having a clean driving record, seem less reasonable, particularly if you are not warned about these restrictions when you make your reservation and first learn of them when you show up to pick up your rental car.

The rental car contract governs the rights and responsibilities of both you and the rental car company. By signing the contract, you agree to abide by its terms. Thus, it is very important to understand all of the terms of the contract and to ask any questions you have before signing.

Some sections of a signed rental agreement may be unenforceable if they are unfair or unreasonable or if you weren't given sufficient notice of the conditions or restrictions. Because the terms of most car rental contracts are nonnegotiable, courts are likely to examine their fairness if you make a legal challenge.

Rental car companies present contracts in a "take-it-or-leave-it" fashion. The type of contract that has no negotiation of the terms is known as an "adhesion contract" and would be subject to more careful review by a judge or jury than a contract where the parties negotiate the terms. Don't let a rental car company bully you by claiming that you are bound by all of the terms, no matter how unfair or unreasonable—particularly if you were tricked or forced into signing without understanding the significance of what you were doing.

Below we discuss some of the common conditions of rental agreements for which you should prepare.

Age

For most major companies, the minimum age to rent a car is either 21 or 25. Many rental car companies won't rent to people under age 25 unless they are an employee with a corporate account using the car for business or are government military personnel traveling on orders. Those companies with an age 21 cutoff usually charge an additional fee for drivers between 21-24, even for additional drivers and corporate customers. (See Young Driver Fees, below.)

Although this condition does discriminate against younger drivers, it is not generally considered illegal. This is because rental car companies are generally allowed to do business with whomever they choose, as long as they do not discriminate based on race, religion, national origin or other categories protected under civil rights laws. (See Chapter 11.) One exception is in New York, where the state's highest court, the Court of Appeals, recently upheld a law preventing rental car companies from refusing to rent to drivers 18 or older solely on the basis of age. Rental car companies usually do not impose a maximum age limit in the U.S., but companies located elsewhere may.

Valid Driver's License

It is illegal to operate a vehicle on public roads without a valid driver's license, and all rental car companies require renters and additional drivers to present a valid driver's license when renting. If you are in an accident involving your rental car, your rental agreement may be voided and any insurance protection rendered ineffective if you used a phony license and your real one is suspended, revoked, invalid or expired. Don't risk it. If you don't have a valid license, don't rent a car.

Credit Card

Most rental car companies require a major credit card as a way to secure a deposit from you at the time of rental, although you can use the card or cash when you actually pay for the car. The company will check your credit limit and "freeze" an amount slightly greater than your estimated rental charges against your card, meaning that this amount is not available for you to charge other purchases. This freeze can last for several days after you return the car, even once the actual amount is charged or you pay with cash.

As an alternative to using a credit card, you can get a prepaid voucher through your travel agent by paying for the rental car first at the travel agency and bringing the voucher to the rental counter. The voucher may not cover taxes, surcharges, additional drivers, upgrades and other charges, so be sure to find out exactly what is included in the price of the voucher before you pick up the car. Many companies require you to present a credit card or provide some other form of deposit even if you are using a voucher, so call ahead to find out.

Cash Deposits

If you don't have either a credit card or a voucher, you will be required to make a substantial cash deposit. Most rental car companies do not accept checks. Some people believe that this is a form of discrimination against poor people, who are less likely to have credit cards than wealthier people, but there is no clear law supporting this point.

Clean Driving Record

In a number of states, certain rental car companies refuse to rent to drivers with drunk driving convictions, citations for speeding or reckless driving or a history of severe or frequent accident involvements. Some rental car companies screen in an effort to reduce costs of liability insurance, and this practice has caused a lot of commotion in the rental car world. Sales agents conduct screening checks when you show up to rent by entering your license number into a computer program that essentially calls up your driver's record as reported by your state department of motor vehicles. If your record doesn't meet the screening criteria of the rental company, the agent will refuse to rent you a car.

Who Will Be Screened?

Screening originated with Hertz in 1992 in New York and Florida, but currently, anyone who lives in a state that makes driver records available to online services is at risk of being screened. As of May 1998, states with online driving records are Alabama, Arizona, California, Connecticut, District of Columbia, Florida, Idaho, Indiana, Kansas, Kentucky, Louisiana, Maine, Maryland, Massachusetts, Michigan, Minnesota, Mississippi, Nebraska, New Jersey, New Mexico, New York, Ohio, Pennsylvania, South Carolina, Vermont, Virginia, West Virginia and Wisconsin. Many companies are developing lists of bad drivers to prevent anyone on such a list from renting from the company anywhere in the country—even in states that do not yet conduct computer checks—until the driver's record is clear.

By the mid-1990's, all companies screened drivers whose records were available online when they rented in popular tourist destinations such as Florida, New York and California. During the past few years, Dollar and Alamo dropped screening (finding it not to be cost-effective), though Avis, Budget, Enterprise, Hertz, National, Ryder, Thrifty and Value still screen. And while screening is almost certain in popular vacations spots, several companies screen anyone (from the states listed above) no matter where the car is being rented.

Screening Standards

Generally, a rental car company will deny you a car if, during the past 36 months, you:

- were caught driving with a suspended or invalid license
- had one instance of drunk driving, hit-and-run, driving a stolen car or other serious offense, or
- had three moving violations or two accidents.

The standards adopted by each rental car company vary and are subject to change, so you must ask about the specific rental screening standards of any company you are considering using. In general, a company will let your know in advance if you will be screened.

Screening Specifics

Some of the most common disqualifying offenses include:

- operating a vehicle without insurance or a valid driver's license within the past 48 months
- conviction for reckless disregard for life and property within the past 36-48 months
- conviction for driving while intoxicated (DWI), driving under the influence (DUI), driving while alcohol impaired (DWAI) or other alcohol- or controlled substance-related convictions within the past 36-72 months
- three or more convictions for moving violations within the past 24-36 months
- failure to report an accident or leaving the scene of any accident within the past 36-48 months
- possession of a stolen vehicle or use of a vehicle in a crime within the past 36-48 months, and
- one or more accidents resulting in a fatality or bodily injury within the past 48 months.

Injustice and Errors in Screening Systems

The driver screening system is difficult to implement fairly and accurately, and has generated much consumer dissatisfaction. You may be unjustly blacklisted for incidents where another party was at fault (such as an accident where you are rear-ended) or for infractions that don't make you a high-risk rental customer. The information that appears on the computer check may be inaccurate, because lists are not automatically updated as driving records change. As we all know, computers may crash, making screening checks haphazard and subject to mechanical failure.

It is very hard to correct an inaccurate blacklisting, because few lists are updated regularly. This means that you can remain on a blacklist indefinitely, since computers at rental car companies aren't linked to motor vehicle departments. (They call up information provided by independent companies.) It is your responsibility to provide the rental company with your updated driving record if you wish to have your name cleared.

Rental car companies won't conduct screening checks at the time you make your reservation, because they have many no-shows and each screening costs money. The delayed screening could cost you money. Because you are screened only when you arrive at the counter to pick up your car, you lose the opportunity to get an advance booking discount rate at another company if the screening system rejects you. (Four to six percent of screened drivers are rejected.)

Swearing Instead of Screening

Instead of screening you when you come to pick up your rental car, some rental car companies require you to sign a statement that you have an acceptable driving record. This shifts the responsibility for providing accurate information away from the company and to you. Thus, if you have an accident and signed a statement that turns out to be incorrect, the rental car company could use it against you by claiming that you acted in violation of the rental agreement.

If Your Driving Record Is Questionable

- Find out whether your state makes driver records available to rental car companies. (Check with your state department of motor vehicles.) If your state doesn't, then relax and don't worry about being screened.
- Get your driver record evaluated by a screening company. Several companies evaluate driving records to determine in advance whether drivers will be disqualified from renting. TML Information Services (800-789-7891), the leading evaluator of vehicle records for rental car companies, operates a program for drivers from states that make driver record data available online. For around $11 (less for AAA members), you can get an evaluation of your driving record against the criteria for screening risky drivers used by major rental car companies.

- If you don't want to pay for an evaluation, get a copy of your driving record from the motor vehicle agency in your home state (allow plenty of time), obtain the screening criteria of the rental car companies you are considering and make an evaluation on your own.

- If you are traveling for business and your company has an agreement with a rental agency whereby your employer assumes liability, the screening company may overlook items that would otherwise disqualify you.

- Finally, if you are disqualified by a screening system, have someone you are traveling with rent the car and do the driving.

Limited Range of Travel

Some rental agreements prohibit you from driving outside the state in which you rent the car, or beyond that state and a few adjacent ones. You may be barred from traveling to certain remote areas because of poor road conditions. Be sure your contract allows you to travel in all of the areas in which you plan to drive. This is particularly true if your trip includes crossing a national border to Canada or Mexico, where special insurance and liabilities may arise. If you ignore the territorial limits, you can be found in violation of your rental contract, which would probably negate your coverage for insurance and any benefit of unlimited mileage. If you have mechanical problems or an accident in an area in which you are not authorized to drive the car, your rental rate may revert to a much higher one, and you may have to foot the bill for repair or towing charges because you were driving in violation of the contract.

Rental Car Rates and Charges

Many cities have a selection of different rental car companies; if you are unhappy with what the first company has to offer, call around and shop for more favorable terms. Follow these key steps to avoid being ripped off by extra rental car charges:

- **When you make your reservation.** Ask about fees, taxes or other charges that might be added to the quoted price. Get the fare quoted in writing.

- **When you return the car.** Ask about additional charges and what they cover. Don't let the desk clerk intimidate you. Have her clearly explain all additional charges you do not recognize. If you have time, have a lot attendant inspect the car for any possible damage and "sign off" on the good condition of the car before you leave the lot, and keep a copy of the sign-off sheet.

- **After the rental.** Retain your receipts and credit card slips. The amount that appears later on your credit card bill may not match the amount charged at the location. Demand an explanation for any difference.

Car rental fees are set by each company and vary depending on the location of the rental office, time period the car will be rented, season, car model, special promotions or vacation packages, as well as the customer's eligibility for discounts (such as frequent flyer discounts, association discounts, a charge card program or travel club). In addition, because many rental car companies have franchises, rates and policies of a central office may vary substantially from those of a local office.

There is nothing illegal about multiple prices, but there is also nothing to stop you from asking about special fares when you rent or for a reduction after the rental if you learn that a better rate was available but was not offered to you. Although not obligated to offer you the lower price, the company may do so to maintain good customer relations.

A 1994 study by a national consumer rights group concluded that a company's national reservation line is likely to give you a lower quote than a local office of the company or a computerized reservation system used by travel agents. When shopping for the best rental terms, check directly with the company that will be providing your car and ask about all potential additional charges and limitations.

Rental Period

One question to ask the reservation or rental counter agent is, "When must I return the car in order to avoid extra charges?" Rental car companies may quote rates that require you to keep a car for a minimum time or during a certain part of the week, such as over a Saturday night. If you do not keep the car that long, your rental rate may revert to a higher regular weekday rate. If you are given notice in advance, this practice is legitimate.

Most rental rates are based on a 24-hour clock—a rental day begins at the time you pick up the car and ends 24 hours later, unless you have secured a weekly or other special rate (a rental car "week" usually equals at least five 24-hour days). Nearly all companies allow a one-hour grace period beyond the rental period, and some companies let you pay for a short extra period at a prorated hourly rate. Other companies

assess severe penalties for late vehicle return, including "extra day" fees that can total as high as 30%-40% of the weekly fee. Optional waivers, insurance and other surcharges are normally applied on a daily basis, so you will likely be charged a full day's rate for these even if you are only several hours late.

When you rent at a weekly or weekend rate, find out the earliest and latest times you can return the car to avoid penalties. If you rent the car at a special rate, keeping it beyond that time or returning it early may negate that rate. Most companies do not prorate an extra day, but instead apply a higher daily rental rate for that one day. If there is any possibility that you will have trouble bringing the car back on time, find out the consequences of a late return before you rent.

> **Example:** Regina showed up at the rental car counter Sunday morning to rent a car until the following Sunday morning. The agent quoted her a special weekly rate of $203 ($29 a day), and she took the car. Because of trouble at home, Regina needed to return the car Thursday afternoon instead of Sunday morning. Due to this change, her rental rate was recalculated at the daily rate of $69 a day for five days, for a total of $345.

Although penalties for early returns of weekly rentals are generally allowed under rental car contracts, ask for a refund (see Chapter 13) if circumstances beyond your control (such as a family illness or death) caused you to change your plans. Some rental companies may be sympathetic in those cases.

Mileage Charges

Mileage charges can add a lot to the price of a rental car. While many companies offer unlimited mileage as the standard in rental contracts, mileage charge policies change frequently, and you should ask each time you rent. A few summers back, for example, several large rental car companies added a charge of about 25¢ a mile for driving in excess of a set cap, typically 100 miles a day. Consumer complaints led most companies to revert to unlimited mileage for most rentals.

If the rental company offers a choice, unlimited mileage may not always be the best option. If you will use a rental car mainly for local driving, a lower daily or weekly rate with a limited number of free miles per day may be a better deal than unlimited mileage.

Renting at an Airport

Renting at an airport may be more expensive than renting at an urban or suburban location, because airports and local governments often add surcharges and taxes (as high as 8.7%) to rental car rates. These charges and taxes are required by state or local law, and the rental company must add them to your bill. Sometimes, a nearby off-airport rental car office may be located in a different governmental jurisdiction and not subject to the same local taxes.

Some rental car companies give better rates to travelers arriving by plane. If you are renting at an airport, but aren't arriving or departing on a flight, check to find out whether the rate you are quoted requires you to have an airline ticket.

Additional Driver Fees

Rental company policies governing additional driver fees vary, but most charge extra for anyone who drives the car other than the person who signs the rental agreement. Often, but not always, additional driver charges are waived for your spouse (but not domestic partner), immediate family member or business associate, as long as he or she signs the rental agreement. The charge for an extra driver may be an added fee per day ($3-$9 per day) or per rental ($20-$25 per rental). California and Nevada prohibit per day charges for extra drivers.

Some local rental offices, especially franchises, may assess a spouse charge even if the official corporate policy would not. Some companies permit a direct business associate to drive, but other companies charge extra, even if the business associate is an immediate family member, and many charge for non-family extra drivers. If the additional driver is not a family member living in the same house as the renter, the other driver usually must provide a credit card.

If you fail to have an additional driver sign up and pay when you rent the car, you will be in violation of your rental contract and could negate your insurance protection. Do not risk it! While your best option is to find a company that charges little or nothing for an extra driver, do not ignore additional driver requirements if another person will be driving the car.

Young Driver Fees

Many companies charge an extra daily surcharge for any driver aged 21 to 24. Because the fee can vary from very little to a whopping $25 a day, it definitely pays to research the daily surcharge policies for drivers aged 21 to 24. To avoid or reduce the fees, have an older driver rent the vehicle and list the younger driver as an additional driver.

Child Safety Seats

All states require children under a certain age to be placed in child car seats. If you don't bring your own seat, you will be required to rent one, usually at a cost of $3-$5 per day or $25 per week. You may be charged more for one-way rentals, and you may be required to make an extra deposit for the seat if you are paying cash for the car rental. Also, you may be assessed a lost seat fee if you damage or don't return the seat. While it might be convenient to rent rather than transport your own child seat, the cost can be substantial on long trips.

All rental car companies are supposed to have an adequate supply of child seats, but to ensure that one is available for each of your small children, double-check the age requirements and that the seats have been reserved when you reconfirm your rental car. Don't wait until you arrive to pick up the car. In addition, the use of metal clips which attach to seatbelts to prevent them from slipping when holding child seats may be required. This requirement is frequently not followed by rental car companies, and many parents recommend bringing the metal clips yourself as a safety precaution.

Child-Safety Seats

Although all states require child-safety seats for small or young children, the rules differ in each state. Some states base their regulations on a child's age, others on a child's weight and still others on a combination of these two. If you plan to transport small or young children in a rental car, ask the rental car company at the time you reserve your car whether a suitable child seat will be available. If you plan to bring your own, consider checking with the highway patrol for the state or states in which you'll be traveling to make sure your seat meets the particular require-ments. In some states, the fines can reach as much as $500 for not comply-ing with the safety-seat requirements, and if your child is injured or killed and was not sitting in a safety seat, it is possible that you could face criminal charges. A guide published by the Automobile Association of America (AAA), *Digest of Motor Laws*, includes a section on the child restraint require-ments of the various states. It is avail-able by mail for $11.95 from AAA, Mail Stop 76, 1000 AAA Drive, Heathrow, FL 32746 or through local AAA auto clubs.

Vehicle Drop-Offs

Rental car company charges vary substan-tially for dropping off a car at a different location from where the car was rented. Some companies with low basic rental rates require you to return the car to the location from which it was rented; others let you return a car anywhere within a state or urban area at no extra charge. Almost all companies let you pick up a car from one office and drop it off at another within the same metropolitan area at no extra charge. Charges for one-way rentals, where you pick the car up in one city and drop it off in another, can be as high as $1,000.

Companies may limit their one-way rentals to certain car models, seasons or dates, and locations may refuse to accept drop-off cars altogether. Some companies offer one-way rates as a cheaper alternative to paying a drop-off fee. Occasionally, a rental car company may be willing to eliminate or reduce drop-off fees on a car that needs to be returned to its original city. While these opportunities are not common, it doesn't hurt to ask.

Refueling Charges

Rental car companies have come up with a variety of clever schemes to make money from charges for gasoline. Most companies require you to return the rental car with a full tank of gas. Customers who can't or forget to fill the tank before returning the car are forced to pay the company's inflated price per gallon, as much as $3 for onsite fill up.

Some companies offer customers the opportunity to purchase a full tank of gas at or below local gas prices when they first rent the car. Although this sounds like a good deal because you can avoid their notoriously high charges, the car company nearly always makes money, because you

break even only by bringing the car back with the gas tank empty. It can be convenient, however, if you have an early morning return time or won't have time to fill the tank before returning the car.

One trick to look out for is a per gallon quote that excludes state and local taxes in order to make the company's gas price look lower than it really is. Another technique is to add an extra charge if any gas had to be added, or to charge you for a minimum of five gallons no matter how much gas is actually added.

Although most companies require you to return the car with the gas tank "full," you are often allowed a little leeway. For example, some companies say that you may fill up the tank within a ten-mile radius of the car rental location. Find out about fill-up requirements ahead of time, and present your gas receipt as proof.

Repairs

If the rental car company discovers damage to the car after you have returned it, you will be liable for the damage unless you have purchased a loss damage waiver (LDW) from the rental car company. Unfortunately, many rental car contracts do not provide for a car inspection to sign off for damages when you return the car, but you are within your rights to ask for and obtain such a sign-off before you leave the premises.

If you damage the car and the bill for repairs is unreasonable, demand proof of the actual repair expenses, including the hours required to make the repair and the cost of the replacement parts. Compare these prices to those charged by other repair shops in the area, and refuse to pay for any amount that exceeds regular market prices. If you are charged for the revenue lost by the company while the car was being repaired, demand proof that all of its similar cars were rented while your car was being repaired, and that the company had to turn down rentals for your type of car. If it didn't, the company didn't lose any revenue.

If You're Misled About Rental Rates

Most states have laws to protect consumers from unfair or deceptive business practices. Some states have laws specifically relating to rental cars, as described just below.[2]

If you are the victim of a misleading price scheme, you can file a complaint with your state law enforcement antifraud office alleging fraudulent misrepresentation. Unfortunately, enforcement of this type of consumer protection law is often not a priority, and the time and expense required to pursue individual cases mean that few are actually tried. Your best defense is to be skeptical of any "great deals" and to ask a lot of questions. If you are taken in by a fraudulent marketing technique, determine which laws described below apply and use this information when demanding a refund or other compensation, as described in Chapter 13.

Common State Laws

State laws regulating deceptive advertising of rental car rates usually dictate the following:

- what is included in the advertised rate
- the kind of language that may be used in the ad
- the size and degree of boldness required for displaying certain terms in printed and video ads, and
- the disclosure requirements concerning LDW and other forms of insurance, the optional nature of insurance and other services and that rental car insurance may duplicate a renter's own insurance.

For example, in New York and California, a rental car company's advertised and quoted rental rate must include all charges except taxes (sales, use, local and vehicle license taxes) and any mileage charge. California also requires a rental car agreement to disclose that the renter's personal insurance policy may provide for all or part of the renter's liability and that the renter should contact his insurer to determine the scope of insurance coverage.

In Texas, all rental car agreements must contain provisions in at least 12-point bold-face type that LDW may not be necessary, that it is not mandatory and that it is not insurance. In Hawaii, rental car companies must use 10-point type in written rental agreements and 12-point type in written advertisements.

> **Example:** Ed rents a car in Hawaii from Volcano Rents and discovers when he returns the car that Volcano always adds a "cleaning and maintenance fee" in addition to the regular rental charges. The charge is described in tiny (7-point) type. Under the Hawaii law, this is misleading and Ed is not required to pay.

Even in the absence of a state law, when companies use "fine print" to hide extra charges, you have a strong argument that you did not have sufficient notice of the terms, and therefore the terms are not enforceable.

Bait and Switch

A common rental car ploy is to lure you in by advertising an inexpensive automobile, and then when you try to make your reservation, to say that all cars in that category are rented, but for a "small additional fee" you can get a car in the next class. Often, only a very, very limited number of cars were ever available at the advertised price.

This is a classic example of bait and switch, and it is unlikely that you can do much about it on your own. If you do experience bait and switch, report it to the state consumer protection office and the Better Business Bureau where the salespeople are located (and where the company has its headquarters). Pressure from a large group of consumers can force companies to discontinue this type of fraud.

Rental Car Insurance

Each year, travelers in the U.S. spend more than $1 billion on rental car insurance, much of it unneeded or unwanted. Rental car insurance options are complex, confusing and rife with potential rip-offs for the unwary consumer. In fact, insurance accounts for about 10% of the rental car industry's revenue, and nearly all rental car companies pay commissions to rental agents for selling insurance to customers. Not only are the terms of rental car insurance options bewildering, but they are often presented by agents engaged in high-pressure sales tactics.

Although states have passed many laws regulating and curtailing the sale of rental car insurance, it remains one of the most confusing and contentious aspects of renting a car. The following sections set forth practical information to help you make it through the rental car insurance labyrinth and get the right coverage to meet your needs. As you read these sections, keep in mind this basic strategy:

- determine what coverage you already have through your insurance or your credit cards
- find out what insurance options the rental car company offers, and
- buy only what you need and don't fall prey to hardball sales tactics.

Your Own Auto Insurance Coverage

Most American drivers carry auto insurance that provides partial protection for rental car driving, with certain limitations, such as a dollar limit and coverage only for rentals within the U.S. Some policies limit their coverage to cars rented while your own car is being repaired, while other policies do not cover certain classes of cars, such as exotic or antique rentals.

In most circumstances, other forms of coverage, such as credit card protection or liability insurance included in a standard car rental contract, will be secondary to your own auto insurance. This means that if you get in an accident, your own insurance will be used first to cover the costs. Only after you reach the maximum on that coverage will the other forms of insurance kick in. As a result, your own auto insurance rates may be affected if you are in an accident while driving a rental car.

California, Texas and Indiana require rental car companies to inform consumers that the rental car insurance may duplicate the consumer's personal automobile policy, although the laws are not clear about how the information has to be conveyed. Alamo and Budget comply with this requirement by offering written guides, available as follows:

- *A Consumer's Guide to Renting a Car,* Alamo Rental Car, Office of Public Affairs, P.O. Box 22776, Fort Lauderdale, FL 33335, tel: 800-445-5664
- *Budget Rent-a-Car Rent Smart Brochure,* P.O. Box 23903, Milwaukee, WI 53223, tel: 800-736-8762 (this number provides automated information on rental car insurance, but does not discuss personal auto insurance).

Don't count on rental car salespeople to help you determine whether the rental car company's coverage will duplicate the terms of your own auto insurance policy. Instead, call your auto insurance company before you reach the rental car counter and find out the following:

- Does your auto insurance policy cover you in the location that you plan to rent the car? Many auto insurance policies cover cars rented and driven only in the U.S. and Canada.
- How much liability coverage does your policy provide? You need liability insurance any time you drive, not just when renting a car. Your own policy may cover you in a rented car, or you may have an extra umbrella policy that does. In recent years, rental car companies have reduced the amount of liability insurance they include in their standard contracts or in some cases have eliminated liability coverage entirely. This change shifts the bulk of accident costs to your own insurance policy. Because the minimum liability insurance requirements of many states may be inadequate to protect your personal assets against a large personal injury claim, you may want to consider purchasing extra liability insurance when you rent a car.
- How high is your deductible? Are you willing to risk paying the deductible if you have an accident in the rental car?
- Does your personal auto insurance policy limit coverage to no more than the value of the vehicle scheduled on the policy? If so, you need to consider how the value of your personal auto compares to that of the car you would be renting. If the value of your personal auto is less than that of the rental car, you could still have some damage responsibility in the case of an accident.

- Does your insurance cover theft?
- Does your policy cover collision damage? Roughly 70% of all personal auto policies offer collision coverage that duplicates the coverage offered by rental car agencies.

See below for more detailed explanations of the types of insurance available.

Credit Card Protection

If you pay for your rental car with a credit card, you may receive some insurance protection automatically. How much and under what circumstances varies from card to card, and you need to scrutinize the fine print of your credit card agreement carefully before relying on this coverage.

Generally, credit cards offer protection against collision damage to a car rented with the credit card, but do not cover liability insurance. Almost all gold or premium cards offer collision insurance, while standard cards may not. Some cards restrict their coverage to certain major rental car companies, some cards limit coverage to the U.S. and some cards restrict the kinds of cars that they cover. All cards require you to decline the rental car company's LDW in order for credit card coverage to be in effect. Some credit cards have a maximum coverage period for a single rental of 15 days, while others allow 30 days; some cards may allow more for corporate rentals (Diners Club covers 59 days). MasterCard and Visa provide 15 days continuous collision coverage on domestic rentals. If you use one of these cards on a monthly rental, however, you may not be covered at all, even for the first 15 days.

Calling All Credit Cards

The specific terms and wording of different credit card agreements can make it difficult to determine whether rental cars are covered, what the extent of coverage is and which models are excluded. If the small print of your credit card agreement has you confused, call the company's help number and speak with a customer service representative:

American Express:	800-528-4800
American Express Gold:	800-327-2177
American Express Platinum:	800-525-3355
Diners Club:	800-234-6377
MasterCard:	contact issuing bank
Gold MasterCard:	800-622-7747
Visa:	contact issuing bank
Visa Gold Cards:	800-847-2911

Most credit card coverage is secondary or excess coverage, meaning it will only cover repair costs owed after you have collected from your personal auto insurance policy. If you have no auto insurance, the credit card coverage will be primary. Only Diners Club provides primary coverage in the U.S. regardless of your own policy. Although the credit card issuer will reimburse you for charges not covered by your auto insurance, the responsibility for the damage remains yours until the credit card issuer makes this payment.

It can be confusing to determine which car models are covered by your credit card. In general, very expensive cars are excluded, as are antique cars, trucks, cargo vans, customized vans, pickups and any vehicle used to carry cargo. With such a wide variety of sport and recreational cars on the rental market, companies make very detailed distinctions in the fine print as to what they will and will not cover. Some cards give specific model numbers they exclude, while others determine what will be covered by where it is used—roads that are regularly maintained by municipal, state or federal government versus off-road.

Example: Rebecca rented a four-wheel-drive Suzuki Sidekick from a rental car company in New Jersey for a trip to the Adirondacks in the winter. She told the agent she did not want the LDW because she was charging the rental to her American Express card, which provides this coverage. The agent said that American Express would not cover the Sidekick, and insisted that Rebecca buy the LDW, with a $1,500 deductible, at $15 a day. Unsure and concerned about snow in the mountains, she bought it and signed a pledge not to drive the car off-road. When she got home, Rebecca called American Express, which said that it did cover such cars, as long as they were not driven off-road.

Sports Utility Vehicle Dilemma

Sports utility vehicles have rapidly become some of the best-selling cars in America. They are also increasingly popular with renters, particularly families. Many credit card policies, however, specifically exclude sports utility vehicles from coverage. This policy is presumably left over from the time when these vehicles were used primarily for off-road transportation. Be sure your credit card agreement or your own car insurance policy covers sports utility vehicles before you rent one. If not, you may be stuck buying expensive LDW coverage when you rent.

This true example demonstrates the importance of knowing the exact terms of your coverage before you go, and watching out for sales agents who sell you what you do not need. As discussed in the next section, some rental car employees are given quotas or commissions to encourage them to sell as much extra insurance and LDW coverage as possible.

Types of Rental Car Insurance

Although not all rental car companies use the same names for insurance policies, their offerings fall under the following main insurance categories.

Loss Damage Waiver (LDW)

Loss damage waiver, or LDW (also known as collision damage waiver or CDW), has gotten more press than any other type of rental car insurance, due primarily to its high cost and to complaints by consumers of pressure from rental car companies to purchase unnecessary LDW. LDW has raised so many concerns that Congress has considered banning the sale of this most expensive and controversial form of insurance.

Rental car companies claim that they are not selling insurance, and that LDW is simply a waiver of the company's right to collect from you if the rental car is damaged or stolen while under your control. In most rental contracts, the rental company shifts all responsibility for collision damage or other loss to the customer; the effect of purchasing LDW is to shift responsibility back to the rental car company. In other words, if you purchase LDW and your rental car is stolen or damaged, the rental car company will be liable for the damage—not you. Three aspects of LDW make its value suspect:

- the high-pressure or deceptive sales tactics used to sell LDW
- the high price for LDW—especially when you may already be protected by your own insurance or credit cards, and
- the number of exclusions (loopholes) in LDW coverage that allow the company to charge you for repairs even if you purchased LDW to protect yourself.

Controversial LDW Sales Tactics

Although LDW is described as an option, the optional nature of LDW is frequently obscured by the sales tactics of rental car sales agents. Because such waivers are commonly not mentioned when you make rental car reservations over the phone, you often hear about LDW for the first time when you pick up the vehicle and have no time to research your existing coverage or to compare prices with other rental companies. Sales agents take advantage of this by trying to make you believe that you will face un-limited liability for all damage to the rental car, regardless of the circumstances, if you don't purchase LDW. When in a hurry in an unfamiliar place, the coercive atmosphere of many rental car counters may make you feel that you have no choice but to purchase LDW.

Many agents are trained to create doubt and insecurity in the rental customer by asking a series of questions and giving specific responses, such as:

- Are you sure you are covered for any accident? (This creates doubt and insecurity in you.)
- Do you know how much a new car costs to replace? (The agent quotes the full price of a car, a factor that is daunt-ing, but irrelevant.)
- Are you traveling on business? (The agent tells you that your company won't cover any part of the trip that isn't related to business, although most companies cover brief side trips.)
- Where are you going? (This suggests that if you are a stranger, you might be vulnerable to car thefts and need theft insurance.)

Rental car agents have been known to coerce renters into purchasing unwanted insurance by threatening to deny or restrict rental privileges or claiming that unless the customer purchases collision protection from the company, the customer won't be able to leave the state after an accident involving the rental car until the bill is settled in full. Other intimidation tactics include offering several kinds of LDW to make it more complex and confusing to consumers, or if a customer declines to buy LDW, refusing to honor reservations, limiting availability of vehicles, requiring an additional deposit or freezing an excessive amount on a renter's credit card. States are cracking down on these practices. If you experience any of them, report it immediately to the consumer protection agency in the state where you rented the car and demand a full refund from the company.

Example 1: When Sam and Sally picked up their rental car, they told the agent that they didn't need the LDW because their own auto insurance covered rentals. The agent told them that if they had an accident, they wouldn't be allowed to leave the state until the claim was settled —which could take weeks. Because they didn't want to run that risk, they fell for the agent's story and bought the wholly unnecessary LDW.

Example 2: When Vince went to pick up his rental car, he was told by an agent in Las Vegas that he would have to put down a cash deposit or have a "hold" put on his credit card if he didn't buy the company's insurance. Vince bought the LDW despite the fact that his credit card offered similar coverage because he needed access to his full credit limit and felt that he didn't have any other choice.

Example 3: Jose and Alvin were told to initial a small box on the rental agreement, but not told what it was for. Only after their trip ended did they realize they had agreed to pay $200 for insurance.

In each of these cases, the renters were forced to pay for unnecessary LDW due to pressure from rental car sales agents. These practices may be in violation of state consumer protection laws or laws governing LDW. In addition, the rental car company could be liable for fraudulent misrepresentation.

High Price of LDW

LDW is the most expensive form of rental car insurance, with typical charges running $10-$15 per day, a price that would add up to more than $5,000 for one year of coverage. Rental companies use LDW as a way to increase profits without increasing apparent rental rates. LDW increases the base price of an economy car rental, and the car rental industry makes an estimated $500 million each year on LDW. Reservation agents often fail to include the cost of LDW when quoting prices for rental cars, so you learn of the cost only when you are at the rental counter and feel pressured to buy it.

Legislative Initiatives Governing LDW

Due to a flurry of consumer protests, several states have enacted laws relating to LDW. These laws cover things such as the minimum property damage coverage required for rentals, dollar limits on the price of LDW, requirements that coverage be included in the base cost of any rental and requirements that the price of LDW reflect its actual cost. Some specific legislative initiatives are:

- Illinois and New York have eliminated the sale of LDW.[3]
- California requires rental car companies to disclose information about the nature and extent of a renter's liability and how it relates to insurance coverage offered by the rental car company. This law also prohibits a rental car company "to induce a renter to purchase damage waiver, optional insurance" by refusing to honor reservations, limiting the availability of vehicles, requiring a deposit or debiting a renter's credit card if he or she declines the insurance.[4]

Should You Purchase LDW?

Keep in mind that if you purchase LDW, any coverage you would otherwise have under your credit card will not apply. Purchasing LDW may be a prudent choice for you in these circumstances:

- **Foreign rentals.** You will be renting a car outside the U.S. and your auto insurance or credit card coverage does not include foreign rentals.
- **No personal car insurance.** You do not own a car and do not want to rely on credit card coverage alone.
- **Insufficient personal auto insurance.** Your policy coverage is for a car that is of significantly lower value than the car you will rent or your policy has insufficient liability coverage.
- **Can't carry credit charge temporarily.** Your credit card issuer will eventually pay for the repairs, but you can't afford

a large charge on your credit card until the credit card issuer reimburses you.
- **Car you rent not covered under your insurance.** You are renting a car that is specifically not covered by your auto insurance or your credit card coverage (such as an antique or exotic car).

Exclusions and Loopholes in LDW Coverage

If you do purchase LDW, be aware that rental agreements may exclude certain kinds of damage, such as broken or cracked glass, or may contain loopholes which exclude coverage for a variety of other forms of damage. Read the terms carefully, and don't let the loopholes catch you off guard. Bear in mind that your protection could be voided if you engage in any of the following:

- carrying people or property for hire
- propelling or towing any vehicle or trailer
- using the vehicle in a race, contest or training activity
- allowing an unauthorized person to use the vehicle
- using the vehicle for illegal purposes
- obtaining the vehicle from the rental agency by fraud or misrepresentation
- operating the car outside of the state without prior written consent, or
- damaging the vehicle intentionally or through "willful, reckless or wanton misconduct," often defined in rental policies as transporting animals, driving off-road, standing or sitting on the hood or trunk or merely failing to require all occupants to comply with seat belt and child-restraint laws.

Personal Accident Insurance, Personal Effects Coverage and Personal Accident and Effects Insurance

These insurance policies can be very confusing. Some rental car companies offer personal accident insurance and personal effects coverage separately, while other companies combine them and simply offer personal accident and effects insurance. Check your homeowners, renters or business insurance, which frequently provides the same or better coverage. In some instances, you may want to purchase this kind of coverage to offset your deductible, increase the limits of your protection or fill in any coverage gaps.

Personal Effects Coverage

Personal effects coverage (PEC) is commonly known as theft insurance because it covers personal belongings if they are lost or damaged due to theft, damage or accident. If you are the primary renter and you buy PEC, it will normally cover you, your immediate family, other authorized drivers listed on the rental agreement and their immediate family members, as long as they are traveling with you.

Before you purchase PEC, check all of the restrictions and limitations carefully. Many PEC policies contain so many limitations on coverage that they become fairly worthless. Most PEC policies reimburse you for the cash value of items only up to a certain limit per person and impose a total combined benefit maximum. In addition, you have to pay a deductible per claim, and some companies put a low maximum reimbursement (maybe $250) on items such as briefcases, cameras or camera equipment. Further,

many of the valuable items most likely to be lost or stolen—such as cellular phones, computers, computer equipment, eyeglasses or contact lenses, currency, hearing aids, jewelry and sporting equipment—may be excluded entirely from coverage.

Personal Accident Insurance

Personal accident insurance (PAI) covers rental car drivers and passengers for certain medical expenses resulting from an accident during the rental period. Specific terms vary, and most PAI policies contain a long list of exclusions from coverage along with a grisly list of the compensation you will get for loss of body parts in various combinations. If you have personal car insurance that covers rental cars, you probably don't need to purchase PAI.

Personal Accident and Effects Insurance

PAI may be combined with PEC and sold together in a policy called personal accident and effects insurance (PAE). PAE provides a combination of PAI for physical injury, as well as PEC for lost, damaged or stolen personal property. If you are offered a combined policy and only need one, ask whether you can get the single policy at a lower price.

Supplementary Liability Insurance Coverage

While collision insurance covers damage to or loss of the rented car, liability insurance covers damage someone in a rented car might do to other people or property. Buying LDW from a rental company does not provide liability coverage, nor do most credit cards, but personal auto policies do provide liability insurance because it is required by law in all states. Your auto liability insurance usually covers you when you are driving a rental car, but you should check the terms of your policy to make sure.

In the past, rental car companies were required to carry primary liability insurance, but some states have allowed companies to cancel their liability coverage entirely. Further, now that most rental companies have switched their coverage from primary to secondary, your own personal auto insurance policy will provide the majority of liability coverage. This results in an increased chance of a claim on your insurance policy. If a rental car company provides liability coverage in its standard contract, it is likely to be only the minimum liability insurance required by state law. This may be enough to cover minor repairs, but may be inadequate to protect you against a large personal injury claim.

What should you do if you want more liability insurance than that included in the standard rental car contract? First, check your own auto policy. Normally, you will not need more liability insurance for a rental car than you need for your own car, unless your personal policy is very low. If your personal policy's liability is too low, consider buying additional coverage through your regular insurance company. If you do not own a car, but rent cars frequently, consider a year-round nonowner policy sold by auto insurers. If you do not want to involve your own liability insurance company in order to avoid premium increases or cancellation, you can buy liability coverage from most car rental companies, but be prepared to pay a daily charge of $8-$10 for the state's minimum legal coverage.

Renting a Car in a Foreign Country

The laws governing car rentals differ in every country, but this section addresses a few common problems encountered by travelers renting cars outside of the U.S.

License Requirements

If you travel abroad, most countries will accept your valid state driver's license with another form of photo ID. (See sidebar.) Some countries may also require an International Driver's Permit (available through AAA offices). Check below or call a AAA travel office to find out if the country you are visiting requires the Permit. You don't need to take a test to get one; all it does is explain (in several languages) the type of license you have, any limitations that apply and when it will expire.

Countries That Honor Each Other's Licenses

The following countries allow visitors from the other listed nations to use their own domestic driver's licenses:

Albania, Algeria, Argentina, Australia, Austria, Bahamas, Bangladesh, Barbados, Belgium, Belize, Benin, Botswana, Brazil, Bulgaria, Cambodia, Canada, Central African Republic, Chile, Colombia, Congo, Costa Rica, Cuba, Cyprus, Czech Republic, Denmark, Dominican Republic, Ecuador, Egypt, El Salvador, Fiji, Finland, France, French Polynesia (Tahiti), Gambia, Ghana, Great Britain, Greece, Grenada, Guatemala, Guyana, Haiti, Honduras, Hungary, Iceland, Israel, Italy, Ivory Coast, Jamaica, Japan, Jordan, Korea, Laos, Lebanon, Lesotho, Luxembourg, Madagascar, Malawi, Malaysia, Mali, Malta, Mauritius, Mexico, Monaco, Morocco, Netherlands, New Zealand, Nicaragua, Niger, Norway, Panama, Papua New Guinea, Paraguay, Peru, Philippines, Poland, Portugal, Romania, Rwanda, St. Lucia and St. Vincent, San Marion, Senegal, Seychelles, Sierra Leone, Singapore, Slovakia, South Africa, Spain, Sri Lanka, Surinam, Swaziland, Sweden, Syria, Taiwan, Tanzania, Thailand, Togo, Trinidad and Tobago, Tunisia, Turkey, Uganda, (nations of former) U.S.S.R.*, United States, Uruguay, Vatican City, Venezuela, Vietnam, (nations of former) Yugoslavia, Zaire, Zambia, Zimbabwe.

* You must check with the consulate or embassy of the specific former nation of U.S.S.R. prior to travel to verify that the country will honor your U.S. driver's license.

Be aware that in some countries, the police will take your license if you are involved in an accident or stopped for a moving violation, and will not return it until you pay any applicable fine. Get receipts for all payments you make, and report any mistreatment or apparent scams to the American embassy or consulate in that country.

For international travelers in the U.S., a valid foreign driver's license plus another form of photo ID (preferably a passport) is sufficient for most U.S. rental companies.

Insurance

Many personal automobile insurance policies have restrictions or limitations on driving in foreign countries. Check your coverage, including the terms of your credit card policy, before you rent in a foreign country. Purchasing additional insurance may be advisable if your coverage is limited.

Some countries, including Mexico, require you to purchase liability insurance coverage while driving there. Even if you believe that your regular insurance covers you, if additional insurance is legally required, you would do well to purchase it to avoid potential difficulties (including a possible visit to the local jail). Check these requirements with the relevant foreign consulate in the U.S. before your journey.

In certain countries, such as Australia, New Zealand and Costa Rica, the purchase of LDW may be required due to government regulations. In certain European countries, such as Italy, purchase of theft insurance for rental cars is required, though the cost of the theft insurance will likely not be included in the advertised price of the rental. Be sure to ask about mandatory theft insurance charges when renting in Europe.

- If you plan to rent a car outside of the U.S., check with your credit card issuer in advance, as some expensive cars not covered in the U.S. may be covered overseas.

- All major credit card companies provide primary coverage for overseas rentals if they cover them at all. No credit card covers rentals in Australia, Italy or New Zealand.

- If you will be renting a car outside of the U.S., be sure to know and document the terms of your credit card coverage. A foreign rental car company may be unfamiliar with the terms of your specific card, so be sure to bring written evidence of the coverage when you pick up the car. Otherwise, you may be refused your rental car unless you purchase insurance from the company.

- The coverage period for credit cards may be different overseas than in the U.S.

Example: When Juan rented a car in Costa Rica, the agent pressed hard to sell him extra collision and liability insurance. He planned to use his credit card's collision protection and showed the rental agent his credit card's brochure. The agent told Juan that if he didn't buy LDW, he alone would be "responsible for the total value of the car," and that if he didn't buy the extra liability insurance, he would be responsible for any injury he caused someone else. In fact, the agent was only partially correct. Juan would have been protected under the terms of his credit card for collision coverage and did not need to buy LDW. But because Juan's regular auto policy covered him only in the U.S. and Canada, and the liability included in the basic rental rate was very low, he may well have been driving without sufficient liability coverage.

Tickets

Certain European countries, particularly Italy and Great Britain, track traffic violations with street cameras that photograph cars at intersections. The police trace the drivers using the license plate numbers of the cars and then request payment from the rental car companies for the tickets. A rental car company is within its rights to collect the fine from you, even if the company is informed of the violation after you have returned and paid for the car.

> **Example:** Lana and Colin rented a car from Hertz while traveling in Europe in May. Five months later, Hertz notified them that they owed an additional $74 because of a traffic violation in Italy. They were not told of any incident at the time, but according to photographs produced as part of the Italian police report, they ran a red light and will have to pay the fine to Hertz.

Control of Foreign Rental Car Offices

Many rental car companies claim that they have a hard time keeping tabs on the practices of their foreign franchisees and licensees, and foreign agents rarely have all the information about policies, such as which credit cards do and do not offer coverage. Therefore, you should be extra cautious about pressure to buy unwanted insurance or services when renting abroad and investigate companies before you travel. Remember that your credit card's coverage agreement is with you—the cardholder—not with the rental car company, so the decision

to accept or decline the rental company's coverage should be your decision alone.

> **Example:** Donna rented a car for a trip to Italy using her Visa Gold Card that provided collision damage coverage. The rental agent in Milan said that a company policy barred the use of her credit card for this protection and would not give Donna a car until she paid $300 for the company's own coverage. In fact, the rental agent was wrong, and there was no such policy. Donna should be able to get back the amount she paid because it was the agent's misrepresentation that caused her to purchase the extra insurance.

In practice, collecting from a foreign company (even a franchise of a major American company such as Hertz or Avis) may be difficult in the U.S. after the fact. Most American rental car companies hide behind the legal formalities of franchises and licenses and claim that they have no control over foreign offices they do not own. While this may be true in a formal, legal sense, most of these companies have a great deal of leverage over their foreign offices and should be able to get your money returned if you were cheated. If the American company refuses to support your claim against the foreign office, you may be able to argue that the American company itself is liable for failing to properly investigate, monitor or supervise the use of its corporate name by licensees and franchisees, and that because you relied on the good name of the American company in making your choice of rental cars, the American company should cover your losses.

When In Europe

 If you will be driving in Europe, the following publications have useful information:

- The *EuroDollar* brochure—includes explanations of procedures in European rental offices, rental conditions, age requirements and insurance options.
- *Autorental Europe*, by Bill Meier (Lansing Publications, Box 1887, Pleasanton, CA 94566)—discusses the rental process and provides detailed specifications of European car models.
- *Exploring Europe by Car*, by Patricia and Robert Foulke (Globe Pequot, Old Saybrook, CT; 800-243-0495)—focuses on driving in Europe, with details on driving conditions and rules in different countries.
- *Motoeuropa*, by Eric Bredesen (Seren Publishing)—includes a lot of specifics about renting and driving both in Europe in general, and country by country.

If Something Goes Wrong: Accidents and Injuries

Rental car companies are not common carriers, and so they are not considered the insurers of your safety when you rent. Rental car companies are required to use at least "reasonable care" when maintaining and renting cars, and they may be held to an even higher standard of care because they are renting something that has the ability to kill or seriously injure the renter and others.

Most rental agreements disclaim any warranties of fitness or safety. In other words, the rental car company is saying that it is not responsible if the car is not safe or in proper condition for rental. It is highly unlikely that any court would let a rental car company get away with this. When you rent a car, you are paying for the use of a well-maintained, safe vehicle. If you are injured or suffer other loss because the car is unsafe, you should be able to recover damages despite the company's disclaimers, because the company is in a much better position than you are to inspect and maintain the rental car. It would be contrary to public policy to require every car renter to be an automotive expert.

If you are injured or suffer other loss because of an unsafe condition in a rental car, document exactly what injury or damage occurred and how it happened, preferably in writing with witnesses. Furthermore, if you suspect that the car was not properly inspected or maintained, demand a copy of the car's maintenance record from the rental car company.

If you are in an accident in a rental car, take the following steps:

- Get the name, driver's license number and insurance policy number of any other drivers involved in the accident.
- Get the name, address and telephone number of any witnesses willing to cooperate.
- If there is any chance of damage or injury, call the police, and keep a copy of the written police report.

- Do not leave the scene of the accident until the police say that you may.
- Inform the rental car company as soon as possible. Many companies require that you drive to one of their offices to fill out an accident report within a certain period of time—often 24 hours.
- Inform your own insurers (including the credit card issuer and insurance carrier) as soon as possible after any accident or injury.

Under the rental agreement, rental car companies require you to "cooperate" with their investigation and any legal action that they take after the accident. You are not required, however, to make a statement to any insurance adjuster or rental car employee before you have a chance to consult with an attorney or otherwise review your legal rights. Do not be coerced into doing so, particularly if you believe that the company may be trying to pin the blame on you.

■

Endnotes

[1] Restatement of Contracts § 329; 11 Williston on Contracts §1338; Uniform Commercial Code § 1-106.

[2] See, for example, California Civil Code § 1936; Hawaii Revised Law § 437D; Illinois Annotated Statutes § 95 1/2-6-305; New York General Business Law § 396.z; Texas Revised Civil Statute § 9026.

[3] Illinois Annotated Statutes § 95 1/2-6-305; New York General Business Law § 396.z.

[4] California Civil Code § 1936.

Chapter 3

Taking a Cruise

An Introduction to Cruises

Ocean cruises are a popular form of vacation travel. Because cruise lines provide not only transportation, but also accommodations, food and often entertainment, the cruise line has a large number of responsibilities to its passengers. As one court put it:

A contract for passage by water implies something more than ship room and transportation. It includes reasonable comforts, necessaries, and kindness .... It is a duty of the common carrier by water to provide his passengers with comfortable accommodations ... unless there is a contract to the contrary or a fair understanding to the contrary; and the carrier must subject his passengers to no suffering or inconvenience that can be avoided by reasonable care or effort.[1]

As a cruise passenger, most of your legal rights are determined by the terms of the cruise ticket you purchase and a special area of law—called maritime law—that is applied to ships and passengers. Most disputes between cruise lines and passengers are not covered by individual state contract or tort laws, or even general federal law. Maritime law supersedes any state law concerning oceangoing cruises. A lawsuit under maritime law, however, can be brought in either a federal or state court.

 In this chapter, we refer to many specific cases against cruise lines. These cases can be used to support your position if you have a similar complaint. But beware—maritime law frequently favors the cruise line, not the passenger. Although you won't choose your ocean cruise based on the terms of the ticket-contract, you need to know your rights before you buy.

Special Laws for Ocean Cruises

 Complaints against cruise lines are generally governed by maritime law—the law of the seas. In some cases, your claim might have to be resolved under the law of a foreign country.

Maritime Law

Maritime law is based on court interpretations of old legal principles covering ships and sailing. Because maritime law is interpreted in different ways by different courts, it is often filled with contradictions, and determining exactly how the law should be applied in your case can be tricky. If you have a dispute with a cruise line, bear in mind that the cruise line's lawyers know the ins and outs of maritime law. Even if you hire a lawyer to represent you, you may have problems unless that lawyer is a specialist in maritime law.

Foreign Law

In some cases, particularly where a cruise begins or ends in a foreign country, the law of the foreign country may be applied if your ticket contains a provision saying so. This is true even if you are a U.S. citizen and you purchased the ticket in the U.S.

You do have some protection in this situation. A U.S. court won't apply foreign law without a good reason. For instance, a cruise from San Diego along the coast of

Mexico could state in its ticket that the laws of Mexico will apply—and a court will enforce that. However, if the ticket stated that the laws of France should be applied (as a cruise line might if the ship owner were French), U.S. courts are not likely to follow the provision. Generally, U.S. courts look to see if the passenger and the cruise line had an understanding about the law that would apply, whether there are sufficient contacts with the country—such as the beginning and ending points of the cruise, the location of the cruise and the citizenship of you and the nation of registry for the cruise line—to warrant application of its law.

Cruises Totally Outside the U.S.

Your legal rights may be different than what's described in the ticket if you are taking a foreign cruise that does not "touch the U.S."[2] The ticket probably states that any dispute will be resolved under the laws of a foreign country, and may require you to sue in a foreign court. You may also be required to make a written claim to the cruise line within a few days or to sue within months. Further, the amount you can recover for injuries is limited by an international treaty known as the "Athens Convention."[3]

The expense and difficulty of making a claim or suing in a foreign country can effectively eliminate your ability to pursue a claim. This is no reason not to take a foreign cruise, but know that you may be sacrificing some of the rights available to you in the U.S.

Before You Book a Cruise

- **Research the reputation of the cruise line.** Check with the Better Business Bureau where the company is based to find out how many complaints have been made against it. Ask your travel agent whether it has had complaints from past passengers or experienced trouble processing refunds or cancellations.
- **Review the sanitation ratings for any cruise ship you might take.** (Getting information on sanitation ratings is covered below.)
- **Ask about special discounts for advance booking** and whether the cruise line will guarantee you a lower fare if it lowers its rates closer to departure.
- **Request a copy of the cruise contract (ticket)** before you buy a cruise and study the contract for the type of questionable terms discussed in this chapter, such as requiring you to bring any lawsuit in a foreign country.
- **Before purchasing cruise insurance, find out about exclusions** such as whether you are covered if you cancel your trip shortly before departure or in the middle of the trip.
- **Bring copies of your medical prescriptions and even medical records,** such as a recent EKG, if you have a chronic problem that might require treatment.
- **Find out about the ship's medical facilities,** whether there will be a doctor on board, whether the doctor speaks English and what his or her qualifications are.
- **Ask what other charges** such as port charges, taxes or fees will be added to the cost of your ticket.

Resolving Problems After You Go

- Study the terms of your ticket carefully, but don't believe everything you read. Cruise lines can limit their liability in a number of ways, but they are still responsible if their negligence leads to a loss, injury or death.
- Remember that usually you cannot rely on the protection of state laws—cruises are covered by maritime law. In some rare cases you may be able to use your state's consumer protection laws, such as those that prohibit false advertising. (See Chapter 7.)
- Check your ticket carefully and meet all time limitations. Each ticket contains the time limits for sending a written claim and suing (see Suing a Cruise Line, below.) If you do not make your claim and file your lawsuit within these time limitations, you may lose your right to recover anything.
- Try to settle your dispute informally first. (See Chapter 13.)
- Understand that it may be difficult to sue. You may have to file your case in a part of the U.S. far from where you live or in a different country.

Cruise Insurance and Cancellation Protection

Taking a cruise often requires the prepayment of a large sum of money, and many cruise passengers purchase cruise insurance. Because of the expense of cruise insurance and the variety of types of coverage avail-

able, it is important to check the terms carefully before you buy. In general, you are better protected if you buy your insurance from an insurance company rather than the cruise line. As with other insurance purchases, check with your credit card companies and regular insurer to see if they offer any free or low-cost protection.

 For details on travel insurance, see Chapter 8.

Cancellation penalty waivers, also known as cancellation protection, are often sold directly by the cruise lines. These waivers are not really insurance; instead, they give you the chance to cancel your cruise without paying the normal penalties for cancellation. The value of these waivers is often questionable, particularly because many are effective only until two or three days before the cruise leaves. If you need to cancel at the last minute or during your trip, the waivers normally do nothing for you, and you must pay the full amount of the cruise. True trip cancellation or interruption insurance that provides more comprehensive coverage (described in Chapter 8) is usually better.

Tickets and Reservations

The Ticket Is a Contract

The ticket issued by a cruise line to you is considered a "contract for carriage" under which the cruise line has a number of responsibilities towards you. Beyond simply transporting you from the starting point to the ending point of the cruise, the line has general obligations to provide appropriate accommodations, food and drink, and to take sufficient steps to ensure that the ship is clean, sanitary and safe. Just because these obligations are not explicitly listed as terms of the contract does not mean that the cruise line can avoid its obligations; these general requirements are considered implied terms.

The Terms of the Ticket-Contract— The Fine Print

Most tickets contain basic information such as the cruise date, price and cabin location on the first page, and paragraphs of small print on the back or additional pages. Because many of the cruise line's obligations to you are defined by the terms of the ticket-contract, most cruise lines use the fine print to try to limit their obligations—by including terms that allow them to change the cruise itinerary, skip ports and limit their liability for lost or stolen baggage. Unfortunately, these fine-print terms are generally enforceable, even if you do not read them.

If you want to review the contract terms before agreeing to them, it is possible to contact the cruise line directly and request a copy of the ticket. It is very unlikely that the cruise line would negotiate any of the terms, however, and you are in a "take it or leave it" situation. U.S. courts are likely to enforce the provisions of a ticket unless the provisions are highly unreasonable or unfair.

Notice of the Terms

In theory, the terms of a cruise ticket cannot be enforced unless you had sufficient notice of the terms. This does not mean that you actually read the fine print or are even able to read the fine print, but there must be a conspicuous statement on the ticket that informs or warns you that the other terms have been "incorporated." Most cruise tickets contain a statement such as:

ISSUED SUBJECT TO THE TERMS AND CONDITIONS PRINTED ON THE COVER OF THIS CONTRACT TICKET WHICH FORM PART THEREOF.

Generally, a court would enforce the terms against you if you "had an opportunity" to read the contract.[4] The fine-print terms of tickets have been upheld even when passengers did not speak English or never actually saw the ticket because it was kept by their agent, traveling companion or spouse.[5]

It may be impossible for you to know the terms of the contract before you pay for your ticket if you make your reservation and payment through a travel agent or travel club and the ticket does not arrive until soon before you sail. In one case, a court ruled that the passengers did not have sufficient notice when they received their tickets only two or three days before sailing because they could not object to the terms without forfeiting the entire price of the cruise.[6] Other courts have ruled the opposite. For example, one couple received their tickets 20 days before sailing and would have had to pay a 40% cancellation penalty if they decided to cancel at that point. Nonetheless, the court determined that they were bound by the terms of the ticket.[7]

If the delay in receiving the tickets is the cruise line's fault, your argument is much stronger than if you delayed in paying for or picking up the ticket from your travel agent.

Remember, the basic test is whether you had "an opportunity" to review the terms, not whether you actually read the contract.

Master Tickets

A passenger who took a cruise as part of a group was able to prove that she did not receive sufficient notice of the contract terms when the limitations were included only on a "master ticket" held by the group leader, and when nothing given to her, including her boarding pass, indicated that she was bound by the terms of the master ticket.[8] Most cruise companies now issue individual tickets to group members.

The Lowest Fare

The cruise industry is famous for discounting fares. In the past, cruise lines did their heaviest discounting right before departure. Knowing this, many cruise passengers waited until the last minute to book. To encourage early bookings, many lines have changed their fare schedules so that fares increase closer to the departure date. In any case, it is likely that another passenger may have paid much more (or less) than you for an identical cabin. Although there is nothing illegal about multiple fares, it can be frustrating to cruise passengers, particularly those who booked early (perhaps to get a better choice of cabin) but paid more. If you want to make sure you are getting the best deal, ask for a written guarantee that you will receive a refund if the same type of cabin is offered for a lower fare after you purchase your ticket. Also, consider using a "cruise only" travel agent or travel club that specializes in finding discounted cruise fares.

In 1996, several lawsuits were filed against many major cruise lines accusing them of deceptive advertising. In addition to the ticket price, the cruise lines were padding their charges with port charges and other fees. In many cases, the cruise lines were adding the cost of wages, fuel and other operating expenses to the ticket price and thus unfairly raising the true price of the ticket. In 1997, most of the major lines agreed voluntarily to itemize port charges and other fees. Be sure to ask about these additional expenses before you purchase your ticket.

Upgrades

One advantage of buying your ticket far in advance of the cruise is that cruise lines will sometimes offer upgrades (better cabins) to passengers who book early. If you are interested in a free upgrade, let the cruise line know when you make your reservation.

Failure to Honor a Ticket or Reservation

Unlike airlines, cruise lines do not routinely overbook. On some occasions, however, a cruise line might not accept your ticket or may put you in a lower-class room than you reserved. If you have a valid ticket and reservation, and the cruise line gives you a different cabin than you reserved, you should be able to recover the difference between the cabin that was promised to you and the cabin that you received. In addition, you may be entitled to compensation for reduced enjoyment (see section on Lack of Enjoyment, below).

Cruise Canceled by Cruise Line

If the cruise line cancels your cruise, you are entitled to a full refund. Cruise lines are required by federal regulations to maintain reserves or have sufficient insurance to cover canceled cruises.[9] Nevertheless, in several recent cruise line failures, the reserves were not large enough to cover all the claims from passengers. If the cruise line cancels your cruise, demand a full refund immediately. A failure or delay in providing a refund could indicate that the cruise line is in financial difficulty, so keep asking. Demand not only your out-of-pocket damages to compensate you for the cruise ticket, but also your consequential damages for additional losses, such as the need to change or forfeit your original airline ticket, or other expenses you incurred specifically because of the cancellation.

If the cruise line goes bankrupt and cancels your cruise, you theoretically have the right to a full refund. But the cruise line won't be able to refund your money because its assets will be tied up by the bankruptcy court. Instead, you will have to file a claim with the bankruptcy court. You have a chance of getting paid if the cruise has assets to be distributed to its creditors, but you may not get very much because you will be at the bottom of the creditor list.

Claims Against Cruise Lines

If you have a problem with a cruise, you should try to resolve it informally following the advice in Chapter 13. (And remember to act quickly.) If that gets you nowhere, you may have to sue.

There are several types of claims that can be brought against a cruise line. When a cruise line fails to provide the types of services promised in the ticket, you may be able to recover compensation because of the cruise line's breach of the contract. If you are injured during the cruise or suffer some loss or damage to your property, you may be able to recover compensation under the legal principles of tort law covering injuries of various sorts. Sometimes, one incident can be the basis for both a breach of contract and a tort claim, such as where you are served contaminated food—the cruise line breached its obligation to provide sanitary food, and you may have been physically hurt by the food.

Another type of claim against cruise lines is fraud or misrepresentation if the cruise line or its agents made promises that they did not intend to keep. (See Chapter 7.)

Itinerary Changes and Port Skipping

Many cruises include stops at several ports, and visiting these ports is often a significant motivation for taking the cruise. If the cruise does not follow the itinerary that was promised, or skips one or more ports, you may not receive what you paid for when you purchased the ticket.

Most tickets contain a disclaimer reserving the right to cancel a scheduled call or to change the itinerary as necessary. Furthermore, maritime law allows a ship's captain to deviate from the scheduled itinerary if necessary—for example, because of bad weather or political problems at a port. If the changes in the itinerary are so significant that they undercut your basic expectations, you may be entitled to compensation despite the disclaimer. For instance, on a trip in the Caribbean where two ports were skipped, the ship arrived very late at night at the third port, and anchored in the harbor at the fourth so far from the shore that passengers had to be ferried back and forth in small boats; the passengers were entitled to compensation.[10]

Cruise tickets usually contain a disclaimer limiting the cruise line's liability in the case of a change in the itinerary. Generally, such disclaimers limit recovery to a pro rata share of the ticket price if the cruise is shortened. That is, if a seven-day cruise was shortened to five days, you may be entitled to a refund of 2/7 of the ticket price. While such a limitation is generally enforceable, there are exceptions. If a major reason for taking a cruise is defeated by the changes or shortening of the trip, you may be able to recover more than the pro rata share for lack of enjoyment. If, for instance, your one-week nature cruise to the Galapagos Islands from Ecuador was shortened to five days, and as a result you were never allowed to go ashore as promised, you would have a good argument that you received much less than 5/7 of the value promised when you purchased your ticket.

Switching Cabins

Sometimes, a cruise line finds it necessary to assign you to a different cabin than you reserved. If the cabin is better than the one reserved, that's great. If, however, you are placed in a smaller or less comfortable cabin than you reserved, you should be able to recover the difference between the price of the original cabin and the one you are given. If the cabin is the same class and size as the one you reserved (and therefore the same price), but simply in a different location, it's unlikely you would get compensation, unless the new location is substantially inferior (for example, next to a noisy machine room). If you are unhappy with your cabin, let the appropriate crew members know immediately. It may be possible to reassign you to a better cabin. This is generally better than complaining after your cruise.

Uncomfortable Cabins

Most cruise cabins are substantially smaller than hotel rooms of similar cost, and many cruise passengers complain about the cramped conditions. Unless the cabin is actually smaller than the one you contracted for, you're stuck. If other basic conditions make the cabin unacceptable or unsafe, such as an overflowing toilet or a door that will not stay locked, you have grounds to complain.[11]

In addition, you have a right to "quiet enjoyment" of your cruise. If a cabin is immediately adjacent to a generator that makes it difficult to sleep, the cruise line may be breaching an implied term of your contract, that is, to provide you with suitable accommodations. A certain amount of noise and motion is to be expected on board a ship, and you must be reasonable in your expectations, particularly if the price of the cabin has been reduced to reflect its short-comings. If the condition of the cabin is so bad that it interferes with your fundamental enjoyment of the cruise, however, inform the onboard cruise staff and ask to be moved.

Failure to Observe Laws and Regulations

Cruise lines operate under a number of laws and regulations, including those covering health, sanitation and safety.[12] Most are enforced by the U.S. Coast Guard. If a cruise line violates these laws and regulations, such as failing to have sufficient life boats on board, generally you cannot demand com-pensation because only the government can sue to enforce those laws and regulations.

If the problem that injured or inconve-nienced you also violated a health or safety regulation (such as too many people on the ship), this would probably be viewed as strong evidence of a breach of your con-tract, thus entitling you to compensation. Reports prepared by crew members or inspection reports prepared by the Coast Guard would be good sources of informa-tion on possible violations. You would have to make a special request to the Coast Guard to obtain copies of these reports, and in some cases you may need a court order.

Sanitation Inspections

All cruise ships that sail from U.S. ports are periodically inspected by the U.S. Public Health Service to insure that the ships meet certain requirements of sanitation. The inspectors check the quality of water and food, as well as the general cleanliness of the ship. Ships are rated on a 100-point scale, and scores of 86 and above are considered satisfactory. Sanitation scores for ships are listed in the U.S. Public Health Service's *Biweekly Summary of Sanitation Inspections of International Cruise Ships.* The *Summary* is available from the Center for Disease Control and reprinted in the following:

- the CDC's Website, at http://www.cdc. gov/nceh/programs/sanit/vsp/scores/ scores.htm.
- travel section of some major newspapers
- travel newsletters, such as *Consumer Reports Travel Letter,* and
- trade magazines, such as *Travel Weekly,* available from your travel agent.

If you became ill during a cruise and sus-pect that the food or water on board was the cause, alert the cruise line and request compensation. If you don't get anywhere, request the most recent detailed sanitation report for that ship (and perhaps for the other ships owned by that cruise line). The report probably won't prove whether the food or water was contaminated, but a low score in those areas could bolster your argument against the cruise line.

Send your request to Chief, Vessel Sanitation Program, National Center for Environmental Health, Centers for Disease Control, 1015 North American Way, Suite 107, Miami, FL 33132; 305-536-4307 (voice); 305-536-4528 (fax). Provide the name of the cruise line, the name of the ship, the ports of departure and arrival and the dates you sailed.

Lack of Enjoyment

You have no legal claim against a cruise line if you simply do not have a good time on your cruise. If, however, you cannot enjoy the cruise because the conditions on board are substantially different from those promised and anticipated, you may have a valid claim. An example of such a claim would be if certain promised facilities, such as a pool or exercise room, were not available, or if the onboard entertainment was substantially different from that promised.

The principle of being compensated for "lack of enjoyment" is based primarily on maritime cases from outside of the U.S., such as where a ship sank or was disabled and the passengers had to be evacuated.[13] Nonetheless, American courts have been allowing compensation when a trip goes seriously awry. A single item, by itself, probably would not constitute a material breach of the contract. But a sufficient number of small failures on the part of the cruise line may, if they are significant enough to prevent you from enjoying your cruise. The items must have been anticipated or controlled by the cruise line; lack of sunshine or grumpy travel companions are not the sorts of things for which cruise lines can be held responsible.

The Sound of Music

A German couple recovered one-third of the price of their cruise because of lack of enjoyment. The couple had signed up for a "folk music" cruise of the Caribbean, expecting to enjoy a variety of Latin American music. What they received was something quite different. Over 80% of the passengers (500 out of 600) were members of the Swiss Union of Friends of Folk Music who spent the entire two-week cruise practicing their Swiss Alpine yodeling.

Service Quality Problems

If you purchase a ticket for a "luxury" or "first-class" cruise, exceptional service is generally implied. If crew members are rude or unresponsive to your legitimate requests, the cruise line may be breaching its obligations. Although it is difficult to describe exactly what luxury or first-class travel entails, these terms suggest a high level of comfort and professional service, and courts have been willing to compensate passengers when the cruise staff falls short.[14] Don't expect to get rich—any recovery is likely to be far less than the cost of bringing the lawsuit.

Injuries or Death

A cruise line has a general duty to provide you with safe and healthy services and facilities. You can recover from a cruise line for injuries connected with the cruise if it was caused by the cruise line's negligent or intentional actions. The cruise line is negligent when it fails to take "reasonable care under the circumstance" to protect its passengers.[15] Courts look at whether the cruise line:

- had actual knowledge of the danger, or
- had constructive knowledge of the danger—meaning that the condition existed long enough that the cruise line should have known about the danger it presented, and the cruise line had an opportunity to prevent the injury.

Because the circumstances of each case are different, the amount of care that the cruise line must exercise depends on considerations such as the extent of risk of danger to the passenger, and whether the circumstances surrounding the injury were linked to ocean travel and different from those normally encountered in daily life on shore.[16] An injury caused by tripping over an unnecessarily large coaming (door sill) in a ship's public bathroom may be the cruise line's responsibility, but an injury caused by tripping while playing on a shipboard basketball court probably is not.

If the cruise line is responsible for your injury, you would be entitled to recover your medical costs, lost earnings, pain and suffering, compensation for any permanent disability and emotional distress.

Death or Serious Injury

Cruise accidents that lead to death or serious or permanent injury may be subject to special laws, such as the Death on the High Seas Act.[17] These cases are quite complex and often involve large amounts of money. If you are seriously injured on a cruise or someone close to you dies from an accident on a cruise, we highly recommend that you consult with an attorney experienced in maritime law. These lawyers will be easier to find in coastal communities than if you live in the center of the country.

To prevent a cruise line from using the fine print in a contract to eliminate or reduce its responsibility to protect its passengers, Congress passed a law which makes it impossible for a cruise line to deny liability for its own negligence.[18] On cruises that "touch the United States," the ticket cannot limit the amount you can recover if the cruise line or any of its employees or agents cause physical injury or death. Keep in mind, however, that strict time limitations can effectively block your claim if you fail to file a written claim or lawsuit within the required time.

In older cases, many courts held cruise lines to a higher standard than "reasonable care under the circumstances," saying that they owed the "highest degree of care" or must exercise "extraordinary vigilance" to protect passengers. This higher standard doesn't apply much anymore, and any older cases you run across (if you do some legal research) may be outdated.

The cruise line's duty of reasonable care includes the requirement to warn you of dangers not apparent and obvious. The warning must be conspicuous and give you effective notice. A sign posted so low that no one is likely to see it is not sufficient. On the other hand, if the danger is obvious, the cruise line does not have to post a specific notice. For example, a passenger who was injured when he jumped into an almost empty ship swimming pool was deemed to have been given adequate notice because the pool was roped off, even though the ship did not post specific warning signs.[19]

Warnings of Storms and Heavy Seas

A cruise line must warn you about dangers such as storms and heavy seas, and must see that its safety instructions are carried out. A passenger thrown out of a chair during a heavy storm recovered from the cruise line because the crew failed to warn passengers of the dangers of sitting in a chair not anchored to the deck during a storm.[20] A cruise line does not have to warn of accidents that it cannot foresee or prevent, such as a large, freak wave causing the ship to roll suddenly. It also does not have to take extraordinary measures such as anchoring all of its chairs to the deck.

Injuries Caused by a "Slip and Fall"

One of the most common injuries aboard ships is caused by slipping and falling on a wet floor or tripping over something constructed to minimize ground water movement. Whether you can recover for this type of injury may depend upon where you were and what you were doing when you were injured. Remember—the cruise line probably owes you a higher level of care if you were injured during an activity that is primarily associated with travel by ship than if your injury came during an activity you would engage in on shore. For instance, if you hurt yourself when you slipped on a ship's dance floor, the cruise line probably would be liable only if it could have foreseen the cause of the injury and done something to prevent it, given that dancing is not an activity unique to traveling by ship.[21]

On the other hand, if you slipped in a ship's hallway during a storm because the ship had no handrail, the cruise line

probably owed you a higher standard of care because of the cruise line's superior experience and knowledge about sailing during storms and its responsibility for having appropriate safety features.[22]

Injuries Caused by an Unsafe Condition

If you are injured by an unsafe condition in your cabin (such as a broken bed), the cruise line's liability generally depends on whether it could have found the unsafe condition if it had done a reasonable inspection of your room, and whether it should have done something to prevent the injury or warn you about the danger.[23] A number of injuries seem to occur in bathrooms (for example tripping over the sill for the shower), and getting in and out of bed. If you discover a problem, report it to the appropriate crew member immediately. Your ability to recover may be reduced or eliminated if the cause of the injury should have been obvious to you.[24]

Injuries Sustained When Entering and Exiting the Ship

The cruise line has a duty to provide a reasonably safe way of entering and exiting the ship. It must take normal precautions to protect you, such as having handrails or ropes along the boarding ramp or plank, and making sure there is no gap between the end of the ramp and the dock—or warning you of such a gap. The cruise line must also provide safe small boats or launches for transporting you to shore when the ship is anchored in the harbor.[25]

Injuries suffered on or near the dock may be the responsibility of the cruise line or some other entity, such as the port authority or the dock owner. If you are injured in that situation, make sure that you consider all of the parties who might be responsible and include all of them separately in any claim or complaint you make. For injuries in foreign ports, particularly where docks are owned or supervised by foreign governments, it may be very difficult to recover against the foreign parties.

Injuries Sustained During Shore Visit

Normally, once you are on shore, the cruise line is not responsible for any harm to you. There are a couple of important exceptions to this general rule, however. If the shore excursion is organized or promoted by the cruise line, it may be responsible for your injuries. The same is true if the cruise line fails to notify you that it is merely acting as a ticketing agent for another company and leads you to believe that it is operating the excursion.

Furthermore, if members of the crew recommend an area to visit, or have told you that an area is safe, the cruise line may be held responsible for any injuries.[26] In one case, several passengers visited a secluded beach at the recommendation of the ship's activities director; they were violently attacked by local thugs and sued the cruise line. The court held that the cruise line was liable for their injuries because it had an obligation to warn the passengers of reasonably foreseeable dangers on shore. The cruise line apparently knew of other violent attacks against other tourists on the island, but did not provide this information to its passengers.[27]

Injuries Sustained During Group Activities and Classes

Many cruises include group activities, such as contests, games or classes. If the activity is organized by the cruise line, or if crew members are significantly involved in the activity, the cruise line is responsible for ensuring that the activity is properly operated and supervised. When a passenger drowned after receiving inadequate scuba diving training from a crew member, the cruise line was found liable to the passenger's family.[28]

If a cruise line organizes potentially dangerous activities, such as scuba diving, it must make sure that the activity is carried out competently and is carefully supervised. A passenger injured during organized group activities can recover if the cruise line was negligent in its supervision, but the recovery may be substantially reduced if the passenger had a medical condition making it unwise for him to participate—especially if the cruise line warned people with that medical condition not to join in.[29]

Injuries From a Safety Feature

The cruise line's duty of care includes taking measures to protect you from unreasonable risks. If a cruise line fails to do so, it may be liable if you are injured. On the other hand, if you are hurt by a safety precaution, the cruise line may have a good defense to any claim you make. For instance, fire doorways are required on most cruise ships. If you trip over the elevated sill of a fire doorway, you cannot claim that the sill is inherently dangerous simply because it is different from other doorways. The same is true for metal tread stairways or coaming on a doorway designed to prevent flooding on board.[30]

The reasoning is that such safety features are there to protect you, and you should expect certain features on a boat to be different from those in your own homes. If the safety feature is not well designed or poses a threat, however, the cruise line does have a responsibility to warn you of the potential hazard by posting a sign.[31]

Injuries From a Ship's Doctor (Malpractice)

Although cruises are not required to have a ship's doctor on board, most do. New voluntary standards for medical facilities and emergency medical care have been adopted by the International Council of Cruise Lines. (The members of the International Council of Cruise Lines include most of the major cruise lines in the U.S.) If a ship's doctor commits malpractice—that is, misdiagnoses or mistreats you—courts usually hold that your complaint is against the doctor and not the cruise line. This is because ship doctors are not employed by the cruise line, but are independent professionals on board for the convenience of the passengers.

You could have a claim against the cruise line, however, if the doctor was incompetent or unlicensed and the cruise line could have discovered this by checking the doctor's background. Cruise lines are required to use reasonable care in selecting a competent and qualified doctor. The doctor does not have to be licensed to practice in the U.S. even if the doctor is likely to be treating American passengers.[32]

A case in Florida suggests that in some instances the cruise line may be liable if the doctor is acting as the cruise line's agent.[33] If you are a victim of malpractice, you (or

your attorney) should study this case to determine whether or not you should pursue
your claim against the cruise line as well as
the doctor. To protect yourself, make sure
you give written notice to the cruise line and
file any lawsuit on time—remember, lawsuits against cruise lines often have to be
filed within six months or a year.

Medical Evacuation

On the average cruise ship, one person
a week is evacuated due to a medical
emergency. Almost one-third of the
evacuations are by medical helicopter.
The U.S. Coast Guard is not obliged to
provide evacuation services, but it does
so in some cases. A medical evacuation
can be extremely expensive. If you have
a chronic medical problem or other
condition that could give rise to the
need for evacuation, this is one situation
where travel insurance, specifically
medical evacuation insurance, might
make sense. See Chapter 8.

Injuries From an Attack on Board

On rare occasions, passengers have been
physically attacked while on a cruise.
Although the cruise line's general duty is to
take reasonable steps to protect its passengers
from harm, the cruise line's liability for an
attack may be greater depending upon the
attacker's relationship with the cruise line.

Attacks by a Crew Member

When the attacker is a member of the ship's
crew, some courts have determined that a
cruise line is "absolutely liable" for a crew

member's assault, regardless of whether the
cruise line could have anticipated the
attack.[34] In a few cases, however, cruise
lines have argued successfully that they
should not be liable if they can show that
they took all necessary precautions in pre-
employment screening, hiring and supervision of crew members, and that other
reasonable precautions were taken to
protect the passengers (such as having good
locks on the cabin doors).[35] In other words,
the cruise line would be liable only if it
were negligent.

Attacks by Another Passenger

When the attacker is another passenger, the
cruise line can be held responsible if the
crew knew, or should have known, that the
attacker was dangerous, and the crew had
an opportunity to do something to prevent
the attack. For example, a cruise line may
be held liable if the crew knows about an
obviously drunk and belligerent passenger
who then makes an unprovoked attack on
another passenger.[36] Similarly, a cruise line
would probably be liable if it sold a ticket to
a passenger who had been belligerent or a
problem with other guests on a previous
cruise.

Attacks by an Outsider

When a passenger is attacked by someone
who does not belong on the ship, some
courts have ruled against cruise lines, saying
they must exercise "extraordinary vigilance"
to protect passengers from criminal attacks.
In one case, where the attacker sneaked
onto the ship while it was in port, the court
said that since the cruise line had a duty to
protect passengers from criminal activity on

board, it didn't matter whether or not the cruise line could have foreseen the attack.[37]

The rarest of attack cases involve terrorism. In the famous incident involving the Achille Lauro, the courts found that the cruise line would be liable only if it failed to take reasonable safety precautions under the circumstances to prevent a terrorist attack, and that the line had no duty to search all passengers for weapons.

If You Are Partially at Fault— Comparative Negligence

A legal doctrine known as "comparative negligence" is applied to passenger injuries under maritime law. This means that if you are partially responsible for your injury, the amount you could recover in court would be reduced by your percentage of negligence. In a trial, the judge or jury would evaluate how much you were to blame for your injury, and any compensation would be reduced by that amount. For instance, if you fall overboard and the jury decides that you were 75% responsible because you didn't look where you were going, you would receive only 25% of the damages that are awarded to you as compensation. This is an important point to keep in mind when you are evaluating your claim against a cruise line.

Baggage and Personal Belongings

Many cruise passengers bring valuable personal belongings on cruises, including jewelry and clothing. This means that you could suffer a substantial loss if your baggage is lost, stolen or damaged. Unlike travel on airplanes, buses and trains, baggage is rarely stowed away by the cruise line. Instead, you normally keep the baggage in your cabin. This makes it difficult for you to recover anything from a cruise line because you—not the line—have effective "control" over your baggage and are in the best position to prevent the loss or damage.

Similarly, when the baggage is being transported on and off of the ship, the cruise line is responsible only if an employee or agent is handling the baggage. The cruise line is not liable if baggage is lost or damaged by an independent porter or longshoreman.

Cruise tickets contain clauses limiting the cruise line's liability when it is at fault for lost, stolen or damaged baggage. These clauses are generally upheld as long as you had reasonable notice of the terms.

The ticket often sets the cruise line's liability at unrealistically low amounts— such as $100 for all of your luggage, clothing and jewelry. For this reason, consider taking additional steps to protect yourself such as:

- declaring the actual value of your possessions to the cruise line when you check in for departure

- purchasing baggage insurance (see Chapter 8), or

- using the ship's safe, if available, to store jewelry and other valuables (the discussion in Chapter 4, on who is responsible if things are missing from a hotel safe, applies here).

If your baggage is lost, damaged or stolen, you must comply with the time periods stated in your ticket for making a written claim to the cruise line or filing a lawsuit. The limitation period for baggage claims is often very short (as little as a few days to notify the cruise line and a few months to file a lawsuit), and failing to meet the deadlines wipes out your chance to recover. In one case where a ship burned and the passenger claimed to have lost $65,000 worth of personal property, the court ruled that the passenger could not recover because she didn't file her claim to the cruise line within ten days of the loss or file her lawsuit within six months.[38]

Suing a Cruise Line

Time Limitations for Suing a Cruise Line

If you want to sue a cruise line, you must act quickly. Most cruise lines require that you give written notice of damaged or lost property, breach of contract or fraud within ten days of the damage; any lawsuit usually must be filed within six months. Written notice of personal injury normally must be given to the cruise line within six months of the injury, and any lawsuit usually must be filed within one year.[39]

 Although states have laws known as statutes of limitations that allow lawsuits to be filed years after damage or injuries occur, these state laws do not apply to cruise injuries. This is important to remember even if you bring your case to an attorney, because many attorneys do not know about the short periods for cruise losses. Check your ticket carefully, and meet all time limitations!

Can You Ever File Your Lawsuit Late?

If you miss the notice or lawsuit-filing deadline even by one day, you will generally have no legal basis to recover against the cruise line. In certain rare occasions, however, you may be able to give notice or file a complaint late. For instance, if you are mentally incompetent or a minor, the six-month and one-year limitation periods for personal injury do not begin until a legal representative is appointed for you. If the passenger died and no legal representative was appointed, the same extension holds.

Furthermore, in some rare cases, the court will find that the cruise line did not provide adequate notice of the time limitations, but don't count on being able to convince a court of this.[40] A warning on the front of a ticket to read all terms is generally considered sufficient notice that you are bound by the limitation periods.

Finally, you may be able to get around the six-month notice period if the cruise line was aware of your particular loss or injury and not prejudiced (placed at a disadvantage) by your failure to make a formal claim in time.[41] All of these are long-shot arguments, however, and your best bet is to make sure you submit your written claim and file your lawsuit within the time limits stated in your ticket.

Negotiations and Settlement— Watch Out!

If you are contacted by the cruise line's attorney or insurance representative after you send in a written claim, and he wants more information or suggests that the cruise line might be willing to settle the dispute, by all means pursue settlement of your claim. At the same time, however, you need to protect yourself in the event negotiations go sour. Always be aware of your time limitation for filing a lawsuit, even if you think you can reach an amicable settlement with the cruise line.

For tips on negotiating a personal injury claim, see *How to Win Your Personal Injury Claim,* by Joseph Matthews (Nolo Press).

You have two ways of protecting yourself. First, you can file a lawsuit within the time limit but agree with the cruise line that neither of you will pursue the formal legal process unless negotiations fall apart. Second, if you don't want to go to the expense of filing a lawsuit, ask the cruise line for a *written* waiver of the time limitations. This does not need to be fancy. Simply have an authorized representative of the cruise line sign an agreement that includes the following type of statement:

> **Example:** We, the ABC Cruise Line, voluntarily waive all time limitations for the filing of a lawsuit based on any claim(s) made by Sally Marx against the ABC Cruise Line, its agents and employees arising from, or in connection with, the Caribbean Creeper Cruise that

departed from Miami, Florida, on July 8, 19XX.

If the cruise line is not willing to sign a written waiver, you must file your lawsuit within the limitation period in order to protect your legal rights.

Where to File a Lawsuit— Forum Selection

Many cruise line contracts contain a provision known as a "forum selection clause" that allows the cruise line to decide ahead of time where passengers who are injured (physically or financially) must file their lawsuits. In most situations, the cruise line designates one place for filing lawsuits in the ticket. The courts in this one place are said to have "exclusive jurisdiction," which means that any lawsuit filed in another place is invalid.

An important case decided by the U.S. Supreme Court said that a provision in a cruise line's ticket stating that all lawsuits had to be filed in Florida was reasonable and enforceable because the cruise line acted in good faith when it chose the place, even though the passengers lived in Washington state, and boarded the ship in Los Angeles and the injury occurred in international waters off the coast of Mexico.[42] Even though it might be difficult or inconvenient for a person to travel a great distance to pursue a lawsuit, the Court said that a forum inside the continental U.S. was not too remote, and that a dispute over an injury while the ship was in international waters was not so local that Florida would be unreasonable.

Forum selection clauses have been upheld even when a U.S. citizen was required to travel abroad to sue. In one case following the terrorist hijacking of the ship the Achille Lauro, a U.S. court upheld the ticket forum selection clause requiring lawsuits to be filed in Italy.[43]

You can argue against a forum selection clause. One argument is that the forum chosen is unreasonable. For instance, if you cruise around the Long Island Sound, you could argue that your dispute was essentially a "local" one and therefore it would be unreasonable to require you to sue in Florida. Similarly, an Italian court might be a suitable forum if the cruise is in the Mediterranean Sea, but it is probably inappropriate for a Caribbean cruise. If the cruise line deliberately chose a forum that would be difficult for most passengers to get to, that provision might be rejected because of bad faith.

You could also argue that the cruise line did not provide sufficient notice that claims would have to be filed at a distant location. As discussed in the section on time limitations for filing claims and lawsuits, however, it is fairly difficult to prove insufficient notice, even if the clause is buried in fine print.

What Type of Court?

Remember, lawsuits against cruise lines are considered maritime claims. A maritime claim can be brought in either a federal or state court. You can sue in a federal court because federal courts have the power to hear cases involving ships and maritime law. Because federal courts do not have "exclusive" power to hear maritime cases, you are also entitled to sue in a state court.

 Suing is discussed in greater detail in Chapter 13. If you sue in a state court, you can choose small claims court or a regular civil court. The court you choose often is determined by the amount of money at stake. Small claims courts (fast, informal and often without lawyers) are for small claims—often a few thousand dollars or less. For larger claims, you will have to file in one of your state's regular civil courts—this may be a municipal or county court for medium-sized claims, or a superior court for a large claim.

■

Endnotes

1 *Kornberg v. Carnival Cruise Lines, Inc.,* 741 F.2d 1332, 1985 AMC 826 (11th Cir. 1984).

2 *Hodes v. S.N.C. Achille Lauro,* 858 F.2d 905 (3d Cir. 1988).

3 The Athens Convention took effect April 28, 1987, and was amended by a 1990 Protocol. Neither the Convention nor the Protocol has been ratified by the U.S., so they are not effective here. See *Mills v. Renaissance Cruises,* 1993 AMC 131 (N.D. Cal. 1992).

4 *Barkin v. Norwegian Cruises,* 1988 AMC 645 (D. Mass 1987).

5 *Reichman v. Compagnie General Transatlantic,* 290 N.Y. 344, 49 N.E.2d 474 (1943); *Marek v. Marpan Two, Inc.,* 817 F.2d 242 (3rd Cir. 1987).

6 *Corna v. American Hawaiian Cruises,* 1992 AMC 1787 (D. Ha. 1992).

7 *Miller v. Regency Maritime,* 824 F. Supp. 200 (N.D. Fla. 1992).

8 *Muratore v. Scotia Prince,* 656 F. Supp. 471 (D.C. Me. 1987).

[9] 46 C.F.R. Part 540, "Security for the Protection of the Public."

[10] *Bloom v. Cunard Line Ltd.*, 76 A.D. 2d 237, 430 N.Y.S. 2d 607 (N.Y. 1980).

[11] *Bloom v. Cunard Line Ltd.*, 76 A.D. 2d 237, 430 N.Y.S. 2d 607 (N.Y. 1980).

[12] 46 U.S.C. § 33.

[13] See, for example, *Baltic Shipping Co. v. Dillon, High Court of Australia,* February 10, 1993.

[14] See, for example, *Owens v. Italia Societa per Azzioni di Navigazioni Genova*, 70 Misc. 2d 719, 334 N.Y.S. 2d 789 (N.Y. 1972).

[15] *Beard v. Norwegian Cruises*, 900 F.2d 71 (9th Cir. 1990).

[16] *Keefe v. Bahama Cruise Lines*, 867 F.2d 1318 (11th Cir. 1989).

[17] 17 U.S.C. §§ 761 and following.

[18] 46 U.S.C. § 183.

[19] *Erdman v. United States,* 143 F.2d 198 (2d Cir. 1944).

[20] *Gerrish v. Panama Canal Co.*, 166 N.Y.S. 258 (N.Y. 1957), *aff'd,* 170 N.Y.S.2d 991 (N.Y. 1958).

[21] *Keefe v. Bahama Cruise Lines*, 867 F.2d 1318 (11th Cir. 1989).

[22] *Compagnie Generale de Transatlantique v. Bump*, 234 F. 52 (2nd Cir. 1916).

[23] *McCormaick Shipping Corp. v. Stratt*, 322 F.2d 648, 1964 AMC 2061 (S.D.N.Y. 1962).

[24] *Luby v. Carnival Cruise Lines, Inc.*, 633 F. Supp 40, 1986 AMC 2336 (S.D. Fla. 1986).

[25] *Lawlor v. Incres Nassau Steamship Line, Inc.*, 161 F. Supp. 764 (D. Mass. 1958).

[26] *Ray v. Transoceanic Shipping Co., Ltd.*, 529 So. 2d 1181 (Fla. D.C.A. 1988).

[27] *Carlisle v. Ulysses Line, Ltd.*, 475 So. 2d 248 (Fla. App. 1985).

[28] *Kuntz v. Windjammer "Barefoot" Cruises, Ltd.*, 573 F. Supp. 1277 (W.D. Pa. 1983), *aff'd*, 738 F.2d 423 (3rd Cir. 1984).

[29] *Hays v. Carnival Cruise Lines, Inc.*, 1982 AMC (M.D. Fla. 1982).

[30] *Carney v. Home Lines, Inc.*, Slip Op. No. 84-Civ. 5629 (S.D.N.Y. Aug. 1, 1985).

[31] *Harnesk v. Carnival Cruise Lines, Inc.*, 1992 AMC 1472 (S.D. Fla. 1991).

[32] *Barberetta v. S/S Bermuda Star*, 848 F.2d 1364 (5th Cir. 1988).

[33] *Fairly v. Royal Cruise Line*, ___ F. Supp. ___ (S.D. Fla. 1993).

[34] *Morton v. De Oliveira,* 984 F.2d 289 (9th Cir. 1993).

[35] *Jaffess v. Home Lines, Inc.*, Slip Op. No. 85-7365 (S.D.N.Y. April 18, 1988).

[36] *Quiqley v. Wilson Line of Massachusetts*, 154 N.E. 2d 77 (Mass. 1958).

[37] *Holland America Cruises, Inc. v. Underwood,* 470 So. 2d 19 (Fla. D.C.A. 1985).

[38] *Shankles v. Costa Armatori, S.P.A.,* 722 F.2d 861 (1st Cir. 1983).

[39] 46 U.S.C. § 183b.

[40] See, for example, *Neiman v. Costa*, 464 So. 2d 228 (Fla. D.C.A. 1985).

[41] 46 U.S.C. § 183b(a).

[42] *Carnival Cruise Lines, Inc. v. Shute*, 499 U.S. 585 (1991).

[43] *Hodes v. S.N.C. Achille Lauro*, 858 F.2d 905 (3d Cir. 1988).

Chapter 4

Hotels and Other Places to Stay

An Introduction to Hotels, Motels and Other Places to Stay

When traveling, you have the choice of many different types of accommodations: hotels, motels, inns, bed and breakfasts, rental houses and other lodging. With some minor variations, the laws governing most types of accommodations are similar. To simplify matters, we use the term "hotel" to cover all types of accommodations.

Before You Book a Room

If you follow these suggestions when dealing with hotels, you may be able to sleep a little easier:

- When you make a reservation, ask about the following:
  - deposits and the hotel's refund policy if you must cancel
  - whether the hotel has an early check-out penalty for leaving before the final date of your reservation
  - possible discounts (such as corporate or off-season)
  - extra fees or charges (such as parking, local taxes and telephone surcharges)
  - the check-in and check-out times—and whether you may be able to check-in early or check-out late
  - whether you must arrive by a certain time to be guaranteed a room
  - amenities, such as a pool, tennis courts and exercise facilities
  - programs for children and the availability of child care, and
  - complimentary meals.

- If one hotel is offering substantial discounts compared to others in the area, do a little investigation (perhaps the hotel is being renovated). Sometimes a "great deal" isn't.
- When you make a reservation, specify exactly the type of room you want (nonsmoking, with two double beds and a view of the ocean) and when you want it. If you are sensitive to noise, ask for a room far from the elevator and ice machines.
- Get a written confirmation of your reservation with as many of the above details as possible (as well as the total price) included. If you will be traveling soon after you make your reservation, give a fax number to get your written confirmation—or at least get a confirmation number.
- If you are traveling to an area for the first time, ask about the hotel's location (how far to the beach?) and safety concerns (is it a high crime area?), as well as its general attributes, such as size, age, traffic noise and garage. The more information you have, the better decision you can make. Travel guides often give good information on hotel rooms; travel brochures are often misleading.

If There's a Problem When You Arrive or During Your Stay

- Hotels have a "duty to receive," meaning they must give you a room if one is available, even if you show up late at night. Hotels can refuse you if they believe you cannot pay or might cause harm to the hotel or other guests, however, so don't give the receptionist any convenient excuse for refusing to accept you (don't park your motorcycle in the dining room).

- **If you have a valid reservation and the hotel claims not to have a room for you, don't meekly go to another hotel.** The hotel created the problem, and it should fix it. With a little perseverance, you may be able to get a better room for the same price. If you believe that a hotel has not honored your reservation because of your race or sex or for another illegal reason, you may have a civil rights complaint. (See Chapter 11.)

- **If you have a reservation, abide by all conditions** (such as arriving by 6:00 p.m.) to protect your rights if the hotel overbooks.

- **Before you check in, ask to see the room the hotel has selected for you.** If it is unsatisfactory, ask for another room immediately. The earlier you make your needs known, the easier it is for the hotel to find a room that suits you.

- **If you have a complaint during your stay, deal with the manager or some-one else in authority who can help.** Keep track of names, dates and other details if you are not satisfied.

- **When you check out, review your bill for additional charges** (particularly telephone charges). You may be able to refuse to pay unreasonable charges if you were not warned about them.

- **If you are traveling with valuable personal property** (such as cash or jewelry), use the hotel safe, but be aware of the legal limitations on the hotel's liability.

- **If you are injured or have your property damaged or stolen**, the hotel may be liable to compensate you if it failed to follow local laws and regulations designed to protect you.

Duty to Receive

The most basic of the legal principles concerning hotels is the "duty to receive." Created hundreds of years ago under the common law of England, the duty to receive required hotel keepers to accept and take care of any traveler who presented himself as a paying customer, as long as the inn had room. Although this basic duty to receive has been modified somewhat by state laws, it is still the basis for many of a hotel's fundamental obligations to its guests.

The duty to receive was created by the English courts because traveling in the 15th and 16th centuries could be quite dangerous, the distance between inns was great, it was very difficult to make reservations in advance and if inns did not accept and protect guests, there was a good chance that guests would be robbed, assaulted or murdered.

Today, although traveling is not completely safe, hotels are abundant, transportation is fast and reservations can be made in advance. Thus, many aspects of the duty to receive that made a hotel keeper liable for any harm to a guest or the guest's property have been relaxed by state law. The relationship between hotel and guest has evolved primarily to one of seller and buyer of a service.

Reservations

When you make a reservation at a hotel, you are entering into a primitive type of contract. Basically, the hotel promises to keep the room available until you arrive, and you agree to pay for the room. But sometimes, the hotel breaks its promise and the room is not available when you show up.

When a Hotel Can Say "No"

If a hotel reasonably believes that you will not pay for your room—for example, there is no money on the credit card you present for payment—you will injure or annoy other guests, or you will physically damage or otherwise harm the hotel (including giving it a bad reputation), the hotel can refuse to give you a room. Common examples are when guests arrive drunk and disorderly or appear to be using the room for prostitution. If you already have a room and fall into any of the above categories, a hotel can eject you. In some situations, such as if you threaten another guest, the hotel may be required to throw you out—in order to protect the other guest.

Prepaid or Guaranteed Reservation

A prepaid or guaranteed reservation is one where you give the hotel a credit card and the hotel promises to have a room for you no matter when you show up, even if it's midnight or 3:00 a.m. The caveat is that if you don't arrive—and haven't canceled your reservation—you will be billed for the room. If you have a prepaid reservation for multiple nights and don't show or cancel your reservation, you may be charged for one night or the entire length of your reservation—policies vary among hotels.

If you have a guaranteed reservation and the hotel does not hold a room for you, the hotel has breached a contract and must do everything it can to find you a room either at the hotel or at a comparable lodging. If you guaranteed your reservation with a credit card, the hotel may be required under the terms of its agreement with the credit card company to pay for your first night's stay at an alternate hotel, to provide free transportation to the alternate hotel as well as a three-minute phone call to let your family or office know where you will be staying and to forward all incoming calls to your new hotel. Be sure to request these services—they may not be offered voluntarily.

If the alternate lodging is more expensive, the hotel should pay the difference for the remaining nights of your reservation—because your contract with the hotel was for lodging at a certain price—as well as any additional transportation costs you incur during your stay—for example, if your original hotel was across the street from the convention center where your conference is being held, staying at a different hotel may mean that you will incur taxi or rental car expenses. If the hotel refuses to pay, write down the name of the hotel employees involved and what they told you, and get receipts for all of your expenses—you will need them to support any later claim against the hotel.

Confirmed Reservation

If you have not paid for the reservation in advance or guaranteed it, but have received a "confirmed reservation" from the hotel, the hotel is still obliged to do its best to find comparable accommodations for you if there is no room when you arrive, unless you haven't kept to the conditions of the reservation.

It is common for a hotel to say, "We will hold the room for you until 6:00 p.m." or "We will hold the room for you if we receive a written confirmation and deposit" by a certain date. If you do not fulfill these obligations, then the hotel does not have to hold the room for you.

> **Example 1:** Van Winkle called the Sleepy Hollow Hotel in July to reserve a room for October 31. The agent took the reservation and informed Van that he had to arrive by 6 p.m. Van overslept and did not arrive until close to midnight—and saw a "no vacancy" sign posted. The hotel manager informed Van that all the rooms had been filled. Even though Van had a confirmed reservation, he did not meet all of the conditions of the reservation because he didn't show up by 6 p.m. The hotel is not obligated to find Van a room and owes him no compensation.

> **Example 2:** This time, Van prepaid for his room and had a guaranteed reservation. When Van arrived, the "no vacancy" sign was posted. If the Sleepy Hollow Hotel hadn't held a room for Van, it would be obliged to find him a room or to compensate him because it did not hold his room as agreed.

Overbooking

If you have a reservation at a hotel and the hotel is full when you arrive, the hotel may be overbooking its rooms—that is, accepting more reservations than it has rooms available. Unlike airlines, which have a legal right to overbook, hotels are not allowed to, and some states impose fines on hotels that do so. Nonetheless, overbooking is a common practice that hotels justify because many people fail to keep their reservations (known as "no-shows").

A hotel will rarely admit that it has intentionally overbooked for a night. In fact, some hotel employee handbooks have specific instructions for desk clerks to explain instead that "certain guests did not leave when they said they would" or that some rooms had "mechanical problems." Sometimes, overbooking is part of a fraudulent "bait-and-switch" ploy. A hotel promises a room at a low price and when you arrive, you are told that the hotel is full but another (more expensive) hotel has room. Frequently, the first hotel is getting kickbacks from the second hotel.

If the Hotel Won't Honor Your Reservation

If you have a confirmed or guaranteed reservation and have fulfilled the conditions of the reservation (such as showing up by 6 p.m.), the hotel is considered to have breached its contract with you if it fails to provide a room for you. Legally, you are entitled to money from the hotel to "put you in the same position you would have been if the hotel had kept its promise." Unfortunately, even if you eventually receive payment from the hotel, it may not be full compensation if what you really needed was a room for the night.

Here are some steps to follow if a hotel will not honor your reservation:

1. **Stay put.** If the desk clerk tells you that there is no room or that your reservation cannot be found, stay at the front desk. If you agree to "step to the side" or to talk to the manager in an office, you are no longer an immediate problem for the hotel. If you stay at the front desk and demand your room, the hotel will probably try to accommodate you to avoid making a negative impression on other guests.

2. **Speak with someone in authority.** If the front desk clerk tells you the hotel is unable to give you a room, don't bother arguing. Ask to speak to the supervisor or manager.

3. **Be persistent.** After you've explained your situation and shown proof of your reservation, ask the hotel manager or supervisor, "What do you plan to do to get me a room?" If you get a series of excuses, but no solution, repeat: "I understand what you said. Now what do you plan to do to get me a room?" Generally, the polite but firm approach works best, although some people swear by the "hysterical tantrum" method, such as, "I just spent ten hours on a plane; I'm utterly exhausted and I have an important business meeting in the morning. Get me a room now."

4. **Suggest resolutions.** Don't just demand a room; also suggest solutions. For example, ask about higher-priced rooms, such as suites, that you could be upgraded to for free. Or ask that the hotel pay for your room at another hotel. In that situation, make sure that you get your deposit back or charges reversed on your credit card. Perhaps the hotel can give you discounts on future stays or free transportation to the other hotel. Whatever you are offered should compensate you for the lost time and inconvenience that you suffered because the hotel did not honor your reservation.

5. **Let the hotel know you will take action.** Threatening to sue the hotel rarely does much good because so few guests carry through. Letting the hotel know that you understand your rights, however, is a good idea, especially if the hotel overbooked illegally. To support any action you might take, get as many details as possible written down, particularly the names of the manager and hotel staff, and the excuses they gave for not providing your room.

Additional steps to take, including sending a letter demanding compensation, getting outside help and possibly suing, are described in Chapter 13. While suing may be drastic, it could make sense if the hotel overbooked, was involved in a "bait-and-switch" scam or otherwise was trying to defraud you. In such cases, you are not limited to the actual damages that you suffered, such as in a breach of contract case, but may be able to recover additional damages that penalize the hotel for its fraudulent behavior. But you must carefully weigh the time, money and energy that go into a formal lawsuit, particularly if it is against a hotel far from your home. Unless the hotel's behavior was truly outrageous, your recovery is likely to be limited to the cost of finding new accommodations.

Rights to Your Hotel Room

In most states, renting a hotel room gives you what is called a "revocable license" to use the room. These rights are much more limited than the rights tenants get in renting an apartment. For example, formal eviction proceedings don't have to be brought if you overstay your welcome. The hotel can simply change the lock (easy to do today because hotels often use preprogrammed entry cards, not keys) and pack up your items.

Also, you don't have the right to a particular hotel room. A hotel manager can move guests from one room to another, as long as it is not done in a discriminatory way. The only exception is if you've reserved a certain room, like the honeymoon suite for your honeymoon.

No matter what rules say, if it's crucial for you to have one particular room, make sure the hotel management knows in advance and that you receive written confirmation for your reservation of that particular room. Otherwise, a hotel would have satisfied its obligations to you simply by providing a room comparable to the one you reserved. If the room you reserved is occupied by other guests, the management may, but is not obligated to, move those guests to another room. If the room is uninhabitable (such as if a water pipe breaks), then the hotel is excused from providing that particular room.

If hotel facilities and amenities—such as swimming pools, tennis courts and dining facilities—fall far short of what was advertised, you may be entitled to compensation. You are likely to get a discount, room upgrade or similar compensation if you complain immediately to the hotel manager.

Right to Privacy

If you are using your room in a normal way, you are not engaging in illegal acts and you are not disturbing other guests, then you have a limited right of privacy in your room. If, however, the hotel management believes that you are carrying out illegal activities (such as dealing drugs), it is entitled to enter and search your room, even without your permission.[1] The hotel management cannot, however, authorize the police to search your room without your permission, unless the police have a search warrant.[2]

The hotel management also has the right to enter your room to clean or perform needed maintenance, or if necessary, to stop you from disturbing other guests (for example, if you are playing the television very loudly) or destroying hotel property. It is generally considered a violation of your privacy if the hotel tells an outside person the number of your room. The hotel can tell an inquirer whether you are a guest at the hotel and connect any caller to your room. If you wish to maintain complete privacy, you must ask the management not to give out this information.

In an effort to maintain complete privacy, some hotel guests give fictitious names when registering. Although this may seem harmless, a few states (Arkansas, Massachusetts, New Hampshire, North Carolina, Ohio and Vermont) make registering under a false name illegal and require guests to show photo identification when registering. If you don't want to be disturbed, you will have to give your name, but make it clear to the management that you are not to be contacted by anyone and that no one is to be told whether or not you are staying at the hotel.

Room Rates

The rates charged for a hotel room must be "reasonable." There is no set formula for determining what amount is reasonable, but many states require hotels to post the maximum charge for a room in a conspicuous place in each room (usually on the back of the door). Although the hotel may not charge more than this maximum rate (often referred to as the "rack rate"), it certainly may rent the room for less. If you are reserving a room, you may be able to get a reduced price simply by asking about corporate rates or other discounts.

Discounted Rates

There are several possible discounted rates available from hotels. All you have to do is ask.

Perhaps the most common discount is the "corporate rate." Many hotels have negotiated rates with large corporations that are 10%-30% lower than their standard rates. These corporate rates are generally available to anyone who asks for them. Few hotels check to see whether or not you are actually employed by a particular corporation, but some may ask for a business card or other ID.

Other possible discounts may be available to:

- seniors
- families with children
- AAA members
- members of certain professional associations (like the American Medical Association or American Bar Association)
- guests paying with certain credit cards, or
- members of frequent flyer or frequent guest programs.

Travel clubs or hotel discount programs often advertise discounts of up to 50% for members. Generally, there is a fee to join. For frequent hotel users, these programs can provide some savings, primarily in large cities, but the savings may not be as good as they appear. The discounts apply to the hotel's inflated standard or "rack rates," and you may be able to get a better deal negotiating directly with the hotel or using one of the discounts listed above.

Always check your hotel bill to see whether it matches the rate you were quoted when you reserved the room. Frequently, additional charges will have been tacked on. Some, such as visitor fees or "bed taxes," may be mandated by local or state law and are probably legitimate. To make sure, you can call the office of the city manager or a local visitors' bureau.

Other fees, such as service charges or telephone charges, may not be legitimate. When you are quoted a room rate when making a reservation, ask for the total per night charge including all additional taxes and charges. A hotel cannot legally charge you more than the rate quoted to you, unless you approve the charges in advance. Many states have laws requiring all additional charges to be posted or approved in writing by guests.

If you are charged more than the price you were quoted for the room and the charges seem illegitimate, use the same techniques described earlier under Overbooking—show proof (if any) of the price quoted, stay at the front desk, speak to someone with authority, be persistent, suggest solutions and let the hotel know you will take action. Most hotels will remove surprise or unfair charges to avoid a negative scene. Remember that hotels have no discretion about taxes or fees imposed by the government, no matter how unreasonable they may seem.

Phone(y) Charges

Hotels have used telephones in a number of ways to gouge customers. One technique is to charge a "telephone rental fee" per day that applies whether or not you use the phone. Other hotels charge 75¢ or more for any call at all, even a local one. Many states require telephone charge policies to be posted in writing in the hotel room. If you have any questions, ask about telephone charges at the hotel desk before you use the phone.

The most common hotel telephone rip-off is to add outrageous surcharges for long distance calls made from your room. In many instances, you will pay three to five times more calling from your hotel room than you would if you used your credit card to call from a pay phone in the lobby. Some hotels will even charge you for access to the 800 "toll free" numbers or for outgoing calls that ring more than six or seven times— even if no one answers. Know the details before you dial!

Getting Less Than You Paid For

All rooms are not created equal. To comply with the requirement of "reasonable" room rates, the size, comfort, location and other qualities of a room should reflect the amount you are charged. If your room does not live up to your expectations, tell the management right away. Many experienced travelers will ask to see the prospective room before registering or making any payment.

The room you receive may not resemble the one described to you or pictured in an advertisement or brochure. If the advertisement or description was intentionally deceptive, the hotel may be guilty of fraud. The law generally allows a limited amount of exaggeration or "puffing" in advertisements, but it does not allow intentional deception. Among the most common complaints against hotels are those concerning the view from the room, the location of the room or hotel, the condition of the room or hotel, the level of luxury, sanitation, noise and security.

Your Point of View

Is that narrow stretch of beach that you can see between two high rises really an "ocean view"? It depends. Although technically correct, this type of deceptive description is annoying and may be fraudulent if it induced you to stay at the hotel. As with most complaints on hotels, your best remedy is to talk to the manager immediately. She may be able to reduce your room charge or move you to a better room. Unless you are paying a substantial premium for the view over a nonview room, it is unlikely that you would be able to recover much if you complain after your stay is completed.

Location, Location, Location

Location of the hotel and room within the hotel can be important variables in selecting where to stay. A "seaside resort" located two miles from the shore is an example of a deceptive description, as is a "luxury" room located next to a noisy elevator shaft that is busy all night. One of the most serious location problems, a hotel located in a dangerous area, is probably not a basis for a legal complaint unless you were promised ahead of time that the area was safe or secure. That is why it is crucial to ask questions about the hotel's location before you make your reservation.

Obviously, it is easier to move your location within the hotel than to move the entire hotel. If your complaint is with the surrounding area, your only solution may be to request a refund and find other accommodations. If your complaint is with the location of the room within the hotel, the manager may have some leeway.

Size, Condition or Comfort of the Room

What may be described as a "cozy" room at a bed and breakfast, you might consider cramped and uncomfortable. Similarly, what is called "luxury" may remind you of your last camping trip. Complaints about the size, condition or comfort of a room are among the most difficult to resolve because of subjectivity in the description of these attributes.

If your room falls below your expectations, identify, as precisely as possible, the differences between what was promised and what was delivered. Advertisements, brochures or videos that contain photographs or precise descriptions of your promised accommodations are most useful. Similarly, you have a right to expect what are considered standard descriptions, such as a "king-size bed" or a "three-room suite." A double bed with a

crown at the top or one room with two closets won't fly.

While certain terms have standard definitions, a comfort level is difficult to state with precision. Terms like "luxury" and "deluxe" are frequently meaningless. Whether or not you have a legitimate complaint with the hotel for using such a term may depend upon the amount you pay. If you pay $29.99 per night, you are not entitled to expect the same level of comfort as someone who paid $299 per night for a room.

To determine the reasonableness of an assertion of "luxury," you'll want to compare the hotel with other hotels in the same area. How large are the rooms? How lavishly are they furnished? How new are the carpets, towels and other materials? What is the ratio of staff to guests? What additional facilities, such as swimming pools, restaurants or health clubs, are available? Although comparisons are usually made only to other hotels in the same area, you can expand your comparison if the hotel does, such as describing itself as one of the "finest in the country."

Nonsmoking Rooms

Hotels may set aside certain rooms for nonsmokers, and in most states they can charge you a fee if you smoke in a nonsmoking room.

If you are guaranteed a nonsmoking room when you make a reservation (this would be rare, as most hotels only promise to "do their best") and no nonsmoking rooms are available when you check in, you may be entitled to some compensation. The amount, however, may be difficult to quantify unless you have asthma or some other medical condition that requires a nonsmoking room. (In such a case, you would go to another hotel to get a nonsmoking room and would be entitled to any difference you had to pay.) Your best bet is to make it clear when you make your reservation that only a nonsmoking room is acceptable. The hotel manager may be able to find someone in a nonsmoking room willing to switch if you are persistent— but don't hold your breath.

If you go to court to settle your dispute, the amount of compensation you can receive for a hotel falling below your expectations is usually minimal, unless there is a gross discrepancy between what was described and what you received. In rare cases, if a hotel is engaged in a pattern of deception, a court might assess damages to punish the hotel for fraud.

Stars in Their Eyes

What is a four-star or five-star hotel? In some countries, such as France, a national body rates hotels and gives out stars depending upon a hotel's level of service and luxury. Although motor clubs such as AAA or Mobil rate hotels, the United States has no uniform national rating system, and hotels frequently claim more stars than an outside observer might give. If a hotel claims it has a five-star rating, ask who gave the mark. Beware of any hotel with no outside validation of a rating.

Cleanliness and Sanitation

If you have a complaint about the cleanliness or sanitary level of your hotel, report it to the manager and the housekeeping department immediately. If they are unable to clean your room to your satisfaction, request a new room or a refund. If you end up in a serious dispute over the cleanliness of a room, the health and safety codes for the city or state where the hotel is located may provide the best support for your argument. Often, there are very detailed regulations, particularly relating to sewage and infestations by rodents or bugs. Failure to clean on a regular basis may also violate the hotel's own rules, as set forth in its employee handbook or management plan. A serious violation should be reported to local health authorities, not only to bolster your claim, but as a service to future guests. Take photographs of the offending conditions if you can.

Safety and Security

The safety and security of guests has long been regarded as a hotel's most important obligation. Early cases often held the hotel to a "strict liability" standard, meaning the hotel was liable for any non-self-inflicted injury suffered by a guest, regardless of whether the hotel knew of the defect responsible for the injury. Although hotels are no longer held to this standard, they still owe you a substantial "duty of care," meaning that they must take great care to make sure the hotel is safe, and that you are not injured by the condition of the hotel, by other guests or by criminals. Negligence, the failure to perform up to this duty of care, is carelessness that contributes to an injury.

A hotel is responsible for warning you about known or probable dangers. The greater the danger, the greater the duty to warn. Some warnings, such as "no lifeguard on duty," are common sights at hotels. Others, such as warnings about crime in nearby areas, are required only when there is some special risk that the hotel knows about but would not be obvious to a guest. If the hotel places you in danger or causes you to be less cautious than you might, such as if a hotel manager assures you that the area is safe and that you can walk around the neighborhood at night, the hotel may be liable if you are assaulted or robbed.

Are You a Guest?

In injury cases, many courts distinguish between a guest at the hotel and other classes of visitors. A guest is someone who is using the hotel facilities with the approval and at the invitation of the hotel. Basically, if you are a paying customer, you are a guest. The next category is known as a licensee, someone who is allowed to come to the hotel, but is not specifically invited by the hotel; an example would be a guest of a guest. The third category, trespassers, are people who have no right to be on the property—such as someone who sneaks into a resort to use their tennis courts.

The hotel owes the highest duty of care to guests. The hotel must use reasonable care to discover actual conditions of premises, make them safe or warn the guest of any dangerous condition.[3] The duty of care to licensees is just a tad lower than that to a guest. As far as trespassers go, a hotel need only exercise ordinary and reasonable care, but does not have an obligation to warn the trespasser of potential hazards.

Slip or Trip and Fall Injuries

A hotel may be liable if you slip or trip and fall on the hotel premises. Common examples include slipping on spilled food or drink in a hotel bar or restaurant, snow and ice that has not been cleared from a walk-way or moisture on tile floors or other slick surfaces. In this situation, the hotel's duty to protect you arises not when the dangerous condition is created, such as when food or drink is spilled, but when the hotel fails to take reasonable care to clean up or remove the cause of the fall.[4]

Other slip and fall claims include design or building flaws (such as steps or a ramp that is too steep), failing to maintain the physical condition of the hotel and even failing to light an area properly.

Example: While walking down a hotel hallway, Wu tripped over a loose edge of carpet, fell and broke her arm. The hotel is liable for her injuries, even though the injury was caused by a careless employee of the carpeting company who forgot to tack the carpeting down. Because the hotel is responsible for the safety of the premises, the hotel cannot simply point the finger at the carpet company. (The hotel might be able to receive reimbursement from the carpet company, but that's the hotel's problem, not Wu's.)

Tripping and falling while walking on stairs is another common accident. A hotel's liability can arise from a number of reasons, including failing to comply with local building codes for length and height of the steps or failing to install a handrail. Failing to use a nonskid surface for stairs that are frequently wet (such as those near a pool), or to remove accumulated water, oil or other slippery substances can also make hotel liable for a guest's injuries.

Know Your Rights Under Local Building Codes

Hotels must adhere to a number of state and local laws and regulations establishing minimum requirements for things like sanitation and sewage disposal, structural design, heating, water supply, fire protection and electrical equipment. If you are injured at a hotel, find out about the building code, fire code and health and safety regulations that apply to the hotel. (The local building or housing authority and health or fire department can provide this information.) If the hotel failed to abide by a code and you were injured because of the failure, it is considered negligence per se. This means that the hotel cannot claim that its action (in not adhering to the law) was reasonable, because the laws are presumed to be reasonable and any failure to abide by the laws makes the hotel responsible.

Example: Carla slipped and fell down a three-step flight of stairs at a hotel in Kentucky. The hotel was liable for her injuries because the local building code required a handrail on stairs and the hotel stairs did not have a handrail. The hotel maintained that handrails were not required on very short flights of stairs; but the code contained no such exception. In fact, Carla had reached for a handrail when she fell. The court ruled that the hotel's failure to abide by the code was a direct cause of her injuries.[5]

In addition to regulations and codes, ask about the hotel's own rules, the procedures set forth in the employees' handbook and industry standards. For example, if a hotel's employee manual requires maintenance workers to remove snow every hour from the walkways, and you are injured when a walkway had not been cleared for several hours, this is strong evidence that the hotel acted negligently.

 For tips if you're injured at a hotel, see *How to Win Your Personal Injury Claim,* by Joseph Matthews (Nolo Press).

Fires

Fire safety is critical in hotels. Fire code requirements for hotels are usually more strict than for other buildings because guests are likely to be unfamiliar with their surroundings and disoriented, particularly if a fire breaks out at night. If you are injured during a fire at a hotel, failure by the hotel to abide by the fire code may make the hotel liable for your injuries, even if the hotel was not responsible for the fire.

Example: At 1:00 a.m., Greg was awakened by shouts of, "Fire! Fire!" Smelling smoke, he jumped from his second story balcony and broke his leg when he landed. The fire, which started when a guest fell asleep while smoking, was quickly extinguished and never reached Greg's room. Nonetheless, the hotel could be liable for Greg's injuries if it failed to (1) use fire retardant blankets, mattresses and curtains in the room where the fire started, (2) have a sprinkler system or (3) have an emergency escape (such as a fire ladder) for guests on the second floor. Although Greg may not have been completely reasonable in jumping from the second floor before he was sure he could not escape on foot, courts are generally sympathetic to guests in such circumstances, and the hotel almost certainly would be liable if it had not complied with the local fire code.

Lack of smoke detectors, emergency lighting, fire alarm systems or clear instructions or signs for exiting during a fire could all form the basis for a hotel's liability.

Swimming Pools

After fire, water is probably the most dangerous substance in a hotel. A great number of slip and fall cases occur in showers or bathtubs, but many of the largest jury awards have come from injuries in swimming pools. Because swimming pools create a potentially dangerous situation, hotels must be especially vigilant in designing, maintaining and controlling access to swimming pools.

Disclaimers such as "swim at your own risk" are unlikely to protect a hotel from liability if it failed to use sufficient care to protect its guests.

Example: After a night of drinking, Al left the hotel bar, took a shortcut across the middle of the hotel grounds and fell into the swimming pool. The hotel's failure to build a fence around the pool and its failure to properly light the area are probably grounds for finding the hotel liable for Al's injuries.

In the above example, the hotel's counterargument—that Al was drunk and that's what caused him to fall—is unlikely to succeed. Most courts require hotels to anticipate that inebriated guests, kids and others might find their way into the pool if safeguards don't keep them out. If local or state law requires a fence around the pool, the hotel would be negligent per se in this situation.

Comparative Negligence

Although hotels are held to a high standard of care, and courts are often sympathetic to guests who are injured at hotels, you do not have an unlimited right to act stupidly or ignore common sense, and then recover from the hotel if you are injured. A doctrine called "comparative negligence," now widely used in the U.S., says that any award to an injured person is reduced by the percentage of the injury caused by that person.

Example: Dee, an interior designer, decides that she does not like the location of the bed in her hotel room and moves it. In the process, she is cut by a sharp corner on the bed frame and sues the hotel. The jury decides that her injury is worth $10,000, but that the hotel was liable 60% for maintaining the bed in a dangerous condition and Dee was liable 40% for carelessly trying to rearrange the furniture. Dee recovers only $6,000.

More information on comparative negligence is in Chapter 1.

Unsafe Furnishings and Accessories

The materials and furnishings used by the hotel must be safe for normal use. For example, a small boy slipped and cut himself badly on a plate glass door that shattered as he fell into it. The hotel was found liable for failing to use safety glass in the door, which would have prevented the injuries to the child.[6] Walking into windows and sliding glass doors is more common than you might think. In some states, laws require a marking or barrier to prevent guests from walking into glass windows.[7]

Hotels must also make sure that the furniture and furnishings they supply are reasonably safe for normal use. As noted above, a hotel's failure to use fire retardant materials can make the hotel liable in the event of a fire.

Example: A guest was injured when he sat down on a wicker chair in a hotel restaurant. The wicker tore, causing him to fall. The court held the hotel restaurant liable because any reasonable inspection of the chairs would have revealed that the wicker had deteriorated and was unsafe.[8]

Even if an inspection by a hotel would not reveal a defect or weakness in furniture, some courts will hold a hotel liable under the theory of "implied warranty of suitability." Basically, this means that in making a chair or couch available to the public, the hotel implicitly promises that you can sit down without being injured.[9] In essence, courts are saying that between the hotel and the guest, the hotel is in a better position to anticipate and prevent such injuries and to obtain insurance against them, and that a guest should not be required to inspect every chair at a hotel before sitting down.

Hotels' Special Duty Toward Children

Hotels, particularly those that cater to families, must take special care to safeguard children against "attractive nuisances" that are interesting to children but dangerous, such as a swimming pool poorly fenced off. The hotel must antici-pate that children will not be aware of certain dangers or be as cautious as adults would be in the same circum-stance. Because young children can't read (and many older children will ignore written warnings), these warnings may not be enough. Hotels may need to place physical barriers between the children and the attractive feature. Even if parents have failed to adequately supervise their children, the hotel may be liable if its negligence caused an injury.

Example: Wally, an inquisitive five-year-old, is injured while playing with a hoe left on the hotel's grounds by a gardener taking a break. The hotel is probably liable if the gardener knew or should have known that kids were in the area and might be injured by the tool. The hotel's argu-ment that Wally's parents should not have allowed him to play by himself on the hotel grounds might reduce the hotel's negligence, but it is un-likely to excuse the hotel's failure to take special care to protect children.

Defenses such as "assuming the risk" —you knowingly engage in a risky activity—cannot be applied against chil-dren who are not old enough to recog-nize the risk that they are running.[10]

Hotels are responsible for injuries that occur on their premises even if the hotel might have had no way to prevent the accident. For example, a hotel was found liable for injuries suffered by its guests on an escalator. Although the escalator was built and maintained by an independent escalator company, the hotel remained liable because it had "control" of the escalator, which was located in its lobby. Hotels cannot force in-jured guests to sue the escalator company.[11]

Injuries Caused by Crime or Assault

Hotels cannot be held liable for crimes committed on or near the hotel unless the hotel should have anticipated the crime and could have prevented it, either by providing sufficient warnings or taking better security measures. Criminal acts are generally viewed as difficult to anticipate, but this may not be true in a very high crime area. In such situations, the hotel's general duty to warn of dangerous conditions may extend to a duty to warn about crime in or around the hotel. Furthermore, the hotel's actions— such as failure to install proper locks on windows and doors, provide adequate light-ing in parking areas or take adequate measures to ensure that pass keys are not used by criminals—may make the hotel at least partially liable.[12]

In one case, the singer Connie Francis was awarded over $2.5 million when she was assaulted in her hotel room. The hotel was liable because the locks on the room doors could be opened from outside the room.[13]

The hotel may be liable if a hotel employee assaults a guest. An employer is responsible for the acts of employees carried out "within the scope of their employment." Because hotels owe a special duty of care to their guests, when an employee commits a crime on the hotel premises, a hotel may be held liable even if the employee was off duty or acting outside of the scope of his employment.[14] The hotel could also be liable for failing to supervise or failing to adequately check the background of the employee. If you are assaulted by another guest, the hotel would be liable only if the assault was foreseeable—for example, the other guest was drunk and belligerent.

Your Belongings

Just as a hotel has a duty to receive guests, it also has a general duty to receive and protect the guest's belongings, although this duty is not unlimited. Hotels can create reasonable rules, such as prohibiting animals (see Chapter 11, section on Traveling With Pets), hazardous or flammable materials or other goods that could cause harm or annoyance to guests or the hotel.

Valuables

Although hotels used to be generally liable for the loss or theft of a guest's property, most states have laws limiting a hotel's liability if it follows certain procedures. For cash, jewelry and other valuables, a hotel is required to provide a safe. Under most state laws, the hotel must tell you that the safe is available, that the hotel has limited liability for valuables left in the safe and that the hotel may have no liability if you do not place valuables in the safe.

Disclaiming Liability

In general, a hotel cannot limit its liability to a certain monetary amount. In some states, however, hotels can limit liability. But hotel managers can defeat their limited liability. For example, if the hotel posts a statement that "the management is not responsible for any loss or damage suffered by the guest or the guest's property," the hotel has tried to avoid all liability. If state law allows the hotel to limit its liability—but not avoid it altogether—the hotel may have tried to get more protection than is allowed by state law. In such a case, the hotel may lose the protection of the state law and be liable for the full amount of the loss or injury, even though state law would have limited it.

Laws limiting a hotel's liability for a guest's valuables often give a hotel discretion to accept valuables over a certain dollar amount. For example, Charles' hotel room contains a posted notice that the hotel is not responsible for money, jewelry, securities or other valuables unless they are deposited in the hotel's safe. It also limits the hotel's liability for deposited valuables to $300, unless the guest specifically declares an excess value. Finally, the notice states that the hotel shall not be required to accept property having a value in excess of $1,000. Charles is carrying financial bond certificates worth approximately $2,000.

- **If Charles doesn't put the bonds in the safe, is the hotel liable if they are stolen or destroyed by fire?** No. The law in this state lets the hotel limit its liability completely if valuables are not placed in the safe.

- **If Charles puts the bonds in the safe, but doesn't declare their value, is the hotel liable?** To a limit. Charles would be entitled to recover $300 because he did not declare a value in excess of $300.

- **If Charles puts the bonds in the safe and declares the full $2,000, is the hotel liable?** Maybe. In this state, the hotel can reject valuables worth more than $1,000. If the hotel accepts goods above the $1,000 limit, the hotel may be "waiving" its right to the $1,000 maximum liability. Some states say that when a hotel accepts goods whose stated value is more than the statutory limit, the hotel accepts the full risk and must pay the full value if the goods are lost or destroyed. Other states allow the hotel to accept the goods, but only pay the statutory amount if they are lost or destroyed.

The point is to use a hotel's safe for cash, jewelry and other valuables, and to be aware of the hotel's maximum liability. If you will be traveling with valuables, also check your homeowner's or traveler's insurance (see Chapter 8) to see if any conditions might prevent you from recovering the full worth of the valuables. For example, an insurance policy might limit your recovery to a certain value, or might exclude coverage if you do not use a hotel safe available for your valuables.

If the loss of valuables was due to a hotel's intentional or negligent acts, the statutory limits on liability may not apply.

Generally, the laws were passed to protect hotels from forces beyond their control, such as fire or theft. If the hotel fails to use reasonable care to protect the valuables, such as leaving the safe unlocked, the hotel would most likely be liable for the full value of the goods.

If you have valuables worth more than the statutory limit and they are lost or destroyed in a hotel, you may be able to recover the full value if the hotel didn't follow all provisions of the law setting out the limitation of liability. For example, certain laws require that the hotel post the limitations of liability in a conspicuous place in the room. If the hotel put a notice on the inside of a closet door or under glass on the desk, this may not be conspicuous enough, and the statutory limit might not apply.

Baggage or Other Personal Goods

The limitation of liability described in the previous section also includes a limitation for clothing and other personal goods brought to the hotel. While you are not required to check expensive suits or mink stoles at the front desk as valuables, clothing and expensive luggage often exceed the statutory limit. If you lose personal goods valued more than the statutory limit, you may be able to recover from the hotel if you can show that it was negligent.

Unfortunately, state laws are far from uniform on this point. In some states, the hotel loses the protection of the statutory limitation if it is negligent, but in other states, the hotel must be "grossly negligent" to lose the protection. If you find yourself in this situation, you may need to do some legal research. First, find out whether the statute says a hotel will lose statutory protection for "negligence" or "gross negligence," and then determine what each of those terms means in your particular state. A hotel that failed to put locks on the doors in a high-crime area would be considered grossly negligent. Few cases are so clear-cut, and the line between negligence and gross negligence can be quite fine.

 For a good research reference, see *Legal Research: How to Find and Understand the Law,* by Stephen Elias and Susan Levinkind (Nolo Press).

Bailment

Bailment is a word usually used only by lawyers and on parking garage tickets. Bailment is a process by which the owner of goods, such as a hotel guest (the bailor), leaves the goods in the care of another, such as a hotel employee (the bailee). The bailee must return the goods to the bailor and is usually liable for the full value of the goods if the bailee does not do so. A common example of bailment is when you store luggage with the front desk and receive a claim check, or when you give clothing to a hotel laundry service for cleaning. If the hotel does not use reasonable care in taking care of the goods, it may be liable for the full value of the goods if they are lost or damaged.

Selling a Guest's Goods

In extraordinary circumstances, if you fail to pay for your room or meals, the hotel can seize your property and sell it to cover the amount owed. In some states, including California, Florida, Nebraska and New York, the hotel must give notice to you before selling your property. Many states require hotels to sell the items at a public auction to ensure that the maximum amount is recovered. Any amount received in excess of the amount owed to the hotel must be refunded to you. If you find some way to make payment before your property is sold, it must be returned to you. Note that the hotel can seize your property only to pay for debts related to a current stay at the hotel.

Example: Jimmy checks into the Ace Motel. Paul, the manager, remembers that the last time Jimmy stayed he skipped town without paying. Paul takes Jimmy's goods, locks them in a storeroom and plans a sale. This is illegal. Paul cannot seize Jimmy's goods to pay for a prior debt. If Jimmy doesn't pay for this visit, however, Paul could seize the goods and sell them. The hotel could keep only the amount equal to the current debt—not to cover the previous stay too.

Automobiles or Other Means of Transportation

Traditionally, hotels were strictly liable for protecting your means of transportation. This meant caring for your horses, saddles, tack and the rest. In modern times, hotels are responsible only for using reasonable care to protect your means of transportation.

Many states have laws setting a monetary limit for loss or damage to a vehicle or its contents. But even in these states, negligence (or gross negligence) by the hotel could make the hotel liable for damage it should have foreseen.

Vehicle Lost or Stolen

Automobiles are not considered the same as baggage and other goods, and generally do not fall under the limitations on liability described above. When a vehicle is damaged or stolen, the question arises of who is liable. If you entrust the car to the hotel, and the hotel fails to use reasonable care to protect the car, then the hotel may be liable. This is the legal theory of "bailment."

When you give your car keys to a valet, you have a reasonable expectation that the valet will take care of the car and park it safely. If the valet damages the car, the hotel has breached its responsibility to take reasonable care of the car. In this case, you (the bailor) entrusted the car to the hotel (the bailee) and can recover the fair market value to fix the damage.

To avoid liability, many hotels now require that guests park their own cars and issue disclaimers saying that "no bailment is created." Because few people understand what bailment means, it is hard to believe that these disclaimers are enforced, but sometimes they are. Many courts just apply a regular negligence standard. The greater the control that the hotel has over the car, the greater the likelihood that the hotel will be liable if the car is damaged or stolen.

Some hotels have attempted to escape liability by claiming that they did not have control or custody of the car, for instance, if the hotel did not own the parking garage. If the hotel could have foreseen the damage or loss and did not take reasonable steps to prevent it, however, the hotel may be liable. If you park a car in a garage provided for guests, even if the hotel does not own it, the hotel's implied control of the premises may be enough to make the hotel liable to you.

Contents of the Car

Whether the contents of the car parked at a hotel are the hotel's responsibility is not clear. Car contents do not fall into the traditional categories of goods within the hotel or transportation. The hotel is most likely to be liable when you are paying for parking and a valet or other employee takes your car, retains the keys and is informed of the value of the contents of the car. In such a case, the hotel is considered a "professional bailee for hire" and is held to a high standard of care.

At the other extreme, if you do not pay for parking but park the car yourself, retain the keys and do not inform the hotel of the contents, the hotel is unlikely to have any liability for the contents. Most cases, of course, will fall somewhere in between; the greater the hotel's involvement and knowledge, the greater the chance that the hotel is liable for the automobile's contents.

Endnotes

[1] *People v. Minervini*, 20 Cal. App. 3d 832 (Cal. 1971).

[2] *Stoner v. California*, 376 U.S. 483, *rehearing denied*, 377 U.S. 940 (1964).

[3] *Silverton v. Marler*, 389 P.2d 3 (Alas. 1964).

[4] *Ashley v. Oclean*, 518 So. 2d 943 (Fla. 1987).

[5] *Whitehead v. Ramada Inns, Inc.*, 529 S.W.2d 366 (Ky. 1975).

[6] *Jenkins v. McLean Hotels, Inc.*, 859 F.2d 598 (8th Cir. 1988).

[7] *Peterson v. Haule*, 23 N.W.2d 51 (Minn. 1975).

[8] *Gary Hotel Courts, Inc. v. Perry*, 251 S.E.2d 37 (Ga. 1978).

[9] *Schnitzer v. Nixon and Heath*, 439 F.2d 940 (4th Cir. 1971).

[10] *Hooks v. Sheraton*, 578 F.2d 313 (D.C. Cir. 1977).

[11] *Blansit v. Hyatt Corp.*, 874 F.2d 1015 (5th Cir. 1989).

[12] *Greil v. Travel Lodge International, Inc.*, 541 N.E.2d 1288 (Ill. 1989).

[13] *Garzilli v. Howard Johnson's Motor Lodges, Inc.*, 419 F. Supp. 1201 (E.D.N.Y. 1976).

[14] *Tobin v. Slutsky*, 506 F.2d 1097 (2nd Cir. 1974).

Chapter 5

Travel Agents and Promoters

An Introduction to Travel Agents and Travel Promoters

Your travel agent is likely to be the person you rely on most to help you make decisions about where, when and how to travel. In the U.S., travel agents arrange 80% of all air travel, 95% of all cruise reservations, 30% of all car rentals and many hotel reservations. A travel agent's legal responsibilities vary depending on the role the agent plays in helping with your plans. In some cases, your travel agent is required to check every detail of your travel plans carefully, while in other cases, the agent is obligated only to avoid using dishonest methods to sell you travel services you don't need or want.

Before You Use a Travel Agent

- **Understand the role of your travel agent.** Is the agent acting as a travel advisor, a tour operator or merely a ticketing agent? These distinctions (explained below) help determine the duties your travel agent owes you.
- **Treat your travel agent as an ally.** Work together to build a relationship that will motivate your agent to make the best possible arrangements for you.
- **Use the right type of travel agent.** Many travel agents specialize in a certain type of travel (such as cruises or business travel). Know the specialties of the agent you work with, and use a different agent if the type of traveling you want to do is outside your agent's areas of expertise.
- **Ask questions.** If you are going to a place you have never been before or using an unfamiliar travel service, ask your travel agent for details and request that the agent do the necessary research to get the answers. But don't rely solely on your travel agent—you can avoid most travel-related problems and disappointments if you take an active role in planning your trip.
- **Be specific in your requests.** If you want the lowest possible rates for travel services, be sure to state this clearly to your agent. If you are interested in specific suppliers (such as no-frills airlines) or package deals that may not be included in your agent's computerized reservation system, ask about them.
- **Find out if your travel agency has a financial reason to recommend a particular airline or hotel.** Sometimes travel agencies get higher commissions for choosing certain carriers over others. (See How Travel Agents Are Paid, below.)

How Agencies Operate— Providing Information, Making Reservations and Issuing Tickets

To understand your travel agent's responsibilities to you, you need to know how travel agencies operate—particularly how the operation could affect your travel agent's obligations to you and the quality of service you receive.

Travel agents normally provide three important services:

- give you information about potential travel options
- make reservations, and
- issue tickets.

Some travel agents also act as tour operators. See Chapter 6.

Providing Information

Travel agents have a range of resources from which they obtain information, including brochures produced by travel suppliers, trade newsletters and magazines, directories of travel services and computer databases. Travel agents also rely on their own travel experiences and word of mouth. A good travel agent uses a combination of these resources to provide travelers with information on a particular trip or destination. An agent is legally required to use reasonable care in gathering this information so that you do not suffer from any unpleasant surprises that should have been foreseen.

Many travel agents specialize in certain types of travel. Travel specialists include:

- purpose of travel (business vs. vacation)
- destinations (such as the Caribbean or South Pacific)
- type of client (for example, families with children or gay couples)
- cruises, or
- adventure trips.

Ask immediately if the agent has a specialty. If it doesn't match your travel needs, ask for a recommendation of some-one whose area of concentration does. If you do a lot of different kinds of traveling, you don't have to use the same agent for all of it. Keep in mind that you don't want to spread yourself too thin, however; building a relationship with a travel agent can be a key to resolving disputes you have with any travel supplier.

Making Reservations

To make reservations, a travel agent contacts the travel suppliers by phone, fax or computer to:

- determine the availability of tickets or accommodations for the date and time you want to travel, and
- clarify the specific terms of your arrangement with the supplier, such as the time, price, number of people and restrictions.

In making reservations, an agent is legally required to make the best effort to match the reservations to your specific requirements and limitations. In some situations, an agent is responsible for confirming reservations directly with a travel supplier, particularly if the agent is making the reservations with an intermediary such as a tour operator and has reason to doubt the reliability or financial stability of that supplier or intermediary.

Issuing Tickets

A ticket (or similar document, such as a voucher) represents tangible proof of your agreement with the travel supplier. It normally indicates the price you paid and the conditions under which you can use the ticket. A ticket is a contract between you and the travel supplier, and you each have obligations under the ticket's terms. The travel agent has no direct rights or responsibilities under the ticket, but the agent is obliged not to mislead you or sell you a ticket for travel services you clearly do not want or cannot use.

 Additional information on tickets is in Chapter 1 and Chapter 3.

How Travel Agents Are Paid

When travel agents issue a ticket or make other travel arrangements for you, they generally receive a commission from the travel supplier. It may range from 7%-15% of the price you pay, but it is usually about 10%.

Sometimes, a travel agency may have an "override" or "preferred supplier" arrangement that would allow the agency to earn an additional 5%-10% if it meets certain sales quotas with a particular travel supplier. Although there is nothing illegal about such arrangements, it might be useful to know if your agent has such an arrangement. For example, if your agent gets a large bonus for booking a certain number of clients on a particular cruise line, the agent has a strong incentive to recommend that line over others, even if that line does not offer you the best value. Ask your agent about her company's override arrangements, particularly if she seems to be steering you toward one supplier and away from all others.

Because agents are paid on a percentage basis, an agent may be tempted to sell you a more expensive service or product than you really need. Most agents, however, recognize

that in the long run they are better off providing you with the best value possible and keeping you as a satisfied customer.

In some cases, an agent may be willing to rebate part of her commission to you. For example, if an agent sold you a tour package for $4,000 and received a commission of $400 (10%), she might be willing to give you $100-$200. It is worth asking, especially on international trips. Most airlines cap the commission on domestic air travel at $50 per ticket, even if the ticket costs more than $500—remember, this commission is paid by the airline, and does not increase the cost of your ticket. It is very unlikely that your agent will rebate any of her commission on domestic flights.

Because of the commission cap, many travel agents charge service fees for certain transactions, such as for changing an airline ticket or making a reservation with a hotel that does not pay a commission. If the agent will charge you, she must tell you about the charge in advance. Some travel agents have printed price lists showing their fees. If you are not told about a fee until after you buy a ticket, you do not have to pay. You have the option to cancel the transaction and look for an agent who does not charge a fee. Realize that agents who do not charge fees are becoming more rare as travel suppliers cut back on commissions.

A travel agent has no legal obligation to find you the least expensive option unless you specify that that is what you want. If you feel that an agent has sold you a product at an inflated rate or deliberately didn't tell you about lower-priced alternatives, address this issue with your agent. If you bring a complaint against the agent with her boss, a professional agency or in small claims court, you may need to obtain proof of the lower-priced options that were available at the time you made your reservation or bought your ticket. Another travel agent can probably get onto a computer and check prices as of the date you made your reservation. You could also use a price list or advertisement offering the same services at a lower price.

Computerized Reservation Systems

Most modern travel agencies are equipped with at least one computerized reservation system (CRS). Using a CRS, the travel agent has access to a wide variety of information, including the availability and prices of airline flights, hotels and rental cars. In most cases, the agent can make reservations and confirm arrangements directly through the CRS.

The CRSs are owned primarily by the airlines. For example, American Airlines owns the Saber system, United owns Apollo, and Delta, TWA and Northwest together own the PARS system. It is worthwhile to know which CRS system your travel agent uses, for two reasons:

- The system may be set up to make the flights of the CRS owner(s) easier to find than others.
- Some airlines, particularly no-frills airlines such as Southwest, are not included on all systems. To contact an airline not listed on the CRS, a travel agent will normally have to spend time and money to call the airline directly.

Unless you specifically ask the agent to check the airlines not included on the agent's CRS system, the agent may book you on the flight that is cheapest and easiest for the agent, rather than cheapest and easiest for you.

Your Relationship With a Travel Agent

If you'll be doing any regular amount of traveling (even just the once-a-year family vacation), it pays to establish a good relationship with a competent travel agent. In shopping for a travel agent, look for someone who has all or most of the following characteristics:

- specializes in the type of travel you do
- committed to service
- accessible and convenient
- reliable, and
- willing to hunt down the best deal.

Dealing With an Agent, Rather Than an Agency

A loyal travel agent can be a tremendous asset. Such an agent can save you money, make your travel more enjoyable and be of great help if you have any problems. Loyalty, however, is reciprocal. It is easy to expect loyalty from a travel agent if you use only one agent for all of your travel plans. A good agent you use regularly will come to quickly understand your needs and preferences, and will be likely to look out for your interests. For instance, if the fare drops on a ticket you have already purchased, a loyal travel agent may let you know that you can be reticketed for a lower fare, even if it reduces the agent's commission. (Of course, you should be checking on this yourself, too.)

Travel agents who do not own their own travel agency frequently change jobs. Some clients choose to continue to deal with the same agent, and will move agencies when the agent does. Doing so builds a strong relationship between the traveler and the agent, which could pay off in the long run.

In some situations, using only one agent may not be your best approach. If your employer uses an excellent business travel agent, this agent may not be able to fulfill your leisure travel needs. For example, an agent who concentrates only on business travel is unlikely to know the ins and outs of discounted ocean cruises. In such cases, ask your business travel agent to recommend someone else who specializes in leisure travel.

Treat the Travel Agent as an Ally

If things go wrong when you are traveling, it is often tempting to blame the travel agent. Resist this temptation. Although lawsuits against travel agents are increasing, they are rarely successful—usually the problem is caused by someone other than the travel agent.

Lawsuits are filed against travel agents because they are nearby. It is often difficult to sue a tour operator or hotel located halfway around the world. Suing the travel agent, however, is only appropriate if the travel agent, or agency, was responsible for your problem. If the agency was not responsible, you are unlikely to win. Furthermore, you will incur the costs of suing and destroy your relationship with your agent. (See

Resolving Disputes With Travel Agents, at the end of this chapter.)

Almost always, treating the agent as an ally will be less expensive and more productive than suing the agent. If you do not have a long-term relationship with the agent or agency involved, mention how much business your friends, family or business associates do with the agency. It is no secret that frequent clients get better service. Yelling and threatening to sue your travel agent or the agency may provoke some immediate action, but will almost certainly destroy your relationship with the agent.

Another reason to treat the agent as an ally is because in many cases, a travel agent is in a much better position to get you compensation (such as complimentary airline tickets, hotel stays or rental cars) than you are. Your travel agent probably does much more business with the travel supplier than you do and, therefore, has more leverage to demand that errors be corrected and compensated. If you treat your travel agent as an ally, your agent may be able—and willing—to help you.

Be Specific

To get the best deals and accommodations and to avoid disputes, travel agents and clients should ask very specific questions and give very specific answers to each other. Often, details that seem unimportant to one person are crucial to another. For example, if you are allergic to cigarette smoke, tell this to your agent. The agent may be able to find you a smoke-free rental car. Don't assume that your agent should know about your allergy just because you requested a nonsmoking room in a hotel.

Good questions to ask your travel agent include:

- Is that the lowest price available?
- Would the fare change if I changed my itinerary by a few days?
- Have you been to that city/stayed at that hotel yourself?
- Do you know if that place is good for families with children?
- How safe is that area?
- What are the passengers on that cruise like?
- Does that tour operator belong to a consumer protection program?
- Have your clients had any trouble getting compensated by that travel insurance company?

Providing specific information about your expectations and getting specific information from your agent can help prevent many common misunderstandings. Further, when you get specific information and promises from your travel agent (ideally in writing, but if not, make notes of your conversation), you have a much better chance of receiving compensation from that agent or the supplier if something goes wrong.

Travel Agent Associations and Groups

Most travel agents belong to one or more professional associations. Each association has a code of ethics that requires its members to remain knowledgeable of developments within the travel industry and not to engage in misleading sales practices. Nonetheless, there are very few formal requirements needed to become a travel agent, and many have learned their trade through "on the job training."

Travel Sellers and Travel Promotion Laws

In some states, travel agents are regulated by special laws known as "travel seller" or "travel promoter" laws. In California, for example, travel agents must register with the state Attorney General and pay an annual registration fee that goes into a fund to help travelers caught when travel agents or other travel businesses go bankrupt. Florida, New York, Oregon, Rhode Island and Washington have similar laws, but weaker laws have been proposed in Maryland, Missouri and New Jersey. Almost all of these laws are under attack and may be substantially changed or repealed by the time you read this book. If you end up in a serious dispute with a travel agent or your agent goes out of business, check your state laws (see Take It to Court—Doing Legal Research in Chapter 13) to see if a travel seller law can bolster your case.

Members of the Institute of Certified Travel Agents must go through a period of training and pass exams on making travel arrangements. An agent who completes the training becomes a "Certified Travel Counselor" (CTC). Ask your agent if he or she is a CTC. Although a CTC designation is no guarantee of good service or good value, it does normally indicate a certain level of experience and professionalism.

If you have a complaint or question about a travel agent, ask him (or someone else in his office) if he belongs to a travel professional association. If he does, you can contact the association as follows:

American Society of Travel Agents (ASTA)
1101 King Street, Suite 200
Alexandria, VA 22314
tel: 703-739-2782
fax: 703-684-8319
Web: http://www.astanet.com

Association of Retail Travel Agents (ARTA)
845 Sir Thomas Court, Suite 3
Harrisburg, PA 17109
tel: 717-545-9548
fax: 606-264-0368

International Airlines Travel Agent Network (IATAN)
300 Garden City Plaza, Suite 342
Garden City, NY 11530
tel: 516-747-4716
fax: 516-747-4462
Web: http://www.iatan.org

Institute of Certified Travel Agents (ICTA)
148 Linden Street
Wellesley, MA 02181
tel: 781-237-0280
fax: 781-237-3860
Web: http://www.icta.com

The association should be able to tell you if the agent is a member in good standing. In some cases, an association may be able to help you if you have a complaint against one of its members. (For example, ASTA has a mediation program, which is described in Chapter 13.) Submit your complaint in writing to the agent's association. Even if the association can't resolve your dispute, you may at least help protect some other unwary

traveler. All legitimate travel agents should belong to at least one travel agent association.

Travel agencies may also be affiliated with other agencies, or be part of a group of agencies, such as the American Express Travel chain. The head office for these groups may be able to offer some assistance if you have a complaint, but most of the agencies affiliated with these groups are independently operated, and belong to these groups only to obtain the benefits of a national affiliation or to improve their negotiating position with travel suppliers. (See Chapter 13 for addresses and phone numbers.)

Travel Agents' Ethical Obligations

If you are involved in a dispute with a travel agent, it may be a good idea to review the code of ethics for the association to which your agent belongs. Call the association and ask for a copy. If your agent has taken actions that violate the organization's code of ethics, this would support your claim that the agent acted wrongfully. Unfortunately, there is generally no legal obligation for the agent to act according to the association's code of ethics. If you believe that the agent is violating a principle of the association's code of ethics, however, you might want to bring this to the agent's attention as a way of applying some leverage. If you send a letter about an ethical violation to your agent, you should send a copy to the agent's association.

For example, the ASTA code of ethics sets a number of rules for their agents, such as that agents must:

- provide their clients with complete details about the terms and conditions they offer

- keep all transactions confidential
- not use any deceptive or misleading sales tactics, and
- promptly respond to any customer complaints.

Consumer Protection Plans and Insurance

When booking any tour package or other travel service, ask your travel agent what type of consumer protection or insurance is available if something goes wrong. If possible, you will want to purchase a consumer protection plan or insurance policy that covers the tour operator's or supplier's insolvency and potential bankruptcy. Many plans provide you with compensation only if the operator actually files for bankruptcy.

 Chapter 6 describes the important considerations regarding consumer protection plans covering tour operators, and Chapter 8 covers travel insurance.

ASTA formerly operated its own consumer protection program known as the Travel Reimbursement Insurance Protection (TRIP). ASTA had suspended the program when we went to print, but a similar type of service could be reinstituted in the future.

Travel Agents' Legal Obligations

To understand a travel agent's legal obligation to you, you must learn a little bit about agency law.

- An agent is someone who acts on behalf of another person (referred to as the principal) in dealing with third parties.

- Agents must exercise a degree of fairness and good faith in all transactions stemming from the principal-agent relationship.
- Agents owe a special duty of loyalty to their principals (referred to as a fiduciary duty) to act in the principal's best interest.

When we use the term "travel agent," we are referring to someone who is authorized to sell travel services to the public on behalf of a certain travel supplier (such as an airline or tour operator). Most people are surprised to learn that a travel agent is generally considered the agent of the travel *supplier*, not the customer. This is because there is an ongoing relationship between the travel supplier and the travel agency whereby the agent represents the supplier and is compensated for providing business to the supplier.

Most travelers feel that a travel agent should be "their" agent and should look out for their best interests, rather than the interests of travel suppliers. The law is changing in this area, and in some cases a travel agent may be considered your agent as well. When a travel agent charges you a service fee (see How Travel Agents Are Paid, above), you have a much stronger argument that the travel agent is acting as your agent. In most cases, however, the travel agent will owe you the normal duties owed by a salesperson to a customer, but not the higher level of loyalty of an agent.

Below are four examples of roles that travel agents can assume when conducting business with clients. In our examples, the client has contacted the travel agent to help with arrangements for a one-week vacation to Quebec. These examples should give you a good idea of your travel agent's duties to you in the most common situations. In general, the more input the travel agent has in your choice of travel suppliers, and the greater the agent's connection to that supplier, the greater the chance that the agent will be at least partially liable if something goes wrong.

Role 1: Ticketing Agent. You call an airline directly and make reservations for a round-trip flight to Quebec. Later, you tell your travel agent about your reservation and have your agent issue a ticket and boarding pass for you. You make your own hotel and car arrangements.

Travel Agent's duties and responsibilities. The travel agent's responsibilities are very limited in this situation. The travel agent is acting as the agent of a disclosed principal (the airline) and has no liability for the actions of the principal. The agent would have no liability, for example, if your flight was overbooked and you were bumped.

Role 2: Travel Advisor and Ticketing Agent. You tell your travel agent that you want to take a one-week vacation to Quebec. The agent asks you some questions, shows you a variety of brochures and suggests particular tour packages that seem to match your requirements. When you make your selection, the agent books the tour for you, reserves the airline tickets, hotels and a rental car for you and issues your airline tickets.

Travel Agent's duties and responsibilities. Determining the travel agent responsibilities in this situation can be tricky. Formerly, as an agent of the supplier only, the agent

would owe you only the duty that a salesperson has, that is, not to intentionally deceive. If the agent let you know the identities of the suppliers involved (such as the tour wholesaler, hotels and airlines) before you bought the package, then she was considered to be acting as the agent of disclosed principals and had no liability for the actions of the principals.

Increasingly, however, courts are holding travel agents to a higher standard. Because the travel agent is acting as your counselor when you make your travel plans, she may also be considered your agent. If so, the agent has a number of responsibilities to you, including to:

- provide information about the travel supplier that would affect your decision (such as the supplier's financial condition)
- warn you of possible dangers of which the agent is aware (such as recent terrorist attacks on tourists or the shaky financial condition of a tour operator), and
- exercise a duty of due care and loyalty in her dealings with you.

Many courts have held that travel agents are not only responsible for disclosing facts known to them, but also facts of which they should have been aware if they had been reasonably diligent. In some cases, being reasonably diligent means doing investigative work, such as calling a new hotel directly to be sure that construction is finished.

The travel agent is not, however, the ensurer of your travel enjoyment. Just because something goes wrong on your trip does not make the travel agent responsible; there must be some proof that the travel agent was at fault.

Role 3: Seller of Travel Services for an Undisclosed Principal. You ask your agent to arrange a one-week vacation for you in Quebec. Instead of booking the hotel reservations, airline tickets and rental car directly, your travel agent contacts a tour wholesaler who sells her a package including those services. She then marks up the price of the package, and without telling you about the tour wholesaler, sells the package of services to you. You believe the travel agent has made the arrangements directly.

Travel Agent's duties and responsibilities. Where the agent is operating for an undisclosed principal (the tour wholesaler), the travel agent takes on the responsibilities of that principal. Therefore, if the principal fails to provide you with the promised services, you would have the right to seek compensation from both the principal and the travel agent. For example, when you arrive, you discover that the hotel you are supposed to stay in is still being built, and you are forced to pay twice as much as you had planned at a neighboring hotel. You would register a complaint with (and seek compensation from) both the tour wholesaler and the travel agent.

Role 4: Tour Operator. You receive a flyer from your travel agent for a one-week tour of Quebec arranged by the travel agency that includes deluxe accommodations and an experienced tour guide.

Travel Agent's duties and responsibilities. Your travel agent is acting like a tour operator and is under the same legal obligations as a tour operator. (See Chapter 6.) In addition to your travel agent's normal duties described in the previous examples, the agent has direct contractual responsibilities to you. If the travel agent is acting as a tour operator and a tour fails to live up to what was promised (for example, your deluxe accommodations are actually in a rundown motel and your guide is an American who only had two years of French in high school), the agent may be liable for breach of contract or fraud. Like any other tour operator, the travel agent may try to limit its liability through a pre-trip contract, release of liability or other documents that you agree to before the trip. To protect yourself, read these documents carefully before signing. Don't sign anything with which you disagree.

If a Travel Agent Makes a False or Misleading Statement

When your travel agent's description of a travel service or destination is false or misleading, the agent may be liable for misrepresentation and the agent's marketing techniques may be considered illegal under consumer protection laws. The more specific and concrete the misleading statements are, the better your chance of recovering against the travel agent. If your agent promises you the penthouse suite of a beachside hotel with an Olympic-size swimming pool, and you get a small room on the second floor of a hotel that is miles from the beach and has no pool, you have a strong case. If, however, your agent describes a hotel as "luxurious" or "deluxe" and it does not live up to that billing, you are unlikely to recover anything. Courts often determine that exaggerated claims are "mere puffing" and not statements of fact upon which you should rely. Before booking, try to nail your travel agent down to specifics and get as much as possible in writing ahead of time.

Specific Duties of Travel Agents

 Very few laws specifically address travel agents' responsibilities to their clients. Generally, a travel agent's legal responsibilities arise out of traditional concepts of contract and tort law. (Torts are sometimes referred to as "civil wrongs," such as negligence.)

As you read this section, keep in mind two important points:

- the specific details of any situation are very important in determining a travel agent's liability, and
- if a court in one state rules that a travel agent is (or isn't) liable in a particular case, a court in your state could decide the same issue very differently.

In general, courts in more recent cases have required a higher standard of care from travel agents than did courts in older cases. In addition, a travel agent is much more likely to be held liable for a problem she created directly, such as failing to provide accurate information or make a reservation, than for an indirect problem, such as recommending a hotel where you are subsequently injured.

Making Reservations

If a travel agent fails to make a reservation for you, and you suffer an economic loss because of it, the agent may be responsible to compensate you.

Example: Vera sees an ad for a discounted cruise vacation that requires 60 days, advance reservation. She contacts her travel agent, Anthony, who, after checking with the cruise line, confirms the price and availability of berths for the cruise that Vera has selected, which leaves in 61 days. Vera enthusiastically tells Anthony to make all of the arrangements for her and gives him her credit card number. Unfortunately, Anthony forgets to make the reservation until several days later, at which time the 60-day advance discount is no longer in effect. If the discounted ticket would have cost $2,000 and the ticket without the discount costs $2,500, Anthony would be liable to Vera for the $500 difference because it was his negligence that led to Vera's loss.

It is important to remember that the travel agent is responsible only if the failure to make the reservation was the agent's fault. In the above example, if the travel agent learns during his initial conversation with the cruise line that the cruise Vera wants is already sold out, Vera cannot recover against the agent, because his inability to make a reservation was not his fault.

Sometimes travel agents simply make the wrong reservations. If you request and pay for a flight to San Jose, Costa Rica, and you find you have a reservation on a plane destined for San Jose, California, your travel agent is probably responsible for the extra expense involved in making arrangements to get you to your proper destination.

More commonly, travel agents will book their clients into the wrong hotel or reserve the wrong type of rental car. If you can show a real difference between the value you would have received had the agent made the reservation properly and what you did receive as a result of the agent's mistake, the agent would be responsible for making up the difference.

Example: Marcos and David asked their travel agent to reserve them a car with an automatic transmission because Marcos couldn't drive a car with a standard transmission. When they arrived at the rental counter, they learned that their agent reserved a standard and that the rental company had no automatics in the lot. They took the car, but David had to do all the driving. Their plan had been to drive both the east and west coasts of New Zealand's North Island, but they had to cut it short because David was too tired to drive the entire way.

This type of situation is a good example of circumstances in which working *with* your travel agent, rather than against her, is likely to serve your interests. When you return from your trip, or even while you are traveling, call or fax your agent and describe the mistake. Stay calm, don't yell and don't be confrontational. The travel agent may be able to arrange complimentary hotel nights, free upgrades, free car rentals or other services to compensate for the inconvenience or loss you experienced. If, instead, you spend your vacation complaining and sue your travel agent when you get back, you will be in the difficult position of putting a monetary value on highly subjective things, such as the service received in one hotel versus another, the quality of your view or the spaciousness of a rental car.

Confirming Reservations

Some travel reservations must be confirmed. Frequently, however, travelers don't know this, or they count on their travel agents to do it for them. If a travel agent has a responsibility to confirm a reservation and fails to do so, the travel agent may be responsible for the harm caused. In one case, a travel agent failed to confirm the clients' hotel reservations for a honeymoon suite. When the couple arrived at the hotel, only standard rooms were available. They sued their travel agent and recovered compensation because of the inferior hotel accommodations that they received.[1]

When travel agents use tour operators or wholesalers to make reservations, they may have an obligation to verify the reservations with the travel suppliers independently. In one case, a customer purchased a charter flight through his travel agent. The travel agent contacted a tour operator to make the reservations, but never investigated the reliability of the tour operator or confirmed the reservations with the airline. The flight never took place, and the court found the travel agent liable to the client because of the agent's failure to confirm the status of the flight and the reservations.[2]

Several years ago, a court held a travel agent liable for relying on computerized reservation information rather than contacting the airline directly.[3] Given the current common usage of computerized reservation systems by travel agents, it is questionable whether a court would now find a travel agent liable for not independently confirming the reservations directly with an airline.

Of course, the very small effort of confirming a reservation yourself is cheap insurance that your seat, room or car will be there when you show up.

Issuing Tickets

When a travel agent makes reservations and issues tickets almost simultaneously, your rights are similar to those on reservations, discussed just above. Among the most common types of ticketing mistakes are charging too much or too little for the ticket or writing a ticket that is inconsistent with the reservation.

For several reasons, the amount indicated on your ticket or tour contract might not equal the actual cost of travel. Your agent might be using outdated information, the travel supplier might change its rates without notice or the agent might make a mechanical or mathematical error in calculating the total price.

If you overpay because of the travel agent's mistake, it is fairly straightforward that the travel agent must reimburse you for the difference between the amount you paid and the actual fare. You must consider the proper fare at the time the ticket was reserved and paid for, not when a subsequent fare change was made.

Although a good travel agent will stay abreast of changes in fares, the agent has no obligation to continually check fares for tickets already issued. For example, although many airlines allow reticketing (for a fee) if a fare drops, your travel agent is not obliged to tell you about the lower fare if you have already purchased your ticket. (If your agent doesn't tell you, you may want to consider changing agents.)

If your travel agent charges you less for a ticket than the actual cost of the ticket, you are not entitled to travel for less than the established fare. For example, Flo purchased an around-the-world air ticket for $699. When she arrives at the airport, the airline agent tells her that the actual fare was $999, and that the travel agent made an entry error when entering the price of the ticket. The airline was within its rights to require Flo to pay the additional $300 before she could start her journey.

Whether Flo could recover the $300 from her travel agent depends on the circumstances. If Flo knew that the price was supposed to be $999 and agreed to that price, and the travel agent simply hit the wrong key on the computer, Flo is not entitled to any compensation from the travel agent. If, on the other hand, Flo can show that she did not know that the price was $999, and that she made her decision based upon the travel agent's statement that the price was $699, then she may be entitled to recoup the $300 from the travel agent.

The client's actual reliance on the travel agent's statement must be reasonable. If Flo's ticket had read $9.99 rather than $999, it would not have been reasonable for her to believe that an around-the-world ticket was available for less than $10.

Researching Airlines, Hotels and Other Suppliers

Travel agents have only a limited responsibility to conduct research on the travel suppliers they use—there is no general duty to investigate suppliers.[4] As noted above, this responsibility increases if the agent is not merely a ticketing agent, but recommends the travel services or acts as a tour operator.

In general, agents are only required to stay current with reasonably available information, such as what is in trade journals and magazines. The most important types of information are often the supplier's reputation, track record and financial condition. A travel agent must provide this type of information, as well as any specific experience that the travel agent has had with that sup-

plier, if it would likely affect your decision to use the supplier.

Although travel agents don't have a general duty to investigate, a travel agent's failure to do a basic investigation and pass the information on to you can result in a travel agent's liability. Travelers have recovered against travel agents who failed to inform them about the following:

- substandard hotels and hotels under construction[5]
- the risk of a charter air carrier defaulting[6]
- the bankruptcy of an airline,[7] and
- the reliability of a tour wholesaler.[8]

If your travel agent books you on a flight that has already been canceled or in a hotel that has not been built, obviously you have a fairly strong argument that the agent was negligent and failed to undertake a basic investigation. If, however, a tour operator suddenly goes out of business or a hotel closes between the time you make your reservation and the time you arrive, the agent's responsibility is less clear. If the agent knew about the impending closure or could have known by reading trade information or calling the supplier to confirm the reservation, then your agent has probably fallen below the basic level of investigation expected of travel agents. In recent years, however, a number of suppliers, particularly tour operators, have folded overnight, giving virtually no warning to customers who had reserved and paid for their services.

Remember that the role the travel agent plays when assisting you will affect the agent's potential liability. If you see a newspaper ad for a "great deal" for a tour and insist that your travel agent book you on that tour, the agent does not have the same responsibility to investigate as when the agent recommends or promotes a travel supplier or package.

Advising of Requirements for Entering a Foreign Country

Many foreign countries require you to obtain a visa prior to entering the country. These visas are generally available at that country's U.S. embassy or consulate. If you arrive at such a country without a visa, you are likely to be denied entry by the country's immigration officials and forced to return home. In some situations, the airline might not even let you on the plane without the proper documents required by the country to which you are traveling.

The law is not clear whether a travel agent has an obligation to warn you about visas and other entry requirements. It used to be assumed that travelers were responsible for learning about the legal requirements for traveling (such as visas), but in at least one case, a court found that a travel agent was negligent in failing to warn a client that a visa was required.[9]

Warning of Risks

If a travel agent knows of a substantial risk to the client, such as an airline that is bankrupt but continuing to fly, the travel agent has an obligation to warn the client of that risk. This obligation has several important limitations.

- A travel agent does not have to warn clients about risks that are obvious and apparent to the traveler.[10] For example, a passenger on a cruise ship cannot claim that she should have been warned of a dangerous condition when it was one that was so obvious that "any person with normal eyesight should have observed it."[11]

- A travel agent is not required to be a fortune teller, particularly concerning factors out of the agent's control, such as the weather. Many courts have concluded that "the law requires only that travel agents be loyal, not prescient."[12] Although a travel agent might be liable for promoting a "sun and fun" vacation in India during monsoon season, the agent does not have a duty to warn you about all possible conditions—such as unannounced strikes, political conditions or bad weather—that could affect your enjoyment of the journey. Courts have found that a travel agent is not required to warn clients traveling to Mexico that it might rain or to warn that access to a ski resort might be blocked by snow.[13] It is not clear whether a travel agent would be responsible for failing to warn of potentially dangerous areas (such as countries subject to State Department warnings) that she knew or should have known about.

- A travel agent does not have to point out disclaimers or other legal elements of an agreement between you and the travel supplier, although a helpful travel agent might do so. The travel agent is not your attorney. If a travel supplier's brochure or contract limits its liability or otherwise restricts your rights, by law you are required to inform yourself about these restrictions. Always review these before you travel.

Claiming that you didn't know, or that your travel agent should have told you, is unlikely to get you very far.

Risk of Physical Injuries

Several cases have been brought against travel agents by clients who were injured while traveling. Unless the travel agent was acting for an undisclosed principal or as a tour operator, such cases are normally unsuccessful. For example, a traveler who slipped on a rock while walking on the beach in Fiji claimed that the travel agent should have warned her of the "known hazardous condition"—that is, the slippery rock. The court disagreed, stating that there was no duty to warn about obvious hazards over which the travel agent had no control.[14]

In another case, a traveler who wanted to go waterskiing asked his travel agent to book a reservation at a particular resort. That resort was full, so the agent showed him the brochures for another resort that offered waterskiing. When the traveler asked whether he had to bring his own ski equipment, the agent looked in a binder of information on the resort and determined that the resort had its own skis.

After skiing successfully on several different days, the traveler was injured when the boat driver made a sharp turn in rough waters. The traveler claimed that the travel agent should have warned him about the unsafe conditions for waterskiing at that resort. The court decided for the travel agent, stating that the traveler, who was an experienced waterskier, was in a much better position to evaluate the safety of the waterskiing program than the travel agent

who was thousands of miles away. The traveler admitted that he had looked at the water skis and boat before going skiing and thought that they were relatively safe.[15]

Basically, a travel agent cannot be expected to know everything about a destination or to warn clients of all potential hazards. An important exception is prior knowledge on the part of the travel agent. If, in the waterskiing example, the travel agent had known that other clients had been injured waterskiing at that resort, there is a good chance that the agent would have been liable for failing to disclose this information to the client.

Risk of Crime

Travel agents are not responsible for warning you about all potential criminal activity at your destination. If the travel agent knows or reasonably should have known about past criminal activity, however, the agent may have a duty to warn you about the risk. In most cases, courts have ruled that a travel agent cannot be responsible for independent criminal acts over which the agent has no control and could not have reasonably foreseen.

A victim of purse snatching in Rome, Italy, claimed that her travel agent was liable because the agent had promised to book her in a first-class hotel and should have warned of the risk of street crime in Rome. The court concluded that there was no evidence that the hotel was substandard or that the travel agent had a particular duty to warn about street crime. In another case, two travelers requested that their agent book reservations for them at a particular hotel. During their stay at the hotel, they were locked out of their room and assaulted by employees of the hotel. The court determined that this type of behavior was not foreseeable, and that the travel agent was not responsible for the acts of the hotel's employees.[16]

In one of the few cases where the court has said that a travel agent could be responsible for criminal acts against a traveler, the particular facts no doubt led to the responsibility of the travel agent. The client was assaulted while going for a night walk on the beach in the Bahamas. Before booking the tour, the traveler had expressed concern about crime to the travel agent, who assured her that the travel agent was going along as a tour guide and that they were staying in a large, safe hotel. In fact, the travel agent did not go along and the hotel was switched at the last moment because the first hotel had been over-booked.

The court held that if the area was not safe and this information was reasonably available to the travel agent, the travel agent could be responsible for the traveler's injuries. What is important about this case is that the travel agent was acting as a tour operator, not just a ticketing agent, and had made some assurances that the traveler would be safe. Furthermore, the court did require that the traveler prove that the area was unsafe and that the travel agent could easily have known that.[17]

Health and Safety Risks in Foreign Countries

In many cases, a travel agent will be in a better position to know about health and safety risks in foreign countries than you will

be. Until recently, travel agents have not had to inform travelers about all health risks in a particular area or about the vaccinations or other medical precautions to take before traveling. Nor have travel agents had to inform travelers about unstable governments, local uprisings or other activities that might threaten safety while traveling. In some recent cases, however, courts have empha-sized a travel agent's superior access to information and claim of expertise as a travel professional in holding the agent responsible for failing to disclose information about particular health risks.[18]

The best ways to protect yourself are to ask your agent specifically whether there are health or safety problems in the area (which may trigger an agent's responsibility to investigate) and to do your own investigation before you travel.

 Information on diseases in foreign countries and appropriate precau-tions to take is available from the Centers for Disease Control in Atlanta, Georgia, at 800-311-3435 or 404-639-2572, or on the CDC's Website at http://ww.cdc.gov/travel/travel.html. Also, you can hear the State Department's evaluation of travelers'

security in particular foreign countries by calling the Citizens' Emergency Center at 202-647-5225 or by visiting the State Department's Web page at http://travel.state.gov/travel_warnings. html. (For further information on agencies that can provide advice on foreign countries, see Chapter 9.)

Outside Agents, Ticket Consolidators and Other Ticket Sellers

Outside Sales Agents

Sometimes, you may deal with someone who is not an employee of a travel agency, but works as an independent contractor or outside sales agent (OSA). OSAs frequently work out of their homes as sideline jobs. An OSA usually contracts with a travel agency that does the actual ticketing, and the OSA gets part of the agency's commission.

There is nothing illegal about dealing with an OSA, but keep in mind two risks:

- The OSA may not have access to a computerized reservation system and, therefore, may not have the most recent information on availability or prices.
- If you pay an OSA for your tickets rather than dealing directly with a travel agency, you may have trouble getting compensation if something goes wrong.

Ticket Brokers

Discounted tickets are often sold by ticket consolidators (sometimes called "bucket shops" or "ticket brokers") who buy blocks of tickets at discounted prices from the airlines, usually for international flights. Many ticket consolidators are legitimate and can offer substantial discounts. Some engage in questionable practices, however, such as reselling tickets purchased with frequent flyer miles, which is a no-no as far as the airlines are concerned. If you are caught using a ticket that wasn't obtained legitimately (under airline rules), your ticket is likely to be destroyed, and it is unlikely you will be compensated by the seller. Investigate ticket brokers (check with the Better Business Bureau, ask your travel agent and ask the broker for the names and phone numbers of references) before purchasing from a ticket broker if you have any doubts about its legitimacy.

Unbelievable Deals

The standard advice on unbelievable deals is, don't believe them. Unfortunately, there are plenty of scam artists who will offer you substantial discounts on airline tickets, cruises, vacation rentals and other travel "bargains" and then take your money and run. These phony deals are often advertised in newspapers, promoted by telemarketing or presented as some sort of prize. Almost always, the seller will try to get you to pay money immediately, "before the deal gets away." If you have any doubts about the honesty or legitimacy of the seller, STOP! Get more information before you commit any money (especially if you are asked to give your credit card number). Chapter 7 has information on how to avoid being the victim of a travel scam.

Your Identification Please

Several companies operate programs that claim to allow you to become an "instant" outside sales agent. They lure travelers by claiming that they can enjoy all of the discounts available to regular travel agents and earn commissions on all the travel they book. The price of these programs ranges from $50 to $3,000. Often, the primary advertised benefit is a "travel agent identification card."

Most of these programs offer little or no training or support, and the ID cards are often useless because the travel industry is moving toward a standard ID card issued by IATAN to travel agents with substantial annual bookings. In at least one case, the court declared one of these programs an illegal pyramid scheme. Similar programs are under in-vestigation by the offices of Attorney General in several states. Although some of these programs may be legitimate methods for you to work as an OSA, most seem to be scams. Investigate very carefully before becoming involved with any OSA program.

Travel agent associations are fighting back against groups that sell false travel agent credentials. According to the ASTA, 29 states and the District of Columbia have laws prohibiting impersonating a travel agent. Information on these laws is available through ASTA's fax-back service at 800-ASTA-FAX and on the Web at http://www.astanet.com.

Hawaiian residents who enrolled in the World Class Network (WCN)—a group that claimed to make people out-side sales agents—obtained a $1 million settlement from WCN in 1997. A Hawaiian court had earlier ruled that WCN had violated Hawaii's laws prohibiting "endless-chain (or pyramid) scheme"; all participants in Hawaii were given refunds. Many other consumers who have tried to obtain the supposed benefits of being an outside sales agent have not been so lucky. Although suits have been brought by the Federal Trade Commission and state attorneys general against WCN and similar organizations, there is frequently no money left to reim-burse people lured into these programs when the organization shuts down.

Resolving Disputes With Travel Agents

Alternatives to Suing

Travel agents are often scapegoated for problems beyond their control. Travel agents cannot guarantee sunny weather, crime-free cities or pleasant travel companions. Nevertheless, there are instances where a travel agent may be at fault for something that goes wrong with your travel arrangements. Keep in mind that there are a number of ways short of suing to resolve disputes with your travel agent.

 Before trying to resolve a dispute with a travel agent, read Chapter 13. That chapter emphasizes the need to:

- attack the problem not the person
- be firm but polite, and
- specifically state the compensation you want.

If you want to maintain an ongoing relationship with your travel agent, you may want to use a mediator or other neutral party to help resolve the dispute before resorting to a lawsuit that will almost certainly destroy your relationship.

If you are considering seeking compensation from your travel agent, first determine whether your agent was directly or indirectly responsible for the problem. This difference determines the travel agent's liability. Furthermore, you will probably want to take different approaches depending on whether the agent is indirectly or directly responsible for a problem.

Travel Agent Directly Responsible

If the agent was directly responsible for the problem by, for example, failing to make necessary reservations, take the following steps to try to resolve the dispute:

- **Speak directly with the agent.** Hear the agent's explanation and the reasoning behind the agent's actions. Explain your concerns, and state exactly why you believe that the agent's actions were responsible for the problem. Request specific compensation from the agent if you feel you are entitled to it.

- **Speak with the travel agency owner.** If you are not satisfied with the results from your discussion with the travel agent, discuss the situation with the agency owner. Bring any relevant documents that help explain your position, and be prepared with specific information such as dates, times and locations that are relevant to the problem. Again, request specific compensation.

- **Prepare a written complaint.** If the situation cannot be resolved through informal discussions, prepare a written complaint outlining the problem and the events leading up to it. Send a copy of the complaint to your travel agent and the travel agency owner. Include copies of any relevant documents or materials that support your claim or help to clarify the situation.

- **Contact the agent's professional association.** Send a copy of the complaint and supporting materials to any professional association to which your travel agent belongs, and make specific note of any violation of the association's code of ethics. This will show the agent that you are knowledgeable about her responsibilities to you. You may get some help from the association, but don't count on it.

- **Seek in-kind compensation first.** When asking for compensation, keep in mind that it is easier for an agent to provide future discounts than it is to refund money for a trip already completed. Despite the glamorous image that many people have of travel agents, most agencies are only marginally profitable and do not have large amounts of money available to settle disputes. If you demand a refund, you are likely to meet stiff resistance from your travel agent or agency. If, however, you are willing to accept complimentary air tickets, hotel rooms or rental cars, or free upgrades on travel services, you may quickly resolve your problem to your satisfaction.

Travel Agent Indirectly Responsible

If your problem was not caused directly by your travel agent, but was caused by a travel supplier—for instance, you get food poisoning in a restaurant included on a package tour sold by the agent—take the following steps:

- **Seek your travel agent's assistance.** You are likely to be most successful resolving a dispute with a travel supplier if you work with your travel agent. Your agent can draw on past experiences to come up with creative ideas as to how to seek compensation from the supplier and how best to approach a given supplier.

- **Use leverage on the agent.** In order to get maximum assistance from your travel agent, remind the agent of your family, friends and business acquaintances who do business with the travel agency. A travel agent may be much more willing to assist you knowing that more is at risk than just your business. A travel agency relies on steady clientele and will most likely go to greater lengths to protect the goodwill of a group of clients.

- **Use leverage on the travel supplier.** Assert any special status, such as your frequent flyer or frequent guest membership. Also, your travel agent is generally in a better position than you are to seek compensation from travel suppliers because your agent does much more business than you do with the suppliers. Work together with your agent to put this leverage to work for you.

Suing Your Travel Agent

If all other efforts to resolve your dispute fail, you may want to sue your travel agent. In many ways, travel agents are easy to sue because they are usually nearby and you are in direct contact with them when making travel arrangements. There are many drawbacks, however, including the need to prove both your damages and the connection between your travel agent's acts and those damages. This will be difficult if the agent is only indirectly responsible for the problem. To avoid wasting your money and time, consider these important questions before filing a lawsuit:

- **Have you exhausted all other alternatives?** Could the agent's professional association or mediation with a neutral party help to resolve the dispute?

- **What was your relationship with the agent?** If the agent acted as a tour operator or arranged services with an undisclosed travel supplier, he may be liable to you. If he merely acted as the middle person for a disclosed travel supplier, he probably is not liable to you.

- **Did the agent make any specific and concrete promises which were broken?** Specific broken promises can be the basis of claims for fraud or breach of contract, but mere exaggerations or minor deviations are unlikely to be enough to support your case.

- **Were the mistakes made by your agent or by some other travel supplier?** You are more likely to succeed if the agent is directly liable (forgetting to make or confirm reservations), rather than indirectly responsible (the hotels on the tour package sold by the agent were not as comfortable as described).

- **Is it worth the time and money?** Unless you can prove that the travel agent should compensate you for the harm caused by the travel suppliers, your recovery is likely to be limited to the compensation received by the travel agent from the suppliers, which may be only about 10% of what you paid.

If, after considering these questions, you want to sue your travel agent, you may be able to prepare your own case, unless it is complex. (Chapter 13 has the basic steps you will need to follow to prepare a case.) Use the principles outlined earlier in this chapter and the relevant cases mentioned to back up your legal claims.

Travelers' Restitution Fund

A fund created by the California Legislature to compensate travelers who lost money from unscrupulous travel sellers paid out over $350,000 in its first year of operation. The fund, administered by the California Travel Consumer Restitution Company, received 757 claims in its first 14 months and granted 185. As of the end of 1997, the fund contained less than $1 million. The average claim paid to travelers was $2,500 per incident.

■

Endnotes

[1] *Van Rossem v. Penney Travel Service, Inc.,* 488 N.Y.S.2d 495 (N.Y. 1985).

[2] *Trip Tours Ltd. v. Zamani,* 22 Aviation Cases 17,425 (N.Y. Civ. 1989).

[3] *Prechtl v. Travel House of Garden City, Ltd.,* 17 Aviation Cases 17,182 (N.Y. Civ. 1980), *modified,* 17 Aviation Cases 17,183 (N.Y. App. 1981).

[4] See, for example, *United Airlines v. Lerner,* 410 N.E.2d 225 (Ill. 1980).

[5] *Josephs v. Fuller,* 451 A.2d 203 (N.J. 1982); *Tuohey v. Trans National Travel,* 47 PA.D.&C. 3d 250 (Penn. 1987).

[6] *Rodriquez v. Cardona Travel Bureau,* 523 A.2d 281 (N.J. 1986).

[7] *Fix v. Travel Help,* 541 N.Y.S.2d 924 (N.Y. 1989).

[8] *Bucholtz v. Sirotkin Travel Service, Ltd.*, 343 N.Y.S.2d 438, *aff'd*, 363 N.Y.S.2d 415 (N.Y. 1974).

[9] *Levin v. Kasmir World Travel, Inc.*, 540 N.Y.S.2d 639 (N.Y. 1989).

[10] *McCollum v. Friendly Hills Travel Center*, 172 Cal. App. 3d 83 (Cal. 1985).

[11] *Stafford v. Intrav, Inc.*, 1994 A.M.C. 939, *aff'd*, 16 F.3d 1228 (8th Cir. 1994).

[12] *McCollum v. Friendly Hills Travel Center*, 172 Cal. App. 3d 83 (Cal. 1985).

[13] *Hervey v. American Airlines and Yucan Travel Market*, 19 Aviation Cases 18,531 (Okla. 1986); *United Airlines v. Lerner*, 410 N.E.2d 225 (Ill. 1980).

[14] *Lavine v. General Mills, Inc.*, 519 F. Supp. 332 (N.D. Ga. 1981).

[15] *McCollum v. Friendly Hills Travel Center*, 172 Cal. App. 3d 83 (Cal. 1985).

[16] *Taylor v. Trans World Airlines, Inc.*, 381 N.E.2d 944 (Ohio 1977); *Sacks v. Loew's Theaters, Inc.*, 263 N.Y.S.2d 253 (N.Y. 1965).

[17] *Loretti v. Holiday Inns, Inc.*, #85-0709 (E.D. Pa. 1986).

[18] *Philippe v. Lloyd's Aero Boliviano*, 589 So. 2d 536 (La. App. 1992).

Chapter 6

Tour Operators
and Tour Packages

An Introduction to Tour Operators and Tour Packages

Organized tours or "vacation packages" that combine several services, such as accommodations, transportation and meals, are popular with many leisure travelers. Tours and packages are often promoted as being more convenient and less expensive for a traveler than if the same services were purchased separately. The companies that plan tour itineraries and put together the packages are known collectively as "tour operators."

Before You Buy a Tour

Before buying any tour, consider the following questions:

- **What is the cost of the tour as compared with buying the services separately?** Be sure to find out exactly what is included in the cost—for example, some tours include breakfast, lunch and some dinners, but for many evening meals you are on your own. Also, ask if tips are included.
- **What if you are traveling alone?** You will probably be assigned a roommate unless you pay extra for a "single supplement." How much is the supplement? If you decide to share a room, find out what, if anything, you can do if you're assigned a roommate with whom you don't get along.
- **Can you get the names, addresses and phone numbers of all the suppliers—** such as the airline, ship operator, hotel or bus operator? Once you have this information, check out the reputation of the providers. If you can't get their names from the tour operator, be wary of buying the tour.
- **Can you get a copy of the contract with the tour operator before you buy?** You should read it and understand all its terms—such as the tour operator's liability and the cancellation policy, changes in price and items excluded.
- **What is the reputation of the tour operator?** How long has it been in business, and are there any complaints on file with the local Better Business Bureau or Tourist Commission?
- **Does the tour operator put your deposit and other payments into an escrow account until after the tour is completed?** If not, why not? If so, how can you make you payment directly into the escrow account rather than to the tour operator?
- **Does the tour operator participate in a consumer protection program that will compensate you if the tour is canceled or the tour operator goes out of business?** If so, what are the limitations of the program, and how much compensation can you expect to receive if the tour operator has problems?
- **What is the tour operator's legal relationship to the other suppliers?** Are they subsidiaries (owned by the supplier) or independent subcontractors (in business for themselves)? The difference may determine who is liable to you if you have a problem.
- **Does the tour operator disclaim any responsibility for the negligence of the suppliers, such as hotels and travel guides?** If so, how will you be compen-

sated for any loss or damage you suffer on a tour?

Types of Tour Operators

The term "tour operator" is used to describe a wide variety of companies that offer travel services. If you purchase a tour package, identifying the type of tour operator you are dealing with is one of the most important steps you can take to protect your rights. As we discuss later in the chapter, the relationship between the tour operator and the suppliers (such as hotels or transportation providers) can be quite important when determining responsibility if problems arise. Generally, the greater the tour operator's control over the elements of your tour, the greater its liability if something goes wrong.

Tour operators come in all shapes and sizes and could provide as little as an airplane ticket and a rental car (such as in "fly/drive" packages) or, in the case of some wilderness tours, provide you with a guide and all of your housing, food and even outdoor equipment and clothing. The range of tours is tremendous, including tours specializing in outdoor activities (biking, hiking, climbing and rafting), walks across European countries, cultural sights (theater, opera, symphony or ballet) and types of museums.

In the U.S., bus tours are the most popular product provided by tour operators. A bus tour operator plans an itinerary, contracts with hotels and restaurants and provides a bus and often a tour guide. Because of the strong association with bus tours, many people assume that tour operators only plan trips for groups. In fact, over 80% of tour packages sold by tour operators are for individual or family trips.

Air Carriers as Tour Operators

Some airlines have become major tour operators. Through subsidiaries or related companies, air carriers often provide organized tours in connection with the sale of their flights. These tour packages range from the simple fly/drive packages that offer a rental car with a flight, to comprehensive group packages. These are particularly popular with vacationers traveling to foreign countries or families with children traveling to theme parks. Because airlines enjoy many legal protections and limitations on liability for damages caused during flight (see Chapter 1), it is important to distinguish between when an airline is acting as only an air carrier (limited liability) and when it is operating as a tour operator (greater liability).

Travel Agents as Tour Operators

Travel agents can operate as tour operators in two ways: they can independently plan an itinerary and make arrangements with the hotels and other suppliers, or they can resell a tour package that has been put together by a tour operator. If the travel agent resells a package and discloses to the client that the package was put together by another tour operator or wholesaler, then, most likely, the travel agent has the limited liability discussed in Chapter 5. If the agent claims to be or gives the impression of being the organizer of the tour, and does not disclose the identity of the other operator or wholesaler, however, the agent will normally be treated like any other tour operator would be—and the liability is as discussed in this chapter.

Example: Terry, a travel agent, offers to put together a tour to France for the local gourmet club. Terry obtains a tour package, including hotel rooms and cooking classes from Eatwell Tours that costs $1,800 per person. Terry marks up the tour by $250 per person and sells it to club members without telling them about Eatwell (or her markup). Terry is now operating as a tour operator, and if the vouchers for the hotel rooms and classes provided by Eatwell turn out to be worthless, the club members can seek a refund from both Terry and Eatwell. Terry would be liable for the entire amount of the tour, not just the $250 per person she received.

Local Tour Operators and Outfitters

Around the world, there are literally millions of bus and cab drivers, tour guides and outfitters who operate tours. From a legal standpoint, these local tour operators, guides and outfitters are the most difficult to reach if you want compensation of some sort. Recently, courts have begun to accept the idea that other travel suppliers up the line, such as the airlines or hotels, may be liable for the actions of a local operator in some instances (see below). This may be the case if the local operator was recommended by the other supplier or if you were given the impression that the local operator was employed or directed by the hotel, airline or other supplier, and you relied on the good reputation of the supplier.

Identifying the relationships among the various travel suppliers can be crucial if you are seeking compensation during or after a tour. There is often no formal contract between you and the local operator setting forth the operator's obligations and responsibilities, and almost no chance of getting court power over that distant tour operator once you return to the U.S.

Furthermore, local tour guides or other small tour operators rarely have the financial resources to compensate you if you are injured because of their mistakes. The U.S.-based tour operator that organized your tour may be the only entity with the resources (including insurance) to cover your losses. A case involving an injury on a camel ride in Egypt demonstrates how attorneys sometimes use the relationships among travel suppliers in order to put liability on someone who can pay.

Example: An American tourist bought a tour package from a major hotel chain which included accommodations at the chain's hotel in Egypt. The bell captain at the hotel recommended that the tourist take a camel ride, which he represented as "being perfectly safe." The tourist was seriously injured and sued the U.S.-based hotel. The hotel argued that it could not be responsible for the actions of an independent third party, such as the camel tour operator. The court determined that the hotel, in this case, was acting as a tour operator and could be liable for the actions of its employee, the bell captain, that may have led to the visitor's injuries.[1]

How Tour Operators Plan and Market Tours

Most tour operators follow a standard format in planning their tours. Based on their experience and estimates of the market demand, the tour operator will reserve blocks of hotel rooms, airline seats and even items such as theater tickets or wilderness permits, often one or two years in advance of the tour date. By buying in bulk and guaranteeing the suppliers a certain amount of revenue in advance, tour operators can obtain a better price than individuals purchasing the same service on their own.

The tour operator then creates a brochure or other marketing device and sells the tour, either directly to the public or through resellers such as travel agents or travel clubs. A company that doesn't create its own packages, but only markets groups of tours to resellers, is generally referred to as a "tour wholesaler" rather than a tour operator.

A one-week itinerary may involve contracts with dozens of different travel suppliers, such as airlines, hotels, restaurants and guides. Tour operators attempt to limit their liability for any problems created by these subcontractors. The limitations of the tour operator's liability are normally set forth in the fine print of the tour brochure, the contracts and any waivers the tour operator will ask you to sign, so pay attention to those documents. Courts are increasingly enforcing these documents in favor of tour operators.

Going Out of Business

In the past few years, thousands of people have purchased tour packages and found themselves part of a tourist's nightmare. Many large tour operators have gone out of business, stranding some tourists at their vacation destination, and leaving others with worthless vouchers, tickets and reservations not honored by the airlines, hotels or other suppliers. Although failure of some smaller operators was common in the past, it was not until the early 1990s that large-scale failures of major operators became common.

Theoretically, when a major tour operator goes bankrupt, you have, as a creditor of the tour operator, the right to receive some reimbursement under federal bankruptcy laws. By the time the tour operator's bank, major creditors, suppliers and attorneys have all taken their share, however, you are likely to receive only pennies on the dollar (if that much), and probably not until several years after the bankruptcy occurs. To avoid this dismal scenario, follow our advice.

Investigate the Tour Operator's Financial Condition

Don't choose any tour operator—or make any deposit—until you carefully investigate the tour operator's financial condition. To check the condition, you can:

- Ask the tour operator if it has posted a performance bond to cover default or bankruptcy.
- Ask whether the tour operator maintains an escrow account where customer payments are deposited until the trip is completed. (This is required for charter operators; see below.)

- Verify the existence of the escrow account with the bank where the funds should be deposited, and inquire how you can make your payment directly into the account rather than to the tour operator.

⚠️ Of course, even a good track record in the past is no guarantee; several tour operators with excellent reputations have failed. One warning sign is a tour operator that is offering last-minute deals and prices that are substantially below the market. Dramatic price reductions are often a sign of a cash-flow problem that eventually will catch up with the company, and possibly with you.

Use a Tour Operator With a Consumer Protection Plan

One way to minimize financial disaster is to use a tour operator who belongs to a consumer protection program, such as those sponsored by the U.S. Tour Operators Association (USTOA) or the National Tour Association (NTA). (The American Society of Travel Agents used to sponsor a travelers protection plan known as TRIP, but withdrew its sponsorship in 1995. A new protection plan may be added, so check with ASTA or your local ASTA travel agent.) Under such programs, the tour operator must post a bond or deposit a certain amount of money designed to compensate you if the tour operator goes out of business. For example, USTOA's consumer protection plan requires a $1 million bond from each member, and members must have been in business for at least three years under the same ownership or management.

But even these programs are no guarantee that you will get your money back. A tour operator who belongs to USTOA could easily have obligations that greatly exceed $1 million, in which case you may receive only partial compensation or nothing at all.

Always verify that the tour operator's membership in a consumer protection program is current. Even if the program is mentioned in a brochure, check directly with the tour operator, and if you are suspicious, check with the bank or other organization sponsoring the program. Remember that the brochure may have been printed far in advance of the travel date, and that each year a number of tour operators are removed from the consumer protection programs or voluntarily drop out.

You can get information about a specific tour operator's membership in a particular consumer protection program by calling:

U.S. Tour Operators Association (USTOA)
342 Madison Avenue, Suite 1522
New York, NY 10173
tel: 212-599-6599
fax: 212-599-6744
e-mail: USTO@aol.com
Web: http://www.USTOA.com

National Tour Association (NTA)
Member Services, 120 Kentucky Street
Lexington, KY 40508
tel: 606-226-4444
fax: 606-226-4414
Web: http://www.ntaonline.com/www/
        nta/pub/cons1.lhtml.

Pay by Credit Card

Use major credit cards, when possible, to pay for your tour. Under the Fair Credit Billing Act (discussed below), you may be able to challenge a charge on your credit card and receive a refund. Although the law requires that you file a written challenge within 60 days of the date that you receive the charge on your credit card bill, some companies let consumers challenge charges up to 120 days after the charge appears. Check with your credit card company for its policy.

> **Example:** Libby paid more than $10,000 for a ten-day tour of Greece for herself, her husband and her mother-in-law. Two weeks before they were to leave, the tour operator informed Libby that the trip had been canceled because of the company's financial problems. Even though the company had posted a bond with USTOA, it had withdrawn from USTOA three months before the tour was to begin, and the bond expired. Libby sued her travel agent and got back the agent's 17% commission of $1,700. She also got back the $1,950 deposit she had put on a credit card, although it was a long, hard battle that took more than a year to settle. She never recouped the remaining $6,350 that she paid by check.

Purchase Travel Insurance

In some cases, travel insurance can cover you for the bankruptcy of the tour operator or other complete failure of a tour. Make sure to check the fine print for exceptions. If you buy travel insurance designed to cover operator failure, buy it from someone other than the operator. Insurance purchased through the operator is likely to be invalid if the operator then goes out of business.

 For more details on travel insurance, see Chapter 8.

Check Your State Consumer Protection Laws

Several states, notably California, Florida and Hawaii, have laws that generally require tour operators and other groups selling or promoting travel to register with a state agency and either establish a trust account or post a bond sufficient to cover deposits made by travelers before their tour. Similar laws are under consideration in other states, including Pennsylvania, Maryland and New Jersey. If you purchase a tour in a state with this type of consumer protection law, you may be able to apply for a refund under that state's law if the company goes out of business.

 To find out if your state has such a law—and how to apply for a refund if it does—you can check with the consumer protection agency in the state where you are considering buying or have bought a tour. Call information for the state capital and ask for the phone number for the state Department of Consumer Affairs, Consumer Protection or Consumer Services, or the Office of the Attorney General.

Even if there is no specific travel promoter law on the books in your state, a travel agent may be liable if she sells you a tour and the operator becomes bankrupt, if the travel agent knew, or should have known, that the tour operator was in financial difficulty, or if the travel agent failed to tell you about travel-trade press reports of a tour operator's financial instability.[2]

Promises, Promises

What happens if the tour operator fails to live up to its promises, short of going out of business? What can you do if the tour operator makes substantial changes or cancels your tour? This section explains a tour operator's liability for changes.

 See Chapter 13 for information on resolving a dispute with a travel supplier. Travel scams, where the tour operator deliberately lies and seeks to cheat you out of your money, are covered in Chapter 7.

Changes and Substitutions

Most tour operators stipulate in their tour materials and contracts that they retain the right to make changes and substitutions when necessary. Sometimes these changes are relatively harmless, such as substituting a comparable hotel, or changing a departure time on a tour by one or two hours.

 If a tour operator makes substantial changes that affect your enjoyment of the tour, the operator may liable for breach of contract or misrepresentation.

Substitution of hotels is one of the most common changes made. If the hotel substituted for the one advertised in the brochure or other materials is greatly inferior or located in a less desirable area, you could have a reasonable basis for claiming compensation from the tour operator.

Changes Before the Tour

If you are notified that a change or substitution is being made before your tour, you have several options—requesting a partial refund, having the tour operator make different arrangements for you (for example, finding a better hotel when an inferior one has been substituted) or canceling your tour and demanding a full refund. You are in your strongest bargaining position before you take the tour. If the operator will not negotiate a settlement and you refuse to cancel, it is almost certain that after the tour the operator will take the position that you were informed of the changes and voluntarily accepted them.

Changes During the Tour

When you learn about changes during the tour, and were not warned of them ahead of time, you should bring your concerns to the attention of the tour operator immediately, in writing if possible. Ask the tour operator to make an immediate effort to accommodate you. The result of a direct request during the tour is generally far superior to any partial refund or credit you might receive after the tour is over.

You must make a judgment call as to whether the changes are significant enough to alter the nature of the tour. Some small changes are almost inevitable, considering the fact that many tour itineraries are planned and reserved years in advance, and most contracts give the operator the right to make such changes. Substantial changes that fundamentally affect your enjoyment of the tour may be a violation of the contract; however, what constitutes a substantial change is open to interpretation. Some legal authorities suggest that the substitution of an inferior tour guide would not be a violation of the contract if the tour guide was not the major reason you decided to take the tour, but if the guide was a major draw (such as a world-renowned botanist on a trip to the jungle), this substitution might defeat the essential purpose of the contract.

Write Your Own Fine Print

If a particular element of a tour is important to you, and a change or substitution would greatly reduce your enjoyment of the tour, put it in writing. Identify the elements especially important to you, demand immediate notification if any of them will be changed and reserve the right to cancel your tour and receive a full refund if any are changed. Whenever possible, get a written agreement to your terms by the tour operator. Without such an agreement, your terms may have no effect. The fine print in the contract may say that no changes to the terms and conditions of the contract are allowed without express written approval of the tour operator.

Changes by a Government Agency or Third Party

One of the most difficult issues concerning changes in a tour are changes made by third parties, such as host governments. For example, often travelers to the People's Republic of China have been subjected to itinerary changes made by the government and enforced by government guides. Such changes are normally out of the hands of tour operators, who are not likely to be held liable for changes beyond their control. This leaves you in a bind because it is virtually impossible for you to seek any sort of compensation from the government agency or other third party that made the changes.

Misleading Claims

What happens when the facilities or services offered on the tour do not match those described beforehand? If your "deluxe" resort turns out to be a run-down hotel you may well feel cheated, but what are your legal rights? Generally, the law allows a certain amount of "puffing" in advertising. Just because the brochure promises "the time of your life," don't expect to get your money back from the tour operator if it's not the best trip you ever took. Terms such as "beautiful," "exciting" or "luxury" are relative, and thus considered as opinion. It is important that you identify *factual* discrepancies between the tour you were offered and the tour you received.

For example, if you were promised a four-star hotel and stay at a hotel that has only a two-star rating, or if you were promised a seaside hotel and are actually located miles from the shore, you may be able to show some reduction in the value of the tour. If certain elements of the tour do not materialize, such as meals, guides or local transportation, you probably have grounds for some compensation.

Practically speaking, unless there is a substantial difference between the promised tour and the tour you received, it is unlikely to be worth your while to do anything other than write a letter to the tour operator (as explained in Chapter 13). This is true even though courts are increasingly recognizing that a traveler's "loss of enjoyment" should be compensated.[3] The reality is that the amount usually awarded in such cases is quite small, and so pursuing a case through the formal legal system is not cost-effective unless you are also claiming other compen-

sation, such as a refund of transportation costs.

A Picture Is Worth a Thousand Words

If you find that the conditions on your tour are quite different from those described beforehand, use your camera. A video or a few photographs of the hotel room with no window or the swimming pool with no water in it are often much more effective in making your point than is a long-winded description.

Misleading Tour Advertisements

Most states have laws against fraudulent or misleading advertising. In some cases, these laws may be part of laws covering unfair business practices or consumer protection. Generally, these laws prohibit businesses from knowingly deceiving customers by making "material misstatements of fact." To prove a case in court, you would have to show:

- an intent to deceive
- misstatements that were "material" (relevant and important), and
- that the misstatements concerned factual matters, rather than opinion.

Some states allow claims for "negligent misrepresentation," meaning that the business should have known that the statements it made were false, even if it didn't actually intend to deceive.

If you sue a tour operator, you would probably want to claim false advertising or misrepresentation as well as breach of contract. If you are attempting to resolve a dispute informally, however, avoid words such as "fraud" and "deception"—at least initially. No one likes to be accused of lying or fraud, and a hostile letter is likely to get a very unsympathetic response. Remember— your objective is to get fair compensation. Focus on facts. Show the differences between what you were promised and what you received. If possible, use the exact words set forth in the tour operator's brochure or advertising.

If the company wants to keep you, your family and your friends as potential customers, it should offer some compensation. If the company simply made an error or bad judgment, a reasoned description of the tour's shortcomings and some concrete suggested compensation are your best bet. On the other hand, if a company's operation is truly fraudulent, it is unlikely that any letter you send will have much impact.

Physical Injuries

Physical (personal) injuries to you or your possessions are a normal occurrence in traveling. If you are injured on a tour and are trying to get compensation from the tour operator, make a realistic assessment of both the extent of your injuries and the probability of recovering from the tour operator. (Most likely, the Solutions Letter™ approach set forth in Chapter 13 will be your best bet for minor injuries and inconveniences.) If your injuries are more serious and you are seeking greater compensation than a tour operator is willing to provide voluntarily,

you may be forced to bring a formal legal complaint.

This section briefly explains the process an attorney might use to analyze a claim and suggests a few legal theories under which a tour operator might be held liable for your injuries. Because of the difficulty of bringing a physical injury case outside of the U.S. (and the impossibility of describing all the different foreign procedures), this section assumes that you can sue within the U.S., even if you were injured while traveling abroad—meaning that the tour operator has some contacts in the U.S., such as a reservation office. If you were injured while touring outside of the U.S. with a completely local tour operator who has no contact with the U.S. (for example, you bought the tour once you arrived at your destination), the best you can probably hope for is that your medical insurance carrier will cover your bills.

Remember, in the case of a serious injury, you may need the help of an attorney. Nevertheless, this section should help you understand the basic elements of a complaint for physical injury.

Obstacles to Bringing a Physical Injury Claim

Two factors make it very difficult to bring a successful personal injury case against a tour operator. First, most elements of your tour, such as hotels, restaurants and transportation, are not owned or controlled directly by the tour operator. Generally, each supplier is treated as an independent contractor, and most U.S. courts will not impose liability on a tour operator for injuries caused by independent contractors. This means you most likely will have to pursue the travel supplier—the hotel, bus line or other company—liable for compensating you for your injury.

Second, you almost certainly were required to sign disclaimers, waivers and contracts in order to participate in the tour. These documents normally disclaim any responsibility for injuries and obligate you to "assume the risk" of any injuries or damage, whether caused by the tour operator, its agents or employees, or independent contractors. For years, people have been told that disclaimers and waivers were "not worth the paper they were written on." This is wrong. When you join a tour, particularly one that involves some inherent element of physical risks, such as a skiing or white-water rafting vacation, you are taking a chance that you may be injured. Attorneys for tour operators have taken great care in drafting these documents, and courts are increasingly willing to enforce them. Don't sign a waiver or disclaimer thinking you can get out of it later. Read the terms carefully and decide whether you are willing to assume the risks involved in the tour.

Tour Operator Responsibility

There are two ways in which a tour operator might be found responsible for a traveler's personal injuries:

- *direct* responsibility if it had ownership or control of the premises, vehicle or activity that caused the injury, or
- *vicarious* responsibility for the actions of others.

Direct Responsibility

Direct responsibility often occurs when a tour operator wears more than one hat, for instance, when the tour operator also owns or operates the hotel or bus used for the tour. In such cases, determine your rights against that particular service or premise. (For example, if you are injured in a hotel lobby during a tour, read Chapter 4. A tour operator who owns or operates the hotel is likely to be held to at least the same standard of care that is required of the hotel itself.)

Vicarious Responsibility

One travel law expert has proposed several theories on how you may be able to get around a signed waiver or disclaimer.[4]

Breach of Warranty of Safety

Many travel brochures or advertisements seek to put travelers at ease by making claims about the safety of the tour. If, in fact, the tour is unsafe, you may be able to claim that the tour operator is liable, even if you signed a waiver, because you relied upon the tour operator's assurances of safety.

> **Example:** The wife of a traveler who died while snorkeling on a tour in Costa Rica successfully sued the U.S.-based tour operator and Cornell University, the sponsor of the tour. She claimed a breach of warranty of safety because the brochure said, "safety and comfort of our clientele is always foremost, and we will do everything in our power to ensure the same." Although neither the U.S. tour operator nor Cornell University was directly responsible for the injury, the court found them vicariously responsible for the actions of the Costa Rican travel suppliers, who were not subject to suit in the U.S.[5]

Assumed Ownership and Control

Even if a tour operator, or a supplier acting as a tour operator, such as an airline, hotel or rental car agency, does not directly own and control a supplier, a traveler may be lulled into a false sense of security by the use of the same company name, or by the apparent control over the operation.

> **Example:** As part of a tour, the Fogels were injured in a rental car accident in Italy and successfully sued Hertz rental car company in the U.S., even though Hertz did not own the particular vehicle or the Hertz franchise in Italy that had rented it. The court held that since Hertz had not made it clear that it did not own or operate the foreign rental car operation, the Fogels were reasonable in relying on the reputation of Hertz's parent company in the U.S., and held that company liable for their injuries in Italy.[6]

In some cases, ownership and control might be reasonably assumed because of language in the tour operator's brochures and other marketing materials. For example, a brochure that talks about "our guides" or "our sister hotel" could reasonably lead you to believe that the tour operator had some control over tour operations and management. If you book a tour relying on the good reputation of a "brand name" tour operator, hotel or other supplier and you don't know that the services are actually supplied by a company with much lower standards of care and safety, argue that even though you signed a waiver or disclaimer, you did not have sufficient information to make an informed decision.

Misrepresentation of Professionalism

Tour operators often advertise their "expert staff" or "professional guides" in an effort to attract customers. Whether these representations are made about employees or independent contractors, if they are untrue, they give you a false sense of security. If you are injured because of mistakes made by inexperienced or undertrained personnel, argue that the misrepresentations of professionalism led you to agree to assume the risks of the tour, and that if you had known the real level of professionalism, you would not have done so.

Negligent Tour Planning or Operation

When a tour operator designs and operates a tour, it has an obligation not to expose you to unreasonable risk. It is negligent if it plans or operates the tour in a way that it knows, or should know, will unreasonably increase the odds of your being injured. One type of negligence is in the design of a tour itinerary.

> **Example:** A tour operator might be liable if it plans a bus tour over a road that is known for activity by bandits when other, safer routes are available. Normally, an "intervening illegal act" by a third person would not be the tour operator's responsibility. If, however, the tour operator knew or should have known about the risk of bandits, it might be liable for negligent design.

Similarly, negligent selection of a supplier may create liability for a tour operator. Tour operators often have the ability to choose between several suppliers, and if they choose one that is incapable or unwilling to carry out its responsibilities, the tour operator may be negligent in selecting this supplier. This is particularly true if the tour operator selects an incompetent or unsafe supplier simply to save money. In such a case, the tour operator would be putting its profit motive ahead of the safety of its customers, a position that is difficult to justify in court.

> **Example:** A tour operator selects a bus operator, knowing that these buses frequently have mechanical problems. It could be liable if you are injured in an accident caused by that bus operator's faulty equipment.

Negligent supervision of personnel, such as tour guides, is closely related to the claim of misrepresentation of professionalism. If you are paying for your tour, you have a reasonable expectation that tour personnel, including tour guides, will not expose you to unreasonable risk, unless it is inherent in the trip.

> **Example:** The Supreme Court of Israel ruled against a tour operator and guide who led an American tourist in Israel onto a path in the woods explicitly marked "forbidden." The tourist was seriously injured, suffered brain damage and recovered a substantial amount for the injuries, pain and suffering and loss of potential earnings.[7]

A tour operator could be liable for negligently designing the tour so that it would go on a forbidden route or negligently supervising the tour guide.

Intentional Injuries

In rare instances, a tour operator or a tour operator's employee or agent intentionally harms a traveler. If such an injury was caused by the tour operator itself, it would invalidate any waiver or disclaimer. More commonly, such acts are carried out by the tour operator's employees or agents. In such a case, the tour operator may be able to protect itself, because tour operators are generally not liable for the unforeseen intervening illegal acts of a third party. If, however, the tour operator could have reasonably foreseen the acts (for example, the employee had committed similar acts in the past), then the tour operator might be liable for negligently selecting or supervising that employee or agent.

Related Topics

Both Chapter 5 and Chapter 7 contain information relevant to the duties and liabilities of tour operators. If you have questions about tour operators that weren't answered in this chapter, check these chapters for additional information. The associations for tour operators mentioned earlier in this chapter are another possible source of information.

■

Endnotes

[1] *MacLachlin v. Marriott Corp.*, 2 Travel Law Journal 46 (1994).

[2] *Marcus v. Zenith Travel, Inc.*, 577 N.Y.S.2d 820 (N.Y. 1991).

[3] *Pellegrini v. Landmark Travel Group,* N.Y.L.J., June 2, 1995, p. 31, col. 5; *Tohey v. Transnational Travel,* 47 Pa.D.&C. 3d 240 (Penn. 1987).

[4] *Judge Thomas A. Dickerson,* 2 Travel Law Journal 44 (1995).

[5] *Mayer v. Cornell University,* 92 Civ. 220 (N.D.N.Y 1992).

[6] *Fogel v. Hertz International,* 141 A.D.2D 375, 529 N.Y.S.2d 484 (1988).

[7] *Israel v Cohen,* 2 Travel Law Journal 47 (1994).

Chapter 7

Travel Scams and Questionable Travel Providers

An Introduction to Travel Scams

Each year, Americans lose billions of dollars in travel scams—such as being sold a ticket for a nonexistent flight or paying for a "prize" that consists of a couple of nights at a run-down hotel in a bad part of town. You can avoid most travel scams by learning to recognize telltale signs. If, however, you fall prey to a scam, you'll want to report it immediately to the appropriate government agencies (listed below) and contact organizations that might be able to help you recoup your losses.

Out of the U.S. May Mean Out of Luck

This chapter covers only scams that occur in the U.S. Unfortunately, we can offer little advice if you are the victim of an illegal money changer (someone who sells you expired or counterfeit currency), a fraudulent local tour operator or a foreign hotel that overcharges you. Short of going to the police, you may simply have to chalk it up to bad luck and a hard lesson learned.

How to Recognize and Avoid Travel Scams

A good rule for protecting yourself against travel fraud is this: If the offer sounds too good to be true, it probably is. Unfortunately, the dramatic discounts provided by legitimate travel services (such as drastically reduced fares on certain flights by major carriers) make travel scam offers seem feasible. This situation leaves consumers particularly vulnerable to fraudulent advertisement scams.

There's No Place Like Home

When you are away from home, you are the most vulnerable to travel scams. If you lose money, it can be very costly and difficult for you to return to the location to try to get it back. Also, the federal Fair Credit Billing Act allows you to contest fraudulent credit card charges only if they were made within the state in which you live or within 100 miles of your home. Finally, the scam artist will benefit from a home court advantage and a greater familiarity with local laws and customs than you have.

Here are some typical signs (red flags) that you are being pitched a scam:

"You have been specially selected or awarded a trip or prize." If you haven't entered any contest, then the prize you have won is probably fraudulent.

The company insists that you pay to collect the prize. Refuse any prizes that require you to pay money. No matter how reasonable the initial payment may seem relative to the value of the prize, there will be many additional requests for money before you ever actually see your prize.

Legitimate sweepstakes and contests do not require payments from winners.

The company pressures you to buy or make an immediate decision. A company offering a genuine bargain should not convey a sense of urgency. Walk away from high-pressure sales presentations or telephone calls that do not give you time to comparison shop.

The company asks for personal information. Legitimate businesses do not need your income, social security number or bank account number—and scam artists have many ways to use this information to their benefit.

The company refuses to give you anything in writing unless you pay first. Insist on receiving material in the mail before you pay anything, and refuse any demands to give money before you receive the material. Request complete details in writing about any trip before you pay, including the total price, service charges, processing fees, cancellation and change penalties, blackout dates and specific details about the components of the package. A reputable company will be pleased to send you information, while a fraudulent fly-by-night promotion may refuse unless you pay first.

Example: Two scam-artist brothers were indicted on charges of cheating some 2,000 would-be vacationers in 43 states out of $800,000 in fees paid for vacations that never took place. The brothers ran newspaper and magazine ads touting exotic vacations at cheap prices in the Caribbean, Cancun and similar locations. Customers were required to pay up front with a certified check, money order or credit card. One woman responded to an ad for a five-day trip from Philadelphia to Cancun, including hotel and airfare. After paying the advertised fee of $250, she was told that she had to pay an additional $200. She refused and demanded a refund of her $250. The brothers first would not take her calls, and then promised a refund—which never materialized. Notably, these master scam artists carried out their operation from the basement of their home with nothing more than a couple of telephone lines and an answering machine.

The company gives vague references to "all major airlines" or "all major hotels" or a collection of airlines or hotels. Fraudulent vacation certificates typically omit the dates for travel, names of service providers or price for the vacation. If a hotel or other travel supplier is listed, contact the supplier directly to determine whether it honors these certificates. Most do not.

The company asks for your credit card number over the phone. *Never* give out your credit card or bank account number unless you initiate the call and you have 100% confidence in the company with which you are doing business. A scam artist who knows your credit card number and expiration date has all the information needed to make fraudulent charges on your credit card.

Preventing Credit Card Fraud

Whenever you travel, play it safe by following these tips:

- Carry only the cards you plan to use on your trip.
- Keep credit cards in your wallet or purse, not in your pocket.
- Keep a list of your credit card account numbers and phone numbers to report a lost or stolen card in a safe place other than your wallet or purse.
- Check sales receipts for accuracy before signing. Make sure the decimal point and numbers following are filled in.
- Make sure the person running the charge returns your card.
- Keep carbon sheets or insist that they be destroyed.
- Don't write your credit card number on a check.
- Keep all credit and ATM card receipts.

The company requires that you wait an unusually long time before taking the trip or receiving the prize. Be suspicious of any company that requires you to wait at least 60 days before taking your trip. Most victims of scams pay for their "prize" on their credit card; scam artists know that the federal Fair Credit Billing Act requires you to dispute any credit card charge within 60 days. If you act quickly, you can contest the charge for a fraudulent deal and recover from the credit card company. But you must protest within 60 days of the date you receive your bill—not the date of your travel. Scam operators are well aware of the limit, and therefore restrict travel to a date more than 60 days from when the charge will appear on your card. Although some credit cards offer extended coverage (typically 120 days), and a few cards give their members up to a year to contest a charge, credit card contest battles can be harrowing.

The company requests a direct bank deposit or certified check or offers to send a courier to your home to pick up your check. Refuse any request to pay by certified check or to have your payment picked up by a courier. Scam operations use private courier services and bank drafts in order to avoid prosecution in federal court at a later date. The Federal Trade Commission (FTC), Federal Communications Commission (FCC), Federal Bureau of Investigation (FBI) and U.S. Postal Service (USPS) investigate travel fraud done via mail or telephone, but do not investigate fraud that bypasses the mail or telephone.

An FTC rule requires telemarketers to have express authorization from a consumer to withdraw money from the consumer's account over the phone.[1] This authorization can be by:

- advance written consent, such as a faxed authorization or a canceled check, or
- tape recording, where the consumer is told and acknowledges the following:
  - number and dates of the withdrawals
  - amount of the withdrawals
  - name of the consumer from whose account the funds will be paid

- a telephone number the consumer can call during business hours with any questions, and
- date of the authorization.

Telemarketer Disclosures

Any telemarketer must tell you the following at the start of the call:

- the identity of the seller
- that the purpose of the call is to sell goods or services
- the nature of the goods or services being sold
- the total cost
- all material conditions, limitations and restrictions
- whether or not a refund, exchange or cancellation is allowed
- an explanation of the refund policy if any representation about it is made as part of the sale, and
- if the offer is a prize, that no purchase is necessary, the odds of winning (or the factors used in calculating the odds) and a toll-free phone number you can call to obtain entry information.[2]

Furthermore, telemarketers cannot call before 8 a.m. or after 9 p.m. and must not call someone who has said not to call again.

These rules do not apply to the fast-growing area of online sales, so use extra caution when responding to online sales pitches. Online services are covered by the general antifraud provisions of the Federal Trade Act.

You are unable to book the deal through a travel agent. If the travel offer must be bought directly and can't be booked through a travel agent, decline—there is a good chance that something is suspect.

You must call a 900 number. Avoid 900 numbers for travel deals and prizes—most are scams. If you insist on calling a 900 number in response to a travel solicitation, understand the cost of the call and risks ahead of time.

The company cannot provide names of references. Avoid any company that cannot provide the names of references.

The references sound too familiar. Be wary of anyone whose glowing reference sounds verbatim like what the travel provider claims in its materials—you may be talking to a shill.

The company is not a member of a professional travel trade association. Even if the caller says yes, call the association to verify the provider's membership. (See the Appendix for addresses and phone numbers.)

Reputation Alone Won't Necessarily Protect You

Even well-established travel companies are not immune to fraudulent acts perpetrated by individuals within the company, as the following example illustrates.

Example: In 1993, two Value Rent-a-Car vice presidents were indicted on charges of committing fraud against customers between 1984 and 1991. Their offenses included padding gas bills of customers, making false car repair claims and pocketing kick-backs related to the scheme. Whenever rental vehicles were damaged in accidents, the VPs would get two repair bills, one reflecting the actual repair costs paid by Value and the other reflecting an inflated price that was passed on to the customer or insurance carrier. The VPs also scammed customers on gas usage by rigging the company's computer system to add five gallons to the fuel capacity of any vehicle returned with a less-than-full tank, causing the company to tag 47,000 customers with phony charges.

Be sure to check all charges carefully and contest anything that seems fraudulent or out of keeping with prior experiences.

Fly-by-Night Travel Operations

Fly-by-night operations typically spring up quickly, make their deals and then fold just as quickly as they appeared. Protecting yourself from the tempting, but risky, solicitations of fly-by-night travel operations can be tricky, since there is little state (and no federal) regulation of these companies. These businesses are some of the main culprits leading to the billions of dollars lost annually on travel deals.

This section alerts you to common schemes used by fly-by-night companies that deliberately seek to cheat you out of your money, as well as some legitimate companies so poorly run or capitalized that they go out of business quickly, having the same effect as the fly-by-night operators.

 Many of the worst "fly-by-night" scammers are tour operators. Be sure to read Chapter 6 before signing up for a tour or if you are cheated by a tour operator.

Getting Your Money Back

Frequently, travelers who lose their money to travel scams or bankrupt travel suppliers have no way to get their money back. To help bail out these victimized travelers, California has created a $1.2 million restitution fund. The fund is administered by the office of the state Attorney General, and is funded by mandatory fees paid by travel agents and other travel sellers. So far, no other state has a restitution fund, but the idea may be taken up elsewhere.

Student Scams

A number of fly-by-night travel operations pitch specifically to students through telemarketing and other hard-sell tactics, hoping to take advantage of inexperienced travelers on a tight budget who are looking to save money. Many companies establish a relationship with a school or bank to try to gain legitimacy in the eyes of students. For example, a company may send promotional materials to a school to display in its guidance office, and many students misconstrue this as a school's endorsement of the company. Most schools do not have the time to stay well informed of the practices of travel companies that their students use, and even companies with a known track record may change hands and become unreliable.

> **Example:** A Minnesota-based company offered teachers an all-expenses-paid trip for every eight students enrolled in a tour through its Intra-American Student Programs (IASP) division. A teacher at a high school had taken students on IASP tours for the past 25 years and assumed that the company would continue to be reliable. Unbeknownst to the teacher, however, the company was under new management, and the trip she and eight students planned to take to Mexico was canceled. Her students and about 250 others who had paid for trips that did not take place lost about $1,000 each.

Having a teacher on a trip is no guarantee of legitimacy; teachers who become tour leaders usually do not risk their own money because they get a free trip as compensation for their services.

Students should find out whether the company meets the standards set by the Council on Standards for International Educational Travel (CSIET). Tour operators must submit a review signed by an independent certified public accountant and must submit extensive documentation concerning government regulations for student exchanges, promotions and student insurance to qualify under CSIET's standards. An annually updated booklet listing companies that meet the standards, *The Advisory List of International Educational Travel and Exchange Programs,* is available from CSIET. For price information and to place an order, write or call CSIET, 3 Loudoun Street, SE, Leesburg, VA 22075, tel: 703-739-9050.

An organization known as the Student and Youth Travel Association of North America tries to provide some guarantees of reliable student trips. The Association's member tour operators must participate in a consumer-protection program, holding at least $450,000 of client payment in escrow and carrying a minimum of $1 million in liability insurance. The Association publishes a free booklet with tips on planning group trips for students. For more information, write to the Student and Youth Travel Association, 730 I Street, Sacramento, CA 95814, or call 916-443-0519.

Senior Citizen Scams

Senior citizens are a favorite target of telemarketer scams. In part, this is attributed to the fact that many seniors grew up in a world where "your word is your bond," and where it is rude to hang up on someone—even a telemarketer.

Tour companies targeting senior citizens are likely to publicize promotional tours in banks, senior centers and other establishments that may add legitimacy in the eyes of a senior. In most circumstances, however, the bank or other establishment has no legal connection to the travel promotion and will not be liable if such a tour is canceled. Only if the bank or other establishment describes itself as a sponsor or organizer of the tour might it be liable under state travel-seller laws. (See Chapter 6.) There is no national body that sets standards for travel companies catering to seniors, so the best course of action is to check out the operator independently before booking.

Charter Operators

Charter airlines aim to attract customers by offering significantly lower fares than major carriers. Typically, a tour operator enters into a long-term contract with a charter air carrier to form a public charter tour operator or "charter operator." Under the arrangement, the charter airline provides air transportation for consumers who purchase a package tour marketed by the tour operator. Although many charter companies provide legitimate low-cost travel options, their reliability is far from uniform. The collapse over the past few years of charter operators, including Skybus, Republic Air and others, left many consumers in the lurch, and various charter operations still in business pose financial risks for their current customers.

Department of Transportation (DOT) regulations set forth a complicated seven-step system for how charter operators must handle consumer funds, and require charter operators to either post a bond or deposit consumer funds in an escrow account.[3] These regulations were designed to protect travelers from undercapitalized charter operators who take payment, but then cancel flights or go out of business before the flight. Nonetheless, charter operators have found ways to shirk these requirements, such as failing to deposit passenger funds into escrow accounts and diverting funds from the escrow account.

> **Example:** Henry booked the cheapest round-trip flight he could find from Los Angeles to New York on Republic Air. When he arrived at the airport, he discovered there was no flight. When he called Republic Air, he heard a recorded message that Republic Air could no longer be reached at that number. Henry contacted CD Travel, a company that had been making reservations for Republic Air, and found that it had failed to deposit customers' money into the Republic escrow fund as required. Republic Air filed for bankruptcy, and customers such as Henry have yet to receive refunds.

DOT regulations require sellers of charter flights to file a prospectus with the DOT, explaining how their business is organized. To find out whether a low-fare carrier has at least done this, call DOT's Consumer Affairs Office at 202-366-2220, send a fax to 202-366-7907 or write DOT, 400 7th St., SW, Suite 10405, Washington, DC 20590 and ask for the carrier's prospectus number.

Although a charter air carrier may delay or cancel a given flight, if your flight is canceled or delayed, you must register any complaint and seek compensation from the charter operator. (See Chapter 6.)

> **Example:** You purchase a one-week package tour to Hawaii from Sunbunny Tours that includes round-trip air travel on Clunkbucket Airways, a charter airline. When you get to the airport, you find that your flight has been canceled and that Clunkbucket can't seat you on another flight for another 48 hours. Even though the airline caused the problem, you would make your claim (for lost enjoyment, extra expenses incurred or whatever) against Sunbunny Tours, not the airline.

While the charter operator is generally responsible to compensate you for cancellations or delays, it is not responsible for physical injuries and property damage you suffer that are caused by the charter air carrier. If you are injured or your property is damaged, you should bring your complaint directly against the charter airline company.

> **Example:** Your Clunkbucket Airways flight to Hawaii (part of your package from Sunbunny Tours) finally takes off. During the flight, a faulty overhead latch breaks and a suitcase hits your head, causing a concussion. Clunkbucket would be liable to you for damage caused by the injury if Sunbunny Tours has included a disclaimer (charter operators usually do) for injuries caused by third parties.

Timeshares

The Resort Property Owners Association reports that 94% of all timeshare owners never intended to buy in the first place. How do so many people end up with timeshares they don't want? High-pressure sales pitches, cleverly disguised promotions and an unreliable resale market make for a timeshare industry rife with fraud.

The timeshare concept originated in the French Alps and arrived in the U.S. in the early 1970s. While the specific terms of timeshares vary, the idea is simple. For a one-time price plus an annual maintenance fee, you can buy the right to use a given vacation property for a certain amount of time (typically one week) each year. By spreading the cost among many people, timeshares provide access to vacation property that may otherwise be unavailable to rent or prohibitively expensive to buy.

In the mid-1980s, timeshare sales slumped as various developers faced charges of financial mismanagement and fraud. Over the past few years, several large-scale developers declared bankruptcy amid investigations into complaints from timeshare owners. Timeshares are widespread in vacation spots such as Hawaii, California and Florida. While a timeshare has the potential to be a satisfactory arrangement, it often yields a variety of pitfalls and frustrations for the unwary purchaser.

High-Pressure Sales Pitches

A new camera, a half-price parasail ride, a free day's rental car—you name it, and timeshare salespeople have offered it. What is the price of all this bounty? The answer to that question depends on how prepared you are. Many timeshare developers lure tourists to sales presentations by selling tours and activities at highly discounted prices, but provide only vague disclosure of what is required to qualify for the discount deal.

In the usual scenario, the catch for these gifts is that you must first sit through a presentation on a timeshare vacation property. The presentations vary by company and by salesperson, but most include high-pressure sales pitches that drone on for hours and leave visitors desperate to get out. These circumstances can lead to the worst case scenario: agreeing to purchase an unwanted vacation timeshare as a result of a salesperson's pressure tactics and false assurances. Timeshare salespeople frequently go over the advertised time allotted for their presentation and are not responsive if you complain. They sometimes refuse to give the promised gift or discount if you don't buy.

> **Example:** Beverly was offered a half-price helicopter ride around the island of Maui if she would first attend a 90-minute presentation describing an "exclusive offer" deal on a luxury vacation property —no strings attached. After an hour, Beverly asked whether she could buy a timeshare for her mother. The salesperson said she could buy only for herself and her husband, then abruptly ended the presentation and canceled the ride.

A timeshare seller who refuses to provide you with the bonus or discount offered may be guilty of breach of contract, fraud or both. Unfortunately, it is rarely worth your time or energy, especially on vacation, to try to get compensation from the timeshare seller. Such deceptive practices can, and should, be reported to the local consumer protection agency, Better Business Bureau, Visitor Information Bureau and even your hotel manager. Your only compensation may be helping to put a sleazy operator out of business. You are unlikely to be able to force the operation to provide the promised gift without substantial effort on your part.

Certain popular vacation spots have become prime targets of timeshare prospectors. For example, in Lahaina on the Hawaiian island of Maui, the local authorities recently identified 17 of the 19 tourist information booths along the town's populated main street as fronts for timeshare companies. As a result, unwary Lahainan tourists are subjected to a battery of timeshare promoters, disguised as tour and activity companies, that offer leisure-activity enticements at a discount only to lure prospective timeshare buyers into their sales presentations.

One condominium near Lahaina posts a sign reading:

> Be careful of surf undertow—and of booths ostensibly offering good deals on activities. Beware: They are really selling timeshare properties. Ignore them.

Hidden Costs

All timeshare arrangements specify a one-time lump payment plus an annual maintenance fee. What you may not be told is the extent to which the annual maintenance fees will increase over time. One timeshare owner in Hawaii saw her annual maintenance fees climb 76% in six years. Timeshare operators may force owners to pay unexpected "special assessment fees," sometimes as high as $1,000, in addition to the purchase price and maintenance fees. Commonly, these fees are charged to owners when timeshare operators have suffered financial difficulties and need to make up for lost reserves.

Resale Problems

A number of potential financial traps face timeshare owners when they try to sell. The first hurdle is the lack of a strong resale market. One of the most effective sales tactics timeshare operators use is to misrepresent timeshares as investments. Because of the timeshare industry's unsavory reputation and negative image, many buyers are reluctant to buy resold units. Although statistics vary, all studies show that there are many more timeshare owners wanting to sell than there are buyers. One study revealed that 58% of the roughly 1.5 million U.S. timeshare owners want to sell, while only 1.8% of all timeshare owners purchased a resale. The fact that owners often deed their timeshares back to the developer is evidence that timeshares are difficult to resell.

The original price of a timeshare (which averages $10,000 for one week's use each year) may include premiums of as much as 40% to cover sales costs. As a result, resale of a timeshare can be a financial black hole. A typical timeshare broker in Hawaii resells units for only 50%-70% of the original purchase price and tacks on a 20% commission to boot, leaving the reseller with only 40%-60% of the original price. Timeshare brokers can get away with charging high commissions because the typical timeshare

property is far away from the owner's home, leaving the owner at the mercy of a distant and relatively unaccountable broker.

Limited Availability

The actual availability of the timeshare may be very limited. Lodging often must be reserved six months or more in advance, requiring a high degree of flexibility and foresight on the part of vacationers and decreasing the actual worth of the timeshare. Holiday times may fill up years in advance. Further, swaps with other timeshares, a much touted option in many timeshare sales pitches, may be severely restricted by limits on availability.

Regulation of Timeshare Operations

Large numbers of consumer complaints have resulted in some efforts to curtail the deceptive practices of timeshare operations, but most action is at the local level. In Maui, the state has sent undercover sleuths to act as tourists and learn about tactics of timeshare companies. The experiences of these sleuths have substantiated consumer complaints. Although Maui has enacted a series of timeshare sign and disclosure laws, officials have noted widespread violations, such as hiding disclosure notices behind shrubs or desks. Further, enforcement has been weak because timeshare operations are numerous and widespread.

Hawaii is considering ways to strengthen its timeshare laws to better protect buyers. State officials have requested that the state attorney general force promoters to use the word "timeshare" at their activity booths. The legislature has considered bills that would prohibit developers from using tourist-related products to sell timeshares, ban timeshare solicitation in public places, prohibit timeshare developers from misrepresenting timeshares as investments and give buyers up to 30 days to cancel a timeshare contract (they now have seven days in Hawaii). Hawaii is a closely watched test site for increased restrictions on timeshare operator scams.

Getting Out of a Timeshare Deal

What happens if you purchase a timeshare and conclude that you made a mistake? If you realize this soon enough after your purchase, you may be able to rescind the purchase contract and demand a full refund. Nearly 30 states have a "cooling off" law which lets you rescind a timeshare contract within a few days after signing. (See chart, below.) If there is no cooling-off period, or if you realize your mistake only after some time has passed, your only recourse may be a formal lawsuit. Timeshare sellers are accustomed to handling claims from unhappy buyers and are unlikely to refund your money unless forced to do so.

Breach of Contract

There are several types of claims that can probably be brought against a slippery time-share seller. The first, breach of contract, involves promises explicitly made and set forth in the sales agreements. If the size, location, condition or some other important fact about the timeshare is materially different from that agreed to in the sales contract, then you may have a basis for claiming breach of the contract. Beware! These contracts are carefully drawn up by the

timeshare sellers' attorneys and are likely to cover almost any contingency—so scrutinize the contract carefully before signing.

Fraud

The other types of claims that can be brought against timeshare sellers relate to the tactics they used and promises they made before you agreed to purchase. These can be covered either under state unfair business practices or as a claim for fraudulent inducement. In both cases, the idea is that the seller used unfair sales tactics or lies to get you to buy the timeshare. In such claims, you have to show:

- what the seller said or did
- why it was misleading
- that you wouldn't have bought if the seller hadn't used the misleading tactics or promises, and
- that you suffered some monetary loss because of the purchase.

Example: When Chip bought his time-share, the seller told him that the annual maintenance fees were $100. In fact, they turned out to be $1,000. Chip would not have bought the timeshare if he had known the fees would be so high. Chip's damages are the $900 more he has to pay each year.

Note that timeshare sales contracts usually include clauses that disclaim any promises made during the sales pitch. The contract you sign will ask you to agree that you are making the purchase only on the basis of the representations in that contract. Prospective purchasers who notice differences between what is in the contract and

State	Number of Days You Have to Cancel Timeshare Contract	Legal Citation
Arkansas	5 days	Code Annotated § 18-14-409
California	3 days	Business & Professions Code § 11024
Connecticut	3 days	General Statutes Annotated § 42-103y
Delaware	5 days	Code Annotated § 6-2824
Florida	10 days	Statutes Annotated § 721.065
Georgia	7 days	Code Annotated § 44-3-174
Hawaii	7 days	Revised Statutes § 514E-8
Illinois	3 days	Annotated Statutes § 765-100/16
Indiana	72 hours	Statutes Annotated § 24-5-9-28
Louisiana	10 days	Revised Statutes Annotated § 9:1131.13
Maine	15 days	Revised Statutes Annotated § 33-592
Maryland	10 days	Annotated Code § 11A-114
Missouri	5 days	Annotated Statutes § 407.620
Montana	3 days	Code Annotated § 37-53-304
Nebraska	3 days	Revised Statutes § 76-1716
Nevada	5 days	Revised Statutes Annotated § 119A.410
New Mexico	7 days	Statutes Annotated § 47-11-5
North Carolina	5 days	General Statutes § 93A-45
Oregon	3 days	Revised Statutes § 94.836
Pennsylvania	5 days	Consolidated Statutes Annotated § 455.609
Rhode Island	3 days	General Laws § 34-41-4.06
South Carolina	4 days	Code of Laws § 27-32-40
Tennessee	10 days (if you made on-site inspection) 15 days (if you did not)	Code Annotated § 66-32-114
Texas	6 days	Property Code § 221.041
Utah	5 days	Code § 57-19-12
Vermont	5 days	Statutes Annotated § 27-607
Virginia	7 days	Code § 55-376
Washington	7 days	Revised Code Annotated § 64.36.150
West Virginia	10 days	Code § 36-9-5
Wisconsin	5 days	Statutes Annotated § 707.41

what was promised by the salesperson are likely to be told that the contract is only "legal jargon." It *isn't*. If a timeshare salesperson is not willing to put a promise in writing, don't go through with the sale. You will be forced to argue afterwards that you relied on that promise, even though you signed a contract that explicitly says you did not rely on any promises.

What Can You Get Back?

If you are the victim of a timeshare scam, you can ask for two things. The first is to rescind the contract. You would get your money back, and the seller would regain title to the timeshare. If the seller (or court) refuses this, you must prove monetary damages, the largest of which is the difference between the amount you paid for the timeshare and its actual value. As you can imagine, it can be quite difficult to determine the actual value of a timeshare, although the amount you could obtain by reselling it is one possible indicator.

Private Investigation

If you enter into a legal dispute with a timeshare seller and the seller is still in business, one of your best techniques may be to use a decoy buyer who can verify and record the sales tactics or false promises made by the seller. Such evidence not only shows a pattern of fraudulent behavior, but also corroborates your version of what transpired before the sale of your timeshare. This technique has been used effectively by some law enforcement agencies to shut down timeshare scams. Be aware, however, that tape recording a conversation without informing the seller may be illegal in some states. To find out if it's illegal in your state, check with your local district attorney or consumer protection office.

How to Avoid Timeshare Scams

First and foremost, beware of all promotional deals in vacation spots, particularly those that offer free or deeply discounted events or prizes. If you suspect that the person is trying to sell you a timeshare, you are probably right. Second, ask questions. When you respond to a promotional piece, ask exactly how much time you will spend viewing promotional information—such as listening to speakers and viewing videos—and how much time you will spend inspecting properties. Do not let up until you have clear answers.

Finally, remember that the deal can wait. Reign in all temptations to purchase on the spot. Take sufficient time to consider any decision to buy a timeshare so that you don't get burned by a (costly) impulse buy.

Fraudulent Vacation Certificates or Coupons

The vacation certificate scam plays on the temptation to get "something for nothing." A national poll found that one in six Americans can't resist the lure of a "free" or "discount" vacation. In this scam, you receive a mailed certificate or coupon offering a deeply discounted vacation. The certificate typically describes a glamorous destination and a long list of vacation benefits, but carries no specific date of travel or service providers. Most phony travel certificates are created in boiler rooms, where scammers do nothing but send out thousands of phony certificates or coupons to a list of leads. (See List of Leads (aka Suckers), below.)

If you call the vacation certificate's hotline to get the details, you'll talk to a telemarketer who has a carefully worded script before her. These telemarketers know what concerns most people have, and are prepared with answers to almost any objection you can raise. Many people, like animals caught in the headlights of a car, can't seem to escape the relentless pitch of these telemarketers. If you don't resist, you'll find either that the certificate is worthless or that the amount you eventually pay for the trip is much greater than what you'd pay for an ordinary package tour through a regular travel agency.

List of Leads (aka Suckers)

If you have been contacted by travel scammers, you may be on a "suckers list." These lists identify people who are likely to be vulnerable to high-pressure sales, especially the elderly and people who have responded to scams before. If you actually send money to a telemarketing scammer, then you are seen as a particularly good prospect for another scam. Travel scammers sell names of good prospects to each other.

For example, if you fall for one travel scam, there is a good chance that you will be approached by timeshare salespeople who buy the names of scam victims from other telemarketers. While the typical travel scam costs the victim less than $1,000, timeshare scams often involve $10,000-$15,000. Beware!

Hidden Charges

In one common scam, you are told you have been selected to receive a highly discounted trip, but are not fully informed of the strings attached. What's the catch? Once you sign up, hidden charges are added step by step so that your "discounted" trip winds up costing the same or more than one you would arrange through a travel agent. Even worse, the conditions described in the advertisement may be grossly misleading.

Example: Ellen received a coupon in the mail advertising a "five-day Bahamas cruise trip" for only $279. When she called the tour promoter, she learned that the "cruise" portion of the trip was a seven-hour boat ride from Florida to the Bahamas (no cabins were provided for the passengers). It still seemed like a good deal to Ellen, and she agreed to buy the tour. Two days later, a courier delivered her vacation packet, for which she paid the $279 and a $20 "delivery fee." The packet contained a slick brochure and video describing the wonders of the sunny Bahamas and the luxury accommodations provided. It also contained a reservation form that Ellen had to return with an additional $179 "reservation fee." Ellen then learned that airfare to Florida was not included, so she had to buy a plane ticket. When she finally arrived in the Bahamas, she found that she had been booked into a horribly run-down hotel with holes in the roof, bars on the windows and piles of garbage scattered on the property. When she complained about the conditions, she was told that she could upgrade to a better hotel for an additional $75 per night. In total, Ellen's $279 vacation ended up costing more than $1,000.

Some companies defend these practices by claiming that they are not cheating any-one—they are only engaged in "creative marketing." Fortunately, most states don't see it this way, and there is an increasing effort by state's attorneys general to put these "creative marketers" behind bars.

Trip to Nowhere

In this scam, there is no intention to provide you with any travel services. It is usually set up by scammers who operate for a short period of time in one place (long enough to cash your check or be paid by your credit card issuer) and then vanish overnight, only to set up a similar scam in another place under another name. Although the specifics of the scams differ, the basic operation is the same, and delay and confusion are the scammers' best tools.

If you send in money in response to the vacation certificate you receive in the mail, you'll be required to fill out a reservation form listing your first-, second- and third-choice dates. The requirements for filling out this form are very complicated (or undisclosed) so that, after a long delay, you receive your form back with an explanation of some technical defect, requiring you to start the process again. Even if the form is filled out perfectly, you'll be told that no reservations are available for the desired date or at the low price advertised on the coupon. By the time you ask for a refund, your check is cashed and the company is gone.

> **Example:** The Federal Trade Commission recently prosecuted a company called Passport Travel. Passport required buyers to fill out extensive reservation request forms. If a buyer chose a date within 60 days of when he filled out the reservation form, the form was rejected; if there were fewer than 30 days between each choice, the form was rejected; if any of the three choices fell into a "blackout period," the form was rejected. None of these restrictions or requirements was ever explained to the consumers before they bought the vouchers. Every time a form

was rejected, the buyer had to start again, giving the scammers at least an additional 60-day delay so they would get paid by the victims' credit card company before the victims had time to dispute the charges.

Spotting Fraudulent Vacation Certificates

How do you spot a fraudulent vacation certificate? This list gives some telltale signs of a bad deal. It is difficult to provide a complete list because the scams change all the time. If you note any of the following on a travel certificate, however, treat the offer with maximum skepticism and send it to the recycling bin.

- An unsolicited vacation offer using words such as "Certificate of Guarantee" and a spread-winged eagle or other prominent symbol designed to convey a sense of legitimacy.
- A variety of possible vacation destinations, with no designated dates or price.
- Exciting descriptions of what you will do, such as "gala cruise," "glittering casino action," "moonlight dancing" or "resort accommodations" with no designated company names.
- A requirement to contact the company within a specified, short period of time, often 72 hours or less via its toll-free "hotline" or "award line."
- A phrase in the fine print indicating that recipients were chosen "using credit

Phony Vacation Certificate Sample

and purchasing criteria to select individuals interested in the many benefits of travel."

- Language identifying your "secret code number" designed to imply that you were specially chosen.
- Fine-print language stating that the receipt of one portion of the offer (for example, the airline tickets) is dependent on purchase of something else (such as hotel accommodations).
- If you call, you are told that you "must act now" or you will lose the opportunity to get the discount price—high-pressure sales tactics almost always are a sign of a travel scam.

First-class postage is no guarantee of a good deal. Many companies use preprinted first-class envelopes to send their certificates. Don't be fooled if the certificate contains a spattering of famous logos from well-reputed travel suppliers apparently endorsing the offer. These logos are easy to obtain and frequently used without the supplier's knowledge. The presence of a respected national travel supplier's logo on a promotion doesn't mean that the supplier even knows about the sales pitch, let alone endorses it.

Fighting Back

If you try to get a refund from the company that issued your travel certificate, you will probably be told that you have to deal with a different company—the one that is handling the travel arrangements. If you can reach this company, you will almost certainly be told that you have to deal with the first company. The first company will repeat its claim that you have to deal with the other

company, and so on. This is not only an effective delaying technique, giving the scammers more time to take your money and skip town, but is often so frustrating that customers just give up.

Many travel certificate scams come from companies based in Florida—check the return address or the company location printed on any travel certificate you receive. A few years ago, the Florida Division of Consumer Services received almost 5,000 consumer complaints about vacation certificates, mentioning 367 different vendors. In response, the Florida legislature is considering a bill which would amend the state's Sellers of Travel law. If it passes, the law would:

- extend from seven to 30 days the period for canceling a certificate contract
- set a maximum of 18 months for a certificate to remain valid
- let you cancel the contract if accommodations or facilities are not available on the dates you request
- require sellers to notify you by phone of the cancellation and refund provisions, and
- require any company that sells vacation certificates from Florida or to Florida consumers to maintain a bond of up to $50,000.

Similar laws called "Travel Promoters" or "Sellers of Travel" laws are under consideration across the country. Unfortunately, most of these laws create extra burdens for legitimate travel agents and tour operators without catching the travel scammers. Nonetheless, if such a law exists in the state where you bought travel services, you may be able to take advantage of the provisions that require a bond to be posted or create a state fund to reimburse travelers who are defrauded by phony travel promoters. Check with the office of the attorney general in the state where you bought your travel services to see if such protections are available.

Phony Contests and Prizes

Several fraudulent mail and telemarketing contests or prizes are similar to fraudulent vacation certificates. Typically, you receive a call or letter saying that you have won a prize. (Some enterprising scam artists even send the phony prize notification by over-night mail to make it seem more legitimate.) You are then required either to make a payment to "cover taxes," "release your prize from escrow" or to cover some other imaginary cost.

Another variation is that you are told you will receive a part of the package free—and then are overcharged for another portion. For example, when you try to redeem a coupon for "free" airline tickets to a destina-tion, you are told that you must purchase hotel accommodations (at an inflated price) through the telemarketing company.

Like certificate scams, prize scams use high-pressure sales techniques forcing you to "claim your prize now or lose it." In the phony prize scam, you are informed by telephone or mail that you are the "lucky winner" of a free vacation package, but you have to call someone (a telemarketer) to get more details or to "claim your prize."

Some people, when told they have won a prize, are confused because they don't remember having entered a contest. If you question them, telemarketers are likely to say, "Sure you did!" They then tell you

information about yourself and ask, "How would I know all this if you hadn't entered the contest?" They know because they purchased the information from other telemarketers.

Hidden Requirements and Purchases

Many scams have hidden costs. For example, you may be told that you have won a free three-night cruise in the Bahamas. What you are not told, but learn quickly, is that you have to stay at a very expensive hotel for two nights before and two nights after this "free" cruise, thus inflating the total cost of the trip to equal or above its market value. Even if you pay the inflated price, you may never get your trip because the scammers never confirm your reservations or never tell you about hard-to-meet hidden or expensive "conditions" of travel. When you learn about them at the last moment, you must either pay more or forfeit the trip and what-ever charges you have already paid.

These "conditions" of travel are often disguised as "processing," "reservation," or "service" charges. You can be sure that the scammers will have a ready explanation for them. You can be equally sure that if you pay once, you'll be targeted to pay again. If you actually take the trip, when you arrive at your destination, you almost invariably find that you are subjected to days of incessant, high-pressure timeshare sales presentations. Some vacation!

Rigged Drawings and False Sweepstakes

In a variation on the prize scam, you are told that you are guaranteed to have won one of several dazzling prizes, such as a car or a home entertainment center, and one travel prize, such as "a trip to a tropical Paradise." The contest is rigged so that you always get the travel prize, which contains the hidden costs or requirements described above.

Another deceptive travel ploy is a sweepstakes sign-up that offers a travel package as the grand prize. Often, these drawings are really a way for telemarketers to develop mailing lists for their travel scams.

In an effort to crack down on telemarketers selling fraudulent vacations and other products, as of January 1, 1996, state attorneys general can get nationwide injunctions against fraudulent telemarketers who sell across state lines, seize the assets of firms engaging in deceptive promotions and put convicted companies into receivership. They can also prosecute people who provide "substantial assistance" to fraudulent telemarketers, such as providing lists of leads.[4]

900 Telephone Numbers

900 telephone numbers, where you pay per minute when you call, have some legitimate uses in travel, particularly when they are run by an office, such as a national tourist board, providing information to consumers. If, however, you are told that you must call a 900 number to get a "special deal" or to claim a "prize," there is a good chance it's a travel scam. In these scams, you lose in two ways. First, the phony "discount" or "prize" is rarely worth the processing fees, service charges and other charges that almost certainly will be imposed. Second, you will have to pay the 900 number charges, which can be substantial, because the telephone operators are trained to keep you on as long as possible to prolong those charges. (A 900 number call lasts an average of five to six minutes and costs an average of $16.)

For a Bad Time, Dial 900

The San Diego Better Business Bureau reports a new scam whereby consumers receive a letter saying they've won a "guaranteed" award of either a new car or cash. They can claim the award by calling a 900 phone number. The consumers aren't told, however, that the odds of winning the car are worse than one in four million and that the cash award is a check for $1. Though we are unaware of this scam being used for travel prizes, tours or cruises are likely targets as the next bait. Beware!

Steering Clear of Phony Travel Prizes and Contests

When anyone tells you that you have won a prize, hold on to your wallet. Any time you are told you have won a prize and are then asked to pay money—forget it! If you did not enter a contest, then you probably haven't won a legitimate prize.

As if being ripped off by a travel scammer isn't enough, a few consumers are victimized twice. Some travel scam companies later call their victims back (using a different company name) to hook them with a phony consumer protection pitch. The telemarketers say to the victims: "We have a list saying that you did business with NoGo Travel. That was a telemarketing scam, but (for a fee) we will help you get your money back or the prize you were promised." Of course, they do nothing other than take the fee. Ironically, publicity over recent crackdowns on travel scams has made this new approach very profitable for the scammers.

Deceptive Pricing and Advertising

If nothing else, the creativity of travel scam artists is remarkable. The panoply of deceptive pricing or advertising tactics used to defraud would-be travelers is staggering. This section describes some of the most common pricing and advertising scams carried out by mail and over the phone, as well as what to look out for when you want to be sure that the deal you are considering is legitimate.

Merchant-Affiliated Travel Scams

A close cousin to fraudulent vacation certificates is the merchant-affiliated travel scam. In these situations, a merchant runs a travel-incentive ad, such as the offer of free airfare with any purchase over a certain price, in order to attract customers. Typically, what you get instead of a free ticket is a voucher for free travel from a third-party travel operation. The merchant pays the travel operation to provide travel vouchers to its customers and then denies any wrongdoing because the situation is out of the merchant's hands. When you try to redeem the vouchers for airline tickets from the travel operation, you run into the obstacles described in the vacation certificate section above: processing fees, time and availability restrictions, response deadlines and hidden costs.

> **Example:** Tad noticed an ad for his favorite furniture store in the newspaper that offered "free airfare for two" with any purchase over $200. With his purchase of a $300 table came a certificate issued by Vacation Vultures of Orlando, Florida. After paying a $15 nonrefundable processing fee and an advanced seven-night minimum hotel fee, Tad and his friend headed off to Daytona Beach, Florida. While there, they noticed that the posted room rates were considerably less than the amount they had paid Vacation Vultures, which pocketed a hefty profit.

When national retailers get involved in travel promotion deals, the resulting fraud can be far-reaching. In 1993, a Michigan judge ordered that more than 32,000 customers of the ABC Warehouse chain be notified that they had been illegally deceived by merchant-affiliated travel scams. Several years ago in California, the attorney general obtained a $100,000 settlement from Mervyn's Department Stores, which runs 266 stores in 17 states, for use of travel-incentive ads that were deemed misleading.

Deceptive Airline Ads

Deceptive airline advertising is so frequent that you may have already learned to read between the lines, scan the fine print and hunt down asterisked references to get the real picture. If you are not so savvy, this section highlights what to watch out for.

Deceptive Two-for-One Offers

A common advertising abuse is to promise two tickets for the price of one, but then restrict the ticket you must buy in order to qualify for the promotion to a class that costs the same, if not more, than two tickets at some other published fare. For example, because Southwest Airlines' "Friends Fly Free" promotion applies only to unrestricted fares (no advance purchase, no Saturday-night stay), it is often cheaper to purchase two tickets at advance-purchase fares than one full-fare ticket plus the free one. Be sure to find out what the airline's lowest individual fare to your destination is before inquiring about a two-for-one offer.

Misleading Discounts

Some airfare promotions advertise drastic price reductions in airfares without specifying the base fare from which the discounts are calculated. The base fare used to calculate the discount is frequently not the airline's lowest presale fare available and may not offer the best deal for that route. Further, for years, airlines have advertised ticket prices at half their true cost. The fine print explains that the fare is "each way, based on round-trip purchase," despite the fact that you cannot buy a one-way ticket at the price shown. While this practice is legal, it has been criticized by consumer groups as deceptive. Don't be fooled by it.

Phantom "Sale" Seats

The classic airline bait-and-switch tactic is to promote low airfares for a given route and then fail to disclose the strict limitations on the availability of seats. Sometimes, airlines fall short in providing sufficient seats to meet demand at the promotional price, and then try to sell you a higher-priced seat. Other times, airlines offer a reasonable number of seats at the promotion fare for the first few days an ad runs, but then retract the seats for the duration of the ad campaign.

Department of Transportation advertising rules require that airlines have a "reasonable" number of sale-fare seats available. This generally means that at least 10% of the seats must be available at the reduced price, although that percentage can be adjusted in certain circumstances. Fortunately, bait and switch is one of the easiest travel scams to avoid—because you can simply refuse to switch. If one airline won't find a seat at the low advertised fare, shop around until you find one that will.

Frequent Flyer Deceptions

Airlines continue to severely limit the number of seats that they allocate to frequent flyers, especially for business and first-class seats. Research by consumer advocates has shown that it is getting harder each year to redeem those miles for the free seats they've earned. (See Chapter 1.)

In addition, by creating two classes of frequent flyer awards—the least costly of which has many restrictions and blackout dates—the airlines are now forcing many passengers to use almost twice as many miles to get a free seat as was required only a few years ago.

Hotels

Hotels, too, can be the source of intentional deceptive practices. When you phone a hotel and ask how much a room costs, often the price you will be quoted is the hotel's "rack rate." The rack rate refers to the hotel's full, no-discount price that very few customers actually pay. Generally, the hotel reservation agent will not tell you this unless you take the initiative. To determine your full range of price options, you need to ask a few questions, such as:

- What is the cheapest room you have available?

- Do you have any special offers available, such as off-season discounts?
- Do you offer any membership discounts (such as AAA, American Bar Association or AARP)?
- Can a I get a lower-price room if I'm in the back of the building, on a lower floor or otherwise in a less desirable location? What if there are fewer beds in the room?
- Do you participate in a half-price program? Many hotels participate in nationwide programs that provide half-price rooms to paying members.

Special Event Scams

A favorite target of tour operators are sports and entertainment fans. For years, scam artists have been exploiting customers by promising tickets to high-demand events as part of a travel package, and then failing to deliver the tickets or requiring fans to pay an additional fee at the last minute in order to receive tickets.

> Example: Don and Deena decided to follow their team from Wisconsin to the Rose Bowl in Pasadena. They bought a travel package promising a sunny southern California vacation and tickets to the game. The night before the big event, a note was slipped under their hotel room door saying there were no tickets for the game.

In an effort to crack down on this form of travel fraud, the Department of Transportation enacted "truth in ticketing" rules.[5] Under these rules, an operator may not accept payment for packages that include air travel to any special event—cultural, sports, social, religious or political—unless the operator has on hand a "substantial" number of tickets to the event. You are entitled to a full refund if the promised tickets are not available. You can also cancel your trip and receive a full refund if the price of a tour increases by more than 10% or if it increases at all within ten days of the scheduled departure.

Fake Travel Agent IDs

Some large (and unscrupulous) travel agencies have been selling kits containing fake IDs that identify purchasers of the kit as "outside agents" of the travel agency. The ads and materials in the kits skillfully avoid outright lies, but imply that buyers can use the ID to get discounts and preferential treatment designed for legitimate travel agents. The packages cost as much as $10,000, but the IDs are often rejected because travel suppliers are catching on and frequently accept only the ID card issued by the International Airlines Travel Agent Network (IATAN). The IATAN card is issued to people who work as travel agents at least 20 hours a week and earn at least $7,000 a year in commissions. While the IATAN ID card is not yet used universally, its use is sufficiently widespread to make the fake IDs easily recognizable by savvy suppliers and, therefore, essentially worthless. (See Chapter 5.)

"No-Price" Restaurant Scams

Travelers in some Eastern Europe countries have reported a new scam designed for foreigners. In restaurants and bars where no prices are listed on a menu, diners have been shocked to be charged almost $400 for an ordinary cafe meal for two or $140 for a bottle of local wine. Be sure to verify prices before you order—particularly in places like Eastern Europe where there is no established tradition of tourism and few laws to protect unwary travelers. In some places, you may be threatened or even injured if you do not pay. Contact the local U.S. Consulate if you become a victim of this or a similar scam while traveling abroad.

Where to Go for Help

Fewer than half of all Americans who feel that they have been cheated by scams actually complain to government agencies. Many people are too embarrassed to admit they were fooled. This attitude plays right into the hands of the travel scammers. Law enforcement officials lament that they often cannot prosecute scammers because victims delay reporting the scam or don't report it at all.

If you are the victim of any kind of travel scam, contact one or more of the appropriate agencies or associations listed in Chapter 13, the section entitled Get Outside Help. Also, send a written demand for a full refund to the scammers and show them that you have written to the law enforcement agencies. Often, the squeaky wheel gets the grease. Sometimes, scammers will pay off people who complain and make reports in order to delay full investigations into their operations. The downside of this approach is that it may alert the scammers that it is time to close this operation and open another one somewhere else.

Report Fraud at Once!!

If you were the victim of a travel scam, contact the National Fraud Information Center. NFIC can help you file a complaint with the appropriate federal agency, give you tips on avoiding becoming a victim again or send you consumer publications. You can reach NFIC as follows: NFIC, 1701 K St., NW, Suite 1200, Washington, DC 20006, 800-876-7060 (voice), 202-835-0767 (fax), 202-347-3189 (electronic bulletin board), 202-737-5084 (TTD), nfic@internet.mci.com (e-mail) or http://www.fraud.org (Web).

Other places to contact or to go for information on fraud include:

- Federal Trade Commission, 6th and Pennsylvania Avenue, NW, Washington, DC 20580, attention: Consumer Protection, 202-326-2222 (voice), 202-326-2050 (fax) or http://www.ftc.gov (Web)—publications include *Telemarketing Travel Fraud, Timeshare Tips* and *Timeshare Resales*

- ASTA Consumer Affairs, 1101 King St., Suite 200, Alexandria, VA 22314, 703-739-2782 (voice), 703-684-8319 (fax) or http://www.asta.org (Web)

- American Association of Retired Persons, Consumer Affairs Section, 601 E St., NW, Washington, DC 20049, 202-434-6030 (voice) or http://www.aarp.org (Web), or

- U.S. Office of Consumer Affairs, 750 17th St., NW, Suite 600, Washington, DC 20006, 800-664-4435—publications include a free handbook with tips on how to avoid scams, as well as the names, addresses, phone numbers and e-mail addresses of state, federal and private consumer affairs contacts.

Endnotes

[1] 16 C.F.R. § 310.

[2] 16 C.F.R. § 310.

[3] 14 C.F.R. §§ 207, 208, 380.

[4] Telemarketing Consumer Fraud and Abuse Prevention Act, 15 U.S.C. §§ 6101-6108.

[5] 14 C.F.R. § 381.

Chapter 8

Travel Insurance
and Travel Assistance

An Introduction to Travel Insurance and Travel Assistance

There are a variety of types of travel insurance, including trip cancellation, trip interruption, emergency evacuation, accidental death and dismemberment and loss or damage to baggage and personal effects. Millions of dollars are wasted each year by travelers who purchase unnecessary travel insurance or travel assistance policies. Although these products may be valuable to some travelers in limited circumstances, you should check the terms and exclusions of any travel insurance or travel assistance policies carefully before purchasing them.

 You may need some kinds of insurance when you travel, such as auto insurance. See Chapter 2.

Buy Only the Insurance You Need

Frequently, several types of insurance are "bundled" together and sold as comprehensive travel insurance. If, after reviewing this chapter and comparison shopping among several travel insurance policies, you decide to buy some type of travel insurance coverage, make sure you purchase only what you need.

Existing Insurance Coverage

The first question to ask yourself when determining what type of travel insurance you need is: "What kind of coverage do I already have?" In particular, consider the following:

- Your homeowner's or renter's insurance policies may provide liability or bag-

gage and personal property protection while you are traveling.
- Your health insurance policy probably provides at least some coverage while you are traveling, but you need to check the specific limitations and exclusions of your policy.
- Your life insurance policy may cover accidental death or injury.
- Your automobile insurance policy may cover you while you are using a rental car.
- Your credit card may offer some protection, including loss damage waiver when you rent a car, or coverage if you want to cancel or change a flight.

Primary Versus Excess Coverage

Many travel insurance policies provide what is known as "excess" or "secondary" coverage. This means that if any other coverage can be applied to the loss first (such as homeowner's insurance if your personal property is stolen), then the travel insurance will provide coverage only for amounts not paid by the primary insurance, such as deductibles. Some travel insurance policies offer primary coverage, which is most useful when your own coverage is insufficient or has a very high deductible. The premiums you pay for primary coverage are generally higher than for excess coverage.

Beware of the Exclusions

The biggest drawback of travel insurance is that most policies contain a number of exclusions—and travelers often don't learn about the exclusions until they try to use the coverage. Whenever you review a travel insurance policy, check the exclusions and definitions carefully to determine how much protection the policy really offers.

Trip Cancellation and Trip Interruption Insurance

Trip cancellation and trip interruption insurance are probably the most important types of travel insurance to consider because they cover losses usually not covered by other insurance you might already have. Although closely related, trip cancellation and trip interruption insurance provide different types of protection:

- **Trip cancellation insurance** covers you *before* you travel and reimburses you for any prepaid, nonrefundable expenses (such as an airline ticket or cruise cabin) that you cannot use because you had to cancel your trip.
- **Trip interruption insurance** covers you *during* your trip and reimburses certain expenses if you are required to change or cut short your trip.

When Does Trip Cancellation Insurance Apply?

Although the exact terms of the policies vary, trip cancellation insurance generally will reimburse you for nonrefundable, prepaid trip expenses when all three of the following things occur:

1. you are forced to cancel your prearranged trip
2. because of an unforeseen accident, illness or other specified event
3. that affects you, a close family member or your traveling companion.

Canceling Your Trip

Trip cancellation insurance applies *before* your departure. Be sure that any trip cancellation insurance you purchase covers you while you are en route from your home to your departure point.

> **Example:** Marge and Ivan planned to drive from their home in Dallas, Texas, to Miami, Florida, to take a five-day cruise. On the way to Miami, they were in a car accident and could not make the cruise. Their trip cancellation policy did not refund the cost of the cruise because their accident did not qualify as "pre-departure" since they had already "departed" from home.

Similarly, some trip cancellation policies expire 48 or 72 hours before the departure time, the period during which many last-minute crises arise. Be certain to find out the exact expiration time and date of any policy you consider buying. If you purchase cancellation insurance, make sure you are covered during the entire period of time before your departure.

Trip Cancellation Penalty Waivers

Cancellation penalty waivers, often sold by cruise lines or tour operators, should be avoided. These waivers are not insurance; they only give you the ability to cancel your trip without the normal cancellation penalties. Generally, cancellation penalty waivers expire two or three days before a trip starts and have a number of exclusions and limitations not properly explained when you buy the waiver. Trip cancellation insurance normally provides more protection for less money than cancellation penalty waivers.

Many trip cancellation policies will not cover you if the tour operator, cruise line or other supplier goes out of business. If you decide to purchase trip cancellation insurance, get the policy with the broadest terms. For example, a policy that covers supplier "failure" or "default" is better than one that covers supplier "bankruptcy," because many suppliers go out of business without formally declaring bankruptcy.

Unforeseeable Events

Most travel insurance policies will cover you only if the accident, illness or other event that caused you to cancel was not *foreseeable*. This is an area where it really pays to do your homework.

Preexisting Condition

Many travel insurance policies are written to exclude most "preexisting conditions." A preexisting condition is generally defined as an illness or injury that existed before you purchased your insurance and that causes you to cancel or interrupt your trip. If you have to cancel because of a preexisting condition, the insurance company will not compensate you for your losses.

> Example: Michael and Priscilla purchased a trip cancellation policy six months before their planned cruise to the Mediterranean. A few days before the trip, Priscilla's asthma, for which she had been treated occasionally throughout her life, suddenly became much worse and she had to be hospitalized. Michael and Priscilla canceled their trip and applied for reimbursement from their travel insurer. The insurer refused to pay because the asthma was a preexisting condition.

Coverage for preexisting conditions differs from policy to policy, and small differences can have a large effect. For example, one policy might exclude coverage for a preexisting:

> injury, sickness or other condition that required medical treatment within 60 days of the departure date.

A more detailed policy might exclude coverage for a preexisting condition:

that within a 90-day period before the trip cancellation coverage began—(a) first manifested itself, worsened, became acute or exhibited symptoms which would have caused one to seek diagnosis, care or treatment; (b) required taking prescribed drugs or medicines, unless the condition for which the drug or medicine was prescribed remains controlled without any change in the required prescription; or (c) required medical treatment or treatment was recommended by a physician.

The first policy is preferable for two reasons. First, it has an exclusion period of 60 days, rather than 90 days. This means that the recurrence of an old illness three months before you leave would not be a preexisting condition under the first policy, but would under the second. Also, the first policy includes only conditions that *required* medical treatment; the second policy includes conditions which, by the insurance company's standards, would have caused you to visit a doctor, even if you didn't feel you needed medical treatment. Don't be caught off guard.

Some policies provide that if your condition was stable and your treatment or prescription did not change within the 60- or 90-day period before you purchased your travel insurance, being under a physician's care and/or taking prescription drugs will not be considered a preexisting condition. If you are under the care of a physician, you should be sure to look for a policy that does not consider an illness that is under control to be a preexisting condition.

Timing Is Everything

Because of consumer complaints and lawsuits, many travel insurance companies will waive their "preexisting condition" exclusions if you purchase your travel insurance within a certain amount of time of making a down payment on a tour or cruise—generally between 24 hours and seven days depending on the terms of the policy. This means that the insurance will cover you if you have to cancel your trip because of a preexisting injury or illness, but only if you purchase your insurance within the allotted time.

This is another reason why you need to shop for travel insurance coverage *before* making your travel arrangements. Otherwise, you may not have enough time to compare policies once you have made your reservations and paid the trip deposit.

Conditions Caused by High-Risk Activity or Elective Procedures

Cancellation policies normally don't cover conditions that arise from activities where personal choice or high risk were involved. For example, many policies won't pay if the accident that forces the cancellation was incurred during skydiving, hang gliding, parachuting, skin diving, scuba diving, competitive sports or contests of speed. Suicide, attempted suicide and intentionally self-inflicted injuries are never covered.

Furthermore, elective, cosmetic or plastic surgery may be excluded, as well as venereal diseases. Common problems such as hernias and dental treatment are often not covered.

Compare lists of exclusions and pick the policy that fits your lifestyle and activities. For example, insurance policy A might exclude mountain climbing, while policy B makes no mention of it. On the other hand, policy B may exclude scuba diving, while policy A does not consider scuba diving a high-risk activity.

Pregnancy

Perhaps one of the oddest and most unfair trip cancellation insurance policy exclusions is that for pregnancy. While one very restrictive policy excludes any coverage relating to "pregnancy, childbirth, miscarriage, elective abortion or any sickness resulting therefrom," a more lenient policy might only exclude "normal pregnancy and childbirth." Given the importance to most people of pregnancy and childbirth, it is somewhat shocking that almost all insurers consider this an illegitimate reason to cancel a trip. Furthermore, because many people plan their trips far in advance, enforcing a pregnancy exclusion can be quite unfair.

> Example: Lisa and Bill decide to celebrate their fifth wedding anniversary with a cruise to Europe. To take advantage of advance purchase discounts, they reserve and pay for their cruise one year before its scheduled departure date, and they purchase trip cancellation insurance a few days later. Six months before the cruise, they learn that Lisa is eight weeks pregnant and will be in no condition to travel at the time of the scheduled cruise.

Under their cancellation policy, they are not entitled to reimbursement for canceling, even for doing so six months before the trip, because pregnancy is not considered a legitimate reason to cancel.

If their policy only excluded pregnancies that began before the policy coverage, Lisa and Bill would be entitled to full reimbursement from the insurance company of the nonrefundable amounts they had paid to the cruise line.

Other Unforeseeable Events

Some policies provide reimbursement if you must cancel because you are hijacked, quarantined, required to serve on a jury or subpoenaed or have your home made uninhabitable by fire or flood. Occasionally, terrorism, political unrest or labor strikes occurring in the place of your travel destination are deemed sufficient reason for cancellation, but in other policies they are specifically excluded.

Read the exclusion clauses of trip cancellation policies carefully. Subtle differences in policy exclusions can be quite important. For example, policy A might contain an exclusion for "treatment arising from alcohol or substance abuse," while policy B may exclude "accidents that occur while you are driving under the influence of alcohol." Under policy A, if you have an accident while driving under the influence, you could probably recover, unless you are also in a treatment program. Checking into an alcohol abuse center might be a valid reason to cancel your trip under policy B, but not under policy A.

Reasons for Canceling Trips

According to a recent travelers' survey, the number one reason for canceling a scheduled trip is personal problems at home or business. Injuries or illness are the second most common reason. Bad weather or political unrest are the next, and the last is the failure of the tour operator, airline or other travel supplier.

Only one of these categories, illness or accident, is covered by most cancellation policies, and fewer than 25% of travelers cancel for that reason. This means that over 75% of travelers who cancel their trips would recover nothing from their trip cancellation policy, because their reasons for canceling are not usually covered by trip cancellation policies. Keep this in mind when deciding the real value of purchasing trip cancellation insurance.

You, Your Family or Travel Companion

The accident, illness or other event that forces cancellation does not have to directly affect the traveler for coverage to apply. Generally, close family members and any companion traveling on the same itinerary can be the reason for the cancellation. Again, the definition of terms is quite important.

Immediate Family Members

Most definitions of an immediate family member include legal or common law spouse, children (including stepchildren), parents, siblings, grandparents, grandchildren, aunts, uncles, nieces, nephews and in-laws (mother-in-law, father-in-law, daughter-in-law, son-in-law, brother-in-law and sister-in-law).

Note that unmarried partners (opposite sex or same sex), roommates, boyfriends, girlfriends and others who might be very significant to the traveler are not included in the definition of immediate family.

> **Example:** Leslie and Chris have lived together for several years. Leslie plans an extended tour to Asia and buys trip cancellation insurance from the tour operator. Chris, who is a homebody, chooses not to go. A week before Leslie's departure, Chris becomes seriously ill and needs to be hospitalized. If Leslie decides to stay home to be with Chris rather than take the tour, the insurance company would almost certainly refuse to reimburse Leslie's prepaid expenses, because Chris does not fall under the policy's definition of an immediate family member.

Some broader definitions of immediate family members add other people, such as guardians or wards. Other policies include business partners within the definition of immediate family members, an important consideration for many people who work in small companies.

Traveling Companion

Some policies limit the definition of traveling companion to one individual who is sharing your room during travel. Other policies are much more liberal and define traveling companion as any number of people with whom you have coordinated travel arrangements and intend to travel during the trip. If you are planning to travel with a group of friends, or plan to travel with different people for different parts of the trip, the broader definition could be quite important to you.

> **Example:** Bob, Ted, Carol and Alice are avid bridge players who never miss a chance to take a cruise together so that they have lots of time to play. They all prefer to stay in separate rooms. If one gets sick and cancels, the others would have no right to reimbursement under a policy that defines a traveling companion as "a person who is booked to share the same accommodations during the trip."

Additional Pre-Departure Coverage

There are two additional types of pre-departure coverage to consider when shopping for travel insurance: occupancy adjustment and pre-departure adjustment coverage.

Occupancy Adjustment

If your prepaid travel arrangements are based on multiple occupancy, and one or more of your travel companions is forced to cancel, occupancy adjustment coverage reimburses you for any additional charges incurred when you change to the next occupancy rate.

> **Example:** Jen and Rob prepay for a cruise on the Nile that offers double occupancy at a rate of $1,000 per person. They purchase occupancy adjustment coverage for the trip. At the last moment, Jen is called away on an emergency, and Rob

is charged a $600 "single supplement" to keep his berth as a single. The insurance company would cover this $600 charge.

Pre-Departure Adjustment

If you must temporarily postpone your initial departure, but wish to continue on your original itinerary, pre-departure adjustment coverage will compensate you for any additional charges needed to rejoin your original itinerary. Some pre-departure adjustment coverage will also compensate you for any unused, nonrefundable fees. Generally, you are required to take the cheapest and most direct route to rejoin your itinerary.

> **Example:** Jack and Sheila book a month-long educational tour through Africa. On the day of their scheduled air flight from San Francisco, they get delayed by a huge traffic jam and miss their flight. The next available flight is three days later. Their pre-departure adjustment policy covers any extra charges they incur for changing flights and even pays for new tickets (at the economy rate) to get them to Africa. In addition, it pays for the cheapest, most direct means of travel to rejoin the tour once they arrive in Africa and reimburses them for the three days of the tour that they missed.

The specific terms of the exclusion provisions are important because if the delay is caused by an event, accident or illness that is excluded from coverage, you will recover nothing and will be forced to pay your own way to meet up with the tour. For example, if Jack and Sheila's policy excluded pre-departure delays caused by acts of God, and they miss their flight because of an earthquake, they might not get any reimbursement.

Trip Interruption Insurance

Trip interruption insurance covers you for injuries, accidents or other events that cause you to change your schedule or itinerary once you have started your trip. Trip interruption insurance is often bundled with trip cancellation insurance, and the elements, limitations and exclusions are usually the same or very similar for the two.

The most basic type of trip interruption insurance covers your additional expenses incurred (such as the fee for changing an airline ticket) if you need to return home for any reason allowed under the coverage. Some policies also reimburse you for any unused prepaid expenses.

If you are delayed in the middle of a trip and wish to meet up with the group later, trip interruption coverage will often pay the cost of economy fare to rejoin your original itinerary. Furthermore, a policy covering travel delay expenses may cover additional living expenses (from $50 to $200 per day) if your travel is delayed.

Example: Betsy, on a tour of Italian villas, is stuck in Florence for three days because of a rare, unannounced train strike. Because unannounced train strikes are covered in her trip interruption policy, she could recover both delay expenses of $100 per day while waiting for the strike to end and compensation for the prepaid hotel nights in Rome that she did not use while she was stuck in Florence.

Emergency Medical Transportation or Evacuation

Many trip interruption policies cover medical evacuation costs if you have a medical emergency during your trip. Initially, the evacuation may consist only of transportation to the nearest adequate medical center. In extreme cases, this may require evacuation by helicopter or private airplane, which can be quite expensive. Insurance coverage for emergency medical evacuation often covers up to $25,000 in expenses. If, after initial treatment, you must be transported home to obtain further medical treatment or to recover, the price of the transportation home is covered.

Doctor's Orders

Many medical evacuation policies require certification by a licensed physician that emergency evacuation was necessary before your evacuation expenses will be reimbursed. Be sure to obtain and save copies of any medical forms or reports related to your treatment and evacuation.

Not all evacuation policies cover the same costs. For example, although most policies will reimburse you for the most direct and economical airfare back to the U.S., some will pay only the difference between the normal airfare and any additional charge that you incur if you must occupy more than one seat on your return flight. In addition, most emergency evacuation policies reimburse transportation costs only;

a few policies cover all necessary transportation, medical services and medical supplies incurred in connection with your emergency evacuation. None of the emergency medical or evacuation policies covers additional medical treatment that you require when you return home. These medical expenses must be covered by special travel accident and illness insurance (discussed below) or by your regular health insurance coverage.

Evacuation coverage can be useful in remote or developing countries where modern medical care is not readily available. Evacuation coverage is almost always bundled with other medical insurance coverage and cannot be purchased separately.

The preexisting condition exclusion can be very important when considering emergency medical or evacuation coverage. If you incur substantial evacuation expenses because of a preexisting injury and the preexisting condition exclusion applies, you could be left with a huge, unexpected debt.

Example: Lois and Kate take a trekking tour of Nepal. At the top of one of the highest peaks, Lois's life-long nasal condition acts up and she must be evacuated by helicopter. If Lois's nasal problem had been treated recently, it could qualify as a preexisting condition, and Lois and Kate would have to pay for the helicopter evacuation out of their own pocket.

Repatriation of Remains

For the real optimist, there is even trip interruption coverage that will cover expenses if you die during your trip. Policies range from the very basic that only cover the actual additional cost of transporting your body home, to the more comprehensive that include expenses for embalming, cremation, coffins and transportation.

How Much Do Trip Cancellation or Trip Interruption Policies Cost?

The prices for trip cancellation and/or trip interruption insurance are normally based on the maximum amount of coverage purchased and may vary depending on the length of the trip. Almost all trip insurance brochures set forth a table which lists coverage amounts and premiums for each type of coverage—normal rates are between 4% to 8% of the coverage amount. For example, if the nonrefundable cost of your trip is $1,000, you can expect to pay between $40 and $80 for $1,000 worth of trip cancellation or interruption insurance.

When comparing different trip cancellation and trip interruption insurance policies, remember that although the premium amounts may not differ very much, the terms and exclusions may vary substantially. Beware of "bargain" insurance that charges a lower premium, but has so many exclusions and limitations that you are unlikely to receive any reimbursement if your trip is canceled or interrupted.

Who Should Purchase Trip Cancellation/Interruption Insurance?

Trip cancellation and interruption insurance should be considered by travelers who are susceptible to illness or who have family members or traveling companions with a higher-than-average chance of becoming ill or injured before or during the trip. Because you pay the same premium no matter when you purchase it, cancellation insurance is a much better deal if you buy it well before the trip begins rather than waiting until just before departure—you get much longer coverage for the same price. Similarly, trip interruption insurance may be a good buy for a long or distant cruise or tour because of the greater chance of interruption and the greater expense involved in stopping the trip and returning home.

Travelers who are risk-averse or who cannot afford to absorb the loss of the entire trip cost should also consider trip cancellation or interruption insurance simply for peace of mind. Remember to check the terms and exclusions before you buy!

Accidents, Disease, Injury and Death

Several types of related travel insurance provide some compensation if you are injured because of an accident or become sick during your trip. Usually, these types of coverage are bundled together, but sometimes accident insurance is separated from sickness insurance and specific reimbursement levels are set for each. Coverage for accidental death, maiming or dismemberment generally offers precise amounts of compensation for death or particular types of injuries.

Travel Accident Insurance

If you are accidentally injured during your trip, travel accident insurance will generally pay up to a preset limit for any medical expenses you incur because of that accident. Generally, it will include the cost of an ambulance, x-rays, medicines and physician and hospital charges.

Such coverage may offer some peace of mind to the accident-prone traveler, but it has a number of important limitations. To begin with, the total amount that you will be repaid under the travel accident insurance is usually small, ranging between $2,000 and $5,000 per trip. If you are seriously injured, the coverage may be quite inadequate. Furthermore, in many cases your own health insurance (or automobile insurance if you are in an auto accident) already covers the expenses more comprehensively than travel accident insurance. If travel accident insurance is bundled with other types of insurance, it doesn't hurt you to have the extra coverage if it is inexpensive; but do not be lulled into a false sense of security about the extent of protection actually offered.

Sickness-Hospitalization Medical Insurance

If you become sick during a trip and must be treated either during or immediately after, some of your costs may be covered by sickness-hospitalization medical insurance. Some policies require that you be hospitalized in order for coverage to apply and only pay a preset amount (from $50 to $100 per day) to help defray your hospitalization costs. Other policies are more comprehensive and cover all types of medical expenses that you incur because of an illness when traveling. Like travel accident insurance, however, most sickness-hospitalization coverage stops at a very low maximum benefit (usually $3,000 to $5,000 total).

Sickness-hospitalization medical insurance presents another instance where you must be cautious of the preexisting condition exclusions. If you become sick during your trip and a preexisting condition exclusion applies, you will not receive any of the benefits offered under the sickness-hospitalization medical coverage.

Who Should Purchase Accident or Sickness-Hospitalization Insurance?

Travelers with limited health insurance coverage, such as students or seniors with Medicare, are the best candidates for accident or sickness-hospitalization insurance. Although the coverage offered by such policies is often limited, it may be better than nothing. Medicare, for example, provides no coverage for medical expenses for seniors traveling outside of the U.S.

Most sickness-hospitalization coverage applies for a set period of time. For example, if you contract a disease during your trip, it must manifest itself during the course of the trip and you must receive medical treatment within 90 days from the onset of the sickness. Otherwise, you won't be covered.

> **Example:** Ian, who had no personal health insurance, contracted a serious illness while traveling in Southeast Asia. His sickness-hospitalization coverage was for $50 per day for a maximum of 30 days. Ian was hospitalized for two months, and his actual hospital costs were $100 per day for a total of $6,000. Because the sickness-hospitalization coverage maximum was only $1,500, Ian had to pay the remaining $4,500 out of his own pocket.

Accidental Death and Dismemberment

Accidental death and dismemberment (AD&D) coverage is a sort of gruesome reverse lottery where if you lose, you win. AD&D coverage normally sets out a maximum coverage amount, and you receive a specified percentage of the maximum coverage depending on the injury you suffer. For example, if the maximum coverage is $50,000 and you die, lose sight in both eyes or lose one hand and one foot, you would receive 100% of the maximum coverage. If, however, you have what the insurer considers a lesser injury, such as loss of only one hand or loss of hearing, then you would receive only a partial payment, such as 50% of the total policy coverage.

AD&D coverage may provide some benefit to those who have no other types of accident, disability or life insurance, but in general, AD&D coverage is simply a way for the insurance company to make money off of a traveler's fear of traveling. Most accidents occur at home, not while traveling, and so any accident insurance you have should probably cover you year-round.

Common Carrier Accident Insurance

Many policies for AD&D coverage only apply to accidents that occur while you are a passenger on a common carrier (such as a bus or plane). AD&D coverage for transportation on a common carrier is probably most useful when you are spending a long time on the carrier, such as on a cruise to Europe, as opposed to when you are spending a very short time on the carrier itself, such as taking a plane to Europe. Once you arrive, you are no longer covered by this type of insurance until you are again a passenger on a common carrier. If, for example, you arrive safely in Rome after a train, plane or boat ride, but are then run over by a car while walking around town, AD&D common carrier insurance would provide no compensation.

Flight Insurance

Flight insurance is the most common type of AD&D coverage sold. It is often sold at airports—usually to nervous travelers who buy it on an impulse. Flight insurance policies often tout large payments of $100,000 to $500,000 to attract customers. Flight insurance generally costs about $3 per trip for $100,000 of coverage—that's about $15 for $500,000 of coverage. For what you get, however, flight insurance is very expensive.

Statistically, insurance companies rarely need to pay out on flight insurance because of the high safety standards of commercial aviation. Other than flight insurance, most AD&D insurance is bundled with other types of travel insurance, so no separate premium is charged for the AD&D coverage. Beware of restrictions of flight insurance policies, particularly regarding flights taken in smaller or private planes.

Baggage Insurance

Lost or delayed baggage is one of the most frequently heard complaints about traveling. To capitalize on the public perception that lost or delayed baggage is a common and serious problem, insurance companies offer various types of baggage protection and personal effects coverage. In general, baggage protection insurance is of limited use if you already have homeowner's or renter's insurance that covers your personal property. Furthermore, if the loss, damage or delay of your luggage is the responsibility of a common carrier (such as an airline), it is normally the carrier's responsibility to provide compensation for the lost luggage.

Chapter 1 contains information on how much compensation you are entitled to receive if your baggage is lost or stolen.

As with most types of insurance, it is very important to examine the limitations and exclusions on any baggage protection insurance. For example, although your insurance may claim to offer $5,000 in lost or stolen baggage protection, it is likely to include a limitation provision such as:

There will also be a combined maximum limit of $500 for the following: jewelry, watches, computers and cameras, including related equipment; or articles made in part or whole of silver, gold, platinum or fur.

With this type of limitation, you could only recover $500 for your lost camera equipment or jewelry, even if these items were worth several thousand dollars. Furthermore, most policies allow the insurer to deduct depreciation on any used items and to pay the lower of the costs of repair or replacement. It is almost certain that if you do lose your luggage, the insurance company will try to repay you substantially less than the full replacement cost to you. Police reports, appraisals and receipts for items lost and items replaced are often necessary in order to receive compensation for lost or stolen items.

The limitations and exclusions included in baggage protection insurance are often quite comprehensive. For example, one policy refuses to make any payments for loss or damage due to:

[W]ear and tear, deterioration, insects, vermin, inherent vice, hostile or warlike action, illegal act, insurrection, rebellion, revolution, any processing or being repaired, nuclear or radioactive contamination, confiscation by order of authorities, contraband, illegal transportation or trade, or property otherwise insured.

The same coverage excludes any compensation for a wide variety of items, including contact lenses, credit cards, documents, professional or business property, securities and tickets. Baggage insurance may seem like a good deal at first glance, but when you read the policies carefully, it often turns out to be very expensive for the limited coverage that it actually provides.

An innovative variation on baggage insurance is baggage delay coverage that reimburses you for necessary purchases of personal effects (up to a maximum of $100) if your checked baggage is delayed or misdirected by a common carrier for more than a certain amount of time (such as 24 hours) after you arrive. Because this coverage usually has a very low maximum payment amount, and because most misdirected luggage arrives within 24 hours, this is another safe bet for insurance companies. When you do make a claim on the policy, you must have a claim check for the delayed baggage and must prove that the items you

purchased were necessary. Toiletries and underwear are normally covered, while expensive clothing probably is not.

You can expect to pay 2%-4% of the declared value of the baggage for one week of baggage insurance. For example, $1,000 worth of baggage insurance will probably cost $20 to $40 for a one-week trip. Most policies offer a slightly reduced rate for longer trips.

Who Should Purchase Baggage Insurance

Baggage insurance is worthwhile in limited situations—for example, when:

- you have no other source of reimbursement for personal property lost or stolen during air travel (such as homeowner's or renter's insurance)
- you are responsible for transporting your baggage (rather than a tour operator or airline), and
- you will be carrying a large number of inexpensive items covered by the insurance (such as clothes) rather than a few expensive items excluded from coverage (such as a camera and jewelry).

Baggage insurance may also give you some peace of mind if you will be traveling in high-crime (theft) areas.

Who Sells Travel Insurance

Never purchase a travel insurance policy just because it is recommended by your travel agent or tour operator. Frequently, the agent or tour operator receives a substantial commission for selling these policies, and the policies may not be the most complete or competitive on the market. Policies designed to be sold as impulse purchases (such as flight insurance sold at airports or cruise insurance sold as part of a cruise package) are likely to provide the least value for your money. Start shopping for your travel insurance early before your book the trip so that you have enough time to make a thorough evaluation of each policy's coverage, exclusions and premium rates.

Buyer Beware

Insurance purchased through a travel agent or tour operator that later goes out of business is frequently void (that is, useless). Travel agents and tour operators currently sell a large amount of travel insurance, and insurers are increasingly offering better policies to travelers who purchase their travel insurance within 24 hours of making a deposit on their tour—meaning that travel agents and tour operators will sell even more travel insurance. Don't be lured into acting quickly. Find out what will happen under the insurance coverage if the travel agent or tour operator goes out of business. If you have any concerns about the agent's or operator's stability, purchase your travel insurance directly from the travel insurer or through an accredited agent.

Travel Assistance Services

Travel assistance or emergency assistance services are not insurance. These services generally provide travelers with information or referrals, but the traveler remains responsible for any costs incurred. The following is a list of typical travel assistance services:

- 24-hour hotlines offering emergency services during your trip, or pretrip information on etiquette, weather, shopping and the like
- emergency cash
- credit card replacement services if your card is lost or stolen
- message center, medical assistance, monitoring or transportation services
- onsite hospital payments
- legal referral assistance
- translation services, and
- prescription drug delivery services

Who Should Purchase Travel Assistance Services

Travel assistance services are most useful if you are traveling in an unfamiliar area where you do not speak the language—and there is no U.S. embassy nearby. They may also be useful to inexperienced travelers who can benefit from the advice of the travel assistance professionals.

Remember that travel assistance will not reimburse you for any costs that you incur; it will only serve as an advisor or go-between.

Example 1: Ricardo is run over by a bicycle while walking through Beijing. His travel assistance service may be able to find an English-speaking doctor in Beijing. It may also be able to provide a guarantee of any immediate hospital costs that he incurs. However, he would be responsible for reimbursing the travel assistance service for any payments made on his behalf. If he were seriously injured, the travel assistance service might arrange for a doctor in the U.S. to monitor his condition by telephone.

Example 2: Bill and Ann lose a backpack containing all of their cash, credit cards and travel documents on a llama trip in Peru. The travel assistance service can provide them with $300 in emergency cash and provide translation services by phone so that they can explain their problem to the local llama tour operator. They would be required to pay back the $300 emergency advance to the travel assistance service and to cover all of their own expenses incurred in having new travel documents prepared or shipped. Most credit card companies would arrange for replacement of lost credit cards free of charge.

If you decide that you want travel assistance services, remember the following:

- Learn the toll-free number for the emergency hotline and write it down in several different places. Bring an original copy of the travel assistance services brochure with you if you are unclear about any details.

- Many gold or premium credit cards will provide assistance for free if you are traveling more than 100 miles away from home. Check the policies.
- Find out (before you travel) what countries are excluded from the travel assistance services. Often the places where you may need the help most, such as where there is political unrest or civil war, are countries where travel assistance services are not offered.

Travel assistance is usually bundled with other types of insurance. If a separate premium is charged, it is usually only $1 or $2 per trip.

If You Have a Dispute With a Travel Insurance Company

Insurance companies make money by maximizing the number of policies they sell and minimizing the amount of money they pay on claims. If you are injured or suffer a loss during a trip and file a claim against a travel insurer, expect a battle. The insurer is likely to require proof (such as written receipts) for any expenses you are asking it to reimburse, or to justify the value of your claim for any lost or damaged items.

In Chapter 13, we set forth a recommended approach for dealing with travel suppliers. That material also applies to travel insurers, but even more diligence may be required to get fair compensation.

You can expect the insurance company to send you many form letters, to deny yours claims or to pressure you to settle for a significantly reduced amount of compensation. Never sign a release or other form offered to you by an insurance claims adjuster unless you are sure that the compensation it offers will compensate you for your losses. If the insurance covers a serious physical injury, you should make sure that any offer covers expenses that might arise in the future. You may want to have a qualified attorney review the offer to make sure that there aren't any loopholes or unpleasant surprises hidden in it.

If you believe the insurance company you are dealing with is acting unethically or illegally, put it in writing and send copies of your letter to the president of the company, the Commissioner of Insurance in the state where you bought the insurance (the office of the Department of Insurance is usually located in the capital city) and the state where the insurance company is headquartered. The company headquarters' address can be found on your copy of the insurance forms or brochure.

For general tips on negotiating with an insurance company, see *How to Win Your Personal Injury Claim,* by Joseph Matthews (Nolo Press).

Chapter 9

Foreign Travel

An Introduction to Foreign Travel

Each year, Americans take over 45 million trips to foreign countries. When you leave the U.S., you also leave the jurisdiction of U.S. law. Although this chapter cannot cover the laws of all foreign countries, it will describe some basic steps you can take before and during travel that will help to keep you out of legal trouble. The section on U.S. consulates describes the type of assistance the consulates can provide to you while you are abroad. (If you plan to travel to a foreign country, you should also read Chapter 10, which discusses your legal rights and responsibilities as you return to the U.S. from a foreign country.)

Information in other chapters of this book can also help if you travel abroad. For example, your rights if you're bumped from your international flight, delayed in your arrival or arrive with damaged luggage are covered in Chapter 1. Similarly, Chapter 2 contains general information on renting a car, which applies no matter where you travel.

Emergency Help for Americans Abroad

American Citizen Services and Crisis Management (ACSCM) is a crucial link between Americans traveling abroad and their friends and family at home. If an American dies, becomes destitute, gets sick, disappears, has an accident or gets arrested, ACSCM (which is a part of the U.S. State Department) can serve as the communication channel to all consular officers abroad. ACSCM receives approximately 12,000 calls a year, mostly from worried relatives who have not heard from a traveler. It also arranges for sending money to destitute Americans and helps make arrangements for returning the remains of Americans who die abroad. In an emergency, a traveler abroad can relay messages through the local U.S. consular officer to ACSCM, which relays the message to the traveler's friends or relatives in the states. Americans at home who need to contact an American traveling abroad can contact ACSCM at 202-647-5225 (Monday through Saturday) or 202-634-3600 (Sundays and holidays). You can write to ACSCM at Main Building #4811, Washington, DC 20520-4811 or send a fax to 202-647-6201. Information cannot be given out about an American traveling abroad unless the traveler has given consent to the U.S. consulate in the country in which the person is traveling.

Before You Travel Abroad

- Allow sufficient time to process all necessary travel documents, including passports, visas and tourist cards.
- Carry photocopies of important documents, in case the originals are lost or stolen, and leave copies of documents and your travel itinerary with family or friends at home.
- Check with the State Department and the Center for Disease Control to learn about potential hazards including outbreaks of civil war, crime against tourists or contagious diseases.
- Make sure your health insurance covers you in foreign countries.
- Inform your credit card company that you will be using your card to make purchases in a foreign country. Many credit card companies have security mechanisms that invalidate a credit card if the card shows "out-of-pattern" buying, such as foreign purchases.
- Find out all foreign entry requirements for the countries you will be visiting, including whether you need to show proof of return ticket, sufficient funds, a hotel reservation or any immunizations or health tests.
- Check with the country's consulate in the U.S. about how much of that country's currency can be imported or exported, or whether you will be required to exchange a certain amount of money.
- Learn about any foreign customs concerning clothing, personal appearance and behavior that may affect your travel plans.

While You Are in a Foreign Country

- Remember that you must respect local laws and customs. Being an American offers no immunity against prosecution in foreign countries.
- Take advantage of services offered by the U.S. Embassy or Consulate, but don't expect them to work miracles. Let them know if you will be traveling in an isolated or high-risk area and when you are planning to return.

Passports and Proof of U.S. Citizenship

If you are going to travel abroad, you should have a passport. Although you can take short trips to neighboring countries, such as Mexico, Canada and some Caribbean islands without a passport, you will need proof of U.S. citizenship when you return to the U.S. A passport is the clearest proof of citizenship and, therefore, is highly recommended for all foreign travel (other acceptable documents are described below). Applications for passports are available from many post offices, courts and travel agencies.

To apply for your first passport, you must appear in person at a U.S. passport agency or a specially designated court or post office authorized to accept passport applications. Children between 13 and 18 must appear in person with a parent or legal guardian. Children under age 13 do not need to appear in person. There are 13 national passport agencies and over 2,500 courts and 900 post offices that accept passport applications. Passport agencies are in Boston, Chicago, Honolulu, Houston, Los Angeles, Miami, New Orleans, New York, Philadelphia, San Francisco, Seattle, Stamford (Connecticut) and Washington, DC. Check the government listings in your telephone book for the exact address or to find a court or post office more conveniently located near you.

All telephone inquiries about passports must be directed to the National Passport Information Center at 900-225-5674. The line is answered 24 hours a day, and the charge is 35¢ per minute when dialed directly. Calls to local passport offices will be referred to the 900 number. Additional information about passports is available at the State Department, Bureau of Consular Affairs' Web page at http://travel.state.gov.

If you were born in the U.S., you will need to bring a certified copy of your birth certificate. If you do not have a birth certificate, you will need a notarized affidavit completed by a blood relative who has personal knowledge of your birth. Also bring as many as possible of the following that contain your full name and date and place of birth:

- baptismal certificate
- hospital birth record
- early census
- school record, and
- family Bible record.

In addition, you need to bring with you two identical 2" x 2" photographs, taken within the previous six months, front view, full face on a light background. You'll also need proof of your identity, such as a valid driver's license, government, military or corporate ID card, current voter's registra-

tion card or certificate of naturalization or citizenship. An adult passport costs $65; a passport for a child under age 18 costs $40. You should apply for your passport several months in advance of your planned departure date or you will have to pay an extra $30 for expedited ten-day service.

Adult passports expire after ten years; passports given out to children under 18 expire after five years. All passports can be renewed by mail if you apply within 12 years of the time that the original passport was issued—that is, you can apply by mail for a renewal up to two years after your passport expires. If you wait longer than that, you have to apply again in person, as if you are applying for the first time. Whenever possible, renew your old passport at least nine months before it expires. Certain countries will not allow you to enter if your passport does not have at least six months of remaining validity. If you return to the U.S. with an expired passport, you may have to pay a $100 fee to the U.S. Immigration and Naturalization Service in order to reenter.

 To reduce the time you have to wait when you apply for your first passport, get a copy of *Passports: Applying for Them the Easy Way* before you apply. You can write to the Superintendent of Documents, U.S. Government Printing Office, Washington, DC 20402, and request U.S. State Department Publication #9915 (enclose a check for 50¢), you can call the U.S. State Department at 202-647-3000 and enter code 1015; or you can read the booklet on the Web at http://travel.state.gov/passport _easy.html. To renew your passport by mail, ask the passport agency, court or post office or your travel agent for form DSP-82, "Application for Passport by Mail."

Make Multiple Copies of Your Passport Photo

If you are having photographs taken for your passport and you plan to travel abroad, it is a good idea to have extra prints made. You often must provide a photograph when you apply for a visa or tourist card for a foreign country.

Other Proof of U.S. Citizenship

You may be able to present documents other than a passport to prove your U.S. citizenship when you travel between the U.S. and Mexico, Canada or some Caribbean islands. Possible acceptable documents include a certified copy of your birth certificate, a certificate of naturalization, a certificate of citizenship or an expired U.S. passport. You will also need some form of identification that has a photo or physical description of you, such as a valid driver's license.

Sometimes, especially when you travel between the U.S. and Canada, you may not be asked for proof of citizenship. If you are asked, and you cannot produce the proof, you may be detained by the U.S. Immigration and Naturalization Service. Again, obtaining a passport is your best bet for hassle-free travel and to avoid unnecessary questions and delay.

If You Are Not a U.S. Citizen

Only U.S. citizens can travel on a U.S. passport. If you hold a green card or are living in the U.S. on a visa or permit, you must travel outside the U.S. on the passport of the country in which you still hold citizenship. Check with the Immigration and Naturalization Service (INS) before traveling outside the U.S. to see what you need to avoid difficulties getting back into the U.S. Also, if the country to which you are traveling imposes requirements or restrictions on entry, you will have to adhere to the requirements or restrictions for nationals of the country in which you hold citizenship, not the U.S.

Protect Your Passport

Your passport is the most valuable document you will carry abroad. Guard it carefully and do not lend it to anyone. Photocopy the data page and keep it separate from the passport. Also leave your passport number, date and place of issuance with a relative or friend in the U.S.

When traveling abroad, you may be required to leave your passport at the hotel reception desk overnight so it may be checked by local police. If your passport is not returned the following day, report it to the local police and the nearest U.S. embassy or consulate. If your passport is lost or stolen in the U.S., report the loss or theft immediately to Passport Services, 1425 K Street, NW, Department of State, Washington, DC 20524, 202-647-5366 (voice), 202-647-0341 (fax), http://travel.state.gov (Web) or to the nearest passport agency. If your passport is lost or stolen abroad, report it to the local police and the nearest U.S. embassy or consulate.

Entry Requirements of Foreign Countries

Visas

Many countries require you to obtain a visa before entering. The visa, usually a stamp or sticker placed directly onto a page in your passport, indicates that you have permission from the government of that foreign country to enter the country. Normally, the government issues a visa for a certain period of time (such as 30 days) or for a specific purpose (such as to conduct business), and charges a fee for it. Visa fees vary depending on the country, type of travel and length of stay. Many popular destinations, such as Canada, Mexico, Western Europe and the Caribbean, do not require visas for tourist or business stays up to 30 days.

Generally, visas can be obtained by mail from the foreign government's consulate in the U.S.; in some cases you may be required to appear in person. Call the consulate to find out how far in advance you need to apply.

 Do not plan on making visa arrangements when you arrive in the foreign country. It is your responsibility to learn about visas and other foreign entry requirements before you travel. In some countries, if you arrive without a necessary visa, you will be deported immediately on the next airplane back to the U.S. This could ruin your travel plans and be quite expensive if you need to change your return ticket or buy a new one.

If You Can't Obtain a Visa in the U.S.

In some cases, visas to certain foreign countries (such as Cuba or Libya) cannot be obtained in the U.S. If you want to travel to one of these countries, you will probably have to obtain your visa in a nearby country (such as Mexico for travel to Cuba). Be aware that such arrangements are often problematic and subject to delays and extra costs.

Tourist Cards

Like a visa, a tourist card is a document obtained from a foreign government showing that you have permission to enter the country. Tourist cards are often less expensive and easier to get than visas and can frequently be obtained a short time before entering the country. A tourist card is not a substitute for a visa, so be sure you understand exactly what documentation the country requires. Airlines flying to the country, and sometimes travel agents, may be authorized to issue tourist cards. You will usually have to pay a fee to obtain a tourist card, and you may need to present one or more passport-style photos.

Other Foreign Entry Requirements

Even if you obtain a valid visa or tourist card, this is not a guarantee that you will be allowed to enter the country. The county to which you travel may have other entry requirements, and customs and immigration officials often have the right to deport you if you do not comply with all requirements, such as:

- proof of your onward or return transportation—for example, a round-trip air ticket or a ticket on to another country
- proof of sufficient funds so that you will not need to work in the country
- proof of a hotel reservation or other place to stay
- health certificates, or proof of immunizations or certain health tests (see below), or
- if you are traveling on business, a letter from your company explaining the purpose of your trip and acknowledging responsibility for your acts.

In addition, some countries require that you change a certain amount of U.S. currency into the foreign currency either before arriving or immediately when you get there. For example, Myanmar requires that tourists change a minimum of $300 into local currency upon arrival.

In certain countries, men with long hair or women wearing clothes that are deemed to be inappropriate (such as pants or clothing that does not cover shoulders, arms and legs) may be refused admittance to the country. It doesn't matter whether you think the foreign government's entry requirements are fair or reasonable; if you do not adhere to them, you may not be allowed to enter the country.

Obtaining Information on Entry Requirements

To obtain specific information by telephone on the entry requirements of a particular country that you plan to visit, contact the embassy or consulate of that country directly. Most countries have embassies in Washington, DC and consulates in New York City. Many countries have consulates in west coast cities, such as San Francisco or Los Angeles, as well.

 Visa and other foreign entry requirements sometimes change, so do not rely on old information. To obtain current information, get a copy of *Foreign Entry Requirements,* which summarizes the requirements for most foreign countries. Write to the Superintendent of Documents, U.S. Government Printing Office, Washington, DC 20402 and request U.S. State Department Publication #9835 (enclose a check for 50¢ to cover postage), call the U.S. State Department at 202-647-3000 and enter code 1007 or read this booklet on the Web at http://travel.state.gov/foreignentryreqs.html.

Information on entry requirements is also available country by country from the U.S. State Department, in documents called Consular Information Sheets. These sheets cover many topics—not just entry requirements—as discussed in more detail just below.

Travel agents can generally provide you with information on visa and foreign entry requirements, but they have no legal obligation to do so. International air carriers have clauses in their tickets specifically stating that they have no obligation to provide you with information about visa and foreign entry requirements. Unless you are certain about the entry requirements, it is well worthwhile to get this information by calling the country's consulate in the U.S.

Travel Advisories and Prohibitions

Consular Information Sheets

The U.S. State Department's Consular Information Sheets are available for every country in the world. They explain foreign entry requirements as well as other topics, including:

- currency regulations
- health conditions
- political disturbances
- reports of criminal activity
- cultural norms, and
- U.S. embassy and/or consulate locations.

Travel Warnings

The U.S. State Department issues a Travel Warning about a country if it believes that Americans traveling in that country run the risk of physical danger, unexpected arrest, serious health or crime hazards and other problems. (Consular Information Sheets, described just above, also include information on health conditions and political disturbances.)

Travel Warnings normally are not issued for isolated incidents of violence. They are issued when there is a trend or a pattern of violence or other danger. Wars, outbreak of serious disease, natural disasters and political uprisings are the most common types of events that trigger a Travel Warning. A Travel Warning stays in effect until the U.S. State Department determines that circumstances have changed sufficiently to eliminate or significantly reduce the danger to Americans traveling in that country. Often, a danger which is not severe enough to warrant a

Travel Warning may be included in the Consular Information Sheet.

 Consular Information Sheets and Travel Warnings are available from American Citizen Services for any country. To hear a recording of that information or to access it by modem, through certain computer networks and over the computerized reservation systems used by travel agents, call 202-647-5225. To request that the information be faxed to you, call 202-647-3000. To ask that the information be mailed to you, send a self-addressed stamped envelope and a list of countries for which you want information to: American Citizen Services, Bureau of Consular Affairs, Room 4811 N.S., U.S. State Department, Washington, DC 20520-4818. If you're making your request over the phone or by computer, you will need to specify a code for each country which you are interested in. The list of codes is at the end of this chapter. You can also find Consular Information Sheets on the Web at http://travel.state.gov./travel_warnings.html.

Travel Bans and Limitations

Travel to certain countries is illegal or severely limited for U.S. citizens. (Remember, non-U.S. citizens travel on the passport of the country of which they are still citizens.) For example, under the Trading With the Enemy Act, only journalists, researchers and people with close relatives are allowed to travel to and spend any U.S. dollars in Cuba. Travelers returning from Cuba who have not obtained the required licenses from the Treasury Department are subject to detention and confiscation of all purchases made in Cuba. As of the summer of 1998, the U.S. restricted travel of its citizens to Cuba, Iraq and Lebanon. In addition, the U.S. does not maintain diplomatic relationships with Afghanistan, Iran, Libya and North Korea. If you want to travel to such a country, you may be required to obtain your travel visa through the embassy of a third country—such as the embassy of Pakistan for travel to Iran.

Traveling to countries with which the U.S. does not maintain diplomatic relations is strongly discouraged by the U.S. government. In many cases, your U.S. passport is not valid for travel to such countries unless you receive authorization from the U.S. State Department and the U.S. Treasury Department. For more information on restrictions on travel to an individual country, review the foreign entry requirements for that country. (See above for suggestions on obtaining that information.)

If you choose to travel to a country that does not maintain diplomatic relations with the U.S., there is very little help that the U.S. government can give you if you run into legal or other difficulties. All communication would have to be passed through a third party, such as the embassy of a neutral country. In addition, if you travel to a country that is subject to a travel embargo, you may risk arrest, fines or other penalties imposed by the U.S. government. The most severe penalties are likely to be reserved for individuals and companies that conduct business in violation of an embargo, but individual tourists are not exempt from these restrictions.

Think Before You Shoot

Some countries have photography restrictions and may be particularly sensitive about foreigners photographing police and military installations and personnel; industrial structures including harbor, rail and airport facilities; border areas; and scenes of civil disorder or other public disturbance. Taking such photographs may result in your detention, the confiscation of your camera and films and the imposition of fines. Check with the country's U.S. consulate before you go for information on photography restrictions.

Prohibited Materials

Each country has its own definition of what is contraband (prohibited) material that you may not bring into the country. Certain items, such as fruit or animal products, are likely to be confiscated and destroyed. Pets are subject to quarantine in many countries. Bringing certain other contraband goods with you, such as weapons or material that could be interpreted as pornography or as politically sensitive, can have more serious consequences, including a jail term. Do your research on each foreign country ahead of time by contacting that country's consulate in the U.S.

Health Concerns

Immunizations and Health Certificates

To enter some countries, you must prove that you have been immunized against certain diseases, such as yellow fever and cholera. You may be required to furnish proof of the vaccination by carrying an international certificate of vaccination, such as the one approved by the World Health Organization. These vaccination booklets can be obtained from your doctor or from the U.S. government.

If you are planning an extended trip to a foreign country, you may be required to be tested for other diseases. In particular, a number of countries now require visitors to undergo testing for HIV if they are staying more than a short time.

Be sure to investigate health conditions in foreign countries *before* you travel. Just because a certain vaccination is not required to enter the country does not mean that you won't need it. Be sure to check the health conditions for the part of the country you will be visiting.

 Immunization and health information is available 24 hours a day on the Internet or by automated fax system from the Centers for Disease Control in Atlanta by visiting the CDC's Website at http://www. cdc.gov or calling 404-332-4565. Faxed information on specific diseases is available by calling 888-232-3299.

In addition, you can request Health Information for International Travel or International Certificates of Vaccination, which contain information on immunization requirements and other health recommendations. Write to the Superintendent of Documents, U.S. Government Printing Office, Washington, DC 20402 (enclose a check for $6 for the first publication; enclose a check for $2 and request Booklet PHS-731 for the second document). Finally, you can call a doctor directly and ask. The International Association for Medical Assistance to Travelers provides a free directory of 850 English-speaking doctors in more than 400 international cities; call 716-754-4883.

Medical Expenses and Health Insurance

Medical expenses incurred abroad are not covered by all U.S. health insurance policies, so be sure to check your own policy before you travel. If your policy does not cover foreign treatment, ask your insurance company about a rider or consider purchasing short-term health insurance as a part of a travel insurance package. (See Chapter 8.) Even if your insurer does cover foreign medical treatment, you may have difficulty getting reimbursed if you do not carry your policy card and the proper insurance claim forms with you.

Medically Needed Drugs

Prescription Drugs

Many countries have strict requirements concerning importing and using drugs, even those issued with a legitimate prescription. If you are taking medications with you when you travel, make sure that you carry all medicines in their original, labeled containers. Certain medicines, such as pain killers or sleeping pills, may be considered illegal drugs in some countries. If you are taking such medications, make sure that you check these details with the country's consulate before you enter the country. The U.S. State Department suggests that in addition to your prescription, carry a note from you doctor explaining your need for the prescription medications.

Be sure to bring any and all prescription drugs you might need while you travel, because certain drugs may be impossible to get or very expensive outside the U.S.

Nonprescription Drugs

Nonprescription drugs, such as cold remedies or over-the-counter sleeping pills, can also get you into trouble. Although they are probably not illegal, a foreign customs officer may be suspicious if they are similar to illegal drugs. To minimize misunderstandings, leave nonprescription drugs in their original packaging.

Traveling in a Foreign Country

Foreign Laws Apply

While traveling abroad, you should not fall prey to the common misconception that being a U.S. citizen gives you some sort of special rights. In a foreign country, you are bound by that country's laws. Ignorance of the law is no excuse. Certain freedoms you take for granted, such as the right to free speech or assembly, may be prohibited and may even land you in jail. Although a comprehensive list of foreign laws is impossible, the following sections provide some tips to consider when traveling abroad.

 Check a guide for the country to which you are traveling. Many publishers, including Lonely Planet, Moon Publications and Insight Guides, have guides that can help you avoid problems in foreign countries.

Identification

In many countries, you are required at all times to carry photo identification that includes your name and address. Your passport is your best bet. A driver's license, credit card or other identification may be insufficient. If you are afraid of losing your passport or having it stolen, some veteran travelers recommend leaving it in your hotel's safe and carrying a photocopy with you. Be aware, however, that a photocopy may not be enough if your identity is challenged. In most countries, the police have the right to stop you on the street (without any probable cause) to ask for your identification. Obviously, such stops are more likely in countries where there is political unrest, high crime or immigration problems, but it can happen almost anywhere—so be prepared.

Drugs

Close to 3,000 Americans are arrested abroad each year. Approximately one-third of those arrested are held on drug charges, many of them for possession of small amounts of marijuana or cocaine. Penalties for a drug conviction in some countries may seem extreme by U.S. standards. Penalties of over ten years of prison time are not unheard of, and you can be forced to do hard labor during much of that time. In addition, some countries have imposed the death penalty for foreigners judged to be trafficking in drugs. In a foreign country, you are subject to foreign drug laws, *not* U.S. drug laws.

Offensive Literature

Books, magazines and even your personal papers may be examined when you enter, leave and travel in foreign countries. In politically or religiously conservative countries, possession of literature that is deemed pornographic or seditious (criticizing the foreign government) could land you in jail. Government documents of any kind are suspect, so be very careful that the literature you carry could not be considered a security risk by the foreign government. Leaving the country with letters, pamphlets or other literature written by local political dissidents may get you detained by the border control. In general, remember that freedom of speech and freedom of the press are not international rights, and that you are subject to the laws of the country that you visit, no matter how much you might disagree with those laws.

Clothing, Personal Appearance and Behavior

A number of foreign countries have laws concerning clothing, personal appearance and behavior that most Americans would consider an unlawful intrusion into their personal lives. For example, Malawi has strict dress codes: "Women must wear dresses that cover their shoulders, arms and knees, and may not wear slacks except in specifically designated areas. Men with long hair cannot enter the country."[1] In Myanmar, government officials have been known to prohibit foreigners from traveling with back-packs; chewing gum is not allowed in public in Singapore.

Although these laws might seem absurd, they are the laws for everyone who lives in or visits these countries, including American citizens. A case involving Singapore's laws against graffiti and vandalism graphically demonstrates this point. Despite protests from U.S. government officials, a young American citizen was beaten with a cane, which might be considered cruel and unusual punishment in the U.S.

Currency Controls

If you are planning on bringing large amounts of cash into or out of a country, be sure that you check with the country's consulate about local currency controls. Many countries have strict limits as to how much local currency can be imported or exported. When you change money as a tourist in some countries, you are obliged to accept a special type of currency, or "tourist scrip." Often, the effect of such scrip is to force foreigners to pay substantially more for their purchases than the local citizens pay.

Although there is no restriction on taking currency out of the U.S., you must obtain and fill out U.S. Customs Form 4790 if you plan to export more than $10,000 in cash or negotiable instruments (such as stocks and bonds). This form is available at all Customs offices, and if you don't complete it, you could be criminally prosecuted.

Changing Money

Changing money in a foreign country can often be an adventure. In most countries, you are supposed to change money only at certain banks, government change offices or other officially approved locations. Many times, the official exchange rate and the black market exchange rate that you can obtain on the street are quite different. Changing money on the street in such instances, although quite common, is frequently illegal. If you want to change money at anything other than the official rate, you will need to balance the financial benefits with the potential risks involved.

⚠️ Changing money on the street may leave you short-changed. Illegal money changing can hit you with a double whammy. Not only is it usually illegal, but you may be short-changed, given counterfeit bills or bills taken out of circulation or even robbed by money changers. If this happens, you will get little sympathy if you go to the police to report a crime that occurred while you were breaking the law.

Using Plastic

When you travel abroad, using plastic—a credit card for purchases and ATM card to withdraw foreign currency—will be cheaper than exchanging money before you go or exchanging cash or traveler's checks in the foreign country. This is because your bank— that issues the credit or ATM card—will give you a much better exchange rate than will local money changers or banks.

Credit cards especially make sense when you are purchasing goods and services abroad because you get the best exchange rate without being charged any hidden fees. ATM cards are your best bet for withdrawing foreign cash. Although you'll be charged a fee for using a bank other than your home bank that issued the card, the fee will be

much less than the interest you would pay by taking a cash advance on your credit card.

Making Purchases

There are two times that making purchases in foreign countries can get you into legal trouble:

- when possession of the item is prohibited in the foreign country, or
- when importing the item into the U.S. is prohibited.

The items that foreigners are prohibited from purchasing or possessing within a given country vary, but weapons, alcohol and drugs are almost always suspect. In addition, art and artifacts that might have cultural or religious significance may be considered to be property of the nation as a whole, and attempts to export them viewed as theft. Purchase and possession of gold, silver or other precious metals may also be prohibited. In certain instances, purchasing products made from endangered wildlife may be prohibited, but more commonly, it is your attempt to bring such products back to the U.S. that will get you into trouble.

If you plan to purchase anything other than ordinary consumer items, investigate the potential prohibitions ahead of time. (The laws covering importing items into the U.S. are discussed in Chapter 10. Chapter 10 also includes references to many U.S. government publications which explain limitations on imports.) "Knock-off" copies of items protected by trademark laws, such as designer clothing or accessories, or pirated copies of recordings, software or literature, are the kinds of items which may be confiscated when you reenter the U.S.

Crime Against Tourists

Before traveling to a foreign country, you may want to investigate whether there is a pattern of crime against tourists. The State Department Consular Information Sheets and Travel Warnings, described above, may contain such information if crime is a serious problem.

Often, the most dangerous time of your trip in an unknown country can be when you pick up your baggage at the airport when you are disoriented and vulnerable: stolen luggage, pickpockets or phony cab drivers who rob their passengers are just some of the risks. To protect yourself, make detailed arrangements ahead of time. Learn how to get to the car rental area or the public transit station, or how to identify a legitimate taxi or hotel van.

In some countries, criminals who special- ize in robbing tourists use road blocks on deserted roads, slip drugs into drinks at night clubs, break into hotel rooms or cut straps to take purses. As a foreigner, you may be seen as an easy (and wealthy) target. Your odds of being a crime victim in a foreign country are probably about the same as being victimized in the U.S., so don't let hypothetical crimes deter you from traveling. But be smart; do the same common sense things you would do at home—avoid flashing large amounts of cash or jewelry, don't give your luggage to anyone unless you are sure of them, avoid walking alone in dark or isolated areas and get information from local sources about high-crime areas to avoid and the kinds of crimes that are committed against tourists. If you are the victim of a crime, report it both to the local police and to the U.S. embassy or consulate.

If You Are Arrested

If you are arrested in a foreign country, immediately inform the police that you are an American citizen and request that the local U.S. consulate be informed of your arrest. Repeat this request whenever appropriate, preferably in front of witnesses. The U.S. consular officers cannot get you out of jail, but they can provide a number of services including:

- visiting you
- providing you with a list of local attorneys
- informing your friends and family of your arrest (if you ask them to do so), and
- arranging for transfer of money, food and clothing if you are imprisoned.

When you are arrested in a foreign country, you may not have many of the rights you would have if you were arrested in the U.S. For example, statements you make to the police may be used against you in some cases, even if you were not informed of your rights or did not have an attorney. Therefore, before making any statements or taking any action, it is almost always best to wait until you can make contact with the local U.S. consulate and/or find a local attorney to represent you. Do not expect special treatment because you are an American.

Bribes

Although bribing police, customs officers and other government officials is rarely legal, you should understand that it is customary in some countries. We do not recommend attempting to bribe any foreign official. Nonetheless, be aware that if you get in trouble, certain officials may require personal payment in order to help you. If you are faced with this difficult situation, you may have to rely on a local attorney or other counselor to guide you. This is a very tricky area, and clumsy or improper attempts to use bribes may get you into more trouble than you were in to begin with.

Bail and Pretrial Detainment

Many countries do not allow you to go free on bail before your trial. Furthermore, you may have a lengthy wait before you get a trial date. Being a foreigner may not get you any preferential treatment, but if you feel you are being discriminated against because you are a U.S. citizen, bring this to the attention of the U.S. consulate.

Hearings and Trials

Procedures in foreign countries may be quite different from those used in the U.S. You will probably need to hire an experienced local lawyer in order to protect your rights. Be aware that in many cases, unless you speak the local language, you may not even understand your trial without a translator. Hearings and trials are held in the official language of that country, not in English (unless it is an English-speaking country). Again, your best source of information for locating a translator and/or local attorney is the U.S. consulate.

Jail or Prison

Conditions in foreign jails or prisons may be harsh. In some countries, even minimal facilities, such as toilets and beds, may not be available. In some cases, food and medicine may be limited or you may be expected to pay for them. Yes, there may be a fine line between payment for services and bribery. Again, be extremely careful before you make a payment to a foreign official. In certain instances, you may petition to have your jail time served in America, but this type of arrangement is rare.

Emergency Passports While Abroad

If your passport is lost or stolen while you are traveling in a foreign country, the nearest U.S. consulate or embassy should be able to issue you a new one in a few days; but you will have to pay for the replacement. In a real emergency, if you have no money, and no access to money from friends or family and need the passport to return to the U.S., a consulate or embassy can issue a limited-duration passport for free. This free passport is issued only in very rare situations.

Assistance From U.S. Consulates

There are U.S. consulates in over 140 countries. One primary job of U.S. consular officers is to assist U.S. citizens in that country. The consular officers can help you in an emergency in a number of ways, including:

- replacing a stolen or lost passport
- providing a list of local doctors and other medical information
- helping arrange for transfer of money from the U.S.
- helping relay important messages from and to your family
- visiting you in jail if you are arrested, to protect your interests and ensure that you are not discriminated against
- providing you with a list of local attorneys and informing you generally about local laws
- transferring money and clothing if you are imprisoned
- helping get relief if you are held under inhumane or unhealthy conditions, and
- rendering assistance and arranging evacuation in the event of death, natural disaster or political uprising.

Consular officers can also provide assistance in a number of nonemergencies, such as supplying U.S. tax forms, notarizing documents, issuing passports and reports of birth, assisting in child custody disputes and providing information on absentee voting.

It is important to note what consular officers cannot do. Contrary to what you have seen in the movies, a U.S. consular officer cannot get you out of jail, pay your bail or act as your attorney. Similarly, consulates do not serve as travel agencies, banks, investigators, employment offices or interpreters. They cannot send or receive messages for you unless it is an emergency.

There are two important things you can do to help the consulate help you.

- If you are going to be in an area for an extended period of time or have concerns about your health or safety, register with the nearest U.S. embassy or consulate. Let it know you are there and how to reach you in an emergency.
- Specifically grant permission to the consulate to provide information about your location, welfare and plans to friends, family or others who might be trying to contact you. Under the federal Privacy Act, consular officers are not allowed to provide information about you, your whereabouts, etc. to anyone, including family members, unless they receive your express consent.

 Several government publications spell out just what U.S. consulates abroad do and don't do. You can request one such publication from the Overseas Citizens Services, U.S. State Department, Room 4800, Washington, DC 20520. Another is *U.S. Consuls Help Americans Abroad,* available from CA/PA, Room 5807, Department of State, Washington, DC 20520-4818 (enclose a self-addressed stamped envelope and request publication #9782) or by dialing 202-647-3000 and entering code 1004. These are also available on the Web at http://travel.state.gov/ consuls_help.html.

Additional Resources—Government Publications

 The following U.S. government publications can help you before you travel outside the U.S. They are available by writing the Superintendent of Documents, U.S. Government Printing Office, Washington, DC 20402 (enclose a check for $1 for each publication), calling 202-512-1800 or requesting a fax copy by dialing 202-647-3000 and entering the appropriate code. They are also available on the Web at http://travel.state.gov/travel_pubs.html.

- A Safe Trip Abroad (code 1000)
- Tips for Business Travelers to Nigeria (code 1044)
- Tips for Central and South America (code 1039)
- Tips for Mexico (code 1042)
- Tips for Middle East and North Africa (code 1009)
- Tips for People's Republic of China (code 1010)
- Tips for Travelers to Canada (no code)
- Tips for Travelers to Mexico (no code)
- Tips for Travelers to Russia and the NIS (code 1011)

- Tips for Travelers to South Asia (code 1118)
- Tips for Travelers to Sub-Sahara Africa (code 1002)
- Tips for Travelers to the Caribbean (code 1003)
- Tips for Americans Residing Abroad (code 1008)
- Travel Tips for Older Americans (code 1012)
- Travel Warnings on Drugs Abroad (code 1014)
- Your Trip Abroad (no code)

In addition, you can obtain the pamphlet *Crisis Abroad—What the U.S. State Department Does* by dialing the above number for a fax copy (enter code 1001), by writing CA/PA, Room 5807, Department of State, Washington, DC 20520-4818 (enclose a self-addressed stamped envelope and request publication #9732) or by visiting http://travel.state.gov/travel_pubs.html on the Web.

Consular Information Sheets

You can obtain a fax copy of Consular Information Sheets for foreign countries by dialing 202-647-3000 and entering the appropriate code or by visiting the State Department's Website at http:// travel. state.gov/travel_warnings.html.

Afghanistan	2344	Canada	22622
Albania	2475	Cape Verde	2273
Algeria	2543	Central Africa Republic	2368
Andorra	2636	Chad	2423
Angola	2646	Chile	2445
Antigua & Barbuda	2684	China	2446
Argentina	2743	Colombia	2656
Armenia	2763	Comoros Islands	2666
Australia	28781	Congo	2664
Austria	28782	Conviction of Sheik Omar	
Azerbaijan	2937	Abdel Rahman	2668
Bahamas	2242	Costa Rica	2678
Bahrain	2247	Cote d'Ivoire	2683
Bangladesh	2264	Croatia	2762
Barbados	2272	Cuba	2822
Belarus	2352	Cyprus	2977
Belgium	23541	Czech Republic	2932
Belize	23542	Denmark	3366
Benin	2364	Detention of Musa Abu Marzouk	3383
Bermuda	2376	Djibouti	3542
Bhutan	2488	Dominica	36641
Bolivia	2654	Dominican Republic	36642
Bosnia & Herzegovina	2676	East Jerusalem, West Bank & Gaza	3278
Botswana	2687	Ecuador & Galapagos Islands	3282
Brazil	2729	Egypt	3497
British Virgin Islands	27481	El Salvador	3572
British West Indies	27482	Equatorial Guinea	3782
Brunei	2786	Eritrea	3748
Bulgaria	2854	Estonia	3786
Burkina Faso	2875	Ethiopia	3844
Burundi	28783	Fiji	3454
Cambodia	22621	Finland	3465
Cameroon	2263	France	3726

Consular Information Sheets (continued)

French Polynesia	37361	Lesotho	5376
French West Indies	37362	Liberia	5423
Gabon	4226	Libya	5429
Gambia	4262	Liechtenstein	5432
Georgia	4367	Lithuania	5484
Germany	4376	Luxembourg	5893
Ghana	4426	Macau	6222
Gibraltar	4427	Macedonia	6223
Greece	47331	Madagascar	6232
Greenland	47332	Malawi	62521
Grenada	4736	Malaysia	62522
Guatemala	4828	Maldives	6253
Guinea	48461	Mali	6254
Guinea-Bissau	48462	Malta	6258
Guyana	4892	Marshall Islands	6277
Haiti	4248	Mauritania	62871
Honduras	4663	Mauritius	62872
Hong Kong	4664	Mexico	6394
Hungary	4864	Micronesia	6427
Iceland	4235	Moldova	6653
India	4634	Monaco	6662
Indonesia	4636	Mongolia	6664
Iran	4726	Morocco	6676
Iraq	4727	Mozambique	6692
Ireland	4735	Myanmar	6926
Israel	4772	Namibia	6264
Italy	4825	Nauru	62873
Jamaica	5262	Nepal	6372
Japan	5272	Netherlands	63841
Jordan	5673	Netherlands Antilles	63842
Kazakstan	5292	New Zealand	6399
Kenya	5369	Nicaragua	6422
Kuwait	5892	Niger	64431
Kyrgyzstan	5974	Nigeria	64432
Laos	5267	North Korea	6678
Latvia	5288	Norway	6679
Lebanon	5322	Oman	6626

Consular Information Sheets (continued)

Pakistan	7254	Sudan	7832
Palau	7252	Surinam	7874
Panama	7262	Swaziland	7929
Papua New Guinea	7278	Sweden	7933
Paraguay	7272	Switzerland	7948
Peru	7378	Syria	7974
Philippines	7445	Taiwan	8249
Poland	7652	Tajikstan	8254
Portugal	7678	Tanzania (Zanzibar)	8269
Qatar	7282	Thailand	8424
Romania	76621	Togo	8646
Russia	7877	Tonga	8664
Rwanda	7926	Trinidad & Tobago	8746
Sao Tome & Principe	7268	Tunisia	8864
Saudi Arabia	7283	Turkey	88751
Senegal	7363	Turkmenistan	88752
Serbia & Montenegro	7372	Uganda	8426
Seychelles	7392	Ukraine	8572
Sierra Leone	7437	United Arab Emirates	86481
Singapore	7464	United Kingdom	86482
Slovak Republic	75681	Uruguay	8784
Slovenia	75682	Uzbekistan	8923
Solomon Islands	7656	Vanuatu	8268
Somalia	76622	Venezuela	8363
South Africa	76881	Vietnam	8438
South Korea	76882	Western Samoa	9378
Spain	7724	Yemen	9363
Sri Lanka	7745	Zaire	9247
St. Kitts & Nevis	7854	Zambia	9262
St. Lucia	7858	Zimbabwe	9462
St. Vincent & the Grenadines	7884		

■

Endnote

[1] Bulletin issued by the U.S. State Department, Bureau of Consular Affairs, Foreign Entry Requirements.

Chapter 10

Returning to the United States From Abroad

An Introduction to Returning to the U.S.

When you return to the U.S. from a foreign country, you are subject to a series of laws that are enforced by two U.S. agencies—Immigration and Naturalization Service (regulating the people who enter the U.S.) and Customs Service (regulating the items that enter the U.S.). This chapter discusses the laws generally applicable to returning U.S. residents. It does not explain immigration law for non-U.S. residents or discuss the special rules for U.S. citizens who have resided abroad for many years.

Going Through Immigration

As mentioned, the U.S. Immigration and Naturalization Service monitors the flow of people entering the U.S. For most U.S. residents returning home, going through immigration is a relatively quick and easy process. If you reenter the U.S. by plane, you pass through immigration after deboarding the plane and before gathering your checked baggage, and then you proceed through customs. If you are arriving by land or boat, immigration and customs inspections are sometimes combined.

U.S. citizens have the right to reenter the country without visas or other requirements. U.S. residents who are not citizens may have certain restrictions dictated by the terms of their residency permit. Nonresidents must pass though a more thorough inspection to ensure that they are entering the country legally.

An immigration official will ask to see your passport to check your identity and stamp the passport with the date and location of your reentry into the U.S. The immigration official may ask you some questions to verify your identity and learn about your travels. You may be asked where you traveled, when you were born or when and where your last trip abroad was. While these questions may be tedious, especially if you arrive in the wee hours of the night feeling jet-lagged, make every effort to respond politely and accurately to the questions. It is against the law to make a false statement to an immigration official, and it is likely to delay your processing if the immigration official becomes suspicious.

Going Through Customs

After you clear immigration, you will normally proceed to customs. The U.S. Customs Service has the dual responsibility of keeping contraband (prohibited) items out of the country and making sure that all duties and taxes are paid on imported items. When you return to the U.S., you will be given a Customs Declaration Form on which you must list certain items you are bringing into the country. If you are flying back to the U.S., you will normally be given this form on board the airplane shortly before you land.

Completing the form is your first step in the customs process. In some cases, you may be allowed to make an oral rather than written declaration (see below), but making a written declaration is often useful to jog your own memory and can speed the process along.

As you go through customs, a customs official will interview you, take your oral or written declaration and determine whether further inspection of you and your luggage is necessary. Most inspections are simple and involve a customs officer opening only one or two bags for visual inspection. More complicated inspections can include a detailed search of everything you are carrying and wearing. There are a few limitations on personal searches that are discussed below.

The final step in the inspection process is paying any duties, taxes or fines that you owe. You have very few rights during a customs inspection. Unlike police inspections, customs officers are not required to have probable cause to search you or your possessions. In general, honesty and cooperation are the best policies when dealing with customs officers.

Customs Declaration

You are required to fill out the identification portion of the Customs Declaration Form when you make either an oral or written declaration. You must state the value of all items you *acquired* during your trip that you are bringing back with you. (Items you ship separately are not included in your declaration; see Mailing Packages Home, below.) You must list the value of any articles acquired based on the value of each article in the country where you acquired it. This can be stated either in that country's local currency or in U.S. dollars. The term "acquired" is much broader than "purchased" and, therefore, you must include not only items you bought, but also:

- items given to you—such as gifts you received while you were traveling
- items you are bringing home for other people
- items you intend to sell or use in your business, and
- repairs or alterations made to any items, whether or not you were charged for the repairs or alterations.

Even if the value of an article you purchased abroad was reduced during the trip (for example, an item of clothing you purchased was damaged), you must declare its original value, and the customs officials will make a reduction if appropriate.

Written or Oral Declaration

A written declaration should be a complete inventory of the items you acquired abroad and are bringing into the U.S. with you. If you make a number of purchases or travel for a long period of time, keep a running list of acquired items and the value of each item. You can transfer the information onto the Customs Declaration Form when you reenter the U.S.

If you do not have much to declare, you may be eligible to make an oral declaration, but only if:

- the value of the articles you are bringing with you does not exceed your personal exemption—normally $400 (see below)
- all items are being brought back for your personal use
- you do not have more than one liter of alcohol, 200 cigarettes or 100 cigars
- there is no duty collectable on what you are bringing into this country because all items come within your

personal exemption or are otherwise exempt from duty (see below), and

- you have not used your personal exemption in the last 30 days.

Even if you satisfy all of these conditions, you must still complete a written declaration if requested to do so by a customs officer.

Family Declarations

The head of a family (you decide who that is) may make a joint declaration for all family members who live together in the same household and are returning together to the U.S. A joint declaration allows you to combine all of the family members' personal exemptions. If you are bringing $550 of goods home with you and your spouse only has $150 to declare, making a joint declaration will save you from paying duty on the $150 that exceeds your $400 personal exemption.

Making Your Declaration

It is against the law to make a false statement to a customs official. This includes misstating the value of articles, omitting articles from your declaration or providing false receipts for the value of articles purchased. (You don't have to provide receipts, but many people do as verification.) The penalties for making false statements are described below.

Remember, you must state the value of all articles acquired, even if you believe you owe no duty. If you believe you are entitled to a deduction because of wear and tear on items, or to a higher exemption than the customs officer has allowed, point this out to the officer. If you believe that the customs officer's evaluation is incorrect, ask to speak to a supervisor. You can raise a challenge after the fact with the U.S. Customs Service, but such challenges are difficult to win and require clear documentation to back up your claims.

Customs Inspectors Are Not Easily Fooled

The officers inspect tourist items day after day and know the normal range of prices for items. In addition, lists of current commercial prices of items are available to customs officers. Furthermore, they are aware of tricks, such as phony invoices or bills of sale showing false or understated prices for items. Attempting to hide articles by wearing them or placing them in inaccessible spots in your luggage is not likely to be successful with customs officers, and you risk being treated as a smuggler.

Customs officers have a great deal of discretion as to how individual cases should be handled. If you make an honest mistake, you are likely to get off with only having to pay the normal duty on the items. On the other hand, if a customs officer determines that your declaration is false and that you are attempting to smuggle goods, you may be hit with steep penalties. Your undeclared or misdeclared articles can be seized, you will have to pay penalties and in serious cases, you face criminal prosecution. If in doubt about an article, declare it.

The Customs Inspection

For most returning U.S. travelers, the customs inspection involves little more than opening one or two suitcases in order to show the inspector the contents. Customs officials, however, have broad powers of investigation and can search you and all of your belongings. If customs inspectors believe that you are concealing something in the lining or in a hidden compartment of your luggage—such as drugs or other contraband—they are authorized to dismantle your luggage to the extent necessary to complete their inspection. Remember that customs officials have the dual responsibility of keeping out contraband and making sure you pay all duties and taxes. Therefore, inspectors are allowed to go through your personal effects, including your receipts and any other financial records, to verify that you have declared all purchases and that the declared value of the goods is accurate.

Although it might be quite frustrating to have a customs inspector rummaging through your personal belongings, getting angry or abusive is likely to be counterproductive. It is a federal offense to obstruct a customs investigation. A customs inspector is allowed to detain you as long as is reasonably necessary to complete an inspection, thus, quiet cooperation will get you through the quickest in most cases. If any of your belongings are damaged during the inspection (which is extremely rare), you can file a complaint with the Department of Treasury, but the Department of Treasury is not legally obligated to compensate you for damage.

Delay

What happens if you are so delayed by the customs inspection that you miss a connecting flight? Unfortunately, you have no recourse against the government. On the other hand, if you explain your predicament to the airline, it is likely to allow you to take a later flight without any penalty.

Physical Searches

Although it is rare, customs officials are entitled to do a "pat down" and search of your body. Such a search, however, may not be done without the approval of a supervisor. Furthermore, two customs officers must be present at the search. Finally, customs regulations prohibit you from being searched by someone of the opposite sex.

Penalties

If, during an inspection, a customs official determines that you did not declare items you brought into the U.S. or that you undervalued the declared items, you may have to pay a penalty in addition to the normal duties owed. Penalties can sometimes be several times the value of the item. In addition, in quite serious cases, the items are subject to confiscation and you are subject to arrest. If you are arrested, you are covered by U.S. criminal law and are entitled to certain rights, such as the right to remain silent and the right to have an attorney. Obtaining a criminal lawyer before you make any statement is highly advisable in such situations.

Customs Duties

Customs duties are a form of tax imposed on articles produced outside of the U.S. and imported to the U.S. Customs duties are a major source of revenue for the U.S. government, particularly from commercial importers. Individual travelers must also pay customs duties, but unless you are making very large purchases or importing goods for commercial, rather than personal, use, you will likely pay a fairly small amount. Payment of duty on articles accompanying you is required at the time of your arrival.

Calculating the amount of duty you owe requires several steps. To begin with, you must determine the value of the goods that you acquired and are importing. You are entitled to a basic exemption of $400—this exemption may be increased to $600 or $1,200, depending on where you acquired the items (see list below.) If the value of your goods is less than the value of your exemption, you pay no duty.

The first $1,000 over the exemption is usually subject to a flat duty of 10%. If the value of the goods you acquired abroad exceeds your exemption by more than $1,000, you must pay anywhere from 2% to 40% of the values of the items, depending on how they are classified. If all of this sounds complicated, don't worry. We break it down below, step by step.

This information relates to customs duties on items you bring back with you for your personal use. Duties on any articles you ship separately, as well as gifts and items you purchase for resale, are discussed later.

 You Cannot Import Certain Goods or Items From Certain Countries. Restrictions apply on importing certain types of goods such as fruit, meat or wildlife. Furthermore, you are forbidden to bring back many items from certain countries such as Cuba and Libya. We discuss these important limitations later in this chapter.

Personal Exemption

Most travelers are entitled to a $400 exemption based on the fair retail value of each item in the country in which it was purchased. You are entitled to a $600 or

$1,200 exemption for items brought back from the countries listed below.

Countries Allowed More Than a $400 Personal Exemption

Countries in the Caribbean or Latin America: $600 Exemption

Antigua and Barbuda

Aruba

Bahamas

Barbados

Belize

British Virgin Islands

Costa Rica

Dominica

Dominican Republic

El Salvador

Grenada

Guatemala

Guyana

Haiti

Honduras

Jamaica

Montserrat

Netherlands Antilles

Nicaragua

Panama

Saint Lucia

Saint Vincent and the Grenadines

St. Christopher/Kitts and Nevis

Trinidad and Tobago

U.S. Insular Possessions: $1,200 Exemption

American Samoa

Guam

U.S. Virgin Islands

Families can file a joint declaration, which effectively combines all of the family members' personal exemptions. (Infants and children are entitled to the same personal exemption amount as adults.)

Example: Rick and Mary are returning from their honeymoon in France. During the trip, Rick purchased $600 worth of crafts, while Mary acquired only $100 worth of clothing. Because their combined declaration of $700 is below the $800 they are allowed ($400 per person), they would be charged no duty.

Conditions on Personal Exemption

To claim your personal exemption from customs duties, you must satisfy *all* of the following conditions:

- You must bring the articles back with you personally—you cannot ship them separately.
- You must declare the articles properly to customs.
- The items you bring back must have been acquired during your trip for your personal or household use.
- Your trip abroad must have lasted at least 48 hours, unless you are returning from Mexico or the U.S. Virgin Islands.
- You cannot have used your exemption within the last 30 days.
- The articles cannot be prohibited or restricted (see below).

Limitations on Exemption

Cigars and Cigarettes

You can include no more than 100 cigars or 200 cigarettes (one carton) in your exemption.

These items may also be subject to state or local taxes.

Alcoholic Beverages

You may include up to one liter (33.8 fluid ounces) of alcoholic beverages in your exemption. The exemption is allowed only if you are at least 21 years old, the alcohol is for your own use or is a gift and the state in which you will clear customs permits the importing of alcohol.

Limitations on Importing Alcoholic Beverages

Just like the 1920s, when revenue men chased down moonshiners, the government seems determined to make it difficult to import alcoholic beverages. To begin with, you are restricted to bringing home one liter (1,000 milliliters) of alcohol. Almost all bottles of wine and hard liquor are 750 milliliters. This means that you are entitled to import one-and-one-third bottles under your exemption. (We do not recommend that you drink two-thirds of the second bottle on the trip home.)

Second, the duties on alcoholic beverages vary from a few cents a liter for beer to almost a dollar per proof liter for certain types of brandy. If you want to find out the exact level of duty, contact the Customs Service before you travel. (Phone numbers are at the end of this chapter.) Furthermore, federal excise taxes are added to the customs duties.

These range from approximately 15¢ per liter to more than $3.50 per proof liter for distilled spirits, liquors and cordials. Finally, customs officials will enforce state and local taxes, as well as state prohibitions on alcohol—which may explain why so few people clear customs in Utah.

If you are contemplating trying to side-step these regulations by shipping your alcoholic beverages home, forget it. Mailing any type of alcoholic beverage is prohibited by U.S. postal laws. You can use certain other freight shippers to send alcohol from foreign countries, but the shipment must go through a licensed and bonded customs broker who will charge you all duties and taxes. In the end, it is likely to be much more expensive to ship it yourself than to pay the retail markup at a U.S. liquor store. It's enough to drive you to drink!

Duty-Free Shops Are Not Always a Bargain

Many Americans are disappointed when they return home to learn that they must pay duty on items they purchased at a "duty-free shop." This is due to a misunderstanding of the use of the term "duty-free." Items sold in duty-free shops are free of duty only for the country in which the shop is located. For example, if you purchase French perfume at the duty-free shop at Heathrow Airport in London, you pay no duty or taxes at the duty-free shop. If you had purchased the same perfume at a shop in downtown London, however, you would have to pay duties and taxes. But no matter where you bought the perfume—a duty-free shop at Heathrow or a shop in downtown London—when you return to the U.S., the perfume is subject to regular U.S. customs duties and, therefore, is not duty-free in the U.S.

Items purchased at duty-free shops are intended for export only, and cannot be brought back into the country of purchase without duty. For example, if you purchase a bottle of alcohol at a duty-free shop in the U.S. before you leave, and return to the U.S. with that same bottle, you will have to pay the applicable duty and taxes on it. To ensure that items from duty-free shops are not resold for a profit within the country of purchase, duty-free shops in some countries require passengers to pick up their purchases when boarding their departing aircraft. For example, on your way home from vacation you realize you need a pair of sunglasses. After ringing up your purchase at a duty-free shop at the airport, the cashier hands you two receipts, but not the sunglasses. A representative from the duty-free shop will give you your sunglasses (in exchange for one of the receipts) at the gateway right before you board your plane for home.

Although items purchased at duty-free shops are supposed to be less expensive because they avoid duty and tax, do some research before you purchase. The markup at duty-free shops, particularly at airports, is so high that often the same items can be purchased for less at discount stores within that country.

Articles for Which No Duty Is Charged

Under certain conditions, the U.S. Customs Service charges no duty on specific types of items or items coming from particular countries. This section includes the most common categories of items that may be imported without U.S. duties. To obtain a more complete list, you must contact the U.S. Customs Service. (Phone numbers are at the end of this chapter.)

Your Personal Belongings

Your personal belongings which you purchased in the U.S. are not subject to duty when you bring them back into the U.S. as long as you can prove their origin. Essentially, the government wants you to prove that you owned the items before you left the U.S., took them with you and are simply bringing them back. If you have valuable items with serial numbers, you can register them with the U.S. Customs Service before you go.

Valuable items such as jewelry, whose origin is not easily determinable and which do not have serial numbers, cannot be registered. You can avoid paying duty upon reentry if you bring proof that you owned such items before you left the country (and therefore did not purchase them during your trip). A bill of sale, appraisal or insurance rider that describes the items is often considered sufficient proof of prior ownership. Bring these documents with you on your trip to show to customs officials on reentry into the U.S.

Register Valuable Foreign-Made Objects

If you take valuable foreign-made articles (such as watches, cameras or video recorders), you should register these items with the U.S. Customs Service before you leave the U.S. (The cities with customs offices are listed at the end of this chapter.) As long as these items have a serial number or permanently affixed marking to identify them, they can be registered. You must bring the items, in person, to a customs office before you go and complete a Certificate of Registration, which will be reviewed and certified by a customs official. Keep the Certificate with you when you travel to show to customs officials upon reentry. The Certificate can be used for multiple journeys.

Items From Canada or Mexico

Under the North American Free Trade Agreement (NAFTA), there is no tax on goods brought into the U.S. from Canada that exceed the $400 exemption. For goods from Mexico, the tax for 1998 is 5% on the first $1,000 of goods over the $400 exemption. The tax rate will be reduced 1% each year until it is phased out in 2003.

Items From Developing Countries

Under a U.S. government program known as the Generalized System of Preferences (GSP), many items brought back from developing countries can be imported with no duty. Approximately 3,000 items have been designated as exempt from duty when imported into the U.S. from approximately 130 countries. (Types of items include certain baskets, cameras, chinaware, furniture, games, jewelry, paper, radios, records and tape recorders.) Because the types of items covered and the countries included by the GSP system change frequently (and in fact, Congress may vote not to authorize the program at all), contact the U.S. Customs Service prior to traveling if you want to take advantage of the GSP elimination of duty. (A list of customs offices is at the end of this chapter.) In addition, you can check with the American embassy or consulate in the country you are visiting to verify the GSP status of any article you are considering bringing back to the U.S.

To be eligible for GSP elimination of duty, the item (or the base material of the item) must have been grown, manufactured or produced in a beneficiary country under the GSP. Items produced in non-GSP countries are not exempt, even if imported from a GSP country. For example, if you buy a camera in Indonesia and bring it back to the U.S., you will pay no duty if that camera was manufactured in Indonesia—assuming Indonesia is still a GSP country and cameras can still be imported from Indonesia without a duty. On the other hand, if the camera you purchased in Indonesia was manufactured in Japan, you are not entitled to the GSP exemption, because Japan is a non-GSP country.

No U.S. customs duty is charged on certain types of articles you bring back into the country, regardless of where they were acquired or produced. The following is a list of items that can generally be imported with no duty—like the GSP list of items, this list changes, so check with customs officials to be certain:

- antiques—certified antiques (over 100 years old) are admitted with no duty; you will need to obtain a certificate of antiquity from the seller
- binoculars, opera and field glasses
- books
- drawings done by hand
- paintings done entirely by hand
- postage stamps
- most printed matter
- sound recordings, and
- diamonds and some other precious stones—they may be cut, but they cannot be set.

Mailing Packages Home

All mail originating outside of the U.S. which is delivered within the U.S. is subject to customs examination. The U.S. Postal Service sends all incoming foreign mail packages to a Customs International Mail Branch for examination and assessment of any applicable duty. Packages that customs passes free of duty are returned immediately to the Postal Service for delivery. Packages that require payment of duty have a customs form attached to the outer wrapper indicating the amount of duty owed and a $5 processing fee. The package is then returned to the Postal Service, which assesses an additional postal handling fee for delivery. The recipient of the package must pay the total amount indicated in order to claim the goods.

When you travel, you are permitted to send packages home to yourself duty-free, as long as you receive no more than $200 worth of goods in the same day. You can also send gifts to individuals in the U.S. free of duty as long as the same person does not receive more than $100 in gift shipments in the same day. This gift exemption does not apply to shipments containing alcohol-based perfume or tobacco products, unless the entire shipment has a retail value of less than $5. Further, the U.S. Postal Service prohibits sending alcoholic beverages of any kind through the mail.[1] You cannot send a "gift" parcel to yourself, nor can people traveling together mail home "gifts" to each other, although enforcement of this is next to impossible.

If the value of any package you mail home to yourself exceeds $200, or if the value of any gift item you send back to someone in the U.S exceeds the $100 limit, both the duty owed and a customs processing fee will be collected by the U.S. Postal Service from the recipient of the package.

Whenever you send a gift package to the U.S. from abroad, you must mark the outside of the package with "unsolicited gift" and write your name, the nature of the gifts, the retail value and the name of the recipient. Gifts for several individuals may be consolidated in one package, but they must be wrapped individually and labeled with the name of each recipient. If any single gift within the consolidated package exceeds the $100 value limit, then the duty will be assessed on the entire package.

> Example 1: Ilene mailed from Ireland a holiday package with gifts for three friends living in Berkeley. She marked the outside of the package "unsolicited gifts" and wrote her name as the donor. She then wrote the name of each of her friends followed by the items she was sending that friend and the items' retail value, as follows: George Barker—one hat, $45, Eva Barker—one sweater, $85, Richard Jones—one belt, $35 and one tie, $25. Her friends will pay no duty on their gifts.

> Example 2: Ilene sent a holiday package to the same three friends, with the following gifts: George Barker—one hat, $45, Eva Barker—one sweater, $125, Richard Jones—one belt, $35 and one tie, $25. Because the value of Eva's sweater exceeds the $100 limit, Ilene's friends will have to pay duty on all of the gifts.

Customs has the authority to open and inspect any packages that arrive from outside of the U.S. and to seize the goods and charge the recipient up to two times the rate of duty, if the indicated value of the goods is not accurate.

There are special rules and greater allowances for shipping items from the U.S. Virgin Islands, American Samoa, Guam or a Caribbean Basin country to the U.S. For further details, contact a U.S. Customs International Mail Branch or refer to U.S. customs publication 512.

Disputing the Duty Imposed

If you disagree with the valuation of an item or believe that the duty imposed on any items you imported was incorrect, you may file a protest with the Customs Service.

- **Items you transport.** To protest the valuation or duty imposed on items you bring back with you, contact a customs office (see end of this chapter).

- **Mailed items.** To protest the valuation or duty imposed on items you mailed home, you must send a copy of the form attached to your package (Customs Service Form 3419) to the customs office at the location and address shown on the left side of the form itself. Explain why you believe the valuation or imposition of duty was wrong, and provide a copy of any supporting evidence you have, such as receipts. Your letter will be reviewed by the office that originally inspected the items, and you will be issued a refund, if appropriate.

- **Appeals.** To appeal an unfavorable result, you must file a lawsuit against the Treasury Department. This can be a long, expensive process and is unlikely to be worthwhile unless the customs inspectors have made a gross mistake in their valuation.

Prohibitions and Restrictions on Imports

Remember that the Customs Service has a second function: enforcing prohibitions and restrictions on imports. A general description of the items that are prohibited or restricted can be found in different U.S. customs publications. (See list at the end of this chapter.) This section describes briefly some of the prohibitions and restrictions, but it is not exhaustive. If you have any doubts, check with the Customs Service before you attempt to import any questionable items.

Items Injurious or Detrimental to the General Welfare of the U.S.

A number of items deemed "injurious or detrimental to the general welfare of the U.S." may not be imported. These include narcotics and dangerous drugs, seditious and treasonable materials, hazardous articles such as toxic or poisonous substances, explosives or fireworks. Pirated copies of books, recordings or other copyrighted articles may not be imported, and are subject to seizure and destruction.

Furthermore, items produced in certain countries, or goods that contain components that come from these countries, may not be imported. As of the summer of 1996, the blacklisted countries were Cuba, Iran, Iraq, Libya and North Korea. Exceptions to the prohibition on items from these blacklisted countries are made for certain informational materials such as books, tapes and films.

In general, anyone traveling with a substantial amount of drugs or medicines is likely to raise the suspicions of customs officers. It is against the law to import any narcotics or drugs classified as dangerous, including anabolic steroids. If you have a medical condition that requires treatment with drugs such as tranquilizers, antidepressants or stimulants, and fear a problem returning to the U.S. with them, be sure they are packed in their original containers, and that you carry a quantity that demonstrates that they are for your personal use and have a prescription or written statement from your physician explaining the need for the medicine while traveling.

Drugs not approved by the FDA may not be imported. This includes a number of experimental or unorthodox drugs which may be legal in other countries, but which have not been approved for use in the U.S. Products to combat diseases such as cancer and AIDS often fall into this category, and all such drugs are subject to confiscation when you enter the U.S. Information on drugs which may not be imported into the U.S. is available from the Food and Drug Administration Import Operations Unit, Room 12-8 (HFC-131), 5600 Fishers Lane, Rockville, MD 20857; 301-443-3170 (voice), 301-443-9767 (fax).

Endangered Species

Endangered species of wildlife and any products made from these species may not be imported into the U.S. The prohibition includes:

- most ivory (unless it is more than 100 years old)
- many products made from crocodile and alligator, and
- products made from sea turtles, marine mammals and primates.

Many other products made from wildlife are subject to certain restrictions. (See below and the list of government publications at the end of this chapter.)

If you are considering purchasing products possibly made from an endangered species, but you are not sure, don't do it! Even though the products may be perfectly legal in the country in which you buy them, it may be illegal to import them into the U.S. Equally important, purchasing these products contributes to the destruction of that species by encouraging further hunting or harvesting to meet market demands.

Automobiles

Unless it was specifically designed to be exported to the U.S., a foreign-built car is very difficult to import. An imported car must meet not only EPA emissions standards and Department of Transportation safety, bumper and theft protection standards, but in many cases even more restrictive standards for the state into which it is imported. More information on importing cars is in U.S.

customs and EPA publications. Some states impose their own taxes, such as use taxes and licensing fees. Contact the Department of Motor of Vehicles in your state if you are considering importing an automobile.

Plant and Animal Products

The U.S. Department of Agriculture restricts the type and amount of plant and animal products you can bring into the U.S., and all such products are subject to inspection. The primary purpose of these regulations is to prevent the spreading of animal- and plant-borne diseases, but they also are used to prevent trafficking in endangered or threatened species. If you plan to bring animal or plant products with you when you return, review government publications on the subject (see the list below), or check with the U.S. consul in the country you are visiting. Plant and animal products that you import unintentionally or accidentally (such as shoes that walked among farm animal droppings) are also subject to confiscation or at least inspection.

Because the regulations have been set up by a number of different government agencies, the requirements may seem complicated and even contradictory, but you must satisfy all of the requirements in order to import plant or animal products.

Pets and Quarantine

All animals imported into the U.S. are subject to inspection and, in some cases, quarantine. Before importing any animal into the U.S., even a personal pet you brought out of the country and are bringing back, be sure you review the restrictions for that type of animal carefully. The best resource is U.S. customs publication 509. (See references above.) (For more information on pets and traveling see Chapter 11.)

 Be Aware of Strict Customs Restrictions on Animals. Be aware of strict restrictions on animals. Customs officials are required to either reexport or destroy animals that do not qualify for importation under U.S. law. If an animal must be held in quarantine during the time that a determination of the animal's status is made, you will have to pay kennel and other fees. Don't place your pet at risk. Make sure that you have complied with all vaccination and other requirements before importing a pet.

Other Restricted Articles

Other restricted articles include textiles, trademarked articles and certain cultural property, such as pre-Columbian art. In most cases, you must obtain specific export certificates or permission from the applicable U.S. government agencies before importing the product.

 Several government publications give you information on import restrictions:

- The Department of the Treasury, U.S. Customs Service, P.O. Box 7407, Washington, DC 20044 or on the Web at http://www.customs.ustreas. gov/travel/pubs.htm publishes:
    - *Know Before You Go: Customs Hints for Returning U.S. Residents* (Publication 512)
    - *United States Import Requirements* (Publication 517)
    - *GSP and the Traveler* (Publication 515)
    - *Pets and Wildlife* (Publication 509)
    - *U.S. Customs: Importing a Car* (Publication 520)
- *North American Free Trade Agreement (NAFTA): A Guide to Customs Procedures,* Superintendent of Documents, Government Printing Office, 732 N. Capitol St., Washington, DC 20402, 202-512-2034 (voice), 202-512-1347 (fax) or visit the GPO's Website at http://www.gpo.gov.
- *Buying a Car Overseas? Beware!* from Publications Information Center, PM-211B, 401 M Street, SW, Washington, DC 20460; 202-260-7751
- *Buyer Beware!* Publications Unit, U.S. Fish and Wildlife Service, Department of the Interior, Washington, DC 20240; 703-358-1711 (voice) or 703-358-2314 (fax). (Additional information on importing wildlife and wildlife products can be obtained through TRAFFIC USA, World Wildlife Fund, 1250 24th Street, NW, Washington, DC 20037.)

- *Travelers Tips on Bringing Food, Plant and Animal Products into the United States,* U.S. Department of Agriculture, Animal and Plant Health Inspection Service, G-100 Federal Building, 6505 Belcrest Road, Hyattsville, MD 20782.
- *Travelers Tips on Prohibited Agricultural Products,* U.S. Department of Agriculture, Animal and Plant Health Inspection Service, G-100 Federal Building, 6505 Belcrest Road, Hyattsville, MD 20782.

Customs Offices

For more information on specific customs regulations and requirements, you can call the nearest District Director of Customs at a phone number, below, or visit the Website at http://www.customs. ustreas.gov:

Baltimore, MD	410-962-6200
Boston, MA	617-565-6210
Buffalo, NY	716-626-0400
Chicago, IL	312-353-4733
College Park, GA	770-994-2306
El Paso, TX	915-540-5800
Houston, TX	713-313-2841
Laredo, TX	210-726-2267
Long Beach, CA	310-980-3100
Miami, FL	305-536-6600
New Orleans, LA	504-670-2404
New York, NY	212-466-4444
Portland, OR	503-326-7625
San Diego, CA	619-557-5455
San Francisco, CA	415-744-7700
San Juan, PR	787-729-6950
Seattle, WA	206-553-6944
Tampa, FL	813-228-2381
Tucon, AZ	520-670-9500

Endnote
[1] 18 U.S.C. § 1716(f).

Chapter 11

Discrimination and Travel Restrictions

An Introduction to Discrimination and Travel Restrictions

Have you ever been discriminated against while traveling? The answer is probably "yes," unless you happen to meet all of the typical travel supplier criteria (or stereotypes) for an "ideal" customer. For instance, if an airline overbooks the economy section, travelers in business suits are more likely than people in casual clothes to be upgraded to first class; similarly, people who stay at a hotel frequently are likely to be given a better room than a first-time guest, even though both guests pay the same amount. These are forms of allowable (or legal) discrimination. Other legal discrimination includes age limitations or certain restrictions for travelers with children or pets.

Some types of discrimination, however, such as discrimination based on race, color, religion, national origin or sex, are clearly illegal in the U.S. Other discrimination, such as that based on physical disabilities, is closely regulated and allowed only in limited circumstances. Both federal and state laws prohibit discrimination, and you will want to research all applicable laws and the possibility of suing if you believe you've been discriminated against. (See Chapter 13.) Remember that U.S. laws have no effect in foreign countries, and various forms of discrimination may either be legal or allowed by custom outside the U.S.

Discrimination Based on Race, Color, Religion or National Origin

Most travel suppliers provide access to places of public accommodation (such as hotels) or are considered common carriers (such as airlines or cruise lines) and are subject to the Civil Rights Act of 1964.[1] Under the Civil Rights Act, these businesses cannot discriminate against you or provide inferior service to you based upon your race, color, religion or national origin.

At least one major rental car company has been charged with discriminating against African-American and Hispanic renters. The Attorney General of Pennsylvania brought a complaint because of a pattern of discrimination which included telling African-American renters that no cars were available while providing cars to white renters, requiring three-day rentals, not allowing them to use a debit card and submitting African-American and Hispanic renters to more rigorous questioning.

If you believe that you have been discriminated against in violation of the Civil Rights Act, you may be able to file a complaint with the U.S. Department of Justice or U.S. Department of Transportation. A violation of the Civil Rights Act may also be the basis for a private lawsuit through which you can collect compensation.

For more information, contact the following:

- U.S. Department of Justice, Civil Rights Division, Public Access Section, P.O. Box 66738, Washington, DC 20035-6738, 202-514-2007 (voice), 202-514-

0293 (fax) or http://gopher.usdoj.gov/crt (Web).

- U.S. Department of Transportation, 400 Seventh Street SW, Washington, DC 20590, 202-366-4570 (voice) or http://www.dot.gov (Web).
- civil rights or human relations division of the office of your state attorney general.

Access for Disabled Travelers

Discrimination based on disability may violate the Americans with Disabilities Act or the Air Carrier Access Act, the two most important pieces of legislation governing the rights of disabled travelers. Determining whether you have been a victim of illegal discrimination often requires careful reading of the terms of each statute.

Americans With Disabilities Act

The Americans with Disabilities Act (ADA) is a comprehensive civil rights law for people with disabilities.[2] Under the ADA, a person with a disability is someone with a physical or mental impairment that substantially limits one or more major life activities. The ADA entitles disabled individuals to the same rights and access to public facilities—including buses, hotels, travel agencies and tour operator services—as other Americans. Both denial of the right to participate and unequal or separate treatment are prohibited by the ADA.

The ADA requires that public accommodations provide their services to people with disabilities in the most integrated setting possible and that reasonable modifications be made to policies, practices and procedures in order to make goods and services available to people with disabilities. Modifications must be made if they are readily achievable and do not fundamentally alter the nature of the goods or services provided. An example would be a ramp providing access for travelers in wheelchairs. Public accommodations must ensure effective means of communication with clients who are deaf or hard of hearing or who have speech or vision impairments.

 Several resources are mentioned in this section that provide information on specific types of travel for the disabled. In addition, the following guides have more general information on traveling and the disabled:

ADA Accessibility Guidelines is a free guide on barrier removal; contact the Architectural and Transportation Barriers Compliance Board, 1331 F Street, NW, Suite 1000, Washington, DC 20004-1111, 800-USA-ABLE.

Disability Express: Travel and Disability Resource Directory lists entities worldwide that serve travelers with disabilities, including tour operators, agencies, associations and suppliers. It's expensive ($50 as of June 1998). Contact Southwest Missouri State University, Office of Leisure Research, 901 S. National Avenue, Springfield, IL 65804; 417-836-4773 (phone), 417-836-4200 (fax) or sfi462f@vma.smsu.edu (e-mail).

Travelin' Talk is a directory aimed at alleviating the travel problems of disabled people by connecting them to a network of advisors in 800 locations. Send $35 (as of June 1998) to *Travelin' Talk* , P.O. Box 3534, Clarksville, TN 37043-3534, 615-552-6670.

Open World is the quarterly magazine of the Society for the Advance of Travel for the Handicapped and Elderly (SATH). It's $13 per year. You can contact SATH at 347 Fifth Avenue, Suite 610, New York, NY 10016, 212-447-7284 (voice), 212-725-8253 (fax), sathtravel@aol.com (e-mail) or http://www. sath.org (Web).

Several guides for travelers with disabilities are available, including *Wheelchair Vaga-bond,* by John G. Nelson; *Directory of Travel Agencies for the Disabled*, by Helen Hecker (audiocassette available); and *Travel for the Disabled: A Handbook of Travel Resources and 500 Worldwide Access Guides*, by Helen Hecker (audiocassettes also available). Check your local bookstore or library, or call the Disability Bookshop in Vancouver, Washington, at 800-637-2256.

Airlines—Air Carrier Access Act

The Air Carrier Access Act (ACAA) of 1986 is intended to eliminate discrimination on the basis of disability in air travel and requires air carriers to accommodate the needs of passengers with disabilities.[3] The Department of Transportation (DOT) has issued rules defining the rights of passengers and the obligations of airlines based upon these principles. The following is a summary.

Prohibited Practices

- Airlines may not refuse transportation to people on the basis of physical or mental disability. Airlines may exclude anyone from a flight, if carrying the person would jeopardize the safety of the flight. If an airline excludes a disabled person on safety grounds, the carrier must provide a written explanation of the decision.

- Airlines may not require advance notice that a disabled person is traveling. Carriers may require up to 48 hours' advance notice for certain services that require preparation time, however, such as hooking up a respirator or supplying a stretcher.

- Airlines may not limit the number of disabled persons on a flight.

- Airlines may not require a disabled person to travel with an attendant, except in certain limited circumstances specified in the Act, such as when the person needs oxygen administered and cannot do it alone. If a disabled person and the airline disagree about the need for an attendant, the airline can require the attendant, but cannot charge for the transportation of the attendant.

- Airlines may not keep anyone out of a seat on the basis of disability, or require anyone to sit in a particular seat on the basis of disability, except as Federal Aviation Administration (FAA) safety rules require. For example, the FAA's rule on emergency exit row seating allows airlines to place in exit rows only persons who can perform the functions necessary in an emergency evacuation.

  Example: A disabled traveler who sued an airline when it refused to allow him to sit in an emergency exit row lost his case. The court agreed with the airline that seating the disabled passenger in the emergency exit row could be a legitimate safety hazard to other passengers in the event of an emergency because the disabled person's inability to maneuver might obstruct emergency evacuation through that exit.

Seats, Lavatories and Wheelchairs

- Airplanes delivered after 1992 with 30 or more seats must have movable aisle armrests on half the aisle seats in the aircraft.
- Widebody (twin-aisle) airplanes delivered after 1992 must have accessible lavatories.
- Airplanes with 100 or more seats delivered after 1992 must have priority space for storing a passenger's folding wheelchair in the cabin.
- Airplanes with more than 60 seats and an accessible lavatory must have an on-board wheelchair, regardless of when the aircraft was ordered or delivered. For flights on airplanes with more than 60 seats that do not have an accessible lavatory, airlines must place an onboard wheelchair on the flight if a disabled

passenger gives the airline 48 hours' notice.

Other Services and Accommodations

- Airlines must assist disabled travelers with boarding, deplaning and making connections. Assistance within the cabin is also required, but not extensive personal services. (This is not defined in the Act.)
- Disabled passengers' items stored in the cabin must conform to FAA rules on the stowage of carry-on baggage. Assistive devices do not count toward the limit on the number of pieces of carry-on baggage. Wheelchairs and other assistive devices have priority for in-cabin storage space over other passengers' items brought on board at the same airport, if the disabled passenger chooses to preboard.
- Wheelchairs and other assistive devices have priority over other items for storage in the baggage compartment.
- Airlines must accept battery-powered wheelchairs, including the batteries, and hazardous materials packages provided by the passenger, when necessary.
- Airlines may not charge for providing required services or products, such as hazardous materials packaging for batteries. Airlines may charge for optional services such as oxygen, however.

Administrative Provisions

- Training on the provisions of the ACAA is required for airline personnel who deal with the traveling public.
- Large airlines and their commuter airline affiliates must submit their procedures to DOT for compliance review with the ACAA.

New Horizons for the Air Traveler with a Disability provides more detailed descriptions of the DOT's rules on the ACAA. For a copy, write to the U.S. Department of Transportation, Office of Regulatory Affairs (P-10), Washington, DC 20590 or call 800-322-7873.

The Paralysis Society of America is gathering reports from passengers on how well airlines are complying with the Air Carrier Access Act of 1986. To report your experiences on a recent air trip, call 800-643-8245.

AIDS Discrimination

Some carriers have refused service or otherwise discriminated against travelers who have or appear to have AIDS. Airlines cannot discriminate based upon fear or prejudice. A passenger can be refused boarding only if the passenger has a contagious disease that creates a health hazard for other passengers. In a recent lawsuit against a major airline, the airline settled out of court with a traveler with AIDS who was removed from a flight because of the airline employee's concern about the man's open lesions and I.V. bag. In addition to the monetary settlement, the airline agreed to increase its HIV/AIDS sensitivity training for its employees.

Airports

As a result of the ACAA rules and the ADA implementing regulations, privately owned ground transportation and concessions selling goods or services to the public at airports must be accessible to people with disabilities. In addition, air carrier terminals are required to make the following services and facilities accessible to the disabled:

- parking near the terminal
- medical aid facilities and travelers aid stations
- restrooms
- drinking fountains
- ticketing systems at primary fare-collection areas
- baggage check-in and retrieval areas, and
- jetways and mobile lounges.

In addition, air carrier terminals must provide:

- amplified telephones and text telephones for use by people with hearing and speech impairments
- level entry boarding ramps, lifts or other means of assisting individuals with disabilities on and off aircraft
- information systems using visual words, letters or symbols with lighting and color coding and facilities providing information orally, and
- directional signs indicating the location of specific facilities and services.

Major airports (the Department of Transportation doesn't identify which airports are "major" or define the term) are required to have shuttle vehicles to transport people between parking lots and terminal buildings, as well as people movers and moving walkways within and between terminals and gates.

Access Travel: Airports, a free guide listing the accessibility of design features, facilities and services at 519 airports, can be obtained by contacting Access America, Washington, DC 20202, 202-484-0533 or the Consumer Information Center, Pueblo, CO 81009.

Travel and Tour Agencies

All travel and tour agencies are covered by the ADA. Even a travel or tour agency that is located within a private residence must make the portions of the home used as a place of public accommodation accessible, if it is readily achievable to do so. Here is a summary of measures travel and tour agencies must take for clients with disabilities:

- Agencies are not required to have a telecommunications device for the deaf, but may rely on the relay systems that telephone companies provide.
- If an agency accepts walk-in traffic, it must make accommodations for blind clients and clients in wheelchairs. For the blind, the agency must have an employee able to guide the client to the appropriate area or read any pertinent information out loud. For clients in wheelchairs, an agency must widen doors to at least 32 inches and rearrange furniture at its expense, unless these actions would fundamentally alter the nature of the services provided.
- Agencies that offer parking are required to provide accessible parking spaces for people with "handicap" tags if the agency owns and operates the parking lot and it is readily achievable to do so. If it is not readily achievable, the

agency must provide other options, such as valet parking.
- A person with a disability may not be denied service because the disability or behavior resulting from the disability may be disturbing to other customers.
- At least one entrance, preferably the main one, must be accessible so that people with disabilities can get through the door. If the main entrance is not accessible, a sign should indicate where the accessible entrance is located.
- Agencies must allow service animals, including guide dogs, to accompany clients into their facilities.

 Access Equals Opportunity contains detailed information on access for the disabled to the services offered by tour operators and travel agents; send $1.50 to the Council of Better Business Bureaus' Foundation, 4200 Wilson Boulevard, Suite 800, Arlington, VA 22203, 703-276-0100 (voice), 703-525-8277 (fax), http://www.bbb.org/bbb (Web).

Motorcoaches

The ADA entitles disabled individuals to the same rights and access to motorcoaches as other Americans, and operators must take measures to make their motorcoaches accessible. Some measures include providing wheelchair lifts and tie downs, and conducting employee training. Motorcoach companies are not required to retrofit all their vehicles to make them accessible, but they must have a sufficient number of properly equipped motorcoaches so that a disabled traveler is not unduly limited. The American Bus Association has a training and technical assistance program for tour operators on ADA-related matters.

Hotels

Hotels are required to make their accommodations readily accessible and usable by people with disabilities. This includes making reasonable modifications in hotel lobbies and restaurants as well as guest rooms. Hotels built since 1990 are required to be built to ADA standards, but older hotels, even historic hotels, must retrofit for accessibility if it is readily achievable and does not fundamentally alter the nature of the hotel. Hotels are not required to make every room accessible, as long as the rooms they designate are clearly not inferior to the other rooms in the hotel.

A hotel that is readily accessible and usable by individuals with disabilities would have the following:

- doors and doorways in rooms and bathrooms wide enough to allow passage by individuals in wheelchairs.
- a percentage of each class of hotel rooms fully accessible, with grab bars in the bath and at the toilet, and with accessible counters in the bathrooms
- meeting areas with audio loops
- emergency alarms with flashing lights
- elevators panels with braille or raised-letter words and numbers, and
- handrails on stairs and ramps.

For newly constructed hotels 4% of the first 100 rooms (and approximately 2% of the rooms in excess of 100) must be suitable for use by people in wheelchairs. The same percentage of additional rooms must be

equipped with flashing lights or other visual alarms for people with hearing impairments.

Cruise Lines

Places open to the public aboard ships must comply with the ADA, including removing barriers to access where readily achievable. Physical barriers, such as a change in grade more than half an inch, must be removed if readily achievable, so that travelers with disabilities are not treated differently from passengers who do not have disabilities. The most common obstacles for passengers in wheelchairs are the "sills" or raised lips on ship doorways. This structural peculiarity (designed to keep water from sloshing from room to room when the deck gets wet) can make getting around quite difficult. Cruise lines are required to make ramps available, but are not required to equip all doorways with ramps; thus passengers in wheelchairs may not have complete mobility on board.

Because cruise lines are retrofitting some of their ships to bring them into compliance with the ADA, contact cruise lines directly to determine which ships have been modified and whether cabins are available "dedicated" to wheelchair users. Dedicated cabins are specifically designed to accommodate disabled passengers and are much easier to use than cabins that are only designated "wheelchair accessible," which may have raised lips on the cabin doorways and even the doorway between the berth and the bathroom.

A cruise ship cannot insist that a person with a disability travel with a companion, but the cruise line does not have to provide services of a personal nature if a person with a disability chooses to travel unaccompanied.

 Cruise Guide for the Wheelchair Traveler details the extent to which a passenger in a wheelchair can get around different cruise lines, but you are better off contacting the cruise lines directly to get precise and current information. Still, to obtain a copy of the *Cruise Guide*, contact Cruise Lines International Association, 500 5th Avenue, Suite 1407, New York, NY 10110, 212-921-0066.

Discrimination Based on Sex

Although sex discrimination is not covered by the Civil Rights Act, travel suppliers may not discriminate on the basis of sex unless there is a legitimate purpose, such as a single-sex dorm. In certain countries discrimination based on sex is commonplace, and it may be difficult for a single woman to rent a car or a hotel room for herself. Certain cultural and religious norms, such as requiring that a woman's legs be covered, are still enforced in some areas. Prepare yourself for these possibilities by researching your destination ahead of time if you are traveling to an unfamiliar area.

On most airlines, women can travel during the first eight months of pregnancy. For travel during the ninth month, you must have a certificate from a gynecologist completed within 24-72 hours of the flight stating that you are physically fit to travel on that particular flight.

Discrimination Based on Sexual Orientation

Gay and lesbian travelers may experience discrimination, particularly in areas where political or religious norms condemn homosexuality. While some politically progressive communities have adopted laws that prohibit discrimination on the basis of sexual orientation, no federal law offers such protection. In most cases, if you are discriminated against because of your sexual orientation, your best approach probably is to never go near the travel supplier again, and let all your friends know in order to join you in your boycott.

If you choose to sue based on sexual orientation discrimination, your legal argument will be that the travel supplier breached a contract or violated a duty to receive or carry. Know that the odds of recovery are low, and even if you do win, the expenses of litigation are likely to outweigh any financial compensation you might receive. Lawsuits may be effective, however, if you are seeking to publicly expose the discrimination.

One of the most effective methods to minimize the chances of discrimination based on sexual orientation is to patronize businesses that cater to gay and lesbian travelers. Many travel agencies, travel clubs, newsletters and magazines provide information on resources for gay and lesbian travelers. A few specialized guidebooks offer lodging, restaurant, entertainment and sightseeing recommendations for gay and lesbian travelers throughout the world. For example, *Out & About*, a monthly newsletter aimed at gay and lesbian travelers, has published a travel guide for warm-weather vacations that cater to gays and lesbians. You can reach *Out & About's* publisher at 800-929-2268. Or, check your local library or bookstore.

Foreign Travel

In some countries, homosexuality is illegal, or at least is grounds for refusing entry into the country. Although there is growing protest to such restrictions, check with the country's consulate or a knowledgeable travel agent or supplier to determine the country's policy on gay and lesbian travelers. You might also check with the International Gay and Lesbian Human Rights Commission, 1360 Mission Street, Suite 200, San Francisco, CA 94103, 415-255-8680 (voice) or 415-255-8662 (fax). In recent years, the fear of AIDS has been commonly used as an excuse to exclude and deport gay men—and some countries do test for AIDS before allowing entry.

Rental Cars

Refusal to rent a car to a gay or lesbian couple would constitute a breach of contract if the couple had a reservation and abided by the conditions of the contract (such as showing up on time for the rental). An absolute refusal to rent to gay and lesbian couples is unlikely, at least with any of the national rental car companies, but you may face more subtle forms of discrimination, such as being assessed a fee for an additional driver that would be waived for mixed-sex couples. Some companies now waive the additional driver fee for same-sex partners; check with the rental company before making your reservation.

Airlines, Cruise Lines and Other Common Carriers

Most common carriers, by definition, must provide transportation for any member of the public, unless the person poses a threat to other passengers or the carrier. There is no legal basis for claiming that an individual's sexual orientation poses a threat to other passengers or the carrier, and in fact, in recent years there have been few discrimination claims based on sexual orientation lodged against airlines and other common carriers. Some cruise lines, however, resist providing one-bed cabins to same-sex couples.

Hotels

Under the duty to receive (see Chapter 4), hotels are required, with limited exceptions, to provide accommodation to all travelers who are able to pay. A gay or lesbian traveler could sue if he or she had a valid reservation and was refused accommodations based on sexual orientation. The more subtle form of discrimination, where a same-sex couple is refused one bed, could provide a basis for a breach of contract claim. Because contract claims are based on economic damage that is suffered, however, it would be difficult to prove that this type of discrimination creates damages that can be calculated in economic terms.

One of the exceptions to the duty to receive is that a hotel is allowed to refuse guests who would give the hotel a "bad reputation." This might be an effective defense for a hotel in a conservative community; however, it is unlikely to fly in a metropolitan area.

Age Discrimination

Age discrimination is not covered by the Civil Rights Act. In fact, many travel-related federal and state laws specifically allow certain types of age limitations and restrictions. Nonetheless, some state regulations prohibit age discrimination. Most age restrictions and limitations apply to younger travelers, but in certain cases, the restrictions may apply to older travelers.

For example, certain operators of specialized transportation, such as helicopter rides or adventure tours, may have an age cutoff point. Also, drivers over age 70 may find that certain rental car companies will not rent to them. On the other hand, seniors are sometimes the beneficiaries of a type of discrimination—such as senior fares not available to younger travelers.

See Chapter 2 for information on car rental regulations concerning renting to people under age 25 and placing children in car seats.

Traveling With Children

Airlines

Children Traveling With Adults
Children under the age of five must be accompanied by a parent or guardian. Under DOT regulations, airlines must allow passengers with approved child seats to carry on the seats for use in the airplane without counting them as carry-on baggage. This regulation applies only when the passenger has paid for an additional seat for the child. If the child is less than two years old, the passenger may hold the child in her lap during the flight and no additional charge for the child is allowed.

The Federal Aviation Administration has banned the use of child booster seats, harnesses and safety vests on airplanes. Only child-safety seats with backs and sides can be used. Newer models of the safety seats should have a label certifying that they are approved for use in airplanes. If you have any doubt whether your child safety seat is acceptable, check with the airline before you go to the airport.

 Tips for Parents Using Child Restraint on Aircraft, which has information on the appropriate type of child seats for flying, is available from the Federal Aviation Administration's consumer hotline at 800-322-7873 or on the Web at http:www.faa.gov/apa/publicat/crstips.htm.

Children Traveling Alone
Children between five and 12 who travel without a parent or guardian are known as "unaccompanied minors" and are accepted

as passengers with certain restrictions and sometimes extra fees. Some airlines only allow younger unaccompanied minors to take nonstop or direct flights. Where a minor must be assisted by airline personnel in order to change planes, a fee of $20-$50 is often charged. Although some airlines offer discounts for kids, unaccompanied minors are usually charged the full adult ticket price.

Millions of unaccompanied minors travel on the major airlines every year. Parents or legal guardians are responsible for bringing the minor to the departure gate and having an authorized parent or guardian pick the child up upon arrival. If you send an unaccompanied minor by plane, you will be required to fill out a form detailing the child's name, age, medical considerations and other relevant information. In addition, you will have to agree that the airline is not taking on any special responsibility of guardianship during the flight. Legally, an unaccompanied minor is treated in the same way as an adult passenger. Requiring parents or guardians to pay an extra fee for services provided by the airline to the unaccompanied minor, however, may provide a legal argument that the airline owes a higher duty of care, because it is being specifically paid for the extra services provided, such as shuttling a child from one gate to another to make a connecting flight.

Airlines are careful to point out that they have no obligations before or after the flight, and, in some cases, children have been turned over to local child welfare authorities or police if no parent or guardian is available to pick up an unaccompanied minor. This can be particularly difficult for children who, through no fault of their own, are stranded in an airport when a flight is delayed or canceled. To avoid potential liability, many airlines have instituted very strict rules for their employees as to what services can be provided for unaccompanied minors. Because unaccompanied minors must be escorted off the plane by airline personnel, they may be some of the last passengers to disembark. Airline personnel are not allowed to turn the minor over to a waiting parent or guardian without seeing the adult's identification and matching it with the information on the form filled out before departure.

Tips for Unaccompanied Minors

To minimize difficulties for unaccompanied minors, airlines have the following recommendations for parents or guardians:

- Fly only nonstop or direct flights so that the child does not need to change airplanes. If a change of planes is necessary, use a small, less intimidating airport for the transfer, if possible.
- Completely and clearly fill out all of the paperwork required for unaccompanied minors, especially the paperwork that must travel with the child.
- Provide information about how flight delays or cancellations should be handled, including emergency contacts and a means to pay for necessities, such as overnight accommodation.

Kids and Teens in Flight, a pamphlet produced by the U.S. Department of Transportation, Office of Consumer Protection, 400 Seventh Street, SW, Dept. C75, Washington, DC 20590, 202-366-2220 (voice), 202-366-7907 (fax), offers advice and outlines general polices for the parents and guardians of unaccompanied minors. It also provides a "Travel Card" with flight information and contact names and numbers that can be filled out by the parent or guardian and carried by the minor during the trip.

Hotels

Many hotels refuse to provide rooms to unaccompanied minors. In the absence of a specific state law on the point, this is a violation of the hotel's traditional duty to receive. If the hotel accepts minors as guests (they are allowed to have "no children" policies), then the hotel is obliged to receive minors even when they are not accompanied by adults.[4] Thus, a minor who is turned away by a hotel probably has a legal claim against the hotel. Minors are legally liable for any expenses they incur at the hotel, even though they may not be old enough to form legally recognized contracts. The obligation to serve children is frequently overlooked because the situation is so unusual, and many hotel employees may be unaware of it.

Other Travel Suppliers

Other types of businesses are frequently not required to provide services for minors. Technically, minors cannot enter into contracts, so there would be no way for the travel supplier to enforce any contract with a minor. It's easier for the travel supplier to simply refuse to provide service.

Restrictions on Smoking

Restrictions on smoking in public areas are on the rise throughout the U.S., and the travel industry is no exception. Particularly dramatic are the changes that have taken place with airlines, but other travel industries are affected as well.

Airlines

Since early 1990, smoking any tobacco product has been banned on domestic flights (including Puerto Rico and the Virgin Islands) of fewer than six hours. The law applies to any airline (U.S. or foreign) flying such routes. On direct flights beginning or ending outside of the U.S., domestic airlines must provide a nonsmoking seat in each class to every passenger who wants one as long as the passenger holds a valid reservation and meets the check-in deadline for the flight. If a nonsmoking section is between two smoking sections, the passengers in the middle are not to be "unreasonably burdened."

Currently, a number of airlines go farther than the legislation requires in their restrictions of smoking on board, so ask when booking to avoid any surprises.

A number of foreign carriers have sharply increased their smoke-free flights. The International Civil Aviation Organization (ICAO) proposed eliminating all smoking flights. Various airlines and organizations support this goal, but because the ICAO has no enforcement power, compliance will be voluntary. In the first agreement of its kind, the U.S., Canada, Australia and New Zealand have agreed to ban smoking on nonstop flights among the four countries. The Department of Transportation reported that in 1997, 97% of flights between the U.S. and foreign countries were smokefree. Beware that once you arrive in a foreign country, your continuing flight may not be. A complete list of countries served by non-smoking flights is on the Department of Transportation's Web page at http:// ostpxweb.dot.gov/policy/safety/smoke.htm.

Very few cases concerning smoking on airlines have been litigated. In one that was, a law professor sued Air France for breach of contract when he was seated among smokers despite being assigned a nonsmoking seat. He sued in small claims court seeking $1,600—the cost of his round-trip ticket. He was awarded $500. The judge ruled that the printed ticket disclaimer that it could not guarantee a nonsmoking seat was ambiguous, and that the professor could rely on the airline's employees and his boarding pass, both of which indicated he would have a nonsmoking seat.

 To obtain a letter outlining the rules governing U.S. airlines' seating policies concerning smoking, send a stamped, self-addressed envelope to Smoking Letter, Action on Smoking and Health (ASH), 2013 H Street, NW, Washington, DC 20006, 800-427-4228, or visit their Website at http:// www.ash.org.

Other Travel Suppliers

An increasing number of hotels, rental car companies and cruise lines provide smoke-free facilities. Generally, it is done voluntarily, as few laws require smoke-free facilities.

Traveling With Pets

Although your pet may be treated royally at home, it is likely to feel quite discriminated against while traveling. Hotels, rental cars, cruises or other travel suppliers are not required to provide a space for Fifi or Fido, with exceptions for working guide dogs. (See Access for Disabled Travelers, above.) Call or write ahead to learn which suppliers accept animals, and get their promise in writing. If you are assured that pets are allowed and you are refused service because of your pet, the supplier may be liable for breach of contract.

Airlines

On most airlines, dogs, cats and certain other domesticated animals can be transported as excess baggage or cargo. Sometimes, pets small enough to be comfortable in a pet carrier that fits under an airline seat may be taken on the plane with you as carry-on baggage. Some airlines, however, allow only one pet as carry-on baggage for the *entire* airplane, so make your arrangements well in advance and get them confirmed in writing. An airline may charge you for transporting a pet, even if it fits under the seat in front of you. Most airlines discourage the transportation of animals in the cabin, citing problems with noise, sanitation and passengers with pet allergies.

Animals transported as baggage (on the same flight as their humans) or cargo (unaccompanied) are protected by the Animal Welfare Act.[5] Your pet must be at least eight weeks old and fully weaned, and must travel in a suitable kennel. Kennels must meet several requirements concerning size, sanitation, ventilation, labeling and the number of animals per kennel. The airline must provide water at least once every 12 hours and food every 24 hours, and you must attach instructions for feeding, watering and administering any medication, and documentation that your pet was fed and given water within four hours before departure.[6]

 A brochure entitled *Air Travel for Your Dog or Cat* is available from the Air Transport Association, 1709 New York Avenue, NW, Washington, DC 20006. It contains several tips, such as planning your pet's itinerary to avoid flights where the kennel has to be transferred between planes or where the plane is likely to spend a long time waiting on the runway before takeoff. *Transporting Live Animals* and *Traveling by Air With Your Pet* provide information on the Animal Welfare Act. Contact the U.S Department of Transportation, Office of Consumer Protection, 400 Seventh Street, SW, Washington, DC 20590.

To report mistreatment of a pet or other violation of the Animal Welfare Act, contact the Animal Care Staff of APHIS at the U.S. Department of Agriculture, Room 565, Federal Building, 6505 Belcrest Road, Hyattsville, MD 20782, 301-436-7833. Direct reports about lost pets to the U.S Department of Transportation, Office of Consumer Protection at 202-366-2220.

Airline Policies

In addition to the requirements of the Animal Welfare Act, each airline has its own policies concerning the transportation of animals. For example, most airlines require that you provide a certificate of health for your pet obtained within a short time before the flight. Furthermore, because animals must be transported in a pressurized cargo hold and some planes have limited pressurized cargo space, most airlines cannot guarantee that your pet will fly on the same plane as you.

Quarantine Laws

Most foreign countries have quarantine laws for animals entering from the U.S.—for example, all dogs entering Great Britain are subject to a six-month quarantine. To avoid any unnecessary delays or hardship for your pet, be sure to obtain in advance all of the information you can from the country's consulate or embassy about required vaccinations, certificates and quarantine periods, and the conditions under which the pet would be held during quarantine. You may decide that Fluffy and Muffy would be better off staying home.

Hawaii also has its own quarantine and health requirements for pets from the mainland and abroad. For details, contact the Hawaii Quarantine Office, 99-770 Moanalua Road, Aiea, HI 96701.

Injured or Lost Pets

No money can compensate for a loved pet that is injured, lost or killed in transit. Nonetheless, because transported animals are legally considered cargo or baggage, the compensation available for a loss or injury is limited to the same cold cash available for the loss of a suitcase. That means that the maximum recoverable is often $1,250 or less. Although people whose pets have been lost or killed on flights have attempted to claim compensation for loss of companionship and mental anguish, courts generally deny compensation other than that for lost luggage. If the airline will accept the higher liability, pet owners might be able to emphasize the value of their pets (and give the airline more incentive to take care) by declaring the maximum "excess value" on the pet that is allowed.

It is possible that intentional and malicious acts by the airline's employees could lead to punitive damages against the airlines, but no cases are reported where this has happened. Airlines have been fined by the USDA for violations of the Animal Welfare Act, but most of the fines are so small as to be only a slap on the wrist.

Hotels

Hotels are not obliged to accept your pet as a guest. Hotels are allowed to establish "house rules" (as long as they are enforced

fairly), and one of these is often "no pets." In some cases, hotels have kennels or other areas for pets. To avoid problems, ask when you make your reservation.

AAA has guide books of hotels that accept pets. The *AAA Pet Books* list 10,000 pet-friendly hotels across the U.S. and Canada. Contact your local auto club or write to AAA, 1000 AAA Drive, Heathrow, FL 32746. If you need a veterinary doctor while you are traveling, the American Animal Hospital Association, 800-883-6301, can provide information on the nearest animal hospital or vet.

 Dog Law, by Mary Randolph (Nolo Press), offers valuable advice on airline regulations, liability limits and international restrictions related to traveling with a pet, as well as a number of other valuable legal tips about "(hu)man's best friend." In addition, a booklet, *Traveling With Your Pet,* is available for $5 from the American Society for the Prevention of Cruelty to Animals, 441 E. 92nd Street, New York, NY 10128.

■

Endnotes

[1] 42 U.S.C. § 201.

[2] 42 U.S.C. § 12182 and following.

[3] 42 U.S.C. § 1374 and following.

[4] *Watson v. Cross,* 67 Ky. 147 (1865).

[5] 7 U.S.C. § 2131 and following.

[6] 9 C.F.R. §§ 3.13 through 3.24.

Chapter 12

Is It Tax Deductible?
Traveling for Business or Charity

An Introduction to Traveling for Business or Charity

Many travelers dream of taking exotic vacations and writing the trip off as a tax deduction. That kind of dream can become a nightmare; the IRS scrutinizes deductions for travel and allows deductions only for legitimate business or charitable travel expenses. To maximize your legal deductions you need to:

- learn the rules on deductibility
- plan ahead, keeping in mind the guidelines set by the IRS, and
- keep good records—for example, retain all receipts, write down cash expenses for which you have no receipts and keep a log.

Most of the text in this chapter is excerpted directly or adapted from IRS publications (referred to throughout the chapter), so you can see exactly how the IRS interprets tax laws and regulations. We do not suggest tax-saving ideas or provide interpretations of the law that differ from the official IRS position. For copies of IRS publications, call 800-829-3676 or visit the IRS Website at http://www.irs.ustreas.gov.

General Rules When Traveling for Business

In most cases, your business travel expenses are likely to be deductible if the following two conditions are met:

- The expenses are incurred for a legitimate business reason while you are traveling away from home. For example, you cannot deduct costs of sightseeing, shopping or similar non-business activities.
- You do not receive other compensation for the expenses, such as a reimbursement or per diem allowance from your employer.

The trick is determining exactly what the IRS thinks is legitimate and how far away you have to go to be "traveling."

Here are some other important rules to consider:

- If you are an employee, you can only claim the deduction for your unreimbursed travel expenses if you itemize your deductions (file IRS Form 1040). Furthermore, your travel deductions will be limited to the amount that exceeds 2% of your adjusted gross income. For example, if your adjusted gross income is $50,000, you could only deduct the amount in excess of $1,000. If your expenses were $1,050, you could only deduct $50.
- Whether you are an employee or self-employed, you can only deduct 50% of your meal or entertainment expenses while traveling.
- If your business travel takes you on a cruise, you are limited in how much you can deduct, as is explained later in this chapter.
- A trip to inspect business property may be deductible, but in most cases travel to "investment seminars" is not. Neither is travel to a stockholders' meeting, unless you have some substantial interest in the company other than merely holding stock.
- Deductions for spouses, family members and significant others are likely to be

scrutinized by the IRS to determine if their presence was necessary for business reasons.

You cannot deduct the costs of taking a bus, trolley, subway or taxi or driving a car between your home and your main or regular place of work. These costs are personal commuting expenses. You cannot deduct commuting expenses no matter how far your home is from your regular place of work. You cannot deduct commuting expenses even if you work during the commuting trip.

Traveling Away From Your Tax Home

The IRS considers you to be traveling away from home if:

- your duties require you to be away from the general area of your tax home substantially longer than an ordinary day's work, and
- you need to get sleep or rest to meet the demands of your work while away from home.

Generally, your tax home is your regular place of business or post of duty, regardless of where you maintain your family home. It includes the entire city or general area where your business or work is located. If you have more than one regular place of business, your tax home is your main place of business. If you do not have a regular or a main place of business because of the nature of your work, your tax home may be the place where you regularly live.

Defining Your Tax Home

 For most people, the following IRS explanation of "tax home" is unnecessary. If you work and live in one area most of the time, that is your "tax home" and you can skip ahead to the section on Travel Expenses.

Your main place of business or work. If you have more than one place of work, your main place of business or work is the place where you spend more of your time and earn more of your income.

If you have no main place of business or work. If you do not have a regular or main place of business or work, your tax home is the home where you regularly live if you conduct part of your business in the home and use it for lodging while doing business there; if you have living expenses at your home that you duplicate elsewhere because your business requires you to be away from the home; and if you have not left the area where your main home is located, your family lives at your main home or you often use the home for lodging. If you meet only two of the conditions, you may have a tax home depending on the circumstances. If you meet only one factor, you are a transient; you do not have a tax home and you cannot deduct travel expenses.

Transient workers. If you move from job to job, maintain no fixed home and are not associated with any particular business locality, each place you work becomes your main place of business and your tax home. You cannot deduct your expenses for meals and lodging.

Living Away From Your Tax Home

If you (and your family) live in an area outside your tax home, you cannot deduct travel expenses between your tax home and your family home. Nor can you deduct the cost of meals and lodging while at your tax home. If you are working temporarily in the same city where you and your family live, you may be considered as traveling away from home.

Example 1: You live with your family in Chicago, but work in Milwaukee, where you stay in a hotel and eat in restaurants during the week. You return to Chicago every weekend. You cannot deduct any of your expenses for travel, meals and lodging in Milwaukee because Milwaukee is your tax home and the travel on weekends is not for a business reason.

Example 2: Your family home is in Pittsburgh, where you work 12 weeks a year. The rest of the year, you work for the same employer in Baltimore, which is considered your tax home. In Baltimore, you eat in restaurants and sleep in a rental apartment. You cannot deduct your expenses for meals and lodging there. When you work in Pittsburgh, however, you are away from your tax home even though you stay at your family home. Therefore, you can deduct the cost of your transit between Baltimore and Pittsburgh and part of your family's living expenses for meals and lodging while you live and work in Pittsburgh.

Temporary Assignment or Job

On temporary assignments away from home, your tax home does not change. You are considered to be away from home for the entire period, and your travel expenses are deductible. For a complete definition, see IRS Publication 463.

Tax-Deductible Travel Expenses

Once you determine that you are traveling away from your tax home, you must determine what travel expenses are deductible on your tax return.

Deductible travel expenses include those ordinary and necessary expenses you incur while traveling away from home on business. The type of expense you can deduct depends on your circumstances. The following discussion is a general guideline. You may have other deductible travel expenses that are not covered here. For complete rules, see IRS Publication 917.

⚠ Remember—if you are an employee, you can deduct your travel expenses only if you itemize your deductions and your travel expenses exceed 2% of your adjusted gross income. Different rules apply to people who are self-employed.

Transportation fares. Generally, you can deduct travel by airplane, train or bus between your home and a business destination. Your cost is the amount you personally paid for your ticket. If you are riding free as a result of a "frequent flyer" or other similar program, you have no deduction. If you travel by ship, the amount you can deduct may be limited. (See below.)

Taxi, commuter bus, train and limousine fares. Generally, you can deduct the cost of transportation between the airport or station and your hotel, as well as between your hotel and the work location of your customers or clients, your business meeting place or your temporary work location.

Baggage and shipping costs. You can deduct the cost of sending baggage and sample or display material between your regular work location and your temporary work location.

Motor vehicle expenses. You can deduct the cost of renting or leasing a vehicle for business purposes while you are traveling away from home. If you lease for 30 days or more, special provisions apply. You can also deduct actual operating expenses for a vehicle you rent or lease, such as gas, oil and repairs. You cannot claim a mileage rate deduction.

For a vehicle you own, you probably have a choice of deducting actual business-related expenses or the standard business mileage rate. The standard business mileage rate for tax year 1998 was 31.5¢ per mile (the amount changes annually). There are limitations on who can use the standard mileage rate deduction—for example, you cannot operate more than one car for business or use the car for hire, such as a taxi.

When you use your vehicle for business, keep records of the business purpose of your travel. The better the records, the better your position if the IRS challenges your deductions.

Lodging. You can deduct the cost of lodging if your business trip is overnight or long enough to require you to stop for sleep or rest to properly perform your duties.

Meals. You can deduct the cost of meals only if your business trip is overnight or long enough to require you to stop for sleep or rest to properly perform your duties. You cannot deduct the cost of meals if it is not necessary for you to rest. The expense of a meal includes the amount you spend for food, beverages, taxes and tips relating to the meal. You can deduct only 50% of the cost of business-related meals. Furthermore, you cannot deduct expenses for meals to the extent they are lavish or extravagant. An expense is not considered lavish or extravagant if it is reasonable based on the circumstances. Having a bottle of champagne with dinner to celebrate the closing of a big business deal would probably not be considered extravagant; ordering a case of Dom Perignon probably would be.

Instead of deducting 50% of your actual costs, you can deduct a standard meal allowance for your daily meals and incidental expenses while you are traveling. In 1998, the allowance ranged from $30-$42 per day, depending on location. The details—and an explanation of when you can use the standard meal allowance—are in IRS Publication 463.

The current rate for each state and for foreign travel is available on the Web at http://policyworks.gov/org/main/mt/homepage/mtt/perdiem/travel.shtml.

There are limitations on using the standard meal allowance. For example, you cannot use it if you are related to your employer, meaning:

- your employer is your sibling or half-sibling, spouse, ancestor or lineal descendant (parent, child, grandparent or grandchild)

- your employer is a corporation in which you own, directly or indirectly, more than 10% in value of the outstanding stock, or

- you and your employer have a fiduciary relationship (high degree of trust and confidentiality).

You may use the standard meal allowance if you are self-employed, which means that the IRS does not consider you to be related to yourself!

 If you use the standard meal allowance, you still must keep records to prove the time, place and business purpose of your travel. The standard meal allowance can be a real tax saver for the frugal traveler who spends less than the standard meal allowance.

Telephone expenses. You can deduct the cost of business calls while you are traveling away from home. This includes the cost of business communication by fax machine or other devices. Calls to your family or friends are not deductible.

Cleaning and laundry expenses. You can deduct reasonable laundry expenses while traveling away from home on business. Cleaning and laundry are considered "incidental expenses" and cannot be deducted if you claim the standard meal allowance—which is actually a standard meal and incidental expense allowance.

Tips. You can deduct tips you pay for meals and other expenses listed here. If you claim the standard meal allowance, however, you cannot also claim the tips you paid on your meals.

Entertainment expenses. In general, you can deduct only 50% of your entertainment expenses. This limit applies to employees or their employers, and to self-employed persons (including independent contractors) or their clients. To deduct 50% of your entertainment expenses (such as taking a client out to a play or night club), you must jump through a number of hoops set up by the IRS, for instance, the entertainment must follow or precede a business meeting or substantial business must be conducted in conjunction with the event. See IRS Publication 463.

Other business expenses. You can deduct other ordinary and necessary expenses related to your business travel. Such expenses might include the costs of operating and maintaining a house trailer, public stenographer's fees or computer rental fees.

Expenses for other people. If your spouse, child or other person accompanies you on a business trip or to a business convention, you generally cannot deduct his or her travel expenses. You can deduct the travel expenses you pay or incur only for an accompanying individual who:

- is your employee

- has a bona fide business purpose for the travel, and
- would otherwise be allowed to deduct the travel expenses.

For a bona fide business purpose to exist, you must prove a real business purpose for the individual's presence. Incidental services, such as typing notes or assisting in entertaining customers, are not enough to warrant a deduction.

> **Example:** Jon drives to Chicago on business and takes his wife, Julie, with him. Julie is not Jon's employee, Julie's presence serves no business purpose and Julie does not otherwise qualify to deduct the travel expenses. Jon pays $115 a day for a double room. A single room costs $90 a day. He can deduct the total cost of driving his car to and from Chicago, but only $90 a day for his hotel room. If Jon and Julie use public transportation, he can deduct only his fare.

The IRS is cracking down on business travelers who deduct expenses for a spouse, child or other person who travels with them. Cruises and conferences in vacation areas are particularly suspect. Don't try to claim a "business reason" for your companion if it is really for social reasons—you may be hit with tax penalties. By planning, however, two may be able to travel as if they were one by:

- using a hotel that charges by the room (not per occupant), and
- using a taxi that charges by the trip, not a shuttle that charges per occupant—for rental cars, everything but an additional driver surcharge should be deductible.

If a hotel or other service charges per person, get some proof of what the single rate would have been. It is often a high percentage of the charge for two or more (not simply 50%), and the entire single rate is deductible.

Trip Within the United States

The tax treatment of your travel expenses depends on how much of your trip was business-related and how much occurred within the U.S.—that is, the 50 states and the District of Columbia.

Primarily for Business

You can deduct all of your travel expenses (assuming you itemize and your expenses exceed 2% of your adjusted gross income) if your trip was entirely business related. If your trip was primarily for business and, while at your business destination, you

extended your stay for a vacation, made a nonbusiness side trip or had other nonbusiness activities, you can deduct your business-related travel expenses. These expenses include the travel costs of getting to and from your business destination and any business-related expenses at your business destination.

> **Example:** You work in Atlanta and take a business trip to New Orleans. On your way home, you stop in Mobile to visit your parents. You spend $630 for the nine days you are away from home for travel, meals, lodging and other travel expenses. If you had not stopped in Mobile, you would have been gone only five days, and your total cost would have been $580. You can deduct 100% of the $580 for your trip not related to meals, including the cost of round-trip transportation to and from New Orleans. Your meals are subject to the 50% limit.

Primarily for Personal Reasons

If your trip was primarily for personal reasons, such as a vacation, the entire cost of the trip is a nondeductible personal expense. You can, however, deduct any expenses you have while at your destination directly related to your business.

A trip to a resort or on a cruise ship may be a vacation even if the promoter advertises that it is primarily for business. The scheduling of incidental business activities during a trip, such as viewing videotapes or attending lectures dealing with general subjects, will not change what is really a vacation into a business trip.

Trip Outside the United States

If part of your trip is outside the U.S. (the 50 states and the District of Columbia), follow the rules described in this section below for that part of the trip. For the part of your trip inside the U.S. (even if you're just stopping at spots in the U.S. to get to spots outside the U.S.), use the rules described just above. Your method of travel will help you determine which part of your trip is considered outside of the U.S.

Public transportation. If you travel by public transportation, any place in the U.S. where the vehicle makes a scheduled stop is a point in the U.S. Once the vehicle leaves the last scheduled stop in the U.S. on its way to a point outside the U.S., apply the rules for traveling outside the U.S.

> **Example:** You fly from New York to San Juan, Puerto Rico, with a scheduled stop in Miami. You return to New York non-stop. For the flight from New York to Miami, apply the rules for traveling within the U.S. For the flights from Miami to San Juan and San Juan to New York, apply the rules for trips outside the U.S.

Private car. Travel by private car in the U.S. is travel between points in the U.S., even when you are on your way to a destination outside the U.S.

> **Example:** You travel by car from Denver to Mexico City and return. Your travel from Denver to the border and from the border back to Denver is travel in the U.S., and the rules for that section apply.

The rules for travel outside the U.S. apply to your trip from the border to Mexico City and back to the border.

Private plane. If you travel by private plane, any trip, or part of a trip, for which both your takeoff and landing are in the U.S. is travel in the U.S. This is true even if part of your flight is over a foreign country.

> **Example:** You fly nonstop from Seattle to Juneau. Although the flight passes over Canada, the trip is considered to be travel in the U.S.

If any part of your business travel is outside the U.S., some of your deductions for the cost of getting to and from your destination may be limited. How much of your travel expenses are deductible depends in part upon how much of your trip outside the U.S. was business-related.

Entirely for Business

If you travel outside the U.S. and you spend the entire time on business activities, all your travel expenses of getting to and from your business destination are deductible. Follow the rules in the section above entitled Tax-Deductible Travel Expenses to determine which of your expenses at your destination are deductible.

Primarily for Business

If you did not spend your entire time on business activities, your trip is considered entirely for business, and you can deduct all of your business-related travel expenses, if you meet at least one of the following four conditions:

- You did not have substantial control over arranging the trip. You are not considered to have substantial control merely because you have control over the timing of your trip. A self-employed person is generally regarded as having substantial control over arranging a business trip. You are considered not to have substantial control over your trip if you are:
  - an employee who was reimbursed or paid a travel-expense allowance
  - not related to your employer (see definition in section above entitled Tax-Deductible Travel Expenses), and
  - not a managing executive—an employee who has the authority and responsibility, without being subject to the veto of another, to decide on the need for the business travel.
- You were outside the U.S. for a week or less, combining business and nonbusiness activities. One week means seven consecutive days. Do not count the day you leave the U.S., but count the day you return.

> **Example:** You traveled to Paris primarily for business. You left Denver on Tuesday and flew to New York. On Wednesday, you flew from New York to Paris, arriving the next morning. On Thursday and Friday, you had business discussions, and from Saturday until Tuesday, you were sightseeing. You flew back to New York, arriving Wednesday afternoon. On Thursday, you flew back to Denver.
>
> Although you were away from your home in Denver for more than a week,

you were not outside the U.S. for more than a week. This is because the day of departure does not count as a day outside the U.S. You can deduct your cost of the round-trip flight between Denver and Paris. You can also deduct the cost of your stay in Paris for Thursday and Friday while you conducted business. You cannot deduct the cost of your stay in Paris from Saturday through Tuesday, however, because those days were spent on nonbusiness activities.

- You can establish that a personal vacation was not a major consideration, even if you had substantial control over arranging the trip.
- You spent less than 25% of the total time you were outside the U.S. on nonbusiness activities, even if the trip outside the U.S. was for more than a week. Now, count both the day your trip began and the day it ended.

Example: You flew from Seattle to Tokyo, where you spent 14 days on business and five days on personal matters. You then flew back to Seattle. You spent one day flying in each direction. Because only 5/21 (24%) of your total time abroad was for nonbusiness activities, you can deduct as travel expenses what it would have cost you to make the trip if you had not engaged in any nonbusiness activity. The amount you can deduct is the cost of the round-trip plane fare and 16 days of meals (subject to the 50% limit), lodging and other related expenses.

If you traveled outside the U.S. primarily for business purposes, but spent 25% or more of your time on nonbusiness activities, your travel-expense deductions are limited unless you meet one of the other three conditions. What follows are the rules on claiming limited deductions.

Travel Allocation Rules—Counting Business Days

If your trip was not entirely for business, you must allocate your travel expenses on a day-to-day basis between your business and nonbusiness activities to determine your deductible amount.

To figure the deductible amount of your round-trip travel expenses between the U.S. and your business destination, multiply the total cost by a fraction. The numerator (top number) is the total number of business days outside the U.S. The denominator (bottom number) is the total number of all days outside the U.S. Your business days include transportation days, days your presence was required, days you spend on business, and certain weekends and holidays.

Transportation day. Count as a business day any day you spend traveling to or from a business destination. If, however, because of a nonbusiness activity, you do not travel by a direct route, your business days are the days it would take you to travel a reasonably direct route to your business destination. Extra days for side trips or nonbusiness activities cannot be counted as business days.

Presence required. Count as a business day any day that your presence is required at a particular place for a specific business purpose, even if you spend most of the day on nonbusiness activities.

Day spent on business. If your principal activity during working hours is in pursuit of your trade or business, the day is counted as a business day. Also count as a business day any day you are prevented from working because of circumstances beyond your control.

Certain weekends and holidays. Weekends, holidays and other necessary standby days are counted as business days if they fall between business days. But if they follow your business meetings or activity and you remain at your business destination for nonbusiness or personal reasons, they are not business days.

> **Example:** You live in New York City. You travel to Quebec, where you have a business appointment on Friday. You have another appointment on the following Monday. Because you had a business activity on Friday and had another business activity on Monday, the days in between are counted as business days. This is true even though you use that time for sightseeing, personal visiting or other nonbusiness activity. If you had no other business in Quebec after Friday, but stayed until Monday before starting home, Saturday and Sunday would be nonbusiness days.

By planning ahead, you can take advantage of this gift from the IRS. If you plan your business travel so that you have legitimate business obligations on either side of the weekend, your weekend

days are counted as business days, no matter how you spend them. In addition, because many cheaper flights require a Saturday night stay-over, the fact that your company saves money if you spend Saturday night is probably enough to make Saturday into a business day, even with no additional business on Monday. The IRS appears to be coming around to this position.

Personal Activity to or From Your Business Destination

If you had a vacation or other nonbusiness activity between the U.S. and your business destination or between your business destination and the U.S., you must allocate your travel expenses between business and nonbusiness days. You do so as follows:

1. Divide the number of business days by the total number of travel days.

2. Multiply the result by the cost of round-trip travel between the U.S. and your nonbusiness destination.

3. Add to the result the round-trip cost of travel between the U.S. and your business destination minus the round-trip cost of travel between the U.S. and your nonbusiness destination. This is

the deductible part of your cost of getting to and from your business destination.

4. Add to the result your business travel expenses while at your business destination. These are your total allowable travel expenses.

Example: You live in New York and flew to Brussels on Thursday, May 19, to attend a conference with a customer that began at noon Friday, May 20. The conference ended at noon Monday, May 23. That evening you flew to Dublin, where you visited with friends until the afternoon of June 5, when you flew home to New York. The primary purpose for the trip was to attend the conference. Had you not stopped in Dublin, you would have arrived home the evening of May 23.

You had substantial control over arranging the trip, were outside the U.S. more than a week and spent more than 25% of your time on vacation, and taking a personal vacation was a major consideration in making the trip. Therefore, you must allocate your expenses. May 19 through May 23 (five days) are business days; May 24 through June 5 (13 days) are nonbusiness days. The cost of round-trip travel between New York and Dublin is $600. The cost of round-trip travel between New York and Brussels is $800.

Your deductible travel expenses are as follows, following the four steps above:

1. 5/18 = 28%.
2. $600 x 28% = $168.
3. $168 + ($800 - $600) = $368.

4. $368 + your meals, lodging and any other business expenses in Brussels.

Personal Activity Beyond Your Business Destination

If you had a vacation or other nonbusiness activity at or beyond your business destination, you must allocate your travel expenses between your business and nonbusiness days. None of your travel expenses for nonbusiness activities at or beyond your business destination is deductible. You must also allocate your round-trip transportation and other costs between the U.S. and your business destination as follows:

1. Divide the number of business days by the total number of travel days.

2. Multiply the result by the cost of round-trip travel between the U.S. and your business destination.

3. Add to the result your business travel expenses while at your business destination. These are your total allowable travel expenses.

Add to this result your other business-related travel expenses at your business destination. The sum is your total deductible travel expenses.

Example: Again, you live in New York and flew to Brussels on Thursday, May 19, to attend a conference with a customer that began at noon Friday, May 20. The conference ended at noon Monday, May 23. This time, instead of going to Dublin for a vacation, you fly to Venice, Italy. You cannot deduct any part of the cost of your trip from Brussels to Venice and Venice to Brussels. Nor can you deduct 13/18 of the airfare and other expenses from New York to Brussels and Brussels to New York.

Your deductible travel expenses are as follows, following the three steps above:

1. 5/18 = 28%.
2. $800 x 28% = $224.
3. $224 + your meals, lodging and any other business expenses in Brussels.

Other Methods of Counting Business Days

You can use another method of counting business days if you establish that it more clearly reflects the time spent on nonbusiness activities outside the U.S.

Primarily for Personal Reasons

If your travel was primarily for vacation or for investment purposes and you spent some time attending brief professional seminars or a continuing education program, the entire cost of the trip is a nondeductible personal expense. You may, however, deduct your registration fees and any other expenses (such as the cost of a taxi getting from your hotel to the program and back) incurred that were directly related to your business.

Example 1: You are a doctor practicing medicine and a member of a professional association. The association sponsored a two-week trip to two foreign countries with three professional seminars in each country. Each seminar was two hours long and was held in a different city. You also made an optional side trip to a well-known tourist attraction in each of the countries visited. At the end of the trip,

you received a Certificate of Continuing Education in Medicine. You paid the cost of airfare, hotel accommodations, meals, a special escort, transportation to and from hotels and tips. No part of the cost you paid was specifically stated for the seminars, which were arranged for you by the sponsoring professional association.

Your participation in the professional seminars did not change what was essentially a vacation into a business trip. Your travel expenses were not related primarily to your business. You had no other expenses that were directly for your business. Therefore, you cannot deduct the cost of your trip as an ordinary and necessary business expense.

Example 2: The university from which you graduated has a continuing education program for members of its alumni association. This program consists of trips to various foreign countries, where academic exercises and conferences are set up to acquaint individuals in most occupations with selected facilities in several regions of the world. None of the conferences is directed toward specific occupations or professions, however, and it is up to each participant to seek out specialists and organizational settings appropriate to his or her occupational interests. Various sessions that include workshops, mini-lectures, skill development and exercises are held each of five days. You spend about two hours at each of the planned sessions, and the rest of the time touring and sightseeing with your family.

Your travel expenses for the trip are not deductible because the trip was primarily a vacation. The specifically stated registration fees and other incidental expenses incurred by you for the five sessions you attended that were directly related and beneficial to your business, however, are deductible business expenses.

Special Limits on Deducting Business Travel Expenses

Conventions

You can deduct your travel expenses when you attend a convention if you can show that your attendance benefits your trade or business. You cannot deduct the travel expenses for your family. If the convention is for investment, political, social or other purposes unrelated to your trade or business, you cannot deduct the expenses. (The exception is if you travel as an official delegate on behalf of a charity. See section on deducting charitable expenses at the end of this chapter.) Nonbusiness expenses, such as social or sightseeing expenses, are personal expenses and are not deductible. Your appointment or election as a delegate does not, in itself, entitle you to or deprive you of a deduction. Your attendance must be connected to your own trade or business.

Convention Agenda

The agenda of the convention does not have to deal specifically with your official duties or the responsibilities of your position or business. It is enough if the agenda is so related to your active trade or business and

your responsibilities that attendance for a business purpose is justified.

Conventions Held Outside North America

You cannot deduct expenses for attending a convention, seminar or similar meeting held outside the North American area (defined in IRS Publication 463) unless the meeting is directly related to your trade or business. Also, it must be as reasonable to hold the meeting outside the North American area as in it.

The following factors are taken into account to determine if it was reasonable to hold the meeting outside the North American area:

- the purpose of the meeting and the activities taking place at the meeting
- the purposes and activities of the sponsoring organizations or groups
- the residences of the active members of the sponsoring organization and the places at which other meetings of the sponsoring organizations or groups have been or will be held, and
- other relevant factors you may present, such as the rationale for choosing the convention's locale.

Cruise Ships (Luxury Water Travel)

In general, the deductibility rules described in this chapter don't apply if you take a cruise. Instead, you are limited to deducting twice the federal per diem rate allowed at the time of your travel. For the purpose of water travel, the federal per diem rate is the highest amount allowed for daily expenses to employees of the executive branch of the federal government while they are away from home but in the U.S. (The amount is set forth in IRS Publication 463.)

> **Example:** Esther, a self-employed travel agent, took an ocean liner from New York to London on business in May. When Esther traveled, the highest federal per diem amount allowed for luxury water travel was $180. Her expense for the six-day cruise was $2,300. Esther's deduction for the cruise cannot exceed $2,160—six days x $360 (twice the federal per diem rate).

If your expenses for luxury water travel include separately stated amounts for meals or entertainment, those amounts are subject to a 50% limit on meals and entertainment before you apply the daily limit.

> **Example:** Continuing the previous example, Esther's cruise had a total cost of $2,300. Of that amount, $1,400 was separately stated as meals and entertainment. Esther computes her deductible travel expenses as follows:

Meals and entertainment	$1,400
50% limit	x .5
Allowable meals/entertainment	$700
Other luxury water travel expenses	$900
Allowable cost before the daily limit	$1,600
Daily limit (per federal law)	$360
Times number of days	x 6
Maximum luxury water travel deduction	$2,160
Amount of allowable deduction	$1,600

> Esther's deduction for her cruise is limited to $1,600, even though the per diem rate is higher.

If your meal or entertainment charges are not separately stated or are not clearly identifiable, you are not required to allocate any portion of the total charge to meals or entertainment.

Conventions Held on Cruise Ships

You can deduct up to $2,000 per year of the expenses of attending conventions, seminars or similar meetings held on cruise ships. You must establish, however, that the meeting is directly related to your trade or business. All sailing ships are considered cruise ships. You can deduct the expenses if all of the following are true:

- The cruise ship is a vessel registered in the U.S.
- All of the cruise ship's ports of call are located in the U.S. or in possessions of the U.S.
- You attach to your tax return a written statement signed by you that includes:
  - the total days of the trip, excluding the days of transportation to and from the cruise ship port
  - the number of hours each day you devoted to scheduled business activities, and
  - a program of the scheduled business activities of the meeting.
- You attach to your tax return a written statement signed by an officer of the organization or group sponsoring the meeting that includes:
  - a schedule of the business activities of each day of the meeting, and
  - the number of hours you attended the scheduled business activities.

Record Keeping When Traveling for Business

When you travel away from home on business, keep records of all the expenses you incur and any advances you receive from your employer. You can use a log, diary, notebook or any other written record to keep track of your expenses.

 The IRS says that you "should" keep a record of your travel expenses. This is an understatement. Without good, contemporaneous records, the IRS is likely to disallow many of your travel expenses. Although it may seem like a chore to keep a written log (particularly if you are self-employed and don't need to report to an accounting department), it is a worthwhile investment of your time.

IRS Records and Forms

The records you keep must conform to the record keeping rules explained in IRS Publication 463. Standard hotel, restaurant and taxi receipts may not be specific enough if they do not break down the expenses sufficiently.

For employees to deduct unreimbursed travel expenses, they must fill out a Form 2106 and attach it to their annual 1040—and remember that the expenses must exceed 2% of the employee's gross adjusted income. Self-employed people can deduct their travel expenses on a Schedule C (or Schedule F for farmers or Schedule E for people who earn royalties).

Proving Business Expenses

The table below summarizes the elements necessary to prove certain business expenses.

General Rules When Traveling for a Charity

Certain travel expenses are deductible if your travel constitutes a contribution to a qualified charity. Like any other charitable contribution, you must itemize your deductions for travel for charitable purposes on Schedule A to IRS Form 1040. A legitimate contribution must be voluntary, and must be made without getting, or expecting to get, any personal benefit of equal value. There are limitations as to the amounts of deduction you can claim. See IRS Publication 526 for details.

When Are Charitable Travel Expenses Deductible?

The IRS allows you to deduct out-of-pocket expenses you incur that are directly connected with services you give to a qualified tax-exempt organization such as a church, synagogue or environmental group—the group should be able to supply proof to you of its charitable status. The IRS does not want you to take a vacation and claim it was for charitable purposes, however, so restrictions apply.

You can claim a charitable contribution deduction for travel expenses necessarily incurred while you are away from home performing services for a charitable organization only if there is no significant element of personal pleasure, recreation or vacation in such travel. On the other hand, the

Element to be Proved	Travel Expense	Entertainment Expense
Dollar amount spent for travel away from home	Amount of each separate expense for travel, lodging and meals. Incidental expenses may be totaled in reasonable categories, such as taxis and daily meals. If your employer reimburses you using a per diem allowance (including a meals-only allowance), you may not need proof of separate amounts spent for meals, lodging or incidental expenses.	Amount of each separate expense. Incidental expenses such as taxis and telephones may be totaled on a daily basis.
Time	Date you left and returned for each trip, and number of days for business.	Date of entertainment. For meals or entertainment directly before or after a business discussion, the date and duration of the business discussion.
Place	Name of city or other destination or the area of your travel, described by the name of the city, town or similar designation.	Name and address or location of place of entertainment. Types of entertainment if not apparent. Place where business discussion was held if entertainment is directly before or after a business discussion.
Business purpose	Business reason for travel or the business benefit gained or expected to be gained.	Business reason or the business benefit gained or expected to be gained. Nature of business discussion or activity.
Business relationship	Not applicable.	Occupation or other information (such as name or title) about persons entertained showing business relationship to you. If all people entertained did not take part in business discussion, identify those who did. You must also prove that you were present if entertainment was a business meal.

deduction will not be denied simply because you enjoy providing services to the charitable organization.

Example 1: You are a troop leader for a tax-exempt youth group and take the group on a camping trip. You can take a charitable contribution deduction for your own travel expenses if you are on duty in a genuine and substantial sense throughout the trip, even if you enjoyed the trip. If you have only nominal duties related to the performance of services for the charity, however, or for significant portions of the trip you are not required to render services, you cannot deduct your travel expenses.

Example 2: You sail from one island to another and spend eight hours a day counting whales and other forms of marine life. The project is sponsored by a charitable environmental organization. In most circumstances, the IRS's official position is that you cannot deduct your travel expenses. (Note that many programs run by charitable organizations do qualify for such a deduction—particularly when you provide services to an established research institution. Check with both the charity and your tax preparer.)

Example 3: You work for several hours each morning on an archaeological excavation. The rest of the day is free for recreation and sightseeing. You cannot take a charitable contribution deduction even though you work very hard during those few hours.

Example 4: You spend the entire day attending a charitable organization's regional meeting as a chosen representative. In the evening, you go to the theater. You can deduct your travel expenses as charitable contributions, but you cannot deduct your theater ticket. (See special rules for conventions below.)

Tax-Deductible Charitable Travel Expenses

You can deduct your reasonable travel expenses, including:

- air, rail and bus transportation
- out-of-pocket expenses for your car (or a standard rate of 13.5¢ per mile plus tolls and parking fees)
- taxi fares or airport shuttles
- lodging costs, and
- the costs of meals.

There is no standard meal allowance while traveling for a charity as there is when traveling for business. On the other hand, you are not restricted by the 50% limitation on deducting business meals— you can deduct the entire cost of the meal. Incidental expenses, such as cleaning and tips, may be deducted if they were necessary because of the services you provided on your trip.

Per Diem (Reimbursed Travel Expenses)

If the charity reimburses you a set amount for each day you travel (called a per diem) and the per diem doesn't cover your actual expenses, you can deduct the difference as a charitable contribution. If you are reimbursed for your actual expenses, you cannot claim any deduction. If you are provided with a per diem and your actual expenses are less, you must declare difference as *income* on your tax return.

> **Example:** You are given $100 per day to cover your expenses for a five-day trip. Your actual total expenses were $300. The following April 15, you will have to declare $200 as income ($500 - $300 = $200).

Conventions

If you are a chosen representative attending a convention of a qualified charitable organization, you can deduct actual expenses for travel and transportation, including a reasonable amount for meals and lodging.

> **Example:** You belong to a local church and spend a weekend out of town in order to attend the church's national convention. If you were not selected by your local church to represent the congregation at the national convention, you cannot deduct your travel expenses. Your

expenses would be considered personal and not charitable. If you are an official delegate, however, you would be able to deduct your expenses.

You cannot deduct personal expenses for sightseeing, fishing excursions, theater tickets, nightclubs or other entertainment. You also cannot take any deductions for the expenses of your spouse, children or another person.

Record Keeping When Traveling for a Charity

As with other types of travel expenses, you will be in a better position to justify your claimed deductions if you keep contemporaneous records of your actual expenses and document the time that you spent providing services during your travel.

If you are attending a convention on behalf of a charity, be sure to get a written statement from your group designating you as the chosen representative. (The IRS does allow multiple representatives to conventions, as it requires you to be "a" representative, not "the" representative.)

Chapter 13

Resolving Your Travel Dispute: Let's Make a Deal

An Introduction to Resolving Your Travel Dispute

You do not need to hire a lawyer to resolve most travel-related disputes. Generally, these disputes concern relatively small amounts of money, much of which you would not see if you had to pay an attorney. Using the techniques discussed in this chapter and your own determination, you should be able to deal directly with the other party in the dispute, whether it is your local travel agent or a major airline, and negotiate a satisfactory resolution of your problem.

Because most companies in the travel industry depend on good customer relations and repeat business, they are often willing to settle disputes with travelers informally. You will not get compensation for your losses, however, unless you assert your rights. And let us repeat—most of the time you will succeed in getting compensation with little or no outside help. We suggest the following six steps to assert your rights and seek a solution:

1. Know your rights. If you haven't yet read the appropriate chapter (or sections) of this book, do so before you assert your right to compensation.

2. Negotiate in person when the problem arises. Don't endure the problem and hope for a solution after the fact. Your best bet is to complain early and get an on-the-spot resolution.

3. Write a Solution Letter™. If you cannot resolve your problem on the spot, put your complaint in writing. Through an effective Solution Letter™, you can explain your problem and seek compensation.

4. Write a second letter. If the travel supplier fails to respond to your first letter or sends a form letter that does not directly address your problem, a well-written second letter often will do the trick.

5. Get outside assistance. If the supplier ignores your second letter, get third-party help from your travel agent, a mediator, a travel industry association or an appropriate consumer or government agency.

6. Take it to court. If all else fails and you want to continue the fight, you'll probably have to file a lawsuit.

It is important to focus on solving the problem, not venting your anger. You are entitled to take action to ensure that no one tramples on your legal rights, but rude or aggressive attacks are likely to be met with equally forceful defensive maneuvers. Whenever you try to resolve a dispute over your travel rights, keep the following points in mind:

- Try to find a solution as soon as the problem occurs. The details will still be fresh in your mind, and your trip will not be ruined.

- Take a firm, but polite approach. Blowing your top may make you feel better in the short term, but it will not help you get a satisfactory solution.

- Document what happened and supply any proof you have. Documentation—such as receipts, photos, tickets, boarding pass, baggage check tags, brochures, and reservation confirmations, as well as the dates, places and times of the dispute, names of people involved and witnesses—strengthens your case and clarifies the situation.

- **Set forth the specific, realistic compensation you want.** Don't just complain. Be direct, clear and specific about what you want.

- **Deal with the person who has the power and authority to resolve your problem.** Avoid the delay and frustration of presenting your thoughtfully crafted case to the wrong person.

Negotiate in Person When the Problem Arises

The best way to handle any travel problem is to complain right away and try to resolve the problem on the spot. Many situations can be improved immediately. Don't be stoic and put up with an unsatisfactory situation in the hope that you'll be compensated later. Even if your problem is not resolved right away, you'll have laid the groundwork for a formal complaint later.

You will be in a weaker position if you wait until after the trip because your bargaining power decreases dramatically once you have returned home and no longer present an immediate obstacle for the travel supplier. Even if you do get your money back after your trip is over, you probably won't be compensated for the suffering, lost vacation days or disruption of your schedule.

Talk to the Right Person

Don't waste your time negotiating with someone who can't help you. Figuring out who has the authority to arrange a solution can save you a lot of time and energy in the long run. If something goes wrong during a trip, speak to the most senior representative of the travel supplier you can find, such as the local manager of the airline, cruise line, hotel or rental car company, or the director of your tour or cruise.

Few travel-related problems are caused by on-the-spot agents such as tour guides or rental car salespeople, and these people usually lack the power to change your situation. Even when the hotel clerk, tour guide or flight attendant is the cause of your problem, you will often have a better chance of reaching a resolution if you talk with the manager. If no onsite representative for the company is available, call your travel agent and ask for help.

Identify How Valuable You Are as a Customer

Let the manager know that you are a valuable customer by explaining how frequently you use this particular supplier and how many of your friends, associates and relatives also use the supplier and will be influenced by your account of the trip (but don't overdo it!). If you're a member of a frequent flyer, frequent renter or frequent overnight-guest program, be sure to mention it.

Travel suppliers don't like to lose regular customers—it is much more expensive for a company to attract a new client than to maintain a current one. Establishing yourself as a regular customer will increase your chance of getting a favorable response because it is in the company's financial best interest to pay attention to and resolve your complaint.

If you are not a regular customer or a member of a "frequent" user program, emphasize how you will be doing more traveling in the future and that you are looking to establish a relationship with a particular travel supplier and possibly join a "frequent" user program. Let the supplier know that the experience colored your view of the supplier and that if your problem isn't resolved to your satisfaction, you will certainly take your future business to its competitors.

Be Firm But Polite

Negotiations take many forms, and negotiators have many different styles, but successful negotiators almost always follow a few basic principles.

Control Your Anger

First of all, try to keep your cool. Yelling at someone yields very little progress toward a resolution and may very well reduce your chances of getting assistance. Instead, take a deep breath and explain to the manager exactly what went wrong and how you propose that it be fixed. If you are very angry, you may find it helpful to jot down a few notes ahead of time in order to help you stay on track.

Focus on Fixing the Problem, Not Blaming the Manager

Second, focus on how to fix the problem—not on who caused it. Your natural reaction may be to vent your anger on the manager or blame him for the problem. It is natural for people to direct their anger toward others; however, verbal attacks invoke defensive responses and slow down the process of negotiation. Your goal is to get the manager on your side so that the two of you can team up against the problem and work toward a solution. If you focus on the problem, explaining it clearly and calmly without casting blame, you are likely to get a more cooperative and prompt response.

> **Example:** You booked a one-week package tour to Baton Rouge through Fun-on-the-Run Tours. You couldn't sleep because of the noise (both on the street and in the hotel) you heard all night. The morning after your first night, you spoke to the desk clerk about the problem. When you said, "You gave me a lousy room," the desk clerk became defensive and insisted that there was nothing wrong with your room. Had you stated, "I had difficulty sleeping last night because of the noise. Is there another room available in a quieter part of the hotel?" you may have gotten a new room.

Stay Flexible

Finally, while you may need to be persistent to get sufficient time and attention from a supervisor to resolve your problem, try to remain flexible and open to different options that are proposed. If you approach the manager with a take-it-or-leave-it stance and are unwilling to listen to alternative suggestions, you may miss out on a solution that meets your interests more fully than the one you suggested. Spend a little time exploring the possibilities before you decide which one is the best for you.

 For a thorough and engaging discussion of principled negotiation, read *Getting to Yes,* by Fisher and Ury (Penguin Books).

Explain What Happened

Tell the manager exactly what the problem is and how it has affected you. Try to refrain from barraging him with a series of details, and keep your explanation focused on the one or two specific events that matter the most and for which you are seeking a solution. Be sure to provide information that will help explain the compensation you are requesting, such as receipts for expenses you want reimbursed or your room number if the manager needs to take a look at its shortcomings. If other travelers are involved in the problem, give their names.

Say What You Want

Decide what you think should be done to remedy the situation and let the supplier know. Ask for something specific that the supplier can actually provide. Many common problems with hotel rooms, rental cars, cruise line cabins or airline seating can be resolved relatively quickly and easily if you describe what you want done. Remember that an upgrade, future credit or other non-monetary solution is much easier for the travel company to supply than a cash refund.

If the Supplier Doesn't Cooperate, Consider Leaving

If your negotiations do not result in an acceptable solution, consider leaving the trip (if this is an option). You may do best to go to a different hotel, get off of the cruise ship at the next port or reschedule your flight in order to avoid wasting more time and money. Although you might not be able to recover all of your money if you leave, by refusing to accept the problem, you strengthen your case for a refund in the

future. Don't accept a host of excuses or delays in the expectation that your problem will be solved eventually. The longer you tolerate a problem, the more difficult it is to make an effective complaint later on.

Write a Solution Letter™

If you are unable to reach a solution by negotiating in person when the problem arises, you'll have to put your demand in writing. Probably the number one fault in letters written to travel suppliers is that they are "complaint" letters, not "solution" letters. Spilling out page after page of your anguished story may provide a satisfying emotional outlet, but it will not help get your desired compensation. Forget revenge. In most instances, the best approach is to send a well-formulated complaint directly to the travel supplier and suggest a reasonable solution.

Identify How Valuable You Are As a Customer

It is important to show the travel supplier why it is in the supplier's best interest to help you out. If you and your family, friends or coworkers use the travel supplier often, be sure to say so, and be specific. Stating that "My family and I took 12 flights on your airline last year" is much more effective than saying, "I fly a lot." Include any other evidence of how important you are as a customer, such as your airline frequent flyer number, proof that you are a rental car frequent renter, a list of the trips you've taken through the tour operator or the number of people you work with who regularly stay at the hotel. As noted above, travel suppliers don't like to lose regular customers. And if you're not a regular customer, be sure to mention that you were considering becoming one.

Take a Firm but Polite Approach

You have almost nothing to gain by losing your temper and sending an irate letter. If you really need to get things off your chest, write your story out in all its glorious detail and emotion, then take that letter, file it far away and *start over*. Your goal is to elicit empathy, not provoke or annoy the reader—and so, you must present your situation in a straightforward and positive way. The odds are that the person reading your letter did not cause your problem, and she is unlikely to sympathize with someone who rants and roars, or threatens to "never use this company again." Instead, your letter should adopt a calm, reasonable approach that outlines what you think is wrong, how you think the problem should be resolved and why you think the supplier should resolve it.

Although the tone of your letter should be calm and reasonable, you do not need to downplay the significance of the events and the negative effect they had on you. Your challenge is to strike a balance whereby you explain the seriousness of the situation, but refrain from making offensive threats or accusations. Let's continue with the example from earlier in the chapter: You booked a one-week package tour to Baton Rouge through Mr. Chas, the owner of Fun-on-the-Run Tours, and were very unhappy with your hotel accommodations. The following examples of two opening paragraphs illustrate the difference between the approach of a complaint letter and a Solution Letter™.

Sample 1: First paragraph of a Complaint Letter

> To Whom It May Concern:
>
> Your company ruined my last vacation in Baton Rouge by sticking me in a run-down, filthy motel just so you could save money. How dare you waste my time like that. I have heard of worthless rip-off artists before, but you really take the cake. I am going to let all my friends know how awful your trips are and tell them never to use Fun-on-the-Run Tours. Exploiting people and luring them into spending their hard-earned cash on a worthless trip is disgusting. You're no better than the common crook on the street.

Sample 1: First paragraph of a Solution Letter™

> Dear Mr. Chas,
>
> As a regular customer of Fun-on-the-Run Tours, I am writing to express extreme dissatisfaction with my most recent trip with your company. Because I have taken two successful previous trips through your company, and my parents and sister have also had positive experiences through Fun-on-the-Run Tours, I relied on your company's good reputation when I took this vacation to Baton Rouge. I am deeply disappointed that the hotel on this trip fell far below acceptable standards and, as a result, I did not enjoy my vacation: The hotel was so noisy I could not get any sleep, and I got food poisoning in the hotel restaurant.

Use "I" Statements When Possible

In your Solution Letter™, avoid making accusations about the actions and motives of the supplier ("you" statements), and instead explain how you were affected by the circumstances of your trip ("I" statements). People who hear inaccurate accusations about themselves often get defensive and angry and are less inclined to cooperate with you. When you use "I" statements, it is easier for the other side to hear what you are saying and be willing to work towards a satisfactory negotiated agreement. In the examples above, the statement, "I am deeply disappointed that the hotel on this trip fell far below acceptable standards and, as a result, I did not enjoy my vacation," is an "I" statement. The statement, "Your company ruined my last vacation in Baton Rouge by sticking me in a run-down, filthy motel just so you could save money," is a "you" statement.

Explain What Happened

Say exactly what the circumstances were that led to your complaint, including dates, times, locations, flight numbers, license plate number, room number, ticket numbers, tour guides and personnel you dealt with. To strengthen your Solution Letter™, submit any proof you can, such as documentation of losses and extra payments, or copies of receipts. Where a problem is visible, enclose photos of the problem. If possible, provide the names and addresses of other travelers who saw the problem or suffered from it themselves. Make a realistic dollar estimate of the damage you suffered, including the value you place on lost time or substantial inconvenience, any services you paid for and did not receive or any extra money you paid in an effort to mitigate the problem.

Try to keep your Solution Letter™ focused on the one or two incidents that matter to you the most. Even if there were numerous problems, stick to the ones that caused you the most inconvenience or financial loss. The best Solution Letters™ are no longer than one typed page. A long list of detailed woes will exhaust and annoy the reader and decrease your chances of compensation.

Let's continue with the above example. Assume that your package vacation to Baton Rouge included airfare and six nights at a hotel (including daily dinner and breakfast), and cost you $3,200. You were extremely dissatisfied with the quality, location and service of your hotel, and you tried unsuccessfully to find a suitable substitute hotel during your trip. The following continuation of the above Solution Letter™ sets forth what happened and why you were dissatisfied.

Sample 1: Solution Letter™ continuation

As you may recall, before I bought this trip, I told you I wanted to take a relaxing vacation in Baton Rouge and to stay in a place where I could be sure to get away from the crowds and noise at night. The package that I purchased from Fun-on-the-Run Tours was described as a "luxury vacation with elegant accommodations and five-star dining." What I received was a loud and uncomfortable room and extremely low quality meals.

First, my room, #205 in the Sandy Sheets Hotel, overlooked the corner of Needle Street and Space Avenue, major thoroughfares that had loud traffic from 6 am until 2 am every day (the enclosed photos show the amount of traffic at various times during the day). My second-floor windows were single-paned glass and provided no protection from the traffic disturbances. In addition, my room was located right next to the elevator shaft, so that I was awakened by loud, drunken hotel guests at various times throughout the night. Even with earplugs, I did not get more than three hours of undisturbed sleep any night the entire week.

Second, the meals at the hotel were inexcusably bad. I had to stay in my room all day on Wednesday because food poisoning from the hotel's shrimp dinner on the second night gave me and five other guests (whose names and addresses are attached) severe gastro-intestinal disorders. My illness was so bad that I had to send for a doctor who prescribed medication (physician's bill and bill for medication attached). Not wanting to risk further illness, I dined at restaurants away from the hotel for the remainder of my stay. Further, the breakfasts served were nothing like what was described in your company's brochure. The brochure stated that there would be a full American-style breakfast buffet, including a variety of hot dishes, meats and homemade regional specialties, served from 7-10 am each day. Instead, the buffet included only milk and two types of cold cereal, plus the same selection of donuts and pastries every morning (see enclosed photos), and was served from 7-8 am. Because I usually sleep until 9 am when on vacation, I missed four breakfasts.

I tried to move to a different, quieter room within the hotel, but I was told this was impossible. I also made ten phone calls to the hotels listed on the attached sheet to try to find a decent room at a comparable rate, but everything was booked. I am very angry and disappointed that I spent so much money on your tour and had to stay in such a terrible hotel.

Say What You Want

A good Solution Letter™ asks for specific compensation that the supplier can deliver. The most vivid and detailed description of what went wrong on your trip will be worth very little unless it also contains an explanation of exactly what you expect the supplier to do for you. A company cannot bring back your lost vacation days or ease your mental anguish, but it can give you a discount, refund, credit towards future travel, apology or host of other things—*if* you ask for it.

Most companies would rather give you credit for future services than a refund. A free trip, some extra frequent flyer miles, some credit or an upgrade on future travel are examples of specific kinds of compensation that may be easier to get than cold cash. Be sure to include specific details of your expectations, such as how much credit you expect, by what date you expect to receive it and in what form.

Sample 1: Solution Letter™ closing paragraphs

I request that you provide compensation in the amount of $1,408. I calculated my out-of-pocket costs as follows:

$185	physician's visit
38	medication
4	earplugs
18	phone calls to alternate hotels
130	meals away from the hotel restaurant (receipts for these expenses are attached)
533	1/6 of the total price for the day I lost due to food poisoning from the hotel's food
500	reasonable compensation for the loss of sleep I suffered during my vacation
$1,408	**Total**

I am sure you will agree that this vacation package fell far below the normal standards of Fun-on-the-Run Tours, and I trust that you will respond to my request for compensation promptly and in full. To show my good faith, I am willing to accept full credit on a future trip with Fun-on-the-Run Tours.

Sincerely yours,

Jan Kincaid

Jan Kincaid

(201) 555-9876

Where to Send Your Solution Letter™

Nothing is more frustrating than having your well-crafted letter wind up in someone's dead letter pile. Avoid this delay by directing your Solution Letter™ to the travel supplier with which you had a contract. If your complaint is about a package tour, send your letter to the tour operator. If you bought your travel services separately, write to the offending supplier. If the supplier is a small business, write directly to the president or manager of the company. Be sure to send a copy to the travel agent who made your travel arrangements.

Many large travel suppliers have offices or individuals who handle complaints. For a list of customer complaint offices of major travel suppliers in the U.S., see the Appendix. These headquarters may have very limited authority to handle complaints about a franchised location, so in that situation write directly to the franchise manager. A franchised travel supplier has the same name as a national chain, but the franchise owner is legally responsible for the facility and only pays a fee for the right to use the name. To find out whether a local travel supplier is owned by the parent company or by a franchise, look in the travel supplier's brochures or other literature. If you can't tell, you will have to ask the management of the particular supplier or the company's national head-quarters.

If your complaint is with an airline, write or call the Department of Transportation (DOT) so your complaint will be counted and published in DOT's monthly complaint summary. (See below, for DOT's address and phone number.)

Finally, whenever you send a Solution Letter™, be sure to include your daytime telephone number so that the supplier can contact you.

When Your Complaint Is With an Airline

Airlines must designate an official to respond to complaints from passengers. Before sending your Solution Letter™, contact the airline, ask for the name of the complaint resolution official, and address your initial complaint to him. Sending a copy of the complaint to the same address, but to the attention of the president of the company, may hasten the handling of your complaint. (Airline addresses and phone numbers are in the Appendix.)

If Your Solution Letter™ Is Ignored—Write a Second Letter

Unfortunately, many travel suppliers respond to letters from unhappy travelers with a form letter. The form-letter response may have very little to do with the substance of your complaint and is frequently used by travel suppliers in an effort to make you give up. Don't! Understand this tactic and try not to let it frustrate you. With very little additional time or effort, a second Solution Letter™ may be your critical step to success. It should reinforce your first letter and show the supplier that you are not just going to give up and go away.

First, attach a copy of your original letter and the supplier's response, then briefly recap your complaint for the supplier. Next, explain how the supplier's first response failed to address your specific problem and why it is unacceptable; then reiterate the compensation that you want to receive. While you should resist the temptation to blow your top and tell the supplier that its failure to respond to your first letter is proof that all the horrible things you have been thinking about it are true, your second letter may include some more forceful language. For example, when you reiterate your desired compensation, you can "demand" instead of "request" that the company provide the compensation you seek.

Finally, be sure to include a specific date by which you expect the supplier to deliver your compensation and the method by which it should be delivered.

Sample 2: Solution Letter™

Dear Mr. Chas,

On (date), I sent you a letter describing the problems that took place during my Fun-on-the-Run package vacation in Baton Rouge (a copy of the letter is attached). I recently received a form-letter response from your office (also attached) that did not address the specific concerns I raised in my original letter. My letter was not a "request for further information," as your response indicated. My letter requested specific, reasonable compensation from your company for the losses I incurred on my trip.

In my letter, I requested compensation for loss of sleep and lost vacation time, and medical expenses related to the food poisoning caused by the hotel, as well as reimbursement for meals that I was forced to purchase outside of the hotel. Your response ignored all of these requests.

As a loyal Fun-on-the-Run customer, I was greatly disappointed to receive this extremely inferior vacation after putting my trust in your company. Your failure to respond to my specific requests angers me even more. I demand that you provide the requested compensation of $1,408.

Please send your response and the compensation to me at the above address by (date).

Sincerely yours,

Jan Kincaid

Jan Kincaid

If the supplier offered any sort of compensation in its original letter to you, it is an admission that your case has merit. If the compensation offered is reasonably close to what you requested, take it. If the compensation falls very short of your expectations, make a counterproposal in your second Solution Letter™.

If you get no satisfactory response to your second Solution Letter™, we suggest that you get outside help (see below). Before doing so, consider sending a threatening letter to the travel supplier. Make sure your threat is specific and plausible. Rantings about million-dollar lawsuits are likely to be ignored as crank letters. By describing exactly what steps you will take (file a lawsuit in Small Claims Court), where (at the clerk's office at Morris County Courthouse) and when (if I do not hear from you by August 1), you may be taken seriously. Having a threatening letter sent by an attorney can help, but you may be able to save money by writing most of it yourself.

Get Outside Help

If the travel supplier ignores your Solution Letters™, you may have to turn to outside help.

Your Travel Agent

If your complaint is against someone other than your travel agent, get as much assistance as you can from the agent. Travel agencies often have much more leverage with suppliers than individual travelers. If your agent refuses to help you, get a new agent.

Travel Industry Associations

If you have a problem with a particular type of travel supplier, contact the travel industry association for that type of supplier.

If your complaint is against a tour operator, contact one or both of the organizations that address consumer complaints against member agencies—the U.S. Tour Operators Association (USTOA) and the National Tour Association (NTA). If your complaint is against a travel agency, the American Society of Travel Agents (ASTA) provides a mediation service for consumer complaints against travel agents who are ASTA members if the situation prompting the complaint took place within the past six months. Other travel agent groups such as ARTA and IATAN (see list below) have no formal dispute resolution program, but may be able to help you sort out a dispute with a member organization by sending the member organization a copy of your Solution Letter™ and requesting a response, or by contacting the member organization for you by telephone.

U.S. Tour Operators Association
(USTOA)
342 Madison Avenue, Suite 1522
New York, NY 10173
tel: 212-599-6599
fax: 212-599-6744
Web: http://www.ustoa.com

National Tour Association (NTA)
Member Services, 120 Kentucky Street
Lexington, KY 40508
tel: 606-226-4444
fax: 606-226-4414

American Society of Travel Agents
(ASTA)
1101 King Street, Suite 200
Alexandria, VA 22314
tel: 703-739-2782
fax: 703-684-8319
Web: http://www.astanet.com

Association of Retail Travel Agents
(ARTA)
845 Sir Thomas Court, Suite 3
Harrisburg, PA 17109
tel: 717-545-9548
fax: 606-264-0368

International Airlines Travel Agent
Network (IATAN)
300 Garden City Plaza, Suite 342
Garden City, NY 11530
tel: 516-747-4716
fax: 516-747-4462
Web: http://www.iatan.org

Institute of Certified Travel Agents (ICTA)
148 Linden Street
Wellesley, MA 02181
tel: 781-237-0280
fax: 781-237-3860
Web: http://www.icta.com

 For a free copy of *Avoiding Travel Problems,* send a self-addressed stamped envelope with your request to ASTA's Public Relations Department at the above address.

Consumer Advocates

If there is a consumer advocacy group in your area (such as a television or radio station consumer action hotline), get in touch with it for advice and support. It may know of others who have encountered your type of problem before and have useful suggestions for reaching a satisfactory resolution. These groups can be found through the telephone book, a local library or your local district attorney's office.

In addition, you can provide a public service to other travelers by filing a complaint with the National Council of Better Business Bureaus, which operates a nationwide system for settling consumer disputes through mediation and arbitration. Check your local telephone book to find a BBB office in your area.

If you were the victim of a travel scam, contact the National Fraud Information Center. See the section Where to Go For Help in Chapter 7.

Two specific consumer organizations may be able to help as well:

- International Airline Passengers Association (IAPA) provides safety reports and other information on airlines to its members. It sends a copy of a member's complaint (and nonmember complaints if very serious), as well as its own letter, to the offending airline to try to reach a solution. Contact IAPA at P.O. Box 700907, Dallas, TX 75370, 214-404-9980, http://www.iapa.com (Web).

- Society for the Advancement of Travel for the Handicapped (SATH) responds to complaints from its members, and occasionally to nonmembers, by writing letters to offending organizations. SATH can be contacted at 347 5th Avenue, Suite 610, New York, NY 10016; 212-447-7284, http://www.sath.org (Web).

Travel Press

Several newsletters, magazines and travel sections in newspapers provide extensive travel information, including useful travel tips. The following resources are especially recommended:

- *Consumer Reports Travel Letter* provides travel information from the consumer's point of view through thoroughly researched articles and letters from travelers that warn of travel traps and inform you of travel bargains. Available from Subscription Director, Consumer Reports Travel Letter, Box 53629, Boulder, CO 80322-3629, tel: 800-234-1970; the cost is $39 per year.

- *New York Times Sunday Travel Section* has several valuable features, including "The Practical Traveler," a priceless resource for travelers who want to stay well informed. This unusually well-written, up-to-date and insightful column tackles a current travel topic each week. In addition, "Q. & A." answers readers' questions on particular destinations and travel suppliers. These and other travel columns, such as "Frugal Traveler," can be accessed online at: http://www.nytimes.com.

- *Condé Nast Traveler Magazine's* monthly column, "The Ombudsman," helps to resolve readers' disputes with travel suppliers. "The Ombudsman" will contact airlines, cruise lines and other travel suppliers directly, and is often successful in obtaining reimbursement or other compensation for the disgruntled traveler. Available from Condé Nast Subscriptions, P.O. Box 57018, Boulder, CO 80322, tel: 800-777-0700; the cost is $18 per year.

Government Agencies

In some states, particularly those dependent upon tourism such as Hawaii and Florida, state and local governments have set up offices to handle travelers' complaints and help travelers receive compensation. These travelers' advocates can be located through a local Better Business Bureau or a local or state tourism office. State or local consumer affairs offices are another potential source of assistance. They are listed in the government section of most telephone books.

The local district attorney or state attorney general's office where you are traveling may be able to help with your problems with a local travel supplier based on information and documentation you provide on the office's complaint form. Unfortunately, these offices usually are short on staff, do not specialize in travel rights and may not consider your ruined vacation a serious problem. The district attorney or attorney general's office in your home state may be more interested in helping, but may lack much authority to address disputes arising out of state.

Other specialized government agencies may be able to help as follows:

- **Department of Transportation.** DOT's *Fly Rights* guide contains information on federal regulations regarding delays, bankruptcy protection, overbooking, smoking and refunds. Copies cost $1.75 each and can be ordered by sending a check or money order to Superintendent of Documents, Consumer Information Center, Department 133-B, Pueblo, CO

81009 and are available on the Web at http://www.pueblo.gsa.gov. In addition, you can register a complaint about an airline by contacting DOT's Office of Consumer Affairs, 400 Seventh St., SW, Room 10405, Washington, DC 20590; tel: 202-366-2220; TDD: 202-755-7687. Passenger complaints are tracked and, at the very least, yours may help someone else in the future. To get DOT documents online, type http://www. dot.gov.

- **Federal Trade Commission.** Although the FTC generally does not intervene in individual consumer disputes, any information you provide might lead to an FTC investigation. Also, the FTC has free consumer publications, including *Car Rental Guide, 900 Numbers, Telemarketing Travel Fraud, Timeshare Resales* and *Timeshare Tips.* Contact the FTC, 6th and Pennsylvania Avenue, NW, Washington, DC 20580; 202-326-3238 or http://www.ftc.gov (Web).

- **Federal Communications Commission.** If you were defrauded by a telemarketer or phone solicitor, or sucked in when a travel service provider aired a fraudulent ad on radio or television, contact the FCC, Common Carrier Bureau, Consumer Complaints, 1919 M Street, NW, Washington, DC 20554; 202-418-0200 (voice), 202-418-0232 (fax), http:// www.fcc.gov (Web).

- **U.S. Postal Service.** If you were cheated by anyone who used the U.S. mail, contact a postal inspector. Look in the government listing of your telephone book white pages for the local address.

If you can't find one, contact the federal office, USPS, Inspection Services, 475 L'Enfant Plaza, SW, Washington, DC 20260; 800-654-8896 or 202-268-4267 (voice), 202-268-4563 (fax).

Mediation

If you'd like outside help in resolving your dispute with a travel supplier but don't want to go to court, mediation may be a good option. Mediators assist disputing parties in negotiating a settlement by helping both sides to communicate effectively, identify issues, generate options and decide on a mutually satisfactory agreement. Mediators, unlike lawyers, do not represent one side or the other; mediators, unlike judges, do not have the authority to impose a decision on either side.

Mediation is particularly appropriate in travel disputes where suppliers or service providers often want to preserve ongoing relationships (such as local travel agents or tour operators who want to keep customers), or want to resolve the dispute in a non-adversarial manner. When disputing parties are located near each other and can meet face-to-face relatively easily, mediation may be a wise choice. Here are some of the advantages of using mediation over going to court:

- **Parties control the outcome.** In mediation, the parties negotiate directly with one another with the help of the mediator. Mediators use normal, everyday language, not legalese, and the parties mutually agree to any final decision.

- **Cost and time effective.** Because the parties don't have to engage in lengthy fact gathering or follow complicated court procedures and pay lawyers' fees, mediation frequently saves parties money, time and stress.

- **Confidential and informal.** Mediation is a private, confidential, flexible process structured by the mediator according to the needs of the parties.

- **Not limited to legal claims.** Mediation focuses on resolving the specific dispute at hand, including relevant nonlegal issues that arise. Mediators are not restricted to following legal precedents and do not have to consider the impact of any given mediation on future disputes.

- **Helps create "win-win" solutions.** By broadening the scope of possible solutions, each side has a greater chance of finding a solution that meets his or her underlying interests.

You can locate mediators through several resources, including:

- ASTA and NTA—both provide mediation services if you have a dispute with one of their member organizations.

- Your telephone directory—look under "Mediators" in the yellow pages.

- *Martindale-Hubbell Dispute Resolution Directory* (Martindale-Hubbell)—if a local public library doesn't have this publication, a law library might.

- *Annual Directory of Alternative Dispute Resolution Organizations in the United States* (Graduate Group, West Hartford, CT)—again, check a local public or law library.

- Society for Professionals in Dispute Resolution (SPIDR), 815 15th Street, NW, Suite 530, Washington, DC

20005; 202-783-7277 (voice); 202-783-7281 (fax)—send $25 for the membership list. You can also visit SPIDR's Website at http:www.spidr.org.

 For more information on selecting a mediator and the entire mediation process, see *How to Mediate Your Dispute*, by Peter Lovenheim (Nolo Press).

Which mediator you should choose depends on the nature of your dispute and the services available in your area. Public or community dispute resolution services using volunteer mediators exist in many metropolitan areas and handle cases at very low cost, but give you little or no say as to who mediates your case. If you would like to find a mediator with particular subject matter expertise or if there is no community service in your area, a private mediator is the best bet.

No matter who you choose to act as your mediator, initiating mediation is generally very simple. You contact the mediator and supply basic information about the nature of the dispute and the entities involved. The mediator contacts the other parties in the dispute to notify them of your desire to mediate and request their participation. (Obviously, they can say "no.") Throughout the mediation process, the mediator establishes a constructive environment for negotiation so that parties can identify important issues, build on areas of common ground and reach agreements. Keep in mind that the purpose of mediation is for the parties to arrive at a mutually agreeable solution—not to determine who is right or wrong.

Take It to Court

You tried negotiating on the spot, wrote your most convincing letters, sought outside help, and explored mediation, and you still haven't received the compensation you believe you deserve. At this point, you have two options —drop the matter (and make sure you and everyone you know never uses the travel supplier or service provider again) or go to court.

Going to court doesn't necessarily mean hiring a lawyer. If the case is relatively simple and the total amount at stake is small —no more than a few thousand dollars— you may be able to handle the case yourself in a small claims court. For more compli- cated cases, where the value of your claim is worth more or where there are serious or permanent injuries, you may have to file your case in a regular civil court. If the case is a large one and involves interstate or international travel, you might have to file your case in federal court.

To determine the value of your claim and to decide on a strategy for going to court, you will need more information than we provide. Several good Nolo Press publications can help you evaluate the merits of your case, and, if you decide to go forward, select the appropriate court, decide whether you need a lawyer and proceed with your complaint:

- *Everybody's Guide to Small Claims Court*, by Ralph Warner—complete information on evaluating and filing a case generally involving less than a few thousand dollars.
- *How to Sue for Up to $25,000 and Win*, by Judge Roderic Duncan— complete information for Californians on evaluating and filing up to $25,000.
- *Represent Yourself in Court*, by Paul Bergman and Sara J. Berman-Barrett—a step-by-step guide to handling a civil trial from start to finish.
- *How to Win Your Personal Injury Claim*, by Joseph Matthews—all the information you need to settle a complaint based on a physical injury.

Don't Delay—
Statutes of Limitation

While you need to allow sufficient time for your Solution Letters™ and other negotiating techniques to work, don't let time drag on too long or you may lose the right to sue in court. Several states, notably California, Kentucky, Louisiana and Tennessee, require that you file a lawsuit within one year of an injury. The laws setting the time within which you must file your lawsuit differ depending on the type of claim you are making and the state where you are filing. These state laws are called the "statutes of limitation" or "limitation of action" provisions; figuring out the applicable statute of limitation is one of the first legal research steps you or your lawyer must take to make sure you have not waited too long.

Pay particular attention to limitation periods for injuries during a cruise. Maritime law, not state law, governs all accidents on cruises and requires that you file a written notice with the company within the periods set forth in your ticket—generally within six months of your injury—and file a lawsuit within one year. If you do not, the court will reject your case because it was not filed on time, even if state law would allow you more time. For property losses on cruises, you must generally file a written claim within ten days of the loss and file a lawsuit within six months.

Whether you are going to bring your own case or get an attorney's assistance, there are several steps you can take to make the process as efficient and inexpensive as possible. If your case involves substantial loss, damage or physical injuries, you should consult a lawyer. Even still, you can save a lot of time and money by knowing your rights as a traveler. Most lawyers do not know a great deal about the laws that pertain to travelers (unless your case is a straightforward injury case), and you may be able to save a lot of unnecessary legal fees by doing the following:

- **Get as much information as you can at the time of the problem.** Get statements in writing from any participants or other witnesses, keep all contracts, receipts and other documents and take photographs that help demonstrate what happened.

- **Get additional information from outside organizations.** Contact consumer protection agencies, travel assistance programs, Better Business Bureaus and other organizations that may be able to provide background information or advice.

- **Find out as much as you can about the company you are considering suing.** Find out about its past practices, whether there have been prior complaints against the company, whether the particular part of the company against which you are complaining is a subsidiary or franchise of a larger company and whether the company does business in your home state. Much of this information is available at a local law library.

- **Prepare a brief summary of the facts of the case and as much of the law as you know.** Whether you decide to handle the case yourself or hire an attorney, your summary will provide a good starting point for any additional research that needs to be done.

Finally, keep in mind that suing can be a real drain on your time, energy and money. Lawsuits should never be filed simply to vent anger or get back at someone. If you've been harmed or treated unfairly by a travel supplier and the supplier refuses to provide fair compensation, a lawsuit may be appropriate. Be sure you sue the party who caused the problem, not the most convenient person, such as your travel agent. In some cases, merely threatening to sue or actually filing the case and serving the complaint may be enough to get the supplier to reevaluate its position. Hopefully, by learning about your travel rights and taking the appropriate precautions before you travel, you'll never be in a position where you have to sue.

Doing Legal Research

The cases and laws referred to in this book are only a starting point if you are in a serious legal dispute with a travel supplier. You'll probably need to do additional legal research. Legal research can seem very intimidating because a great deal of abbreviations and technical terms are used, but with a little patience and practice you will be surprised at how much information you can find. If you decide to hire a lawyer or someone else to do research for you, make sure that you show her the parts of this book you think are relevant. Even very experienced

lawyers may not be familiar with some of the specialized aspects of travel law.

For an excellent overview of what you need to know to do legal research, consult *Legal Research: How to Find and Understand the Law*, by Stephen Elias and Susan Levinkind (Nolo Press). Use the step-by-step procedures in that book to supplement the basic legal principles, cases and laws mentioned in this book.

Using a Lawyer

As pointed out several times in this book, in certain situations you should consult an attorney for advice. If the other side is represented by an attorney, you may want to hire a lawyer to represent you. But before hiring someone, weigh the cost of legal representation against your likely recovery. Some lawyers will charge you on a flat per-hour basis, while others will represent you for a percentage of the final recovery (known as a "contingency fee" arrangement).

 If you hire a lawyer and the relationship turns sour, we recommend *Mad at Your Lawyer*, by Tanya Starnes (Nolo Press).

Travel and Tourism Lawyers

Unfortunately, there are very few travel and tourism lawyers—at least for members of the general public. Travel suppliers hire specialists to handle their cases, but it is unlikely that you'll find anyone in your home town (or even your home state) who spends a great deal of time on travel and tourism law. Therefore, if you decide that you need an attorney, select an attorney who has experience representing plaintiffs (the people who sue) with the type of consumer complaint that you have, such as contract disputes or personal injury claims. Familiarity with travel and tourism law is a big plus, but don't waste a lot of time trying to find a travel and tourism specialist.

Choosing a Lawyer

If your case is not very complex and you are willing to put in some time and work on your own, you can hire a lawyer to look over your research and the forms you have prepared to advise whether any other legal course is required in your situation. At a minimum, a lawyer should listen to a description of your situation, analyze it, educate you about your rights and options and help you decide on a course of action. Make sure that you get an estimate of the amount of time this will take and the fee you will be charged *before* you agree to the consultation.

When selecting a lawyer, keep in mind these important points:

- Initial consultations should be free or very inexpensive. You may want to interview two or three lawyers before deciding on one to help you with your case.

- If you are told that you need a signifi-cant amount of paid legal services, get a second opinion before you agree to the recommended services.

- If you need a limited amount of advice, your most important consideration is finding someone with direct expertise and experience with your kind of case. If you anticipate needing ongoing legal services (for example, if your complaint involves serious loss, injury or death), consider how easy it is for you to work

with the attorney, as well as the attorney's willingness for you to do some of the legal work on your own.

- The most expensive lawyers and the largest law firms are not necessarily the best—in many instances, plaintiffs' lawyers work on their own or in small group practices.

How to Find a Good Lawyer

The best way to find a lawyer to help you with your travel dispute is through a personal referral from a friend or relative who was pleased with the lawyer's work on a similar case. If you cannot get a personal referral, try one of the following:

- **Community services.** Many county bar associations and law schools have free clinics or other programs that offer basic legal advice. In many cases, you can learn what it takes to handle your own legal work and get help finding the most relevant laws for your case.

- **Prepaid legal insurance.** If you belong to one these programs, you may be able to receive some initial advice on your case. Beware that extensive services, such as representation in court, are unlikely to be included.

- **Lawyer referral panels.** Most county and state bar associations maintain a list of attorneys with different specialties. As noted above, it may be difficult to find someone who specializes in travel law, so you may want to describe the nature of your case in order to find a good match.

- **Commercial law clinics.** High-profile law clinics, some of which advertise on television, claim they can handle your case for very little money. Warning: the initial consultation may be inexpensive, but additional services needed to resolve your case often cost a substantial amount.

- **Yellow Pages.** The Yellow Pages in every telephone book have an extensive number of lawyers listed under "Attorneys," both by specialty and by alphabetical order. Many of the ads quote initial consultation rates. If all else fails, let your fingers do the walking.

Travel Law Online

Every day, a growing number of basic legal resources are available online through the Internet. The Internet is a worldwide network of computers that share rules for collecting and organizing data so that others can use the information easily. There are a number of different ways to use the Internet to search for material, but by far the most important and common tool for doing research on the Internet is the World Wide Web, or the Web. The Web provides links among documents and makes it easy to jump from one resource to another. Each resource is organized graphically like a book, allowing you to skip around by topic.

A wide variety of legal source materials is also available online through large commercial services such as America Online, Prodigy and Microsoft Network. These services have their own collections of resources and ways of organizing that information. These days, commercial services tend to include more information related to popular culture than legal and reference materials. But they also provide links to the Internet, including the Web.

The following resources can help you locate legal materials on the Web.

- *Law on the Net,* by James Evans (Nolo Press), provides basic instructions on how to understand and get into the extensive library of legal information available on the Internet.
- *Government on the Net,* by James Evans (Nolo Press), explains how to find government documents, including federal and state codes, available on the Internet.
- http://www.nolo.com, the Nolo Press online site, includes a vast amount of legal information for consumers. This includes sets of FAQs (frequently asked questions) on a wide variety of legal topics and articles on legal issues.

In addition, a wide variety of secondary sources intended for both lawyers and the general public have been posted on the Net by law schools and firms. If you are on the Web, for example, a good way to find these sources is to visit any of the following Web sites, each of which provides links to legal information by specific subject.

- http://www.yahoo.com/law/. This is the site to Court TV's Law Center. You can find links to many federal and state laws.
- http://www.law.cornell.edu/lii.table.html. This site is maintained by Cornell Law School. You can find the text of the U.S. Code, federal court decisions and some state court decisions. You can also search for material by topic.
- http://www.law.indiana.edu/law/v-lib/lawindex.html. This site is maintained by Indiana University's School of Law at Bloomington. You can search by

organization, including the U.S. government, state governments and law journals, or by topic.

 This section does not provide the basic instruction that some readers may need in order to understand and "get into" the services and information available on the Internet. There are several books that serve this purpose. For an exhaustive treatment of the subject, see *Law on the Net* or *Government on the Net,* both by James Evans (Nolo Press).

Despite an explosion of travel information on the Internet, very little of it has to do with law—mostly it is commercials. If you have a problem with a travel supplier, however, the Internet can be useful. For example, if the supplier has a Web site, you can compare what the site says to the service or product you actually received. Disparities between what was promised and what was delivered may be persuasive to a judge or jury. Another way to get information is to visit an Internet news group or chat room set up by online providers. You can find out whether other travelers have had problems with a particular travel supplier and, if so, how the problems were resolved.

It may be tempting to use the Internet to "flame" (say nasty things) about a travel supplier, but be very careful—anything untrue that you say may qualify as libel, and you may be sued by the travel supplier for injuring its reputation.

Travel Information Online

You can find a searchable collection of the "What's Doing," "Frugal Traveler," "Practical Traveler" and "Q. & A." columns in the *New York Times* at http://www.nytimes.com.

■

Appendix

Contacting a Travel Supplier

Chapter 13 outlines a number of techniques you can use to resolve your dispute with a travel supplier. This Appendix contains the contact information for most major airlines, rental car companies, tour operators and other travel suppliers.

Airlines

Air Canada
Box 14000
St. Laurent, Quebec H4Y IH4
CANADA
tel: 514-422-5070; fax: 514-422-5077

Air France
Customer Service
125 W 55th St.
New York, NY 10019
tel: 800-375-8723; fax: 914-365-1150

Air New Zealand
1960 E. Grand Ave., Suite 900
El Segundo, CA 90245
tel: 310-648-7000; fax: 310-648-7917

Alaska
Consumer Affairs
Box 68900
Seattle, WA 98168
tel: 800-828-9328, 206-431-7286
fax: 206-439-4477

Alitalia
666 5th Ave.
New York, NY 10103
tel: 212-903-3461; fax: 212-903-3507

All Nippon (ANA)
630 5th Ave., Suite 537
New York, NY 10111
tel: 212-956-8200; fax: 212-969-9022

Aloha
Box 30028
Honolulu, HI 96820
tel: 808-836-4115; fax: 808-836-4206

America West
4000 E. Sky Harbor Blvd.
Phoenix, AZ 85034
tel: 800-235-9292, 602-693-6019
fax: 602-693-3707

American
Consumer Relations
Box 619612, Mail Drop 2400
Dallas/Ft. Worth Airport
Dallas, TX 75261
tel: 817-967-2000; fax: 817-967-4162

American Trans Air
Consumer Affairs, Box 51609
Indianapolis International Airport
Indianapolis, IN 46251
tel: 317-243-4140; fax: 317-487-4808

British Airways
75-20 Astoria Blvd.
Jackson Heights, NY 11370
tel: 800-422-9101, 718-397-4300
fax: 718-397-4395

Canadian International
700 2nd St., SW
Calgary, Alberta AB2T P2W2 CANADA
tel: 800-426-7000; fax: 403-294-2066

Carnival
1815 Griffin Rd., Suite 205
Zania, FL 33004
tel: 305-923-8672; fax: 954-922-3961

Cathay Pacific
300 N. Continental Blvd., Room 500
El Segundo, CA 90245
tel: 310-414-6400; fax: 310-615-0042

Continental
2929 Allen Pkwy
Houston, TX 77019
tel: 800-523-3273; fax: 713-590-2150

Delta
Consumer Affairs
Box 20980
Hartsfield International Airport
Atlanta, GA 30320
tel: 404-715-1450; fax: 404-715-1400

Finnair
10 E. 40th St.
New York, NY 10016
tel: 800-950-5000, 212-689-9300
fax: 212-499-9037

Hawaiian
Consumer Affairs
Box 30008
Honolulu, HI 96820
tel: 808-835-3424; fax: 808-838-5333

Iberia
6100 Blue Lagoon Dr., Suite 200
Miami, FL 33126
tel: 800-772-4642; fax: 305-262-0594

Icelandair
360 W. 31st St.
New York, NY 10001
tel: 800-223-5500; fax: 410-715-3547

Japan (JAL)
655 5th Ave.
New York, NY 10022
tel: 800-525-3663; fax: 212-310-1258

Kiwi International
Hemisphere Center
U.S. Routes 1 & 9 S.
Newark, NJ 07114
tel: 800-538-5494; fax: 201-624-0537

KLM
565 Taxter Rd.
Elmsford, NY 10523
tel: 800-556-1800; fax: 914-784-2545

Korean Air
Customer Service
6101 W. Imperial Hwy.
Los Angeles, CA 90045
tel: 310-417-5200; fax: 310-417-8841

Lufthansa
750 Lexington Ave., 23rd Floor
New York, NY 10022
tel: 800-645-3880, 718-895-1277
fax: 212-479-8817

Midwest Express
Consumer Affairs
6744 S. Howell Ave.
Milwaukee, WI 53207
tel: 800-452-2022, 414-747-3910
fax: 414-570-0199

Northwest
Dept. C 5270, 5101 Northwest Dr.
St. Paul, MN 55111
tel: 612-726-2046; fax: 612-726-0776

Qantas
Customer Service
841 Apollo Street
El Segundo, CA 90245
tel: 310-726-1400; fax: 310-726-1401

Reno Air
220 Edison Way
Reno, NV 89502
tel: 800-736-6247; fax: 702-858-4957

Sabena
1155 Northern Blvd.
Manhasset, NY 11030
tel: 516-562-9303; fax: 516-562-9323

Scandinavian (SAS)
1270 6th Ave.
New York, NY 10020
tel: 800-345-9684; fax: 201-896-3735

Singapore
Public Affairs
5670 Wilshire Blvd., Suite 1800
Los Angeles, CA 90036
tel: 213-934-8833; fax: 213-939-6727

Southwest
Box 36611
Dallas, TX 75235
tel: 214-904-4223; fax: 214-792-5099

Swissair
608 5th Ave.
New York, NY 10020
tel: 800-221-6644; fax: 310-335-5935

Thai Airways
222 N. Sepulveda Blvd., Suite 1950
El Segundo, CA 90245
tel: 310-640-0097; fax: 310-322-8657

Tower Air
Hangar Customer Relations Dept.
Hangar 8, JFK International, Airport
Jamaica, NY 11430
tel: 718-553-4300; fax: 718-553-4312

TWA
1 City Center
515 N. 6th Street
St. Louis, MO 63101
tel: 314-589-3600; fax: 610-631-5280

United
Box 66100
Chicago, IL 60666
tel: 847-700-6796; fax: 847-700-2214

USAir
Consumer Affairs
Box 1501
Winston-Salem, NC 27102
tel: 919-661-0061; fax: 910-661-8031

Virgin Atlantic
96 Morton St.
New York, NY 10014
tel: 212-206-6612; fax: 203-750-6490

Rental Car Companies

Alamo
Box 22776
Ft. Lauderdale, FL 33335
tel: 800-445-5664; fax: 954-468-2108

Avis
Customer Service
Avis World Headquarters
900 Old Country Rd.
Garden City, NY 11530
tel: 800-352-7900, 516-222-4200
fax: 516-222-4381

Budget
Box 111580
Carrollton, TX 75011
tel: 800-621-2844; fax: 214-404-7067

Dollar
Consumer Services
100 N. Sepulveda Blvd., 6th Floor
El Segundo, CA 90245
tel: 800-800-5252; fax: 918-669-3009

Enterprise
600 Corporate Park Dr.
St. Louis, MO 63015
tel: 314-512-5000; fax: 314-512-4722

Hertz
Box 26120
Oklahoma City, OK 73126
tel: 800-654-4173; fax: 405-728-6516

National
Consumer Affairs
7700 France Ave. S.
Minneapolis, MN 55435
tel: 800-468-3334, 612-830-2121
fax: 612-830-2936

Payless
Customer Service
Box 60669
St. Petersburg, FL 33784
tel: 813-321-6352; fax: 813-323-3529

Rent-a-Wreck
Customer Service
6053 W. Century Blvd., Suite 550
Los Angeles, CA 90045;
tel: 800-535-1391; fax: 410-581-1566

Snappy
Customer Service
Box 21018
Tulsa, OK 74121
tel: 918-621-1100; fax: 918-621-1192

Thrifty
Consumer Service
Box 35250
Tulsa, OK 74153
tel: 800-334-1705; fax: 918-669-2765

U-Save
7525 Connelley Dr., Suite A
Hanover, MD 21076
tel: 800-272-8728, 410-760-8727
fax: 800-438-2300

Value
Customer Service
Box 5040
Boca Raton, FL 33431
tel: 800-327-6459; fax: 407-998-7445

Cruise Lines

American Hawaii
1380 Port of New Orleans
New Orleans, LA 70130
tel: 800-543-1949; fax: 504-586-0690

Bergen
405 Park Avenue
New York, NY 10022
tel: 800-666-2374; fax: 212-319-1390

Carnival
Passenger Service
3655 N.W. 87th Ave.
Miami, FL 33178
tel: 800-227-6482; fax: 305-471-4718

Celebrity
Customer Service
5201 Blue Lagoon Dr.
Miami, FL 33126
tel: 800-437-3111; fax: 800-437-9111

Classical
132 E. 70th St.
New York, NY 10021
tel: 800-252-7745, 212-794-3200
fax: 212-774-1544

Clipper
Customer Service
7711 Bonhomme Ave.
St. Louis, MO 63105
tel: 800-325-0010; fax: 314-727-6576

Commodore
Passenger Relations
4000 Hollywood Blvd., Suite 385
Coral Gables, FL 33134
tel: 800-237-5361

Crystal
Guest Relations
2121 Ave. of the Stars, Suite 200
Los Angeles, CA 90067
tel: 800-446-6620; fax: 310-785-3891

Cunard
Customer Affairs
6100 Blue Lagoon Dr., Suite 400
Miami, FL 33126
tel: 800-528-6273; fax: 305-463-3010

Delta Queen Steamboat: *See* American
Hawaii.

Discovery
Customer Service
1850 Eller Dr.
Ft. Lauderdale, FL 33316
tel: 800-937-4477; fax: 954-779-3887

Dolphin
Passenger Service
Box 025420
Miami, FL 33102
tel: 800-222-1003, 305-358-3005
fax: 305-358-4807

Epirotiki
551 5th Ave., Suite 605
New York, NY 10176
tel: 800-221-2470, 212-599-1750
fax: 212-765-9685

Fantasy: *See* Celebrity.

Holland-America Westours
300 Elliot Ave. W.
Seattle, WA 98119
tel: 800-426-0327; fax: 206-281-7110

Norwegian
Customer Relations
7665 Corporate Center Dr.
Miami, FL 33120
tel: 800-327-7030; fax: 305-463-4106

Premier
Customer Service
P.O. Box 573
Cape Canaveral, FL 32920
tel: 800-990-7770; fax: 407-784-0954

Princess
Passenger Relations
10100 Santa Monica Blvd.
Los Angeles, CA 90067
tel: 800-774-6237; fax: 310-284-2857

Regency
260 Madison Ave.
New York, NY 10016
tel: 212-268-1868; fax: 212-687-2290

Renaissance
Customer Service
Box 350307
Ft. Lauderdale, FL 33335
tel: 800-525-2450; fax: 954-356-0146

Royal
Passenger Service
1 Maritime Plaza, Suite 1400
San Francisco, CA 94111
tel: 800-216-2174, 415-956-7200
fax: 415-956-1656

Royal Caribbean
Passenger Relations
1050 Caribbean Way
Miami, FL 33132
tel: 800-327-6700; fax: 800-659-7225

Royal Viking
Customer Service
95 Merrick Way
Coral Gables, FL 33134
tel: 305-436-4000; fax: 305-567-9173

Seabourn
55 Francisco St., Suite 710
San Francisco, CA 94133
tel: 415-391-7444; fax: 415-391-8518

Spice Island
c/o Esplanade Tours
581 Boylston St.
Boston, MA 02116
tel: 800-426-5492; fax: 617-262-9829

Sun Line
Customer Services
1 Rockefeller Plaza, Suite 315
New York, NY 10020
tel: 800-445-6400, 212-397-6400
fax: 212-765-9685

Windjammer Barefoot
Customer Affairs
1759 Bay Rd.
Miami Beach, FL 33139
tel: 800-327-2601 ext. 3327
fax: 305-674-1219

Windstar
300 Elliot Ave. W.
Seattle, WA 98119
tel: 800-626-9900, 206-281-3535
fax: 206-281-7110

World Explorer
555 Montgomery St., Suite 1400
San Francisco, CA 94111
tel: 800-854-3835, 415-393-1565
fax: 415-391-1145

Hotel Chains

AmeriSuites
Customer Service
1775 The Exchange
Atlanta, GA 30339
tel: 800-833-1516; fax: 770-955-3806

ANA
725 S. Figueroa St., Suite 815
Los Angeles, CA 90017
tel: 213-955-7688; fax: 213-955-7678

Aborgate: See Economy Lodging.

Best Western
Customer Service
Box 10203
Phoenix, AZ 85064
tel: 800-528-1238; fax: 602-780-6199

Budgetel
Guest Services
250 E. Wisconsin Ave., Suite 1750
Milwaukee, WI 53202
tel: 800-428-3438, 414-365-9444
fax: 414-302-1310

Canadian Pacific
Customer Service
1 University Ave., Suite 1400
Toronto M5J 2PI CANADA
tel: 800-828-7447, 416-341-7100
fax: 416-341-5091

Choice International
Guest Relations
10750 Columbia Pike
Silver Spring, MD 20901
tel: 301-236-5122; fax: 301-681-7478

Circus Circus
Guest Relations
Box 14967
Las Vegas, NV 89114
tel: 702-734-0410 ext. 3165
fax: 702-794-3876

Clarion: See Choice International.

Club Med
Consumer Affairs
40 W. 57 St.
New York, NY 10019
tel: 212-977-2115; fax: 212-315-5392

Colony and Interstate Hotels
Foster Plaza, Bldg. 10
680 Anderson Drive
Pittsburg, PA 15220-8126
tel: 412-920-5700; fax: 412-920-5757

Comfort: See Choice International.

Concorde
1414 Ave. of the Americas
New York, NY 10019
tel: 800-888-4747; fax: 212-752-8916

Conrad: *See* Hilton (US).

Courtyard by Marriott
Consumer Affairs, Dept. 93337
1 Marriott Dr.
Washington, DC 20058
tel: 301-380-4478; fax: 301-897-9014

Days Inn
Guest Services
339 Jefferson Rd
Parsippany, NJ 07054
tel: 973-428-9700; fax: 973-428-5027

Doubletree
Customer Service
410 N. 44th St., Suite 700
Phoenix, AZ 85008
tel: 800-222-8733; fax: 602-244-0213

Downtown Inns: *See* Hospitality International.

Econolodge: *See* Choice International.

Economy Lodging
Guest Services
26650 Emery Industrial Pkwy.
Cleveland, OH 44128
tel: 800-843-5644 ext. 217
fax: 602-389-5588

Embassy Suites
Guest Assistance
755 Crossover Lane
Memphis, TN 38120
tel: 901-374-5000; fax: 901-374-5934

Fairfield Inn by Marriott
Consumer Affairs, Dept. 93337
1 Marriott Dr.
Washington, DC 20058
tel: 301-380-2617; fax: 301-897-5629

Forte
420 Lexington Ave., Suite 1718
New York, NY 10170
tel: 800-253-0861

Four Seasons
Operations
1165 Leslie St.
Toronto, Ontario M3C 2K8 CANADA
tel: 416-964-0411; fax: 416-964-2301

Friendship Inn: *See* Choice International.

Hampton Inn
Guest Assistance
8245 Tournament Drive
Bldg. A, Suite 300
Memphis, TN 38125
tel: 901-680-7200; fax: 901-680-7230

Harrah's: Contact individual hotel.

Hilton International
Reservation Sales
2050 Chennault Dr.
Carrollton, TX 75006
tel: 800-445-8667 ext. "Customer Service,"
214-770-6000; fax: 214-867-9863

Hilton (US)
Customer Service
Box 5567
Beverly Hills, CA 90209
tel: 310-278-4321; fax: 310-205-3640

Holiday Inn
Guest Relations
3 Ravinia Dr., Suite 2000
Atlanta, GA 30346
tel: 770-604-2000; fax: 770-604-2782

Homewood Suites
Guest Assistance
850 Ridge Lake Blvd.
Memphis, TN 38120
tel: 800-225-5466; fax: 901-680-7230

Hospitality Franchise System: *See* Days Inn.

Hospitality International
Consumer Affairs
1726 Montreal Circle
Tucker, GA 30084
tel: 800-247-4677, 404-270-1180
fax: 770-270-1077

Howard Johnson: See Days Inn.

Hyatt
Customer Service
200 W. Madison St.
Chicago, IL 60606
tel: 800-233-1234; fax: 402-593-9838

Inter-Continental
1120 Ave. of the Americas, 19th floor
New York, NY 10036
tel: 800-442-7375, 212-852-6400;
fax: 212-852-6463

Knights: See Economy Lodging.

La Quinta
Guest Assistance
112 E. Pecan St., Suite 200
San Antonio, TX 78279
tel: 800-531-5900, 210-302-6000
fax: 210-302-6151

Marriott
Guest Services
1 Marriott Dr.
Washington, DC 20058
tel: 801-468-4032; fax: 801-468-4088

Master Host Inns: See Hospitality
International.

Meridien
888 7th Ave., 27th Floor
New York, NY 10106
tel: 800-543-4300; fax: 212-805-5047

Motel 6
Guest Relations
14651 Dallas Pkwy., Suite 500
Dallas, TX 75240
tel: 214-386-6161; fax: 214-716-6540

National 9 Inns
Customer Service
2285 S. Main St.
Salt Lake City, UT 84115
tel: 801-466-9820; fax: 801-466-9856

Nikko
Marketing
320 N. Dearborn St.
Chicago, IL 60610
tel: 312-744-1900; fax: 312-527-2650

Omni
Guest Relations
420 Decker Lane, Suite 100
Dallas, TX 75062
tel: 972-730-6664; fax: 972-887-9240

Outrigger
Guest Relations
2375 Kuhio Ave.
Honolulu, HI 96815
tel: 808-921-6802; fax: 808-921-6901

Pan Pacific
VP of Operations
177 Post St., Suite 80
San Francisco, CA 94108
tel: 415-732-7747; fax: 415-732-5800

Park Inn: See Days Inn.

Passport Inns: See Hospitality International.

Plaza International: See Days Inn.

Presidente: See Inter-Continental.

Prince
700 S. Flower St., Suite 604
Los Angeles, CA 90017
tel: 800-542-8686; fax: 213-627-8702

Pullman
2 Overhill Rd.
Scarsdale, NY 10583
tel: 800-221-4542; fax: 914-472-0451

Quality: *See* Choice International.

Radisson
Customer Service
Box 59159, Carlson Pkwy.
Minneapolis, MN 55459
tel: 800-333-3333, 612-540-5697
fax: 402-498-9166

Ramada International
Guest Services
2655 LeJeune Rd., Suite 800
Coral Gables, FL 33134
tel: 800-468-1902; fax: 216-349-3159

Ramada (US)
Guest Services
Box 29004
Phoenix, AZ 85038
tel: 800-828-6644; fax: 602-389-5588

Red Carpet Inn: *See* Hospitality International.

Red Lion: *See* Doubletree.

Red Roof
Customer Service
4355 Davidson Rd.
Hilliard, OH 43026
tel: 800-554-4555, 614-876-3200
fax: 614-777-8927

Residence Inn by Marriott
Guest Relations, Dept. 851.91
1 Marriot Dr.
Washington, DC 20058
tel: 800-899-7244; fax: 402-397-9218

Ritz-Carlton
Guest Relations
3414 Peachtree Rd. N.E., Suite 300
Atlanta, GA 30326
tel: 404-237-5500; fax: 404-365-9643

Rodeway: *See* Choice International.

SAS Hotels
1270 6th Ave.
New York, NY 10020
tel: 800-345-9684; fax: 201-896-3735

Scottish Inns: *See* Hospitality International.

Sheraton
Corporate Services
60 State St.
Boston, MA 02109
tel: 800-325-3535; fax: 617-367-5676

Shoney's Inn
Customer Service
130 Maple Dr. N.
Hendersonville, TN 37075
tel: 800-222-2222 ext. 231
fax: 615-442-5355

Sleep Inn: *See* Choice International.

Sofitel: *See* Pullman.

Stouffer: *See* Inter-Continental.

Super 8
Guest Relations
1910 8th Ave., NE
Aberdeen, SD 57401
tel: 800-800-8000; fax: 605-229-8908

Tokyu
777 S. Figueroa St., 3rd Floor
Los Angeles, CA 90017
tel: 800-624-5068, 213-622-0245
fax: 801-975-1846

Thriftlodge
Customer Service
1973 Friendship Dr.
El Cajon, CA 92020
tel: 800-835-2424; fax: 619-258-6619

Travelodge: *See* Thriftlodge.

Viscount: *See* Thriftlodge.

Vista: *See* Hilton International.

Walt Disney World
Resort Guest Relations
Box 10,000
Lake Buena Vista, FL 32830
tel: 407-824-4321; fax: 407-828-4903

Westin
Guest Relations
Westin Bldg.
2001 6th Ave.
Seattle, WA 98121
tel: 206-443-5007; fax: 206-443-3142

Woodfield Suites
Customer Services
250 E. Wisconsin Ave., Suite 1750
Milwaukee, WI 53202
tel: 414-272-8484; fax: 414-272-3547

Wyndham
2001 Bryan St., Suite 2300
Dallas, TX 75201
tel: 800-347-7559; fax: 214-863-1342

Tour and Travel Agencies

Abercrombie & Kent
Customer Service
1520 Kensington Rd.
Oak Brook, IL 60521
tel: 800-323-7308, 630-954-2944
fax: 630-954-3324

African Travel
Safari Bldg.
1100 E. Broadway
Glendale, CA 91205
tel: 800-421-8907, 818-507-7893
fax: 818-507-5802

Apple Vacations East
7 Campus Blvd.
Newtown Square, PA 19073
tel: 215-359-6500; fax: 215-359-6650

Apple Vacations West
Client Services
25 N.W. Point Blvd.
Elk Grove Village, IL 60007
tel: 800-727-3400, 800-365-2776
fax: 847-640-1950

ATS
100 N. 1st St., Suite 301
Burbank, CA 91502
tel: 800-423-2880, 818-841-1030
fax: 310-643-0032

Australian Pacific Tours/AAT King's
512 S. Verdugo Dr., Suite 200
Burbank, CA 91502
tel: 800-290-8687, 818-840-9122
fax: 818-840-8039

Bennett Tours
270 Madison Ave.
New York, NY 10016
tel: 212-532-5060; fax: 212-779-8944

Brendan Tours
15137 Califa St.
Van Nuys, CA 91411
tel: 800-421-8446, 818-785-9696
fax: 818-902-9870

Central Holiday Tours
206 Central Ave.
Jersey City, NJ 07307
tel: 800-935-5000, 201-798-5777
fax: 201-963-0966

Certified Vacations
110 E. Broward Blvd.
Ft. Lauderdale, FL 33301
tel: 800-233-7260, 305-522-1440
fax: 954-357-4687

Collette Tours
162 Middle St.,
Pawtucket, RI 02860
tel: 800-832-4656; fax: 401-727-4745

Contiki Holidays
Customer Service
300 Plaza Alicante, Suite 900
Garden Grove, CA 92640
tel: 800-466-0610, 714-740-0808
fax: 714-740-2034

DER Tours
11933 Wilshire Blvd.
Los Angeles, CA 90025
tel: 800-782-2323, 310-479-4411
fax: 310-479-2239

Donna Franca
470 Commonwealth Ave.
Boston, MA 02215
tel: 800-225-6290, 617-227-3111
fax: 617-266-1062

Funway Holidays Funjet
8907 N. Port Washington Rd., Box 1460
Milwaukee, WI 53201
tel: 800-558-3060, 414-351-3553
fax: 414-351-2831

General Tours
245 5th Ave.
New York, NY 10016
tel: 800-221-2216, 212-685-1800
fax: 603-357-4548

Globus & Cosmos Tourama
Customer Service
5301 S. Federal Circle
Littleton, CO 80123
tel: 800-221-0090, 303-797-2800
fax: 303-798-5441

Haddon Holidays
1120 Route 73, Suite 375
Mt. Laurel, NJ 08054
tel: 800-257-7488, 609-273-8777
fax: 609-273-0031

Insight International Tours
Customer Service Dept.
745 Atlantic Ave., Suite 720
Boston, MA 02111
tel: 800-257-7488, 617-482-2000
fax: 617-482-2425

Islands in the Sun
760 W. 16th St., Suite L
Costa Mesa, CA 92627
tel: 800-828-6877, 714-645-8300
fax: 310-536-6266

Isram World
630 3rd Ave.
New York, NY 10017
tel: 800-223-7460, 212-661-1193
fax: 212-983-8497

Japan & Orient Tours
Customer Service
3131 Camino del Rio N., Suite 1080
San Diego, CA 92108
tel: 800-377-1080, 619-282-3131
fax: 619-283-3131

Jet Vacations
1775 Broadway, Suite 2405
New York, NY 10019
tel: 800-538-0999; 212-474-8740
fax: 212-586-2069

Jetset Tours (North America)
5120 W. Goldleaf Circle, Suite 310
Los Angeles, CA 90056
tel: 800-638-3273; 213-290-5800
fax: 213-294-0434

Maupintour
1515 St. Andrews Dr.
Lawrence, KS 66047
tel: 800-255-4266, 913-843-1211
fax: 913-843-8351

Mayflower Tours
1225 Warren Ave.
Downers Grove, IL 60515
tel: 800-323-7604, 708-960-3430
fax: 708-960-3575

MLT Vacations
5130 Highway 101
Minnetonka, MN 55345
tel: 800-934-3707, 612-474-2540
fax: 612-470-3192

MTI Vacations
Customer Service
1220 Kensington Rd.
Oak Brook, IL 60521
tel: 800-323-7285, 800-635-1333,
708-990-8028; fax: 708-990-3353

Olson-Travelworld
Customer Service
970 W. 190 St., Suite 425
Torrance, CA 90502
tel: 800-421-2255; fax: 715-345-2394

Pacific Delight Tours
132 Madison Ave.
New York, NY 10016
tel: 800-221-7179, 212-684-7707
fax: 212-532-3406

Pacific/Global Bestour
228 Rivervale Rd.
Rivervale, NJ 07675
tel: 800-688-3288, 201-664-8778
fax: 201-722-0829

**Pleasant Hawaiian/Pleasant
Mexican Holidays**
2404 Townsgate Rd.
Westlake Village, CA 91361
tel: 800-242-9244; 818-991-3390
fax: 805-374-9899

Runaway Tours
Customer Service
120 Montgomery St., Suite 800
San Francisco, CA 94104
tel: 800-622-0723; 415-788-0224
fax: 415-391-1957

Special Expeditions
720 5th Ave.
New York, NY 10019
tel: 800-762-0003, 212-765-7740
fax: 212-265-3770

Tauck Tours
Customer Service, 11 Wilton Rd.
Westport, CT 06880
tel: 800-468-2825; fax: 203-221-6828

TBI Tours (JTB International)
787 7th Ave., Suite 1101
New York, NY 10019
tel: 800-223-0266; fax: 603-357-4548

Trafalgar Tours
Customer Service
11 E. 26th St., Suite 1300
New York, NY 10010
tel: 800-854-0103, 212-689-8977
fax: 212-725-7776

Credit Cards

American Express
Consumer Card Group
TRS Co.
American Express Tower C
World Financial Center
New York, NY 10285
tel: 800-528-4800 (Green),
     800-327-2177 (Gold),
     800-525-3355 (Platinum),
     800-528-2122 (Corporate),
     800-635-5955 (Optima)
fax: 954-473-6851

Carte Blanche
Customer Service
183 Inverness Dr. W.
Englewood, CO 80112
tel: 800-234-6377; fax: 303-649-2891

Diners Club: *See* Carte Blanche.

Discover Card
Box 32905, Columbus, OH 43232, or
Box 15184, Wilmington, DE 19886, or
Box 5008, Sandy, UT 84091, or
Box 29031, Phoenix, AZ 85038;
tel: 800-347-268, 614-860-1200,
602-516-1897; fax: 602-516-3679

MasterCard: Contact issuing bank.

Visa: Contact issuing bank.

If you're looking for contact information concerning a travel association, travel supplier or the like, consider checking the Website maintained by ASTA, the American Society of Travel Agents, at http://www.astanet.com/www/asta/pub/link/travelassocs.htmlx.

■

Index

CATALOG
...more from Nolo.com

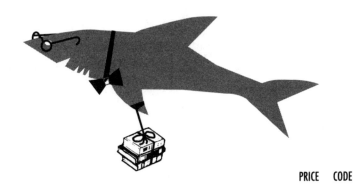

PRICE   CODE

BUSINESS

	PRICE	CODE
⊙ The CA Nonprofit Corp Kit (Binder w/CD-ROM)	$39.95	CNP
⊑ Consultant & Independent Contractor Agreements (Book w/Disk—PC)	$24.95	CICA
⊑ The Corporate Minutes Book (Book w/Disk—PC)	$69.95	CORMI
The Employer's Legal Handbook	$31.95	EMPL
⊑ Form Your Own Limited Liability Company (Book w/Disk—PC)	$34.95	LIAB
⊑ Hiring Independent Contractors: The Employer's Legal Guide (Book w/Disk—PC)	$29.95	HICI
⊑ How to Create a Buy-Sell Agreement and Control the Destiny of your Small Business (Book w/Disk—PC)	$49.95	BSAG
⊑ How to Form a California Professional Corporation (Book w/Disk—PC)	$49.95	PROF
⊑ How to Form a Nonprofit Corporation (Book w/Disk —PC)—National Edition	$39.95	NNP
⊙ How to Form a Nonprofit Corporation in California	$34.95	NON
⊑ How to Form Your Own California Corporation (Binder w/Disk—PC	$39.95	CACI
⊑ How to Form Your Own California Corporation (Book w/Disk—PC)	$34.95	CCOR
⊑ How to Form Your Own Florida Corporation (Book w/Disk—PC)	$39.95	FLCO
⊑ How to Form Your Own New York Corporation (Book w/Disk—PC)	$39.95	NYCO
⊑ How to Form Your Own Texas Corporation (Book w/Disk—PC)	$39.95	TCOR

⊑ Book with disk
⊙ Book with CD-ROM

How to Write a Business Plan	$24.95	SBS
The Independent Paralegal's Handbook	$29.95	PARA
Legal Guide for Starting & Running a Small Business, Vol. 1	$24.95	RUNS
🖳 Legal Guide for Starting & Running a Small Business, Vol. 2: Legal Forms (Book w/Disk—PC)	$29.95	RUNS2
Marketing Without Advertising	$19.00	MWAD
🖳 Music Law (Book w/Disk—PC)	$29.95	ML
Nolo's California Quick Corp (Quick & Legal Series)	$19.95	QINC
⊙ Open Your California Business in 24 Hours (Book w/CD-ROM)	$24.95	OPEN
🖳 The Partnership Book: How to Write a Partnership Agreement (Book w/Disk—PC)	$34.95	PART
Sexual Harassment on the Job	$18.95	HARS
Starting & Running a Successful Newsletter or Magazine	$24.95	MAG
Take Charge of Your Workers' Compensation Claim (California Edition)	$29.95	WORK
Tax Savvy for Small Business	$29.95	SAVVY
Trademark: Legal Care for Your Business and Product Name	$34.95	TRD
Wage Slave No More: Law & Taxes for the Self-Employed	$24.95	WAGE
Your Rights in the Workplace	$21.95	YRW

CONSUMER

Fed Up with the Legal System: What's Wrong & How to Fix It	$9.95	LEG
How to Win Your Personal Injury Claim	$26.95	PICL
Nolo's Everyday Law Book	$24.95	EVL
Nolo's Pocket Guide to California Law	$12.95	CLAW
Trouble-Free Travel...And What to Do When Things Go Wrong	$14.95	TRAV

ESTATE PLANNING & PROBATE

8 Ways to Avoid Probate (Quick & Legal Series)	$15.95	PRO8
9 Ways to Avoid Estate Taxes (Quick & Legal Series)	$22.95	ESTX
How to Probate an Estate (California Edition)	$39.95	PAE
Make Your Own Living Trust	$24.95	LITR
Nolo's Law Form Kit: Wills	$14.95	KWL

🖳 Book with disk
⊙ Book with CD-ROM

TO ORDER CALL 800-992-6656

🖬 Nolo's Will Book (Book w/Disk—PC)	$29.95	SWIL
Plan Your Estate	$24.95	NEST
Quick & Legal Will Book (Quick & Legal Series)	$15.95	QUIC

FAMILY MATTERS

Child Custody: Building Parenting Agreements That Work	$26.95	CUST
The Complete IEP Guide	$24.95	IEP
Divorce & Money: How to Make the Best Financial Decisions During Divorce	$26.95	DIMO
Do Your Own Divorce in Oregon	$19.95	ODIV
Get a Life: You Don't Need a Million to Retire Well	$18.95	LIFE
The Guardianship Book (California Edition)	$39.95	GB
How to Adopt Your Stepchild in California	$34.95	ADOP
How to Raise or Lower Child Support in California (Quick & Legal Series)	$19.95	CHLD
A Legal Guide for Lesbian and Gay Couples	$25.95	LG
The Living Together Kit	$29.95	LTK
Nolo's Pocket Guide to Family Law	$14.95	FLD
Using Divorce Mediation: Save Your Money & Your Sanity	$21.95	UDMD

GOING TO COURT

Beta Your Ticket: Go To Court and Win! (National Edition)	$19.95	BEYT
Collect Your Court Judgment (California Edition)	$29.95	JUDG
The Criminal Law Handbook: Know Your Rights, Survive the System	$24.95	KYR
Everybody's Guide to Small Claims Court (National Edition)	$18.95	NSCC
Everybody's Guide to Small Claims Court in California	$18.95	CSCC
Fight Your Ticket ... and Win! (California Edition)	$19.95	FYT
How to Change Your Name in California	$34.95	NAME
How to Mediate Your Dispute	$18.95	MEDI
How to Seal Your Juvenile & Criminal Records (California Edition)	$24.95	CRIM
How to Sue For Up to $25,000...and Win!	$29.95	MUNI
Mad at Your Lawyer	$21.95	MAD
Represent Yourself in Court: How to Prepare & Try a Winning Case	$29.95	RYC

🖬 Book with disk

⊙ Book with CD-ROM

TO ORDER CALL 800-992-6656

HOMEOWNERS, LANDLORDS & TENANTS

▣ Contractors' and Homeowners' Guide to Mechanics' Liens (Book w/Disk—PC)	$39.95	MIEN
The Deeds Book (California Edition)	$24.95	DEED
Dog Law	$14.95	DOG
▣ Every Landlord's Legal Guide (National Edition, Book w/Disk—PC)	$34.95	ELLI
Every Tenant's Legal Guide	$26.95	EVTEN
For Sale by Owner in California	$24.95	FSBO
How to Buy a House in California	$24.95	BHCA
The Landlord's Law Book, Vol. 1: Rights & Responsibilities (California Edition)	$34.95	LBRT
The Landlord's Law Book, Vol. 2: Evictions (California Edition)	$34.95	LBEV
Leases & Rental Agreements (Quick & Legal Series)	$18.95	LEAR
Neighbor Law: Fences, Trees, Boundaries & Noise	$17.95	NEI
Renters' Rights (National Edition—Quick & Legal Series))	$15.95	RENT
Stop Foreclosure Now in California	$29.95	CLOS
Tenants' Rights (California Edition)	$21.95	CTEN

HUMOR

29 Reasons Not to Go to Law School	$9.95	29R
Poetic Justice	$9.95	PJ

IMMIGRATION

How to Get a Green Card: Legal Ways to Stay in the U.S.A.	$24.95	GRN
U.S. Immigration Made Easy	$44.95	IMEZ

MONEY MATTERS

▣ 101 Law Forms for Personal Use (Quick & Legal Series, Book w/disk—PC)	$24.95	SPOT
Bankruptcy: Is It the Right Solution to Your Debt Problems? (Quick & Legal Series)	$15.95	BRS
Chapter 13 Bankruptcy: Repay Your Debts	$29.95	CH13

▣ Book with disk
◉ Book with CD-ROM

TO ORDER CALL 800-992-6656

Credit Repair (Quick & Legal Series)	$15.95	CREP
▣ The Financial Power of Attorney Workbook (Book w/disk—PC)	$24.95	FINPOA
How to File for Chapter 7 Bankruptcy	$26.95	HFB
IRAs, 401(k)s & Other Retirement Plans: Taking Your Money Out	$21.95	RET
Money Troubles: Legal Strategies to Cope With Your Debts	$19.95	MT
Nolo's Law Form Kit: Personal Bankruptcy	$16.95	KBNK
Stand Up to the IRS	$24.95	SIRS
Take Control of Your Student Loans	$19.95	SLOAN

PATENTS AND COPYRIGHTS

▣ The Copyright Handbook: How to Protect and Use Written Works		
(Book w/disk—PC)	$29.95	COHA
Copyright Your Software	$24.95	CYS
How to Make Patent Drawings Yourself	$29.95	DRAW
The Inventor's Notebook	$19.95	INOT
▣ License Your Invention (Book w/Disk—PC)	$39.95	LICE
Patent, Copyright & Trademark	$24.95	PCTM
Patent It Yourself	$46.95	PAT
Patent Searching Made Easy	$24.95	PATSE
◉ Software Development: A Legal Guide (Book with CD-ROM)	$44.95	SFT

RESEARCH & REFERENCE

◉ Government on the Net (Book w/CD-ROM—Windows/Macintosh)	$39.95	GONE
◉ Law on the Net (Book w/CD-ROM—Windows/Macintosh)	$39.95	LAWN
Legal Research: How to Find & Understand the Law	$24.95	LRES
Legal Research Made Easy (Video)	$89.95	LRME
◉ Legal Research Online & in the Library (Book w/CD-ROM—Windows/Macintosh)	$39.95	LRO

▣ **Book with disk**

◉ **Book with CD-ROM**

SENIORS

Beat the Nursing Home Trap	$21.95	ELD
The Conservatorship Book (California Edition)	$44.95	CNSV
Social Security, Medicare & Pensions	$21.95	SOA

SOFTWARE

Call or check our website at www.nolo.com for special discounts on Software!

⊙ LeaseWriter CD—Windows/Macintosh	$99.95	LWD1
⊙ Living Trust Maker CD—Windows/Macintosh	$79.95	LTD2
⊙ Small Business Legal Pro 3 CD—Windows/Macintosh	$79.95	SBCD3
⊙ Personal RecordKeeper 5.0 CD—Windows/Macintosh	$59.95	RKD5
⊙ Patent It Yourself CD—Windows	$229.95	PPC12
⊙ WillMaker 7.0 CD—Windows/Macintosh	$69.95	WMD7

SPECIAL UPGRADE OFFER
Get 35% off the latest edition
of your Nolo book

It's important to have the most current legal information. Because laws and legal procedures change often, we update our books regularly. To help keep you up-to-date we are extending this special upgrade offer. Cut out and mail the title portion of the cover of your old Nolo book and we'll give you 35% off the retail price of the NEW EDITION of that book when you purchase directly from us.

For more information call us at 1-800-992-6656.
This offer is to individuals only.

⌨ Book with disk
⊙ Book with CD-ROM

ORDER FORM

Code	Quantity	Title	Unit price	Total

			Subtotal	
		In California add appropriate Sales Tax		
		Basic Shipping ($3.95)		
		UPS RUSH delivery $8.00-any size order*		
		TOTAL		

Name

Address

UPS to street address, Priority Mail to P.O. boxes
* Delivered in 3 business days from receipt of order. S.F. Bay Area use regular shipping.

FOR FASTER SERVICE, USE YOUR CREDIT CARD & OUR TOLL-FREE NUMBERS

ORDER 24 HOURS A DAY   1-800-992-6656
FAX US YOUR ORDER   1-800-645-0895
ONLINE   www.nolo.com

☐ Check enclosed

☐ VISA   ☐ MasterCard   ☐ Discover Card   ☐ American Express

Account #   Expiration Date

Authorizing Signature

Daytime Phone

Send to: Nolo.com, 950 Parker Street, Berkeley, CA 94710

PRICES SUBJECT TO CHANGE

VISIT OUR OUTLET STORE!

You'll find our complete line of books and software, all at a discount.
Berkeley • 950 Parker Street • Berkeley, CA 94720 • 1-510-704-2248

VISIT US ONLINE!

www.nolo.com—You'll find our complete line of books and software, all at a discount.

TO ORDER CALL 800-992-6656

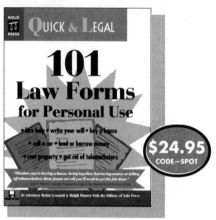

$24.95
CODE—SPOT

101 LAW FORMS FOR PERSONAL USE

"Whether you're buying a house, living together, borrowing money or telling off telemarketers, these forms are all you'll need to get the job done."

--Laurel Pollock, Consumer Protection Investigator, San Francisco District Attorney's Office and Host of Bay TV's "All Consuming"

101 Law Forms for Personal Use gives you plain-English, step-by-step instructions and all the forms you'll need to cover the legal issues you're most likely to face every day. Forms include:

- bills of sale & promissory notes
- a basic will form & general power of attorney
- child care contracts & authorizations
- contracts for home repair & remodeling
- and much, much more

All forms are provided as tear-outs and on disk.

101 Law Forms for Personal Use is authored by veteran Nolo editors Attorney Robin Leonard, a personal finance expert, and Marcia Stewart, a real estate and consumer specialist.

TRAV 2.0

TO ORDER CALL 800-992-6656
OR USE THE FORM IN THE BACK OF THIS BOOK

Take 2 minutes
&
Give us your 2 cents

Your comments make a big difference in the development and revision of Nolo books and software. Please take a few minutes and register your Nolo product— and your comments—with us. Not only will your input make a difference, you'll receive special offers *available only to the registered owners of Nolo products* on our newest books and software. Register now by:

 or

CALL
1-800-992-6656

E-MAIL
NOLOSUB@NOLO.com

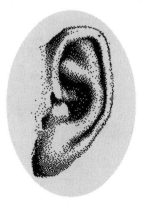

REMEMBER:
Little publishers have big ears.
We really listen to you.

NOLO
IN THE
NEWS

"Nolo helps lay people perform legal tasks without the aid—or fees—of lawyers."

—USA TODAY

Nolo books are ..."written in plain language, free of legal mumbo jumbo, and spiced with witty personal observations."

—ASSOCIATED PRESS

"...Nolo publications...guide people simply through the how, when, where and why of law."

—WASHINGTON POST

"Increasingly, people who are not lawyers are performing tasks usually regarded as legal work... And consumers, using books like Nolo's, do routine legal work themselves."

—NEW YORK TIMES

"...All of [Nolo's] books are easy-to-understand, are updated regularly, provide pull-out forms...and are often quite moving in their sense of compassion for the struggles of the lay reader."

—SAN FRANCISCO CHRONICLE

NOLO.COM
950 PARKER STREET
BERKELEY CA 94710-9867